THE PMP® EXAM
How To Pass On Your First Try

6th Edition

Andy Crowe, PMP

Velociteach

Although the author and publisher have made every effort to ensure accuracy and completeness of information entered in this book, we assume no responsibility for errors, inaccuracies, omissions, or inconsistencies included herein. Any slights of people, places, or organizations are completely unintentional.

"PMI," "PMP," and "PMBOK" are certification marks in the United States and other nations, registered to the Project Management Institute, Inc.

Velociteach is a Global Registered Education Provider with the Project Management Institute.

All inquiries should be addressed to (e-mail): info@velociteach.com

First Edition, May, 2003; Second Edition, June, 2004; Third Edition, October, 2005; Fourth Edition, April, 2009; Fifth Edition, May, 2013
Sixth Edition, First Printing: February, 2018, Second Printing, May 2018, Third Printing, July 2018, Fourth Printing, August 2018, Fifth Printing, August 2018, Sixth Printing, October 2018, Seventh Printing, January 2019, **Eighth Printing, May 2019**

International Standard Book No.   ISBN-13: 978-0-9909074-7-3

ATTENTION CORPORATIONS, UNIVERSITIES, COLLEGES, AND PROFESSIONAL ORGANIZATIONS. Quantity discounts are available on bulk purchases of this book. For information, please contact info@velociteach.com.

Contents

Contents

Contents

Contents

The sixth edition of the PMP Exam: How To Pass On Your First Try is the most expansive update to date. This book has helped people all over the world to pass the infamous PMP exam.

In order to pass the PMP exam, you have to demonstrate your knowledge and your ability to apply that knowledge in difficult situations. In the most frustrating scenarios, there is no answer that is clearly correct, or if there is, it is not represented in the choices. Studying for PMP certification takes a significant amount of commitment and effort, but knowing what to study should be effortless. That's where this book comes in.

With the introduction of agile concepts, *the PMBOK® Guide* has folded in a perspective that can frequently be at odds with the traditionally predictive, "waterfall" approach. Understanding how to read and decode the questions is one of the most important skills you can develop.

This sixth edition also introduces video segments. People learn through a variety of styles, and this one has been added to highlight key points in a new way.

Several resources exist for PMP exam preparation, so why should this be the one volume you use? Because it's designed from page one to be better. It is clearly organized and presents the material in an easily understandable format without insulting the reader's intelligence. Every process, input, tool and technique, and output is clearly explained, and the reasons underlying each are addressed. There is also a glossary of terms in the back that is an excellent reference by itself.

Combined with the online companion website, insite.velociteach.com, you'll find more than enough to help you prepare to pass the PMP exam. I believe you will find this end result to be the most complete, concise, and up-to-date study resource.

Here's to your success!

ANDY CROWE, PMP, PgMP, PMI-ACP

About the Author

About the Author

Andy Crowe, PMP, PgMP, PMI-ACP speaks, writes, and researches prolifically on project management. In addition to this book, he has authored <u>Alpha Project Managers: What The Top 2% Know that Everyone Else Does Not</u> and <u>The PMI-ACP Exam: How To Pass On Your First Try</u>. Crowe is founder and CEO of Velociteach, a company passionate about the sharing the best practices in project management, headquartered in Kennesaw, GA. He spends much of his time writing in the Blue Ridge Mountains.

About Velociteach

Velociteach, a Kennesaw, GA company, was recently named The Project Management Institute's Continuing Professional Education Provider of the Year and one of the US Chamber of Commerce's top 100 small businesses. As a Global Registered Education Provider (R.E.P.), Velociteach offers training around the world, teaching certification and advanced project management theory and practice.

Velociteach offers live classroom, distance, and e-learning courses around the world. Full details on this and other course offerings are available online at www.velociteach.com.

Stay Current

Get updates from Velociteach at twitter.com/velociteach.

Ask exam-related questions, participate in discussions, and stay on top of trends and best practices in project management by communicating with Andy and the Velociteach team via their project management blog at savvypm.velociteach.com.

Get exam tips, free content, and special offers by liking this book at facebook.com/PMPExam

 "Manage This, the Podcast by Project Managers for Project Managers", is an easy and free way for you to earn your PDUs while listening to thought leaders in the project management industry. Start earning free PDUs today! https://www.velociteach.com/category/podcast/

Introduction

The best part of my job has to be hearing from people who bought this book, took an online class, or attended one of our project management boot camps. Practically every day I get email from someone who passed the PMP exam, and it always brightens my day. I read them all, and I try to respond to each of them. Being on the receiving end of hundreds of thank you letters each year is incredibly rewarding and also quite humbling.

I wrote the first edition of this book in 2002, and I have worked on it constantly since then to keep it accurate and relevant. It is a labor of love.

The 6th edition is packed with new content, new questions and more diagrams. The questions that were added were carefully crafted to be compatible with the 2018 exam changes. Those who are familiar with earlier editions should find this edition to be an upgrade in virtually every way.

There is an old saying, "If it were easy, everyone would do it." Among the many certifications available today, the PMP stands out as the most prestigious, in part because it is considered highly difficult to attain.

This book will cut down on the difficulty factors and demystify the material. In the following chapters, you will find exactly what you need to study for the test, how to learn it, how to apply it, and why it is important. The PMP Exam: How to Pass on Your First Try is a complete resource to help you prepare fully for the PMP certification exam.

In order to get the most from your efforts, you should read the material in this book, practice the examples, and then take and re-take the sample exam, reading the explanations that accompany each question. Additionally, Chapter 14 was written to help you know when you are ready to take the exam.

All in all, you should find your preparation for PMP certification a highly rewarding experience. Aside from the financial and career benefits that accompany it, PMP certification is a very worthy goal. The PMP is one of the most recognizable certifications you can earn, recognized by nearly every industry and in over 120 countries around the world.

Conventions Used in this Book

The 6th edition of <u>The PMP Exam: How to Pass on Your First Try</u> is structured differently than other exam preparation materials. Some of the key features that will help you get the most from this book are listed below:

- In order to create a comprehensive reference, every process, input, tool and technique, and output is included, but to help you prioritize your study, key information for the exam is designated by a symbol next to topics of particular importance.

- There is a structure and priority to the material. The book will guide you, and by the time you have read a chapter or two and taken a couple of the quizzes, you will start to understand. By studying the right information with the proper emphasis, you can be confident of passing. You will also find many topics not even mentioned in the *PMBOK® Guide* expanded on quite heavily in this book. These come from recognized sources and volumes on which the exam relies.

- The philosophy behind each knowledge area and many of the sub-topics is explained. Because several questions on the PMP Exam require you to apply the information instead of simply regurgitating it, you must understand "why" the information is structured the way it is, instead of merely memorizing it.

- A large portion of the PMP Exam relies on understanding key terms related to project management. Many test-takers go awry by relying on their own experiences to interpret terminology instead of understanding PMI's definitions. PMI's use of a term or concept may be very different than that of someone who has not had exposure to PMI's philosophy. Key terms are given special attention where necessary to help readers become acquainted with PMI's usage of project management terms and concepts.

The Exam

This chapter will explore the PMP certification exam, what it is like, and the material it covers. It will clarify exactly what the test is, how it is structured, and an overview of the contents. Specific strategies on how to pass the exam will be discussed in Chapter 14 – How to Pass the PMP on Your First Try.

Watch The Video
http://**prep.pm/1**

WHAT THE EXAM TESTS:

Before we discuss what the PMP certification exam does test, let's clear up a few misconceptions about the exam.

The PMP certification exam does not test:

- Your project management experience or competence
- Your common sense
- Your knowledge of industry practices
- Your knowledge of how to use software tools
- What you learned in management school
- Your intelligence

The PMP certification exam does test:

- Your knowledge of PMI's processes
- Your understanding of the many terms that are used to describe the processes
- Your ability to apply those processes in a variety of situations
- Your ability to apply key formulas to scheduling, costing, estimating, and other problems

Chapter Notes:

_____

_____

_____

_____

_____

_____

_____

_____

Chapter Notes:

_____

_____

_____

_____

_____

_____

_____

_____

_____

_____

_____

_____

_____

A PASSING GRADE:

Not to scare you right away, but the cold, hard truth is that many who take the PMP Exam do not pass. Those who do not pass come from a broad cross-section of people, ranging from those who have approached the exam with extensive preparation, including books and training classes, to those who have barely expended any effort. By using this book, you are tilting the scales decidedly in your favor!

Although PMI no longer discloses the exact score you will need to pass, it is estimated that you need to correctly answer at least 106 questions out of the 175 graded questions on the test (more on graded questions later). That translates to 61%, and if your first reaction to the 61% mark is that it does not sound very impressive, consider that the 2018 exam revision is tougher than the one many people took in years past. 61% is a great score, and each year, tens of thousands of project managers do not pass.

Some people find it very difficult to understand why they cannot study and make a perfect score on the PMP. It is a good thing to want to do well on the exam, but considering the incredible breadth of material, simply passing it is a terrific accomplishment! Experts disagree over some of the questions, and there will be some that you will feel absolutely certain you got right that you likely missed. This has more to do with the way the questions are constructed and worded than it does with the study effort you put in, your intellectual powers, or your test-taking abilities.

Your goal in taking the PMP should be to do your absolute best and to make sure that your best effort falls within PMI's passing score limits.

THE EXAM MATERIAL:

Your PMP Exam will be made up of exactly 200 questions, covering a broad variety of material, but only 175 of those questions will count toward your score. The other 25 questions are considered experimental questions that PMI is evaluating for use on future exams. The good news is that these 25 questions do not count toward your grade. The bad news is that you will never know which questions count and which do not since they are scattered randomly throughout the exam.

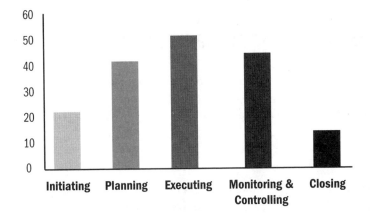

PMI does provide some guidelines as to how the material will be presented. The exam was significantly updated March 26, 2018, and the updated material and questions are allocated as shown in the table below.

Process Group	Number of Questions	% of Exam
Initiating	23	13%
Plannning	42	24%
Executing	52	31%
Monitoring & Controlling	44	25%
Closing	14	7%
Total Graded Questions	**175**	**100%**

The terms used here - initiating, planning, executing, monitoring and controlling, closing, and professional and social responsibility - will be explained in Chapter 3 – Process Framework.

Chapter Notes:

_____

_____

_____

_____

_____

_____

_____

_____

_____

_____

_____

_____

_____

_____

_____

This fact shocks many people preparing for the exam, but the *PMBOK® Guide* (pronounced "pim-bock"), which stands for a Guide to the Project Management Body of Knowledge, is not a single study source for the PMP Exam. The *PMBOK® Guide* does provide an excellent definition and presentation of the overall processes, but it does not give you much help in knowing how that material will translate to the exam. Many of those who do not pass the PMP Exam tried to use the *PMBOK® Guide* as their study guide and were surprised that there were questions, terms, and concepts on the exam that were not in the *PMBOK® Guide*.

GETTING TO THE TEST (APPLICATION)

It is highly recommended that you join the Project Management Institute prior to signing up to take the test. At publication time, the new member fee was $139.00 ($129.00 membership + $10.00 new member activation fee). Application may be made online at www.pmi.org, or you may obtain an application from PMI by calling (610) 356-4600.

After joining PMI, you will receive a membership number that you can use to receive a $150.00 discount on the exam's non-member fee, so you instantly save money by joining. The Examination Fee will be $405.00 for a member in good standing. If you elect not to join PMI, it will cost $555.00 to apply to take the test.

In addition to the financial advantage, there are many other benefits that come with joining PMI, including a subscription to PMI's publications, PM Network and PM Today; discounts on books and PMI-sponsored events; and access to a wealth of information in the field of project management.

When you get ready to apply for eligibility for PMP certification, you can apply online or use printed forms. If at all possible, you should apply online. Depending on the time of year, wait times have been known to stretch out for weeks when using printed forms through the mail, while online applicants usually report turnaround times within one to two weeks. The length of time can vary, depending on the volume of applications that PMI is processing. In any case, you must have your letter of eligibility from PMI to sit for the PMP certification exam.

To be eligible for PMP certification, you will need to demonstrate that you meet certain minimum criteria. The current qualifications that PMI requires are summarized below.

In short, if you hold a university degree, you should apply under the first category. If not, you should apply under the second. See PMI's official guide, available online at www.pmi.org, for more details on this point.

Minimal Requirements to Apply with a College Diploma

- A University Degree

- 36 months (3 years) of project management experience

- 4,500 hours managing projects

- 35 hours of project management education (note that the online class included on the key card in the back of this book can provide you with eight of those contact hours)

Minimal Requirements to Apply without a College Diploma

- A High school diploma or equivalent

- 60 months (5 years) of project management experience

- 7,500 hours managing projects

- 35 hours of project management education

ONGOING EDUCATION

PMPs are expected to demonstrate not only knowledge and experience but also their ongoing commitment to the field of project management. To promote such commitment, PMI requires that all PMPs maintain their certification status by completing at least 60 Professional Development Units (PDUs) every 36 months. The requirements for PDUs are defined in further detail in the PMI Continuing Certification Requirements Program Handbook given to all PMPs, and these requirements are similar in nature

Chapter Notes:

Ongoing Education

Chapter One

to requirements that legal, medical, and other professions have adopted. In order to maintain the value of this certification, PMI requires its PMPs to maintain a project management focus and a continued commitment to the field of project management.

THE TESTING ENVIRONMENT

The PMP certification exam is administered in a formal environment. There is no talking during the exam, and you cannot bring notes, books, paper, cell phones, PDAs, or calculators into the examination room with you. The PMP is considered a "high-stakes" or "high-security" exam and is very carefully monitored. Test-takers are constantly observed by the test proctor and are under recorded video and audio surveillance. This can be distracting as well as unnerving, so it is important to be mentally prepared as you walk into the exam.

The test is delivered on a Windows-based PC that runs a secure, proprietary testing application. The computer setup is very straightforward, with a mouse and keyboard and a simple graphical user interface used to display the test. PMI can arrange special accommodations for those test takers who have special physical needs. To get a feel for how the real PMP Exam looks and feels, use the key found in the back cover of this book to gain access to insite.velociteach.com for simulated PMP Exams and other content.

Recently, PMI has also made provision for certain test-takers who do not live near a testing center to take a paper version of the exam. While this book focuses on the computerized version of the exam, the content of both versions of the exam is identical, and your preparation should not be any different. More information on the paper-based exam may be found online at www.pmi.org.

The exam ends either when your 4-hour time limit has been reached (more on this in a moment) or when you choose to end the exam. Once the exam is over, you will know your score within a few seconds, and those results are electronically transmitted to PMI. If you passed, you are immediately a

"PMP," and you may start using that designation after your name. PMI will mail you all of the official information, including your PMP lapel pin and certificate, within a few weeks. If you did not pass, you may take the exam up to three times in a calendar year. If you do not pass on your third attempt, you must wait one year from your last attempt to reapply.

THE TIME LIMIT

Taking a test while the clock is ticking can be unnerving. The PMP Exam is a long exam, but you are given a significant block of time to complete the test. From the time you begin the exam, you will have 240 minutes (4 hours) to finish. For most people, this is enough time to take the test and review the answers. The allocation works out to 72 seconds per question if no breaks are taken. While a few of the more complicated questions will certainly require more than 72 seconds, most will take much less time.

The subject of time management for the exam, along with a suggested strategy for managing your time, is covered later in Chapter 14 - How to Pass the PMP on the First Try.

Chapter Notes:

The Time Limit

QUESTION FORMAT

Exam questions are given in a multiple choice format, with four possible answers, marked A, B, C, and D, and only one of those four answers is correct. Unlike in some exams, there is no penalty for guessing, so it is to your advantage to answer every question on the PMP Exam, leaving none of them blank.

Many of the questions are quite short in format; however, the PMP Exam is famous (or infamous) for its long, winding questions that are difficult to decipher. To help you prepare, you will see different question styles represented in this book. Going through all the sample questions provided in this volume is an excellent way to prepare for the types of questions you will encounter on the actual exam.

Chapter Notes:

_____

_____

_____

_____

_____

_____

_____

_____

_____

_____

_____

_____

_____

_____

_____

Question Format

Foundational Terms and Concepts

The best place to begin preparing for the PMP Exam is for you to understand exactly what a project is and how it differs from operations, a program, or other activities your organization might undertake. You will also need to understand what a project manager does and how different organizational structures can influence a project manager's role and power. A solid grasp of these and a few other concepts will help you absorb the rest of the material in this book.

Most of the chapters in this book focus on the 49 processes of project management, but this chapter will help you build an important foundation. The concepts in this book will make more sense once you understand this chapter.

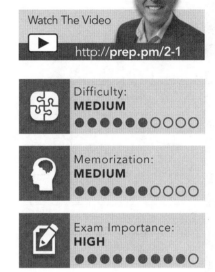

Watch The Video
http://**prep.pm**/2-1

Difficulty:
MEDIUM
●●●●●●○○○○

Memorization:
MEDIUM
●●●●●●●○○○

Exam Importance:
HIGH
●●●●●●●●●○

PHILOSOPHY:

Projects are carried out by organizations. Sometimes this is referred to as the "organizational context." It is important because the type of organization and other environmental factors can greatly influence how the project is carried out.

Every project is going to be unique in its own way. They may have different stakeholders, different team members, or unique goals. An effective project manager must be able to navigate these differences and still get to a successful outcome. Even apparently slight differences between organizations can have disproportionately large impacts on the project. For example, if your senior management strongly supports the project team, that can provide a tremendous advantage over a senior manager that only offers lukewarm support.

Chapter Notes:

_____

_____

_____

_____

_____

_____

_____

Chapter Two

Chapter Notes:

_____

_____

_____

_____

_____

_____

_____

_____

_____

_____

_____

_____

IMPORTANCE:

This chapter is foundational to your understanding, so it is highly important.

There will be many questions on your exam that test your understanding of project managers, stakeholders, and sponsors. You will also need to be able to identify the different types of organizations and to recognize the difference between a project and other activities. Take the time to understand the terms in this chapter.

PREPARATION:

There is a lot of material to learn in this chapter, and much of it is marked as important. Memorizing these terms will help, but understanding and applying them will benefit you even more.

ESSENTIAL TERMS:

Let's begin by mastering a few terms that you will see frequently throughout this book.

→ Process - Most of this book is about the 49 processes of project management, and you will see this term a lot. A process does or creates something necessary and valuable for the project. For example, there is a process we will cover in chapter four named Develop Project Management Plan, and it does exactly what it sounds like. Another process named Identify Risks is the process where the list of risks is created.

Processes consist of only three types of ingredients: inputs, tools and techniques, and outputs. The outputs of one process often become the inputs to one or more other processes. To make it easier, some of the most common inputs, tools and techniques, and outputs are covered in this chapter.

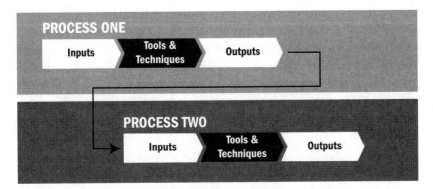

One important thing to understand, and one that trips up many learners, is that every process may be performed more than one time on a single project. In fact, you could conceivably perform most of the processes more than one time within a single phase (don't worry, phases are covered next). For example, just because you have created the project's schedule, it does not mean that you will not revisit the process of Develop Schedule if the scope of the project increases or if the budget were changed. In reality, you may perform that process multiple times, and most processes are the same way.

Do not think about these 49 processes happening sequentially or by themselves. Many processes may be carried out in parallel and may be revisited often.

Chapter Notes:

_____

_____

_____

_____

_____

_____

_____

_____

_____

_____

_____

_____

_____

_____

_____

Foundational Terms and Concepts

Chapter Two

Chapter Notes:

_____

_____

_____

_____

_____

_____

_____

_____

_____

_____

_____

_____

_____

_____

_____

Phase - Most larger projects are broken down into units known as phases. These phases may have names like "requirements gathering," "design," "construction," "testing," and "implementation." When preparing for the exam, it is easiest to think of phases as being carried out one after the other even though they could possibly have some overlap in real practice.

Each phase of a project should produce one or more deliverables, and those deliverables are evaluated to determine whether or not the next phase may be begun. The following illustration shows how deliverables are reviewed to determine whether the project should continue. This decision point is known as an exit gate (sometimes called a stage gate). An exit gate is the point at the end of a phase where the deliverables from that phase will be evaluated to determine whether or not the team completed the phase acceptably and the next phase may be started. This should be performed using exit criteria defined in advance so that the project team is aware of how each phase will be judged.

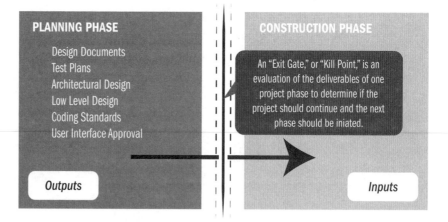

A kill point is very similar to a phase gate with one key addition: Kill points are points in the project's life cycle where a team or individual external to the project makes the decision whether to continue the project or to stop (kill) it. Typically these are carried out at the same point as an exit gate and often using the same or similar criteria.

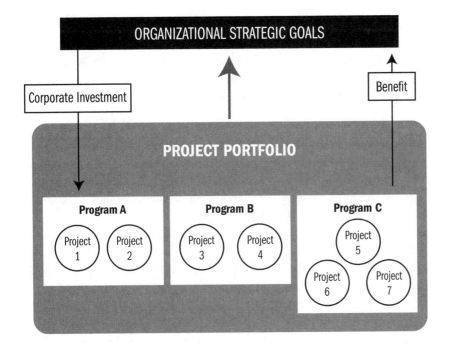

Project - As you might guess, the definition of a project is very important for the exam. A project is a temporary (finite) endeavor undertaken to create a unique product, service, or result. You may encounter a question on the exam that describes a situation and asks you whether that situation represents a project. For something to be a project, it needs to have the following characteristics:

- A project is time-limited (it has a definite beginning and end). This means that projects do not include operations, since operations may go on perpetually, and projects are finite.

- A project is unique (it has not been attempted before by this organization).

Even though projects do not include operations, you should consider operations when you are planning for your project. This means that the project team should understand the needs of the group that takes over operations or maintenance once the project team has delivered its product.

Chapter Two

Chapter Notes:

_____

_____

_____

_____

_____

_____

_____

_____

_____

_____

_____

_____

Foundational Terms and Concepts

For the sake of space, this book often refers to the project's result as a product, but it could be any product, service, or result. The point is that projects ultimately create change, and that change can take on many forms. Projects are the means by which organizations get things done, whether or not the changes are visible or tangible.

Program - A program is a group of related projects that are coordinated together. Unlike projects, programs may also include operations. Organizations often group projects into programs in order to realize some benefit that could not be achieved if those projects were not undertaken in concert.

For example, building a new airport might be viewed as a program, made up of numerous component projects, and this program would certainly take the ongoing operations into consideration in order to make things run smoothly and to keep ongoing costs under control.

Not every project will necessarily belong to a program, but all programs are made up of projects.

Portfolio - A company's project portfolio represents its entire investment in projects and programs. Project portfolios should always be directly aligned to the organization's strategic goals. In fact, an organization's portfolio might be considered the truest expression of its real strategic goals.

Projects contribute to the organization's portfolio, and ideally, the benefit of project investments should be expressed in how they meet or support the organization's strategic goals.

Progressive Elaboration - The concept of progressive elaboration has always been important for the exam, but it just got a lot more important in the latest updates. The reason has to do with the deeper incorporation of agile methodologies.

The term "progressive elaboration" simply means that you do not know all of the characteristics of a product when you begin the project. Instead, they may be revisited and refined often. You may gather some requirements, perform some preliminary design, take the results to the stakeholders for feedback, and then return to gather more requirements. The project is accomplished through several iterations, or "progressively."

Using progressive elaboration techniques, whenever you can, is highly favored on the exam.

➔ **Project Management** - There is nothing special or tricky about the definition of project management, but you will need to be able to recognize it on the exam. Project management is the application of knowledge, skills, tools, and techniques to project activities to meet the project requirements.

➔ **Success** - The definition of project success is delivering the product and the project within the set boundaries of scope, cost, schedule, quality, and customer satisfaction.

➔ **Historical Information** - Historical information is an important concept that runs throughout the exam, usually under the heading of "Organizational Process Assets." Historical information is found in the records within your organization that have been kept on previous projects. These records can be used to help benchmark the current project. They may show previous estimates, what resources were used, and what lessons were learned. More than anything, historical information is used to help predict trends and avoid mistakes for the current project and to evaluate the project's feasibility.

Because continuous improvement and learning matter so much, historical records are extremely important in project management, and they are used heavily during planning activities. They can provide useful metrics, be used to validate assumptions, and help prevent repeated mistakes.

The term "historical information" is as old as project management itself, but the term has recently given way to the more comprehensive "organizational process assets," covered under common inputs a bit further on in this chapter. You may well see "historical information"

Chapter Two

Chapter Notes:

_____

_____

_____

_____

_____

_____

_____

_____

_____

_____

_____

_____

_____

_____

_____

pop up on the exam, but know that it now fits neatly under the broader heading of organizational process assets. That is because any historical information you have is actually an asset for the organization to use on future projects.

 **Baseline** - The term "baseline" is used for certain plans: scope, schedule, cost, performance management, and the project plan itself.

A baseline is simply a version of the plan that exists once the plan is stabilized. While the plan is in its early development, you would not have a baseline, but at some point it is put under control. This means that the plan cannot just be changed at will but that any changes need to be approved and documented through some kind of change control process. Baselining does not mean that the process has to be difficult or bureaucratic.

A plan's baseline is simply the original plan plus all approved changes. Many people get tripped up on the concept that the baseline includes all approved changes. Baselines are used as tools to measure how performance deviates from the plan, so if changes to the plan are approved, the new plan becomes the baseline.

Suppose you were running a one-mile race. That distance of one mile would be your baseline.

Your plan was to run at a pace of just under eight minutes per mile. Now suppose that the race length was changed to a three-mile race. You ran the race and still finished in a very respectable 26 minutes. Would you want your progress measured against the original distance or the updated one? If you did not update your baseline to three miles, your pace of 26 minutes against the original distance of one mile would not be very impressive to most people. Your performance measurements would only be meaningful if you had an accurate baseline.

Remember that your project's baseline is defined as the original plan plus all approved changes. Even though the baseline changes as the plan changes, it is a good idea to keep records that show how the plan has progressed and changed over time.

Lessons Learned - The key word for you to remember when you think of lessons learned is "variances." Lessons learned are gathered at the end of each phase or at the end of the project, and they focus on variances between the plan and the results. The goal is to detail any information that should be shared with future projects. Lessons learned from past projects are another organizational process asset, which is an input into many planning processes. It is important that lessons learned put a special emphasis on what was planned to happen, what actually happened, and what you would have done differently in order to avoid any variances. Lessons learned are collected throughout the project for continuous improvement efforts and for use on future projects.

In a lessons learned meeting, the team essentially asks "what would we do differently if we had this project (or part of a project) to do again."

Regulation - A regulation is an official document that provides guidelines that must be followed. Compliance with a regulation is mandatory (e.g., in the United States, wheelchair ramps are required for many streets and buildings). Regulations are issued by government agencies or another official organization.

You should expect never to see a question on the exam where the correct answer has you skirt, bend, or break a regulation.

Standard - A standard is a document approved by a recognized body that provides guidelines. Compliance with a standard is not necessarily mandatory but may be helpful. For example, the size of copy paper is standardized, and it would probably be a very good idea for paper manufacturers to follow the standard, but there is not a law in most countries requiring that copy paper be made the standard size. The *PMBOK® Guide* provides a standard for project management.

For the exam, you should view standards as a good thing and as helpful. This means that the correct answers will reflect this perspective.

Chapter Notes:

_____

_____

_____

_____

_____

_____

_____

_____

_____

_____

_____

_____

_____

_____

Foundational Terms and Concepts

Chapter Notes:

_____

_____

_____

_____

_____

_____

_____

_____

_____

_____

_____

_____

_____

System - There are several instances of "systems" in this book. A system incorporates all the formal procedures and tools put in place to manage something. The term "system" does not refer only to computer systems, but to procedures, checks and balances, processes, forms, software, etc. For instance, the project management information system (discussed in Chapter 4 – Project Integration Management), may include a combination of high-tech and low-tech tools such as computer systems, paper forms, policies and procedures, meetings, etc.

PROJECT ROLES:

Another area of study regarding the project context is that of the roles and responsibilities found on projects. You should be familiar with the following terms related to project roles:

Project Manager -The project manager is the person ultimately responsible for the outcome of the project. The project manager is:

- Formally empowered to use organizational resources

- In control of the project

- Authorized to spend the project's budget

- Authorized to make decisions for the project

Project managers are typically found in a matrix or projectized organization (more about types of organizations shortly). If they do exist in a functional organization, they will often be only part-time and will have significantly less authority than project managers in other types of organizations.

Because the project manager is in charge of the project, most of the project's problems and responsibilities belong to him or her. It is typically a bad idea for the project manager to escalate a problem to someone else. The responsibility to manage the project rests with the project manager, and that includes fixing problems.

Project Coordinator - In some organizations, project managers do not exist. Instead, these organizations use the role of a project coordinator. The project coordinator is significantly weaker than a project manager. This person may not be allowed to make budget decisions or overall project decisions, but they may have some authority to reassign resources. Project coordinators are usually found in weak matrix or functional organizations.

Project Expeditor - The weakest of the three project management roles, an expeditor is a staff assistant who has little or no formal authority. This person reports to the executive who ultimately has responsibility for the project. The expeditor's primary responsibility lies in making sure things arrive on time and that tasks are completed on time. An expeditor is usually found in a functional organization, and this role may be only part-time in many organizations.

Senior Management - For the exam, you can think of senior management as anyone more senior than the project manager. Senior management's role on the project is to help prioritize projects and make sure the project manager has the proper authority and access to resources. Senior management issues strategic plans and goals and makes sure that the company's projects are aligned with them. Additionally, senior management may be called upon to resolve conflicts within the organization.

Functional Manager - The functional manager is the departmental manager in most organizational structures, such as the manager of engineering, director of marketing, or information technology manager. The functional manager usually "owns" the resources that are loaned to the project, and has human resources responsibilities for them. Additionally, he or she may be asked to approve the overall project plan. Functional managers can be a rich source of expertise and information available to the project manager and can make a valuable contribution to the project. Be aware that functional managers are the most likely persons with whom project managers experience conflict on a project.

Chapter Notes:

Project Roles

Chapter Notes:

_____

_____

_____

_____

_____

_____

_____

_____

_____

_____

_____

_____

_____

_____

Stakeholder - Stakeholders are individuals who are involved in the project or whose interests may be positively or negatively affected as a result of the execution or completion of the project. They may exert influence over the project and its results. This definition can be very broad, and it can include a vast number of people! Often when the term "stakeholders" appears on the exam, it may be referring to the key stakeholders who are identified as the most important or influential ones on the project.

Sponsor - The sponsor is the person paying for the project. He may be internal or external to the company. In some organizations the sponsor is called the project champion. Also, the sponsor and the customer may be the same person, although the usual distinction is that the sponsor is internal to the performing organization and the customer is external.

The sponsor may provide valuable input on the project, such as due dates and other milestones, important product features, and constraints and assumptions. If a serious conflict arises between the project manager and the customer, the sponsor may be called in to help work with the customer and resolve the dispute.

Project Office *(also referred to as Project Management Office or PMO)* - This term refers to a department that can support project managers with methodologies, tools, training, etc., or even ultimately control all of the organization's projects. Usually the project office serves in a supporting role, defining standards, providing best practices, and auditing projects for conformance.

→ **Program Manager** - As the title suggests, program managers are responsible for programs. Earlier in this chapter, we covered the fact that a program is multiple projects coordinated together, and the program manager organizes and manages these at a higher level than the project manager does. For instance, the project manager may be responsible for the daily management of a given project, while the program manager is responsible for coordinating several projects at once in order to create a common benefit. For the exam, you should think of it this way: you (the project manager) manage the details of a project and report status and other relevant information to the program manager.

PROJECT CONTEXT

Another area of study for the PMP Exam is the concept of a project context, which is the organizational environment where the project is carried out. A large part of the project context is determined by the organization's structure or type of organization.

Paying attention to the context is important since projects do not take place in a vacuum. Practically every activity that occurs and every resource that is used will touch the performing organization in some way.

For the exam, your general attitude should be that the project needs to respect and adapt to the performing organization whenever possible. That is true so long as the organization does not pressure you to cut corners, misrepresent the truth, or to sidestep any of the processes covered in this book. The best answers on the exam allow you to do things the right way and in the right order but in such a way that fits with the organization.

Chapter Notes:

Project Context

Chapter Two

Types of Organizations - The way in which an organization is structured will have an impact on the way its projects are managed.

The chart that follows summarizes essential information regarding the various types of organizations. You should be very familiar with this information before taking the exam, as you may see several questions that describe a project or situation and require you to identify what type of organization is involved.

Types of Organizations

Type	Description	Who is in Charge?	Benefits	Drawbacks
Organic	Teams and groups naturally form to address priorities	Varies based on corporate priorities and personalities	Can be adaptive to environment	Lack of organizational maturity. May be driven by the short-term urgent rather than the longer-term important.
Functional	Very common organizational structure where team members work for a department, such as engineering or accounting, but may be loaned to a project from time to time. The project manager has low influence or power and could even be part time.	Functional (departmental) manager	Deeper company expertise by function. High degree of professional specialization. Defined career paths for the team.	Project manager is weak. Projects are prioritized lower. Resources are often not dedicated to a project.
Matrix	A hybrid organization where individuals have both a functional manager for human resources and a project manager for projects. In a strong matrix, the project manager carries more weight. In a weak matrix, the functional manager has more authority. In a balanced matrix, the power is shared evenly between the functional and project managers.	Power shared between project manager and functional manager	Can be the "best of both worlds." Project managers can gain the deep expertise of a functional organization while still being empowered to manage the resources on the project.	Higher overhead due to duplication of effort on some tasks. Resources report to a functional manager and they have a "dotted line" to a project manager, sometimes causing conflict and confusion. High possibility for contention between project managers and functional managers. Because resources do not report to the project manager, they may be less loyal to him or her.

Type	Description	Who is in Charge?	Benefits	Drawbacks
Projectized	Organization is structured according to projects instead of functional departments. The project manager is both the manager of the project and of the people. The project manager is highly empowered and has a strong level of control. This is more commonly found in consulting environments.	Project Manager	Project manager has complete authority.

Project communication is easiest since everyone is on a single team.

Loyalty is strong, to both the team and the project.

Contention for resources does not exist. | Team members only belong to a project - not to a functional area.

Team members "work themselves out of a job" - they may have nowhere to go when the project is over.

Professional growth and development can be difficult. |
| Virtual | A project environment consisting of a distributed team. Members may be part time and may report and communicate peer to peer instead of to a project manager. | Varies | Engages experts without the cost of transportation.

May allow projects to continue around the clock, depending on where team members are located. | Team relationships may be weak since some team members never meet in person.

Project accountability can be challenging. |
| Composite | An organization that has more than one type of reporting structure. Many larger organizations have both functional and projectized structures across the enterprise | Varies according to the group that contains the project | May include any of the benefits from other organizational structures. | Added organizational types may introduce more complexity. |

Types of Organizations

23

Chapter Notes:

_____

_____

_____

_____

_____

_____

_____

_____

_____

_____

_____

_____

_____

Project Manager's Power - Once you are comfortable in your understanding of types of organizations and the roles that various types of stakeholders play in a project, you can see that the organizational context in which a project is carried out will have a great deal of influence on that project. One way that the type of organization affects the project manager in particular is in how much power he or she has to carry out decisions, apply resources, and negotiate. The chart below illustrates the relationship between a project manager's level of empowerment and the type of organization in which he or she works.

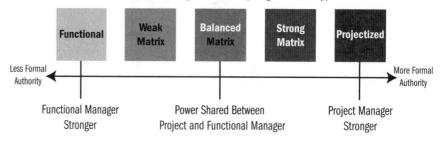

The Project Manager's Power by Organization Type

Project Manager's Management Skills - Project management includes many other disciplines. Since most projects are performed within an organization, there are other management skills that make up the foundation of project management. The way the project manager uses these skills will probably have a significant effect on the projects. The project manager should have experience in:

Leading - Setting direction, aligning people to that direction, motivating them, and inspiring them to commit and perform.

Communicating - Exchanging information clearly and correctly. Communication skills are important to everyone involved with the project, and they are critical to its success.

Negotiating - Working to reach a mutual agreement. Negotiations may happen with groups or individuals inside and outside the organization. The goal of negotiating is to create a win-win outcome that is sustainable for all parties.

Problem-Solving - Defining the problem and dealing with the core factors that contribute to or cause it. Problem-solving is such an important and highly favored skill for project managers that if it appears as one of the choices on the exam, is quite likely the correct answer. At the very least you should give that answer very careful consideration.

Influencing - Accomplishing something without necessarily having formal power. Influencing the organization requires a keen understanding of the way the organization is structured, both formally and informally. Influencing is an important skill, especially in organizations where the project manager does not have a high degree of authority.

Project Governance - Oftentimes there is a group, either within the performing organization or outside of the organization, that looks at how the project work is being performed to ensure that it is being carried out the right way. This typically takes place throughout the entire project life cycle.

Project governance may be used to define processes used across the project and to rate the project manager's performance.

In some organizations, this may be known as the Project Office or the Project Management Office (PMO). The project manager may formally report to the PMO, or it may exist solely to help and support project managers.

Chapter Notes:

_____

_____

_____

_____

_____

_____

_____

_____

_____

_____

_____

_____

Project Context

Chapter Two

Chapter Notes:

_____

_____

_____

_____

_____

_____

_____

_____

_____

_____

_____

_____

_____

_____

_____

Project Life Cycle - The project life cycle is simply the phases that a project typically goes through. These phases are general, but they show the expected flow of activities on a project.

The six phases represented in the following graphic describe the way in which a project typically progresses. It should be noted, however, that this depiction is very general, and different phases and phase names are used by different industries and projects.

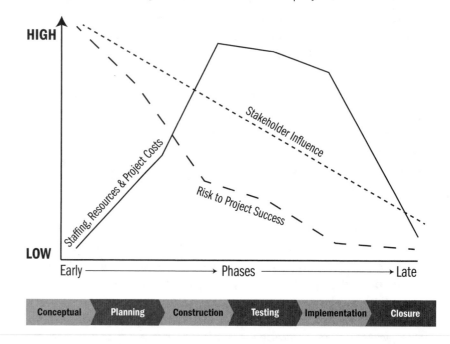

The image also shows some other facts about the project life cycle that often appear on the exam in the form of questions. These questions typically focus on the fact that resource and cost levels rise early in the project and drop over time, or how risk and stakeholders' ability to influence the project is highest early in the project and decreases as the project progresses.

The Triple Constraint - Another fundamental topic in project management is commonly referred to as "the triple constraint." It is based on the realization that while changes do occur during a project, they do not happen in a vacuum. When the scope of a project is changed, schedule and cost are also affected. Of course, the same is true when changes are made to cost or schedule. Those changes will have some impact on the other two areas.

As many different types of changes will be requested in most projects, it is essential in project management to be mindful of the triple constraint and to help keep others aware of it. The project manager should not simply accept all changes or change requests as valid; rather, the project manager should evaluate how those changes affect the other aspects of the project.

The triple constraint, or as some know it, the iron triangle, is simply the concept that scope, time, and cost are closely interrelated. Just as you cannot modify one side of a triangle without changing one or both of the other lengths, you cannot simply change one part of the triple constraint without affecting the other parts.

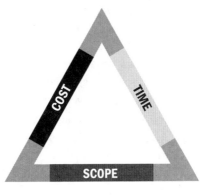

However common a practice it may be in some organizations to slash a budget without revisiting the scope or the schedule, the project manager should not simply accept these mandates. The triple constraint is in place whether or not the organization recognizes and accepts it.

Quality and risk are also factors that are linked to the triple constraint.

A good rule is this: whenever change is detected on the project, the project manager should carefully investigate and review the other areas of the project plan that may be affected and consider which components of the plan should be updated.

Chapter Notes:

_____

_____

_____

_____

_____

_____

_____

_____

_____

_____

_____

_____

_____

_____

The Triple Constraint

Chapter Two

Chapter Notes:

_____

_____

_____

_____

_____

_____

_____

_____

_____

_____

_____

_____

_____

_____

Project Management Methodology - The topic of a project management methodology is important because it underscores something that is vital for you to understand as you prepare for the exam. The *PMBOK® Guide* does not describe a methodology. The *PMBOK® Guide* describes 49 processes used to manage a project. These processes are used by an organization's project management methodology, but they are not the methodology.

To illustrate the difference between the 49 project management processes and a project management methodology, consider the analogy of two baseball teams. The Atlanta Braves and the New York Mets both have the same set of rules when they play, but they likely have very different strategies of how they will capitalize on those strengths and use those rules to their advantages. In this analogy, the rules would equate to the processes, and the strategy to methodology.

Different organizations will employ different project management methodologies, while they will all adhere to the 49 processes. And just as a team's strategy may be more nuanced and rich than the simple rules on which it is based, an organization's methodology may be a very rich and detailed implementation of the project management processes.

Work Authorization System (WAS) - This concept is very important, even though it is not a formal part of any process. The Work Authorization System (WAS) is part of the overall project management information system (PMIS). The WAS is used to ensure that work gets performed at the right time and in the right sequence. It may be an informal e-mail sent by the project manager to a functional manager or a formal system used to get an assigned resource released to complete scheduled work.

COMMON INPUTS, TOOLS, TECHNIQUES, AND OUTPUTS

Throughout this book, several inputs, tools and techniques, and outputs of the 49 project management processes are referenced repeatedly. Since there are 1444 inputs, tools and techniques, and outputs (including their sub-points), the decision was made to discuss the most frequently used of these in the following paragraphs rather than repeat explanations time and again throughout the book. This section should serve as a reference as you encounter them, and spending extra time here should help improve your overall understanding of the material.

In fact, this section is so important that you should read it now, and then come back to reread it after you have read chapters 4–13.

⊙ Project Management Plan - The project management plan is likely the most important document discussed in this book. It may be thought of as the culmination of all the planning processes. It is crucial that you understand what it is, where it comes from, and how it is used.

For the purpose of the exam, the definition of the project management plan is a single approved document that guides execution, monitoring and control, and closure. The use of the word "single" in this definition is a bit unusual, since the project management plan is actually made up of several documents; however, once these component documents become approved as the project management plan, they become fused together as one document. Don't assume that the project management plan is always overly formal or detailed. The project management plan should be appropriate for the project. That means that it may be documented at a summary level, or it may be very detailed.

Chapter Notes:

_____

_____

_____

_____

_____

_____

_____

_____

_____

_____

_____

Common Inputs

Following is a list of the components that make up the project management plan. The project management plan is covered in more detail in Chapter 4 - Integration Management under Develop Project Management Plan. Additionally, each of these components is covered in later chapters of this book.

- Scope management plan
- Requirements management plan
- Schedule management plan
- Cost management plan
- Quality management plan
- Resource management plan
- Communications management plan
- Risk management plan
- Procurement management plan
- Stakeholder engagement plan
- Change management plan
- Configuration management plan
- Development approach
- Scope baseline
- Schedule baseline
- Cost baseline
- Performance measurement baseline
- Project life cycle description

Chapter Notes:

_____

_____

_____

_____

_____

_____

_____

_____

_____

_____

_____

_____

_____

Common Inputs

➜ Organizational Process Assets - What information, tools, documents, or knowledge does your organization possess that could help you plan for your project? Some of these might be quite obvious, such as the project plan from a previous, similar project performed by your organization, while some may be more difficult to grasp at first, such as company policy. Consider, however, that both of these assets will help you as you plan. For instance, company policy adds structure and lets you know the limits your project can safely operate within, so you do not have to waste time or resources discovering these on your own. Organizational process assets are typically divided into the categories of processes, procedures, and corporate knowledge.

A few examples of organizational process assets are:

- Templates for common project documents

- Examples from a previous project plan

- Organizational policies, procedures, and guidelines for any area (risk, financial, reporting, change control, etc.)

- Software tools

- Databases of project information

- Estimating data for budget or schedule components

- Historical information

- Lessons learned

- Knowledge bases

- Special corporate competencies

For the exam, consider anything that your organization owns or has developed that can help you on a current or future project to be an organizational process asset. An important part of your job on the project is to contribute to these assets wherever possible on your project.

Chapter Notes:

_____

_____

_____

_____

_____

_____

_____

_____

_____

_____

_____

_____

Common Inputs

Chapter Notes:

_____

_____

_____

_____

_____

_____

_____

_____

_____

_____

_____

_____

_____

_____

➔ **Project Documents** - Almost all projects regularly produce and update documentation. Even though "project documents" shows up throughout the PMBOK® Guide, it is not particularly important for the exam (remember – the exam tries to exploit your knowledge and understanding, and project documents is not an area where that is particularly easy to do in a fair way). For your preparation, review and understand this list, but do not try to memorize it.

Project documents includes any and all of the following:

- Activity attributes
- Activity list
- Assumption log
- Basis of estimates
- Change log
- Cost estimates
- Cost forecasts
- Duration estimates
- Issue log
- Lessons learned register
- Milestone list
- Project calendars
- Project communications
- Project schedule
- Project schedule network diagram
- Project scope statement
- Project team assignments

- Quality control measurements
- Quality metrics
- Quality report
- Requirements documentation
- Requirements traceability matrix
- Physical resource assignments
- Resource breakdown structure
- Resource calendars
- Resource requirements
- Risk register
- Risk report
- Schedule data
- Schedule forecasts
- Stakeholder register
- Team charter
- Test and evaluation documents

→ **Enterprise Environmental Factors** - This input can cover a lot of ground, and it appears as an input into many planning processes. In fact, it is used so frequently that you may be tempted to just skim right over it, but be careful! Enterprise environmental factors are important to your understanding of the exam material, and you should make sure you have a solid grasp of why they are used so commonly.

Consider the things that impact your project that are not part of the project itself. Just a few of these include:

- Your company's organizational structure

- The corporate culture

- Your organization's values and work ethic

- Laws and regulations where the work is being performed or where the product will be used

- The characteristics of your project's stakeholders (e.g., their expectations and willingness to accept risk)

- The overall state of the marketplace for your project

- Your organization's infrastructure

- The stakeholder or organization's appetite for risk

In fact, enterprise environmental factors can be anything external to your project that affects your project. That is why it is so important to consider these factors when planning your project and to explore how they will influence your project.

Common Inputs

Chapter Notes:

_____

_____

_____

_____

_____

_____

_____

_____

_____

_____

_____

_____

_____

Common Tools

Expert Judgment - If in doubt, ask someone who knows! The tool of expert judgment is used time and again throughout this material. The tool is exactly what it sounds like, and the reason it is so common is that it can be used whenever the project team and the project manager do not have sufficient expertise. For the exam, you do not need to worry about whether the experts come from inside the organization or outside, whether they are paid consultants or offer free advice. The most important things to remember are that this tool is highly favored and is very commonly used in planning processes.

Data Analysis - There is a saying that "nothing speaks louder than data." Data analysis is a tool used in monitoring and controlling processes to help you make sense of the work that has been carried out.

Data analysis is a versatile tool that is used in about two thirds of all processes. It is used in initiating, planning, executing, and monitoring and controlling processes.

Do not fall into the trap of making this tool unnecessarily complicated. Think of data analysis as simply carefully reviewing information in order to make a decision, and as you will discover in this book, taking regular time to review and analyze is a good mindset to carry into the exam.

Meetings - Like it or not, meetings play an important part in the management of a project, and this tool appears frequently in the 49 processes. These meetings may be colocated or virtual in nature, and they are almost unrestricted in terms of what is discussed and who attends.

Meetings do not automatically solve things by themselves, but they do give the project manager and the team time to get input from stakeholders and experts on various aspects of the project.

➔ **Project Charter** - The charter is the project's official birth certificate. It is an important document and one that you will use many times throughout its life cycle. The charter documents much of what is known at the time the project is initiated, particularly if that information informs the reasons why certain decisions are being made. For example, some requirements will certainly be known, and a summary budget or key milestone dates may already be specified.

The project charter is created once an organization has selected a project or a contract is signed to perform a project. Following are the key facts you need to remember about the project charter.

The Project Charter:

- It is created during the Develop Project Charter process.

- It is created based on some need, and it should explain that need.

- It is usually written by the sponsor and/or customer, but the project manager who will be working on the project may assist in developing it in some cases.

- It is signed by the performing organization's sponsor or other senior management.

- It names the project manager and gives him or her the authority to spend money and to allocate resources to accomplish project goals.

- It should document risk as it is understood at this point.

- It should include the high-level project requirements.

- It often includes a high-level milestone view of the project schedule.

- It is a high-level document that does not include project details; the specifics of project activities will be developed later.

- It includes a summary-level preliminary project budget.

Chapter Notes:

_____

_____

_____

_____

_____

_____

_____

_____

_____

_____

_____

_____

Common Inputs

Chapter Two

Chapter Notes:

_____

_____

_____

_____

_____

_____

_____

_____

_____

_____

_____

➜ **Agreements** - For purposes of the exam, you should equate agreements to contracts.

Think of agreements as miniature project plans that are binding. They specify what is important (similar to a project plan). In addition to these project plan-like components, agreements will also often include formal specifications for how the agreement may be amended or terminated, specific quality targets, how much things will cost, how and when payments will be made, as well as any insurance or bonding requirements.

For purposes of the exam, you want to follow agreements in all circumstances. You will never want to choose an answer that has you break an agreement even if it benefits the project.

➜ **Work Performance Data** - There is a general flow in this book that will help you. It starts with (raw) data, which is processed into information and eventually becomes reports.

Think of work performance data as raw data gathered as project work is completed. It may include data about the work itself or about how the work was performed such as the actual hours or costs it took to complete items, any problems that the team encountered, or key performance indicators (KPIs).

Work performance data is an output of the executing process, Direct and Manage Project Work, and it is a common input to 10 monitoring and controlling processes where it is refined into the more useful and understandable form of work performance information.

Interpersonal and Team Skills - The concept of interpersonal skills and team skills, commonly referred to as soft skills, has become increasingly more important in the field of project management. These skills include team leadership, communications and language, and persuasive ability.

Soft skills generally correlate to overall emotional intelligence (abbreviated as EI or EQ).

For the exam purposes, soft skills most generally refer to the project manager building productive relationships with team members and other stakeholders and persuading others to the benefit of the project.

Data Gathering - When it comes to data gathering, keep two points in mind:

1. Data gathering is a preferred technique since it feeds into the contemplative, evaluative approach that is so favored on the exam. You cannot fully consider something that you do not fully understand, so getting more data is almost always a good choice.

2. Data gathering includes brainstorming, focus groups, interviews, and checklists, but do not worry about memorizing this list for the exam. Data gathering includes any technique used to get more information about something.

The technique of data gathering is used across initiating, planning, executing, and monitoring and controlling processes.

Decision Making - It has been pointed out earlier in this chapter (and it will be stressed many times throughout this book) that you should favor a contemplative approach on the exam. This means that gathering data or thinking about a problem is a preferred option, but at some point after the experts have been consulted, the data have been gathered, and the meetings have concluded, it is time to make a decision and take action.

Chapter Notes:

_____

_____

_____

_____

_____

_____

_____

_____

_____

_____

_____

_____

_____

_____

Common Tools

Chapter Notes:

_____

_____

_____

_____

_____

_____

_____

_____

_____

_____

_____

_____

⊙ Project Management Information System (PMIS) - The Project Management Information System (abbreviated PMIS) is an important tool to know for the exam. It is an automated system to support the project manager by optimizing the schedule and helping collect and distribute information. It is your system that helps you produce and keep track of the documents and deliverables. For example, a PMIS might help your organization produce the project charter by having you fill in a few fields on a computer screen. It might then create the project charter and set up project billing codes with accounting. While the PMIS usually consists primarily of software, it will often interface with manual systems.

Another important element of the PMIS is that it will contain the configuration management system, which also contains a change control system.

The point of a configuration management system is to manage different configurations of a product. Typically, a product will be baselined at a point, and different configurations, versions, products, or branches, are managed from that point.

For example, a software company may create a base package that must be implemented for each customer. The configuration management system is used to ensure that new base functionality does not break existing custom features and that changes are evaluated across all relevant versions of the product.

The PMIS can be considered to be an enterprise environmental factor, since it is part of the environment in which the project is performed.

➜ **Updates (All Categories)** - Various updates as process outputs occur so often that it makes it very difficult for the test taker to keep it all straight. For purposes of the exam, know that updates to plans come out of planning, executing, and monitoring and controlling processes. Most of these are common sense, and rather than take up valuable brain space looking at each individual one, the concept is addressed here and referenced throughout the book.

You may reasonably update most of the documents throughout the life of the project. This is not only acceptable; it is encouraged. The team's understanding of nearly everything will grow and change as the project progresses. Documenting that evolving understanding is a good thing.

➜ **Change Requests** - As work is performed, it is common for changes to be requested. These changes can take on many forms. For instance, there may be change requests to increase the scope of the project or to cut it down in size. There may be change requests to deliver the product earlier or later, to increase or decrease the budget, or to alter the quality standards.

Change requests occur frequently for most projects as work is executed or monitored and controlled. Like the previous example, all requested changes are brought into the process of Perform Integrated Change Control where they will be evaluated for impact on the whole project and ultimately approved or rejected. Approved change requests often modify the project management plan and components such as the schedule, cost, and scope baselines.

Change requests are typically related to corrective action (any change to bring future results in line with the plan), preventive action (changes made to avoid the occurrence of a problem), or defect repair.

➜ **Work Performance Information (WPI)** - Work performance information is different from the aforementioned "work performance data" in that it has undergone some analysis or processing. If you are dealing with a summary figure, a percentage, or another useful statistic, you are likely looking at work performance information.

Chapter Notes:

_____

_____

_____

_____

_____

_____

_____

_____

_____

_____

_____

_____

Common Outputs

UNDERSTANDING AGILE

Chapter Notes:

_____

_____

_____

_____

_____

_____

_____

_____

_____

_____

_____

_____

_____

We'll begin the thrust of this book by looking at the agile philosophy and how agile projects differ from the traditional way of managing projects. Exploring the similarities and differences between agile and traditional project management will help you as you prepare for the exam.

Things can change slowly in the world of project management. Mostly, it's a straightforward profession. Needs are defined and are formed into goals. The goals are translated into features and functionality. This, in turn, is broken down into the tasks it would take to create the desired components. Progress is communicated, work is performed, and everything is tested and delivered to the customer. The beauty is that regardless of the methodology your project follows, the aforementioned steps have to be accomplished.

Given the previous sentence, you may wonder how different methodologies can be? After all, with so much in common, they must look more alike than different; however, in actual practice, methodologies can differ so greatly that they bear almost no resemblance to each other. People who attempt to switch from one methodology to another often find it very challenging to make the transition. It can require not just a change in practice, but also a radical change in thinking.

METHODOLOGIES

Before we go any farther, let's define what we mean by the word "methodology." A methodology is a set of processes and practices performed a specific way in order to accomplish a project. For example, an organization may have a particular methodology that prescribes a series of meetings with defined deliverables that need to be produced. These deliverables may follow a workflow to get approval. There may be checklists and policies that are followed regarding how the requirements are defined, how development and testing is conducted, how plans are approved, and how payments are authorized, and all of this needs to be done for each project of this type. All of these would make up the organization's methodology.

Methodologies are incredibly important. An organization which has a mature, effective, and repeatable methodology has an advantage over competitors who do not have this level of process. Some consulting organizations prize their methodologies much the way top chefs treasure their recipes (and for many of the same reasons), and some even build entire marketing strategies around them.

Organizations with no methodology tend to rely on the heroic effort of their employees. Successes are not repeatable, and lessons from failures are not implemented back into future efforts.

A methodology can be thought of as being similar to a professional team's game strategy. It's a way of working within the rules to achieve results and goals, and it needs to provide focus for planning for an end result while being flexible and adaptable to the present situation.

When we talk about "agile," we are essentially referring to a family of methodologies. You can make some assumptions about what an agile project is like, but there are numerous agile methodologies (this book covers Scrum, XP, and Lean), and sometimes how they differ is as striking as are the things they have in common.

Chapter Notes:

_____

_____

_____

_____

_____

_____

_____

_____

_____

_____

_____

_____

Methodologies

TRADITIONAL WATERFALL PROJECTS

The focus of this section of the book is the agile approach, but before we go too far down that path, let's take a moment and discuss the traditional way. If you've never practiced traditional project management, this will help you to understand some of the reasons that agile is the way it is.

Since the end of World War II, project management has primarily followed a path that became known as the "waterfall" approach. It derived its name from the linear way in which activities flow from high level to low level. Waterfall, like agile, really represents a whole family of methodologies that follow that approach.

Much of waterfall came into being with the Deming Cycle of Plan-Do-Check-Act. What may seem like common sense today was quite revolutionary at the time it was introduced.

Deming's Plan-Do-Check-Act Cycle

Waterfall methodologies generally rely on a heavy up-front analysis and documentation of the need and problems, along with the proposed solution. A plan is formed, and then all or part of the solution is constructed, the results are compared with the plan, and corrective action is taken as necessary.

Chapter Notes:

_____

_____

_____

_____

_____

_____

_____

_____

_____

_____

_____

Perhaps no methodology illustrates the waterfall approach better than the Systems Development Life Cycle (SDLC).

SDLC is a robust methodology that breaks the life cycle down into phases, with the analysis, design, implementation, testing, and evaluation carried out in each phase. Specific activities and deliverables are prescribed for each phase.

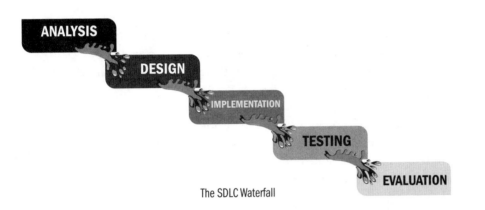

The SDLC Waterfall

While traditional waterfall project management does have its strong points, practitioners began to notice that there are also corresponding weaknesses. Projects often become rigid and resistant to change, even if that change is good for the project. Others noted that waterfall projects can sometimes become more about the process than the product. Organizations that practice this for years can often become more interested in how something is done rather than why it is done or what the results are. Another criticism of waterfall projects is that they require so much up-front analysis that the team commits to technical solutions too early in the project, and many traditional projects keep the customers at bay, requiring them to sign off on a requirements document that they may not fully understand and wait months before they can put their hands on a product. By the time they see and touch a product, it may be what they asked for but far from what they wanted or needed.

THE AGILE WAY

Chapter Notes:

_____

_____

_____

_____

_____

_____

_____

_____

_____

_____

_____

_____

_____

One significant update in the current standard is the way that agile philosophies are incorporated. Agile represents a newer way of managing projects that differs markedly from the traditionally predictive, or waterfall, methods. While agile is still treated as somewhat of an afterthought in this version of *The PMBOK® Guide*, it has made a significant entry that will likely only be increased in future editions.

When agile project management came into being in the mid 1990s, it represented a true shift, both in thinking and in practice for project managers. Many argue that it was the first significant shift within project management in recent history.

This new approach changes quite a bit. Under the old way, management generally told everyone what to do. The manager was often euphemistically referred to as the "smartest person in the room" (and the smartest person must also be the most senior person – right?).

That is not the agile way. Agile turns that approach around. Rather than the smartest or most senior person dictating the work that is done, a team may conduct a dozen experiments to see which way works best. The theory is that one person may be smarter than any one of us, but no one is smarter than all of us.

Teams are no longer organized hierarchically with direction coming from the top down. Instead, agile projects value self-organizing teams with no formal project manager. This means that the work is distributed by team consensus rather than by an authority. After all, who is better to decide what to work on than the people who will be doing the work? The project makes decisions as a team with a continued focus on delivering value to the customer. Meetings and the project work itself are conducted out in the open, with communication flowing freely among all team members.

As work progresses, communication is out in the open. Daily stand-up meetings are held each morning so that each team member can communicate what they worked on yesterday, what is planned for today, and what obstacles they are encountering. Information radiators (covered later) are posted in highly visible locations and are kept updated to communicate the project's progress to everyone who sees them.

When problems arise, rather than escalating these to a manager, the team works to resolve them internally, and because of the high degree of visibility and transparency, it is difficult for team members to hide any poor performance.

Agile projects are welcoming to change, and when product or functional changes are introduced, the team embraces them. This is true even if the changes are introduced late in the project or if they affect the architecture. The team will meet, evaluate the change, and look at the impact and ways in which it can be incorporated into the project.

Customer involvement is a key part of any agile methodology. This means that the customer participates in meetings and has complete visibility into the team's progress. Customers communicate priorities by focusing on the value a feature would provide and then balancing that against the amount of work it would take to implement the functionality. Customers are not punished or penalized when they change their minds. It is not only accepted that priorities shift and change; it is expected.

Work is delivered to the customer and to users in small, frequent releases. This has numerous benefits. For one, it keeps the team's focus very sharp by giving it an immediate priority (to build a set of functionality into the next iteration). Another benefit is that it gets that functionality into the hands of the customer quickly, allowing it to be used, tested, and providing a rapid feedback loop. Still another benefit is that the team integrates various functions back into the overall system quickly, bringing any potential architecture or integration issues to the surface more rapidly (e.g., if one feature breaks or conflicts with another feature, this should be discovered relatively quickly).

Chapter Notes:

The Agile Way

Chapter Two

Chapter Notes:

_____

_____

_____

_____

_____

_____

_____

_____

_____

_____

_____

_____

_____

If a question arises about which path to take, the agile team may execute a "spike," or rapid experiment, to determine the best way to proceed. Spikes are encouraged so that the team is highly dynamic, regularly reviewing the best way to proceed, trying new practices and measuring the outcomes, and generally experimenting and adapting.

When practicing agile, a retrospective is held at the end of each iteration and each release. This provides time for the team to reflect and communicate what worked well in the previous cycle and what did not work. The point of this is not merely to discuss any issues, but to address them with the ultimate goal of continuous improvement (Kaizen).

All of this leads to an entirely new approach. Instead of the traditional way where a product is planned extensively and then executed and finally tested, the agile way more closely follows the model of envisioning and then evolving and adapting.

You may notice here that one of the key differences is that while the traditional model favors anticipation, the agile model favors adaptation.

This is a significant departure from the way things have been done. To contrast it, keep in mind that about half of the processes identified in _The PMBOK® Guide_ are planning processes, with many of these focused on producing relatively heavy documentation before executing the work packages.

Another key difference is that traditional methods of project management typically involved the customer early in the process but tended to keep the customer at arm's length once the project team began executing work packages. Agile projects are different. The customer is more closely involved at the time the work is being performed.

By this time, you may be thinking that the agile approach sounds more like "Ready. Fire. Aim!", but that is not the case. Agile projects take small steps, getting the information in the hands of the customer as quickly as possible and evaluating not only the quality of the product but the quality of the overall process. Work is still planned, but the steps are much smaller, reducing the risk and the opportunity for mistakes.

So is agile always the best choice for managing a project? Not necessarily. Agile works well in projects where there is a need for complex decision making. If a project team already knows most of the details and things are close to agreement and close to certainty, then a waterfall methodology may be the best choice. The same argument can be made for a chaotic project environment, since a commanding and controlling style of leadership could bring order. The illustration, known as a Stacey Diagram, illustrates this spectrum of environments.

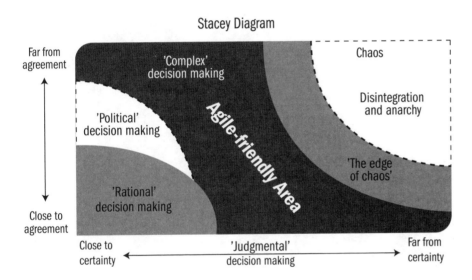

Stacey Diagram

This book is generally oriented toward a more traditional, waterfall approach to project management, but agile concepts are present, and it is necessary to know the agile perspective on the various knowledge areas.

Chapter Notes:

The Agile Way

Chapter Two

Chapter Notes:

_____

_____

_____

_____

_____

_____

_____

_____

_____

_____

_____

_____

_____

Process Framework

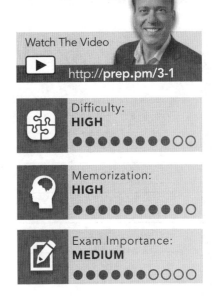

The process framework is the structure on which all of the material in this book is built. All of the processes are organized into ten knowledge areas and based on five foundational process groups:

1. Initiating
2. Planning
3. Executing
4. Monitoring and Controlling
5. Closing

Each of the 49 processes performed as part of a project can be categorized into one of these process groups. Additionally, every question you will see on the exam will tie back to one of these five groups.

This chapter describes what processes, knowledge areas, and process groups are, explains how they are structured, and provides an overview of the project management framework.

IMPORTANCE:

This chapter is essential to your understanding of how this material is organized and structured. Do not be discouraged if you find the material somewhat confusing at first. The more you read and study from this book, the better you will understand these terms and how they are applied.

Watch The Video
http://**prep.pm/3-1**

Difficulty:
HIGH
●●●●●●●●○○

Memorization:
HIGH
●●●●●●●●●○

Exam Importance:
MEDIUM
●●●●●●○○○○

Chapter Notes:

_____

_____

_____

_____

_____

_____

_____

_____

Chapter Three

Chapter Notes:

_____

_____

_____

_____

_____

_____

_____

_____

_____

_____

_____

_____

_____

PREPARATION:

There is significant memorization that accompanies this chapter. You need to understand these terms and the overall organization of this material. This chapter contains only a little that will actually show up on the exam, but it has to be mastered before you will fully comprehend chapters 4 – 13.

Essential Terms

The essential information here builds on what you learned in the previous chapter by adding a few more important terms. It is not necessary to memorize all the definitions, but make sure that you do understand them. They are foundational to the rest of the book and highly important for the exam.

Processes - The term "process" is one of the most important and frequently used terms you will encounter when studying for the PMP Exam. Processes are composed of three elements: inputs, tools and techniques, and outputs.

The different inputs, tools and techniques, and outputs are combined to form processes, which are performed for a specific purpose. For instance, Develop Schedule is a process, and as its name implies, it is performed to develop the project schedule. Identify Risks is another process, with different inputs, tools and techniques, and outputs, where (you guessed it) you identify the risks which could affect the project. There are 49 unique processes, and you will need to be familiar with all of them.

Inputs - The inputs are the starting points for the processes. Just as ingredients are the building blocks for recipes, there are specific and unique inputs into each project management process that are used as building blocks for that process. You might think of inputs as your raw materials. They are what we will use to get things done.

Tools and Techniques - Tools and techniques are the actions or methods that are used to transform inputs into outputs. Tools can be many things, such as software, which can be used as a tool to help plan the project and analyze the schedule. Techniques are methods, such as flowcharting, which help us to frame, approach, and solve the problem. We combine tools and techniques since they are both used to solve problems and create outputs.

Outputs - Every process contains at least one output. The outputs are the ends of our efforts. The output may be a document, a product, a service, or a result. Usually the outputs from one process are used as inputs to other processes or as part of a broader deliverable, such as the project plan.

Knowledge Areas

The knowledge areas in this material have been organized into ten groups. Each of the 49 project management processes fits into one of these ten knowledge areas. They are:

Integration Management (covered in chapter 4)

Scope Management (covered in chapter 5)

Schedule Management (covered in chapter 6)

Cost Management (covered in chapter 7)

Quality Management (covered in chapter 8)

Resource Management (covered in chapter 9)

Communications Management (covered in chapter 10)

Risk Management (covered in chapter 11)

Procurement Management (covered in chapter 12)

Stakeholder Management (covered in chapter 13)

Each of the knowledge areas listed above has a chapter dedicated to it.

Chapter Notes:

_____

_____

_____

_____

_____

_____

_____

_____

_____

_____

_____

_____

Process Framework

Chapter Notes:

_____

_____

_____

_____

_____

_____

_____

_____

_____

_____

_____

_____

_____

_____

Process Groups

The project management processes defined and described here are not only presented according to the ten different knowledge areas; they are also arranged according to process groups. The same 49 processes that are included in the ten knowledge areas are organized into the five process groups.

The five process groups are:

Initiating - processes that begin the project

Planning - processes that create the plans that will govern the work

Executing - processes that execute the plans and produce work

Monitoring and Controlling - processes that compare the work results to the plan and make adjustments for the future

Closing - the process that completes the project, phase, or component of a project

Every process that takes place on the project also fits into one of those five groups.

Think of process groups as categories for processes. They tell what kind of process it is. The following diagram may help you to understand the process groups by giving you some verbs most commonly associated with each one. You will notice some overlap between the groups, and this mirrors the fact that there is occasionally some overlap between processes. When learning each process, it is important that you understand the group to which it belongs.

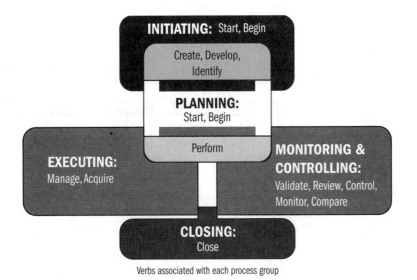

Verbs associated with each process group

Organization

As hinted at in the previous paragraphs, each process has two homes. It fits into a process group and a knowledge area. As the chapters in this book are aligned to knowledge areas, you will be able to see how processes are associated with different knowledge areas.

> **Understanding the Flow** - Do not fall into the trap of thinking that the first step is to do the processes in initiation, the second step is to do the processes in planning, and so on. Although projects may flow very roughly that way, you need to understand that the scope of a project is "progressively elaborated," which means that some processes are performed iteratively. Some planning must take place, then some executing, then some controlling. Further planning may be performed, further executing, and so on. The five process groups are by no means completely linear. More importantly, a process may be repeated multiple times throughout a project's life cycle.
>
> Perhaps one of the biggest misconceptions people have of this material is believing that these process groups are the same thing as project phases. Understand that all 49 processes could be performed one or more times in each project phase.

Chapter Notes:

Process Framework Organization

Chapter Three

Chapter Notes:

_____

_____

_____

_____

_____

_____

_____

_____

_____

_____

_____

_____

_____

_____

···· PROCESS GROUP ONE

INITIATING

Integration	Scope	Schedule	Cost	Quality
⟳				

Resource	Communications	Risk	Procurement	Stakeholder
				⟳

The Initiating Process Group is one of the simpler groups in that it is made up of only two processes: Develop Project Charter and Identify Stakeholders. These two processes are described in further detail in Chapter 4 – Integration Management, and Chapter 13 – Stakeholder Management. This is the process group that gets the project officially authorized and underway.

The way in which a project is initiated, or begun, can make a tremendous difference in the success of subsequent processes and activities.

Although many processes may not be performed in a strict order, the initiating process should be performed first or at least very early on. In initiation, the project or phase is formally begun, the project manager is named, and the stakeholder register is produced.

If a project is not initiated properly, the end results could range from a lessened authority for the project manager to unclear goals or uncertainty as to why the project was being performed.

A project that is initiated properly would have the business need clearly defined and would include a clear direction for the scope as well as information on why this project was chosen over other possibilities, along with a list of the project's stakeholders.

Initiation may be performed more than once during a single project. If the project is being performed in phases, each phase could require its own separate initiation, depending on the company's methodology, funding, and other influencing factors. There is a reason why this might be advantageous. On a longer or riskier project, requiring initiation to take place on each phase could help to ensure that the project maintains its focus and that the business reasons it was undertaken are still valid.

- Develop Project Charter
- Identify Stakeholders

Chapter Notes:

_____

_____

_____

_____

_____

_____

_____

_____

_____

_____

_____

_____

_____

_____

Process Group 1: Initiating

Chapter Three

···· PROCESS GROUP TWO

PLANNING

Chapter Notes:

Integration	Scope	Schedule	Cost	Quality
☼	☼	☼	☼	☼

Resource	Communications	Risk	Procurement	Stakeholder
☼	☼	☼	☼	☼

Planning is the largest process group because it has the most processes, but do not make the leap that it also involves the most work. Although this is not a hard and fast rule, most projects will perform the most work and use the most project resources during the executing processes.

Project planning is extremely important, both in real life and on the PMP Exam. The processes from planning touch every one of the knowledge areas. You should be familiar with the 24 processes that make up project planning.

The order in which the planning processes are performed is primarily determined by how the outputs of those planning processes are used. The outputs of one process are often used as inputs into a subsequent planning process. This shows a general order in which they must take place. For instance, the project scope statement (created during Define Scope) is used as an input to feed the work breakdown structure (created during the Create WBS process). The work breakdown structure is then used as an input to create the activity list (created during Define Activities). You may, for example, encounter a question similar to the one below:

What is the correct sequence for the following activities?

A. Create project scope statement. Create work breakdown structure. Create activity list.

B. Create project scope statement. Create activity list. Create work breakdown structure.

C. Create work breakdown structure. Create project scope statement. Create activity list.

D. Create activity list. Create project scope structure. Create work breakdown structure.

In this example, the correct sequence is represented by choice 'A'. This question requires an understanding of concepts introduced throughout this chapter, such as how scope items (the work breakdown structure) are created first, time-related planning processes (the activity durations) are performed second, and cost planning processes (the budget baseline) are performed third.

Chapter Notes:

- Develop Project Mgt. Plan
- Plan Scope Management
- Collect Requirements
- Define Scope
- Create WBS
- Plan Schedule Management
- Define Activities
- Sequence Activities
- Estimate Activity Durations
- Develop Schedule
- Plan Cost Management
- Estimate Costs
- Determine Budget
- Plan Quality Management
- Plan Resource Management
- Estimate Activity Resources
- Plan Communications Management
- Plan Risk Management
- Identify Risks
- Perform Qualitative Risk Analysis
- Perform Quantitative Risk Analysis
- Plan Risk Responses
- Plan Procurement Management
- Plan Stakeholder Engagement

Process Group 2: Planning

Chapter Three

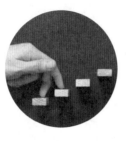

.... PROCESS GROUP THREE

EXECUTING

Integration	Scope	Schedule	Cost	Quality
○				○

Resource	Communications	Risk	Procurement	Stakeholder
○	○	○	○	○

Chapter Notes:

_____

_____

_____

_____

_____

_____

_____

_____

_____

_____

_____

_____

_____

On a project, the 10 executing processes typically involve the most work and expend the most resources. You do not need to memorize a list of executing processes like the one for planning, but you should know that the executing process group is where the work actually gets carried out. In this group of processes, parts are built, planes are assembled, code is created, documents are distributed, and houses are constructed. Other elements are also included here, such as knowledge management, procurement, and team development. These all happen during the executing processes.

Some of the processes in the executing process group are intuitive, such as Direct and Manage Project Work. Others, such as Manage Quality and Manage Communications, often catch test-takers by surprise because they had different preconceptions of what was involved.

As chapter 1 disclosed, there are currently 52 questions on the exam covering these 10 processes, so it is important to learn them well. The key to understanding the executing processes is remembering that you are carrying out the plan.

- Direct & Manage Project Work
- Manage Project Knowledge
- Manage Quality
- Acquire Resources
- Develop Team
- Manage Team
- Manage Communications
- Implement Risk Responses
- Conduct Procurements
- Manage Stakeholder Engagement

···· PROCESS GROUP FOUR

MONITORING & CONTROLLING

Integration	Scope	Schedule	Cost	Quality
○	○	○	○	○
Resource	**Communications**	**Risk**	**Procurement**	**Stakeholder**
○	○	○	○	○

Chapter Notes:

_____

_____

_____

_____

_____

_____

_____

_____

_____

_____

_____

_____

_____

_____

_____

_____

_____

_____

Monitoring and controlling processes are some of the more interesting ones. These processes touch every knowledge area. Activities that relate to monitoring and controlling simply ensure that the plan is working. If it is not, adjustments should be made to correct future results. In monitoring and controlling processes, things are measured, inspected, reviewed, compared, monitored, verified, and reported. If you see one of those key words on a question, there is a good chance it is related to a monitoring and controlling process.

Planning processes are easy enough to grasp for most people. Executing processes are simply carrying out the plan, and monitoring and controlling processes are taking the results from the executing processes and comparing them against the plan. If there is a difference between the plan and the results,corrective action is taken, either to change the plan or to change the way in which it is being executed (or both) in order to ensure that the work results line up with the plan.

Monitoring and controlling processes present another rich area for exam questions. There will be 44 questions on the PMP Exam, covering the 12 processes in this group.

Process Group 4: Monitoring & Controlling

Chapter Three

Chapter Notes:

A helpful fact to remember is that all monitoring and controlling processes will have at least two inputs. One of these will be something that was planned, and the other will be an actual result. The monitoring and controlling process will compare those two to see if any changes are warranted.

Keep in mind that monitoring and controlling processes look backward over previous work results and the plan, but corrective actions, which often result from these processes, are forward-looking. In other words, monitoring and controlling is about influencing future results and not so much about fixing past mistakes. It is very important that you understand the previous statement for the exam. That concept is reinforced throughout the next several chapters.

- Monitor & Control Project Work
- Perform Integrated Change Control
- Validate Scope
- Control Scope
- Control Schedule
- Control Costs
- Control Quality
- Control Resources
- Monitor Communications
- Monitor Risks
- Control Procurements
- Monitor Stakeholder Engagement

CLOSING

Integration	Scope	Schedule	Cost	Quality
Resource	Communications	Risk	Procurement	Stakeholder

Chapter Notes:

The project does not end with customer acceptance. After the product has been verified against the scope and delivered to the customer's satisfaction, the project records must be updated, the team must be released, and the project archives and lessons learned need to be updated (Close Project or Phase).

This lone process is an important part of the project since the files, lessons learned, and archives will be used to help plan future projects.

Although there is only one process in the Closing Process Group, the 14 questions about it make up 8% of the exam. You would do well to build a thorough understanding of what it is, how it works, and how it relates to the other processes.

If you find that you need more help in understanding the content of this chapter, review it again before you go on.

> • Close Project or Phase

Process Group 5: Closing

Chapter Three

The 49 Processes of Project Management

	Initiating	Planning	Executing	Monitoring & Controlling	Closing
Integration	Develop Project Charter	Develop Project Management Plan	· Direct & Manage Project Work · Manage Project Knowledge	· Monitor & Control Project Work · Perform Integrated Change Control	Close Project or Phase
Scope		· Plan Scope Management · Collect Requirements · Define Scope · Create WBS		· Validate Scope · Control Scope	
Schedule		· Plan Schedule Management · Define Activities · Sequence Activities · Estimate Activity Durations · Develop Schedule		Control Schedule	
Cost		· Plan Cost Management · Estimate Costs · Determine Budget		Control Costs	
Quality		Plan Quality Management	Manage Quality	Control Quality	
Resource		· Plan Resource Management · Estimate Activity Resources	· Acquire Resources · Develop Team · Manage Team	Control Resources	
Communications		Plan Communications Management	Manage Communications	Monitor Communications	
Risk		· Plan Risk Management · Identify Risks · Perform Qualitative Risk Analysis · Perform Quantitative Risk Analysis · Plan Risk Responses	Implement Risk Responses	Monitor Risks	
Procurement		Plan Procurement Management	Conduct Procurements	Control Procurements	
Stakeholder	Identify Stakeholders	Plan Stakeholder Engagment	Manage Stakeholder Engagement	Monitor Stakeholder Engagement	

Integration Management

When you look at a project, do you see the forest or the trees? In other words, do you look at the big picture, focusing on the deliverables and the workflow, or the smaller and more numerous tasks that must be performed in order to complete the project?

When it comes to the processes of project management, most of it is made up of trees; however, this chapter represents the whole forest. These seven processes focus on the larger, macro things that must be performed in order for the project to work and for the organization to learn from it. Whereas much of this material is organized around the smaller processes that produce a plan or update a document, the processes of integration are larger and more substantial.

Integration management is the practice of making certain that every part of the project is coordinated. In integration management, the project is started, the project manager assembles the project plan, executes the plan, and verifies the results of the work, and then the project is closed. The appropriate knowledge is captured for the organization. At the same time, the project manager must prioritize different objectives that are competing for time and resources and also keep the team focused on completing the work.

This chapter focuses on seven integration management processes and how they fit together and interact with each other.

One important note as we get started: this is the one knowledge area where responsibility cannot be delegated to someone else. These seven processes are at the heart of managing the entire project, and because the project manager is ultimately responsible for the entire project, he or she is also responsible for carrying out these processes.

Watch The Video
http://prep.pm/4-1

Difficulty:
HIGH
●●●●●●●●○○

Memorization:
MEDIUM
●●●●●○○○○○

Exam Importance:
HIGH
●●●●●●●●●○

Chapter Notes:

_____

_____

_____

_____

_____

_____

_____

_____

Chapter Notes:

_____

_____

_____

_____

_____

_____

_____

_____

_____

_____

_____

_____

_____

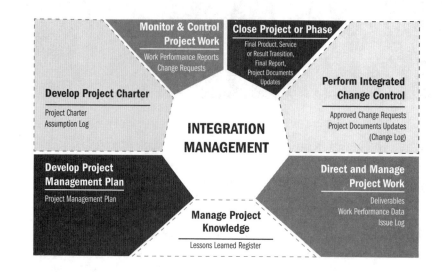

PHILOSOPHY:

Integration management takes a high-level view of the project from start to finish. The reason that the word "integration" is used is that changes made in any one area of the project must be integrated into the rest of the project. For instance, the human body's various systems are tightly integrated. What you eat and drink can affect how you sleep, and how much sleep you get can affect your ability to think clearly. When viewing your physical health, it is wise to look across your diet, exercise, sleep, stress, etc., since improvements in one area will probably cross over into others.

Integration management is similar. Changes are not made in a vacuum, and while that is true for most of the processes in this book, it is especially true among the processes covered in this chapter.

The philosophy behind integration management is threefold:

1. During the executing processes of the project, decision-making can be a chaotic and messy event, and the team should be buffered from as much of this clamor as possible. This is in contrast to the planning processes where you want the team to be more involved. You do not want to call a team meeting during execution every time a problem arises. Instead, the project manager should make decisions and keep the team focused on executing the work packages.

2. The processes that make up project management are not discrete. That is, they do not always proceed from start to finish and then move on to the next process. It would be wonderful if the scope were defined and finished and then went to execution without ever needing to be revisited; however, that is not the way things typically work. Even the most rigorously managed projects will revisit processes across the spectrum of planning, execution, and control. This is similar to the way a musician in a symphony will tune an instrument at the beginning of a concert but will likely retune and make small adjustments multiple times throughout the performance. Variables and circumstances change over time, and when they do, a plan or the way in which a project is being carried out needs to be updated.

3. Integration processes need to be tailored to fit the size and complexity of a project.

IMPORTANCE:

The importance of this section is high; you should expect several questions on the exam that relate directly to this chapter.

PREPARATION:

The difficulty factor of this material is considered high primarily because there is so much information to understand. In earlier versions of the exam, integration management was not considered to be overly difficult, but much of the material that was in other knowledge areas has been moved into integration management. While the material may not present as much technical difficulty as other areas such as schedule, quality, or cost management, it may be new to you and thus present a challenge. This chapter will guide you on where to spend most of your time and how to focus your study efforts.

Chapter Notes:

Chapter Four

Chapter Notes:

_____

_____

_____

_____

_____

_____

_____

_____

_____

_____

_____

_____

INTEGRATION MANAGEMENT PROCESSES:

There are seven processes in the integration management knowledge area. These are: Develop Project Charter, Develop Project Management Plan, Direct and Manage Project Work, Manage Project Knowledge, Monitor and Control Project Work, Perform Integrated Change Control, and Close Project or Phase. Below are the breakouts that show the group to which each process belongs:

Process Group	Integration Management Process
Initiating	Develop Project Charter
Planning	Develop Project Management Plan
Executing	Direct and Manage Project Work, Manage Project Knowledge
Monitoring & Controlling	Monitor & Control Project Work, Perform Intergrated Change Control
Closing	Close Project or Phase

It is also essential that you know the main outputs that are produced as a result of each process. The key outputs that are created in each process are summarized in the following table.

Process	Primary Outputs
Develop Project Charter	Project Charter, Assumption Log
Develop Project Management Plan	Project Management Plan
Direct and Manage Project Work	Deliverables, Work Performance Data, Issue Log
Manage Project Knowledge	Lessons Learned Register
Monitor & Control Project Work	Work Performance Reports, Change Requests
Perform Integrated Change Control	Approved Change Requests, Project Documents Updates (Change Log)
Close Project or Phase	Final Product, Service or Result Transition, Final Report, Project Documents Updates

···· INITIATING

DEVELOP PROJECT CHARTER

WHAT IT IS:

Think of the project charter as the project's birth certificate. It is the document that officially starts the project, and this is the process that creates it. Expect the charter to have a prominent and important role on the exam.

6th Edition PMBOK® Guide
Cross Ref. pg 75

WHY IT IS IMPORTANT:

The charter is one of the most important documents on a project because it is essential for creating the project. If you don't have a charter, you don't have an official project. As you will see later in this section, skipping this process can cause problems for the project manager that may not show up until much later.

Watch The Video

http://prep.pm/4-2

WHEN IT IS PERFORMED:

This process is one of the earliest ones to be performed. It is common for some pre-planning to take place on a project before it becomes official, but it will not be an official project until the charter is issued.

Chapter Notes:

_____

_____

_____

_____

_____

_____

_____

_____

Chapter Four

Chapter Notes:

_____

_____

_____

_____

_____

_____

_____

_____

_____

_____

_____

_____

_____

_____

_____

_____

HOW IT WORKS / INPUTS:

 Business Documents - The general term "business documents" really refers to the business case and the benefits management plan. This input includes documents that describe the need and how the project is going to satisfy or address that need and benefit the stakeholders.

The business case explains why this project is being undertaken, the problem it will solve, and its benefit cost analysis.

The other part of these business documents is the project benefits management plan. This describes how the project contributes to the organization's strategy and the expected benefits the project will yield and how to maximize those benefits. This document is generally provided to the project manager at the project's start.

Reasons A Project May Be Undertaken

Projects may be initiated for several reasons, and those reasons should be explained in the business case. Before going further with this process, it is important to cover some of these reasons as well as some of the ways benefits may be calculated.

Projects are undertaken for a reason, and understanding that reason can contribute to the project's success. Some of the most common reasons to undertake a project are covered below:

 Market Demand - A common scenario is for a business to identify a market need that they can satisfy through a project such as an electronics company creating a new consumer device to meet a need.

 Organizational Need - If senior management is in need of a new reporting tool to allow them to analyze trends, that would be a good reason to initiate a project to accomplish this.

Customer Request - A customer paying for a new project is the most common scenario for new projects being initiated.

Technological Advance - New technological discoveries make new products and services possible. The auto industry is just one example of how new advances in battery technology have made their ways into cars and trucks around the world. Each of these projects was begun because of a technological advance.

 Legal Requirement - New laws or a new interpretation of an existing law will often give rise to the need for a project in order to be in compliance.

 Ecological Impact - Some companies are undertaking projects to reduce their carbon footprint or ecological impact. This is considered to be a valid reason to initiate a project.

 Social Need - As an example of addressing social needs, numerous organizations are springing up to bring entrepreneurship to some of the most impoverished regions on earth. Many of these goals are also largely accomplished through projects.

Project Selection Methods

Companies select which projects to perform using a variety of methods. The most common methods seek to quantify the monetary benefits and expected costs that will result from a project and compare them to other potential projects to select the ones that are most feasible and desirable. Such methods are called benefit measurement methods.

Technically, the project manager may not have been formally assigned at this point in the project, but he or she may already be involved in other ways such as writing the business case and pitching the project to the selection committee or senior management.

Other methods apply calculus to solve for maximizations using constrained optimization. Constrained optimization uses a variety of programming methods. If you see the terms linear programming, or non-linear programming, on the exam, you will know they refer to a type of constrained optimization method and that the question is referring to techniques of project selection. You do not need to know how to calculate values for constrained optimization or linear programming for the exam, but you do need to know that they are project selection methods.

Chapter Notes:

_____

_____

_____

_____

_____

_____

_____

_____

_____

_____

_____

_____

Develop Project Charter

Chapter Four

Chapter Notes:

_____

_____

_____

_____

_____

_____

_____

_____

_____

_____

_____

_____

_____

_____

The following are additional concepts in the fields of economics, finance, managerial accounting, and cost accounting that are sometimes used as tools for project selection. It is not necessary to memorize these definitions word for word; however, it is important to understand what they are and how they are used.

Benefit Cost Ratio (BCR) - The BCR is the ratio of benefits to costs. For example, if you expect a construction project to cost $1,000,000, and you expect to be able to sell that completed building for $1,500,000, then your BCR is $1,500,000 ÷ $1,000,000 = 1.5 to 1.

In other words, you get $1.50 of benefit for every $1.00 of cost. A ratio of greater than 1 indicates that the benefits outweigh the costs.

Economic Value Add (EVA) - When you look at the value of a project, it is sometimes easy to lose sight of the big picture of adding value to shareholders. Economic Value Add, also called EVA, looks at how much value a project has truly created for its shareholders. It does more than simply look at the net profits. It also looks at the opportunity costs. By taking all of the capital costs into account, EVA can effectively show how much wealth was created (or lost) over a period of time. It takes into account the fact that there are opportunity costs to every financial expenditure, and that if a project does not make more money than those opportunity costs, it has not truly added economic value to the organization.

To calculate EVA, start with the after-tax profits of the project. Then subtract out the capital invested in that project multiplied by how much that capital cost.

For example, company XYZ invested $175,000 in a project, and that project returned a net profit of $10,000 in the first year of operation. Accountants would probably celebrate the net profit, but what does the EVA tell us about shareholder value? First, we need to determine the real cost of that capital. In this case, we will estimate 6%, since the organization could have invested that same $175,000 and earned a 6% return. When we calculate EVA, we apply the following formula:

After tax profit − (capital expenditures × cost of capital),
or $10,000 − ($175,000 × .06) = −$500.

Even though the project returned an accounting net profit, it would have been better for XYZ to bank the money instead. In other words, XYZ actually passed up $500 as far as EVA is concerned, since they would have earned $10,500 in interest if they had invested the money elsewhere instead of in the project.

Internal Rate of Return (IRR) - IRR, or "Internal Rate of Return," is a finance term used to express a project's returns as an interest rate. In other words, if this project were an interest rate, what would it be? Do not worry about the formula for the exam, but you should understand that just like the interest rate on a savings account, bigger is better when looking at IRR.

Net Present Value (NPV) - See Present Value, explained later in this section, for an explanation of Net Present Value (NPV) and Present Value (PV).

Opportunity Cost - Based on the theory that a dollar can only be invested in one place at a time, opportunity cost asks "what is the cost of the other opportunities that were passed up by investing our money and resources in this project?" For project selection purposes, the smaller the opportunity cost, the better, because it is not desirable to miss out on a great opportunity.

Payback Period - The payback period is how long it will take to recoup an investment in a project. If someone owed you $100, you would prefer that they pay it to you immediately rather than paying you $25 per month for 4 months. As you want to recoup your investment as quickly as possible in order to free that money up for another investment opportunity, a shorter payback period is always better than a longer one, all other things being equal.

Chapter Notes:

Develop Project Charter

Chapter Four

Chapter Notes:

_____

_____

_____

_____

_____

_____

_____

_____

_____

_____

_____

_____

_____

Present Value (PV) and Net Present Value (NPV) - PV is based on the "time value of money" economic theory that a dollar today is worth more than a dollar tomorrow. If a project is expected to produce 3 annual payments of $100,000, then the present value (how much those payments are worth right now) is going to be less than $300,000. The reason for this is that you will not get your entire $300,000 until the 3rd year, but if you took $300,000 cash and put it in the bank right now, you would end up with more than $300,000 in 3 years.

PV is a way to take time out of the equation and evaluate how much a project is worth right now. It is important to understand that with PV, bigger is better.

Net Present Value (NPV) is the same as Present Value except that you also factor in your costs. For example, you have constructed a building with a PV of $500,000, but it cost you $350,000. In this case, your NPV would be $500,000 – $350,000 = $150,000.

Remember that a bigger PV or NPV makes a project more attractive, and that NPV calculations have already factored in the cost of the project.

Return On Investment (ROI) - Return On Investment is a percentage that shows what return an organization makes by investing in something. Suppose, for example, that a company invests in a project that costs $200,000. The benefits of doing the project would save the company $230,000 in the first year alone. In this case, the ROI would be calculated as the (benefit – cost) ÷ cost, or $30,000 ÷ $200,000 = 15%.

Note that you should not worry about memorizing this calculation for the exam, but you do need to understand that for ROI, bigger is better.

Return on Invested Capital (ROIC) - The measure of ROIC looks at how an organization uses the money invested in a project, and it is expressed as a percentage. It asks "for every dollar of cash I invest in a project, how much should I expect (or did I earn) in return?" This invested money could be cash on hand or cash that was borrowed. For the purposes of project management, the calculation is fairly simple. Use the formula:

ROIC = Net Income (after tax) from Project ÷ Total Capital Invested in the project

For example, Fictional Enterprises invested $250,000 in a project that generated $60,000 top line revenue in its first year, with $20,000 in operational costs and a tax liability of $8,750. To calculate the ROIC, first calculate the after tax profits by subtracting the costs from
the revenue.

This is: $60,000 – $20,000 – $8,750 = $31,250.

Now apply the ROIC formula as follows:
ROIC = $31,250 ÷ $250,000 = 12.5%

This means that Fictional's project is returning 12.5% annually on the cash it invested to perform the project.

Agreements - It is easiest to think of an agreement as being a contract. Not all projects are performed under contract, so this input may or may not be relevant. When a project is performed under contract for another organization, it is common for the contract to be signed prior to the project beginning. As we are ready to start the project and create the charter, the contract provides an essential input.

Enterprise Environmental Factors — See Ch. 2, Common Inputs

Organizational Process Assets — See Ch. 2, Common Inputs

Chapter Notes:

_____

_____

_____

_____

_____

_____

_____

_____

_____

_____

_____

_____

_____

_____

Develop Project Charter

Chapter Four

Chapter Notes:

_____

_____

_____

_____

_____

_____

_____

_____

_____

_____

_____

_____

_____

HOW IT WORKS / TOOLS:

Expert Judgment — See Ch. 2, Common Tools

Data Gathering — See Ch. 2, Common Tools

Interpersonal and Team Skills — See Ch. 2, Common Tools

Meetings — See Ch. 2, Common Tools

HOW IT WORKS / OUTPUTS:

→ Project Charter - Once an organization has selected a project or a contract is signed to perform a project, the project charter must be created. Following are the key facts you need to remember about the project charter.

The Project Charter

- Think of this as your project's birth certificate.
- It is created during the Develop Project Charter process.
- It is created based on some need, and it should explain that need and how the end result will address it.
- It is usually written by the sponsor and/or customer, but the project manager who will be working on the project may assist in developing it in some cases.
- It is signed by the project's sponsor or possibly other senior management in the organization.
- It names the project manager and describes his or her level of authority to apply resources and make decisions.
- It describes under what circumstances the project may be completed, closed, or canceled (i.e. the exit criteria).
- It should include the high-level project requirements.
- It should include a high-level milestone view of the project schedule.
- It is a high-level document that does not include project details; the specifics of project activities will be developed later.
- It includes a summary-level preliminary project budget.
- It contains the objectives and measurements for success and who determines if the project is successful.
- It has a list of the key stakeholders.
- It specifies who should sign off on the final product.

Chapter Notes:

_____

_____

_____

_____

_____

_____

_____

_____

_____

_____

_____

_____

Develop Project Charter

Chapter Four

Chapter Notes:

_____

_____

_____

_____

_____

_____

_____

_____

_____

_____

_____

_____

Develop Project Charter

➔ **Assumption Log** - The assumption log is a document that is created here and will live on and be updated throughout the project. It is a place to capture all of the assumptions and constraints.

Think of an assumption as any unknown that you treat as true for the purpose of planning. At the time the charter is written, the assumptions may be broad and general. Later in the project, they will be updated to be lower level and more specific.

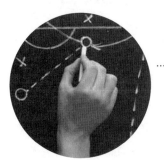

.... PLANNING

DEVELOP PROJECT MANAGEMENT PLAN

WHAT IT IS:

When many people think of a project plan, they mistakenly think only of a Gantt chart or a schedule. The project managers who have carried this misconception into the exam have been chewed up and spit out by the test! As you will see in this section, the project management plan is a comprehensive document that guides the project's execution and control, and it is much more than a schedule chart.

6th Edition PMBOK® Guide
Cross Ref. pg 82

WHY IT IS IMPORTANT:

This one should be easy. The project plan guides the team's work on the project. It specifies the who, what, when, where, and how. This document is referenced throughout this book, so a solid understanding of it will be a big help as you study.

Watch The Video
http://**prep.pm**/4-3

WHEN IT IS PERFORMED:

The question of when the process of Develop Project Management Plan is performed is an interesting one since the project management plan is not developed all at once. This plan is *progressively elaborated*, meaning that it is developed, refined, revisited, and updated. Ultimately, it represents the sum of the other major planning outputs, so it will need to be assembled after the component plans have been created.

Eventually, when the project management plan is approved, it will be put under control, meaning that it is stabilized, and further changes require a change control process.

Chapter Notes:

_____

_____

_____

_____

_____

_____

_____

_____

Chapter Four

Chapter Notes:

_____

_____

_____

_____

Brainstorming, focus groups and ← *Interviews & checklist*

Conflict Management, Facilitation ←

meeting management

kickoff meetings

Small project:

18 components go into

Project managmat plan

_____

_____

_____

HOW IT WORKS / INPUTS:

Project Charter — See Ch. 2, Common Inputs

→ Outputs from Other Processes - The project plan represents 18 component plans, fused together in this process.

Enterprise Environmental Factors — See Ch. 2, Common Inputs

Organizational Process Assets — See Ch. 2, Common Inputs

HOW IT WORKS / TOOLS:

Expert Judgment — See Ch. 2, Common Tools

Data Gathering — See Ch. 2, Common Tools

Interpersonal and Team Skills — See Ch. 2, Common Tools

Meetings — See Ch. 2, Common Tools

HOW IT WORKS / OUTPUTS:

→ Project Management Plan - The project management plan is the sole output of this process, and it is one of the most important outputs from any process.

To understand the project management plan, consider its definition. The project plan is "a formal, approved document that defines how the project is managed, executed, and controlled. It may be summary or detailed and may be composed of one or more subsidiary management plans and other planning documents."

The keys to understanding this are:

- The project management plan is formal. It is important to think of the project management plan as a formal, written piece of communication.

- The project management plan is a single document. It is not 18 separate plans. Once those separate documents are approved as the project plan, they become a single document.

- The project management plan is approved. This process is where these separate plans officially become the project plan. The people who approve it will differ based on the organizational structure and other factors, but typically it could include:

    1. The project manager

    2. The project sponsor

    3. The functional managers who are providing resources for the project

    4. The team who will be doing the work

- It is best not to think of the customer or senior management as approving the project plan. The customer will sign an agreement but will often leave the inner workings to the performing organization (ideally, anyway). The organization's senior management usually cannot get down to the level of reviewing every component document and approving the project plan, and especially not for each and every project.

- Once the project plan is approved, it is not changed on a whim. There is a change control process in place for making changes and updates.

- The project management plan defines how the project will be managed, executed, and controlled. This means that the document provides the guidance on how the bulk of the project will be conducted.

- The project management plan may be summary or detailed. Even though this wording is in the definition, you will do much better to think of the project management plan as always being detailed!

- The project management plan is made up of several components, which you may think of as chapters in the overall plan. More formal and mission-critical projects will have longer and more formal components. On actual projects, not every project management plan will contain every one of the 18 components shown in the graphic at the end of this section, but you should be familiar with the components illustrated before taking the exam.

- Another important thing to note about the project management plan is that most of its components are developed in other processes. For instance, the project risk management plan is developed in Plan Risk Management. This process is where all of these plans are brought together.

Chapter Notes:

_____

_____

_____

_____

_____

_____

_____

_____

_____

_____

_____

Develop Project Management Plan

Develop Project Management Plan

Chapter Notes:

10 Subsidiary

3 Baselines √Q³
S

5 additional

= 18 components

Important.

Which process components
are created.

Project plan components and their associated processes.

Component	PROCESS
Scope Management Plan	Plan Scope Management
Requirements Management Plan	Plan Scope Management
Schedule Management Plan	Plan Schedule Management
Cost Management Plan	Plan Cost Management
Quality Management Plan	Plan Quality Management
Resource Management Plan	Plan Resource Management
Communications Management Plan	Plan Communications Management
Risk Management Plan	Plan Risk Management
Procurement Management Plan	Plan Procurement Management
Stakeholder Engagement Plan	Plan Stakeholder Engagement
Change Management Plan	Develop Project Management Plan
Configuration Management Plan	Develop Project Management Plan
Scope Baseline	Create WBS
Schedule Baseline	Develop Schedule
Cost Baseline	Determine Budget
Performance Measurement Baseline	Develop Project Management Plan
Project Life Cycle Description	Develop Project Management Plan
Development Approach	Develop Project Management Plan

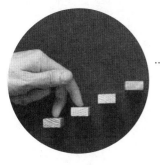

···· EXECUTING

DIRECT AND MANAGE PROJECT WORK

WHAT IT IS:

When learning the processes of project management, it is easy to take away the impression that the project manager must spend most of his or her time planning. Thankfully, however, that is not the case. Most of a project's time, cost, and resources are expended right here in the Direct and Manage Project Work process. This is where things get done!

In Direct and Manage Project Work, the team is executing the work packages and creating the project deliverables.

WHY IT IS IMPORTANT:

The Direct and Manage Project Work process is where roads get built, software applications get written, buildings are constructed, and products roll off the assembly line.

WHEN IT IS PERFORMED:

This process is difficult to put a time frame on, and it is important that you understand why. It is easy to fall into the trap of thinking about project management as occurring linearly. That is, you do your planning, then you execute all of the tasks, then you monitor and control, and finally you close, all in that order. However, that is not the way most projects are performed.

On a real project, you may do some planning, some execution, and then monitor and control, only to return to more planning, more execution, and more monitoring and controlling. In reality, you may repeat this cycle numerous times.

6th Edition PMBOK® Guide
Cross Ref. pg 90

Watch The Video
http://**prep.pm**/4-4

Chapter Notes:

_____

_____

_____

_____

_____

_____

_____

_____

_____

81

Therefore, when looking at the process of Direct and Manage Project Work, you should not think of it as a single occurrence, but understand that it occurs any time you are following the project management plan to create project deliverables.

Chapter Notes:

Carry out the plan &
creating the deliverables

We do the work.

HOW IT WORKS / INPUTS:

Project Management Plan - Remember that the project management plan guides the management, execution, and monitoring and controlling of the project. In this process, we are focused on the execution of the project plan, so it should come as no surprise that it is the essential input into this process.

Project Documents — See Ch. 2, Common Inputs

Approved Change Requests - The approved change requests come out of the Perform Integrated Change Control process and flow as inputs into Direct and Manage Project Work.

Enterprise Environmental Factors — See Ch. 2, Common Inputs

Organizational Process Assets — See Ch. 2, Common Inputs

HOW IT WORKS / TOOLS:

Expert Judgment — See Ch. 2, Common Tools

Project Management Information System — See Ch. 2, Common Tools

Meetings — See Ch. 2, Common Tools

HOW IT WORKS / OUTPUTS:

⊙ Deliverables - A deliverable is any product, service, or result that must be completed in order to finish the project. Some projects also must develop capabilities in order to finish a project, and these may be deliverables as well. For instance, a project may need to develop a new manufacturing technique before it can create a product. In that case, the capability that the team develops would be considered a deliverable. It is also important to understand what happens to the deliverables that are created. They flow through the processes of Control Quality and Validate Scope until they meet specifications for correctness and completeness. After that, the deliverables are also used in the process of Manage Project Knowledge.

⊙ Work Performance Data - If the deliverables are the most important output of this process, this one is the second most important. It isn't only the deliverables that flow out of this process, but also the data about how those deliverables are being produced.

As we covered in chapter two, the work performance data is eventually converted into work performance information after it has been analyzed and understood. The data collected here is raw and unprocessed at this point.

⊙ Issue Log - An issue is an unresolved threat or problem on the project or a point of disagreement, and the issue log is the document where these are recorded. The issue log is important, because it not only helps organize issues, but it lets the stakeholders and the team know that these are actively being reviewed.

Change Requests — See Ch. 2, Common Outputs

Project Management Plan Updates —
　　　See Ch. 2, Common Outputs

Project Document Updates — See Ch. 2, Common Outputs

Organizational Process Assets Updates —
　　　See Ch. 2, Common Outputs

Chapter Notes:

_____
_____
_____
_____
_____
_____
_____
_____
_____
_____
_____
_____
_____
_____

Direct And Manage Project Work

···· EXECUTING

MANAGE PROJECT KNOWLEDGE

6th Edition PMBOK® Guide
Cross Ref. pg 98

WHAT IT IS:

Manage Project Knowledge is a newly recognized process with this edition. This process benefits the project by leveraging lessons learned from previous projects, and it also benefits the performing organization so that it can hold onto the lessons learned on this project.

WHY IT IS IMPORTANT:

Your project can learn from previous projects, and others in your organization can benefit from the lessons you learn on this project. Put another way, "those who fail to learn from history are doomed to repeat it."

Watch The Video

▶ http://**prep.pm**/4-5

WHEN IT IS PERFORMED:

Technically you may perform this process any time a project lesson is learned; however, the most logical time is after the deliverables for each phase have been completed but before the phase or project has been closed.

Chapter Notes:

_____

_____

_____

_____

_____

_____

_____

_____

HOW IT WORKS / INPUTS:

Project Management Plan — See Ch. 2, Common Inputs

Project Documents — See Ch. 2, Common Inputs

➔ **Deliverables** - The deliverables produced in the preceding process, Direct and Manage Project Work, are brought into this process. The reason is that the type of deliverable will shape the learning that needs to be captured.

For example, a new pharmaceutical product or a new type of automobile might have significant regulatory lessons learned, while a new road might have more environmental or stakeholder-related lessons learned.

The deliverables don't automatically determine the lessons learned, but they will definitely flavor them.

Enterprise Environmental Factors — See Ch. 2, Common Inputs

Organizational Process Assets — See Ch. 2, Common Inputs

HOW IT WORKS / TOOLS:

Expert Judgment — See Ch. 2, Common Tools

➔ **Knowledge Management** - Knowledge management has two main components: explicit knowledge and tacit knowledge.

Explicit knowledge include things that may be written down or drawn and easily archived for future lessons learned.

Tacit knowledge includes beliefs, opinions, and abilities. These may be difficult to put into a format for archiving.

The idea behind knowledge management is to get people to interact and share knowledge and experience. This can include a lot of different things like networking, facilitated workshops, and meetings to name just a few.

Chapter Notes:

Tatic knowledge

Manage Project Knowledge

Chapter Four

Chapter Notes:

_____

_____

_____

_____

_____

_____

_____

_____

_____

_____

_____

_____

_____

➔ **Information Management** - It may be slightly confusing to see the tool of information management right alongside knowledge management. Even if it does get nuanced, the two are somewhat different. If you think of knowledge as often being experiential, think of information as being more concrete.

The easiest way to think about information management would be to imagine using a collaboration and document management system such as SharePoint. This would allow you to share documents, tools, templates, and lessons learned with other people on your team and in the organization.

The point of this tool is to be intentional about capturing this explicit, codified information.

Interpersonal and Team Skills — See Ch. 2, Common Tools

HOW IT WORKS / OUTPUTS

➔ **Lessons Learned Register** - This output captures the main point of Manage Project Knowledge. The lessons learned register is a document that spells out what worked well and what did not. It focused on what the team would do differently if they had this project to do over again, knowing what they know now.

It will be updated throughout the project and used as an input both in this project and in future projects performed by this organization.

The team that is performing the work should be very involved in its development.

Project Management Plan Updates —
　　　　See Ch. 2, Common Outputs

Organizational Process Assets Updates —
　　　　See Ch. 2, Common Outputs

···· MONITORING & CONTROLLING

MONITOR AND CONTROL PROJECT WORK

WHAT IT IS:

The process of Monitor and Control Project Work takes a look at all of the work that is being performed on a project and makes sure that the deliverables and the way in which they are being produced are in line with the project plan and meet the objectives.

Monitor and Control Project Work is important because it is another macro integration process even though most of the inputs, tools, and outputs to this process are common ones. It looks at how the overall project is progressing and takes corrective action as needed through change requests. For instance, if the project is trending late, you might decide to trim the scope for the first release or to potentially add more resources. If you are significantly ahead of schedule, you might reduce the number of resources you are using. Both of these would be examples of the kinds of activities involved in Monitor and Control Project Work. The project manager makes large, macro decisions about the project based on how things have been progressing and how they are forecasted to continue.

6th Edition PMBOK® Guide
Cross Ref. pg 105

Watch The Video
▶ http://**prep.pm/4-6**

Chapter Notes:

_____

_____

_____

_____

_____

_____

_____

Chapter Four

Chapter Notes:

_____

_____

_____

_____

_____

_____

_____

_____

_____

_____

_____

_____

_____

_____

WHY IT IS IMPORTANT:

All monitoring and controlling processes fulfill an important role on the project. They compare the work results to the plan and make whatever adjustments are necessary to ensure that the two align. Any necessary changes to the work or the plan are identified and requested here in this process.

Monitoring and controlling processes like this one also keep an eye on all project information to ensure that risks are being identified and managed properly and to make sure that performance is on track.

WHEN IT IS PERFORMED:

Monitor and Control Project Work is closely tied to the process Direct and Manage Project Work, and it takes place as long as there is work on the project to be carried out.

Integration Management

HOW IT WORKS / INPUTS:

➡️ **Project Management Plan** - The project management plan is the main guiding input to this process, and it is key. It will provide the plan against which the results will be measured.

Project Documents – The project documents are covered generally in chapter 2, Common Inputs; however, there are some particular components to focus on.

Assumption Log – to have a record of all of the uncertainties the team was treating as true for planning purposes.

Basis of Estimates – backup information that shows how the team arrived at estimates.

➡️ **Cost Forecasts** – to create earned value calculations to show how the project is progressing against the plan.

Issue Log – to show which issues are arising on the project, who is responsible for them, and when a response to these issues is expected.

Lessons Learned Register – to leverage lessons learned on this project and previous ones.

Milestone List – to give an easy way to measure high-level progress against the schedule.

Quality Reports – to show actual quality versus planned quality. Trends may be visible that would require corrective action.

Risk Register – to show identified risks and risk events that have occurred that may require corrective action.

Risk Report – to show information about high-level risks and detailed risks affecting the project.

➡️ **Schedule Forecasts** – to create earned value calculations to show how the project is progressing against the plan.

Chapter Notes:

output of control cost process

Summary view of schedule

Reference

output of control schedule process.

Monitor and Control Project Work

Monitor and Control Project Work

Chapter Notes:

_____

_____

_____

_____

_____

_____

Variance Analysis

Alternative Analysis

Cost Benifit analysis

_____

_____

_____

_____

_____

➔ **Work Performance Information** - The work performance information, or WPI, is a common input covered in Ch. 2. It is marked as a key fact here because it provides actual results that can be compared against the project management plan.

Agreements — See Ch. 2, Common Inputs

Enterprise Environmental Factors — See Ch. 2, Common Inputs

Organizational Process Assets — See Ch. 2, Common Inputs

HOW IT WORKS / TOOLS:

Expert Judgment — See Ch. 2, Common Tools

Data Analysis - There is a saying that "nothing speaks louder than data." In this case, data analysis is used to look at the data and spot trends, determine root cause, to analyze buffers, review variances, and to ensure that the project is operating within performance and risk tolerances.

Decision Making — See Ch. 2, Common Tools

Meetings — See Ch. 2, Common Tools

HOW IT WORKS / OUTPUTS:

Work Performance Reports - Notice that work performance information is an input into this process, and the work performance reports come out. They are used to create awareness and to help with decision-making. Examples include dashboards, heat reports, burndown charts, and traffic lights, to name a few.

The important thing to remember about reports is that they should be actionable.

Change Requests — See Ch. 2, Common Outputs

Project Management Plan Updates —
> See Ch. 2, Common Outputs

Project Documents Updates — See Ch. 2, Common Outputs

Chapter Notes:

_____

_____

_____

_____

_____

_____

_____

_____

_____

_____

_____

_____

_____

_____

Monitor and Control Project Work

Chapter Four

···· MONITOR & CONTROLLING

PERFORM INTEGRATED CHANGE CONTROL

6th Edition PMBOK® Guide
Cross Ref. pg 113

Watch The Video
▶ http://**prep.pm/4-7**

Chapter Notes:

_____

_____

_____

_____

_____

_____

_____

WHAT IT IS:

Some processes are more important than others for the exam, and this one qualifies as one of the most important.

Every change to the project, whether requested or not, needs to be processed through Perform Integrated Change Control. It is in this process where you assess each change, whether it already occurred or it has been requested, to assess the impact on the project.

WHY IT IS IMPORTANT:

Perform Integrated Change Control brings together (i.e., integrates) all of the other monitoring and controlling processes. When a change occurs in one area, it is evaluated for its impact across the entire project.

For example, suppose you came in to work one morning and found that a new legal requirement meant that the quality of your project's product needed to be improved. Would you only look at the quality processes on the project? No. After understanding the quality impact of this change, you would likely need to evaluate the impact on the scope of the project, the activity duration estimates, the overall schedule, the budget estimates, the project risks, contract and supplier issues, etc. In other words, you would need to integrate this change throughout the other areas of the project.

One way in which Perform Integrated Change Control differs from the previous process, Monitor and Control Project Work, is that Perform Integrated Change Control is primarily focused on managing change to the project, while Monitor and Control Project Work manages the way the work is carried out.

For example, consider a new construction project for a hospital. If a change request were submitted that added a new wing to the hospital building, then that change request would be evaluated through Perform Integrated Change Control to understand its impact on the whole project. If, however, the project team members were performing slower than planned, that would be factored into Monitor and Control Project Work, and corrective action would be requested to ensure that the plan and the execution lined up. Even though both are monitoring and controlling processes, each has a different focus.

WHEN IT IS PERFORMED:

Like the integration processes Direct and Manage Project Work and Monitor and Control Project Work, the process of Perform Integrated Change Control takes place as long as there is work on the project to be carried out.

Some organizations have a Change Control Board (CCB) that reviews change requests and formally approves or rejects them.

HOW IT WORKS / INPUTS:

Project Management Plan — See Ch. 2, Common Inputs

Project Documents — See Ch. 2, Common Inputs

Work Performance Reports — See Ch. 2, Common Outputs

Change Requests - Although change requests are a common input and output of some processes, they are the key to Perform Integrated Change Control. They provide the main content here.

Enterprise Environmental Factors — See Ch. 2, Common Inputs

Organizational Process Assets — See Ch. 2, Common Inputs

Chapter Notes:

Perform Integrated Change Control

Chapter Four

Chapter Notes:

_____

_____

_____

_____

_____

_____

_____

_____

_____

_____

_____

_____

_____

_____

_____

HOW IT WORKS / TOOLS:

Expert Judgment — See Ch. 2, Common Tools

Change Control Tools - Tools here are used to manage the flow of information for the Change Control Board and the project manager. The number of tasks and the associated workflow may become difficult to manage without some type of system in place.

Data Analysis — See Ch. 2, Common Tools

Decision Making — See Ch. 2, Common Tools

Meetings - The Change Control Board is a formally constituted committee responsible for reviewing changes and change requests. The level of authority of a Change Control Board varies among projects and organizations; however, its level of authority should be spelled out in the project management plan. The change control meetings are the forums for formally evaluating these changes.

HOW IT WORKS / OUTPUTS:

 Approved Change Requests - This output would more aptly be named "approved or rejected change requests."

All formally requested changes must be approved or rejected. The approved change requests are channeled back into Direct and Manage Project Work. Rejected change requests should be routed back to the requesting party.

The change log is the central place to keep track of all changes and change requests that occur on a project. They are documented as part of this output and are communicated to the stakeholders.

Project Management Plan Updates — See Ch. 2, Common Outputs

Project Documents Updates - The project's change log is the most important document that gets updated as a part of this process.

···· CLOSING

CLOSE PROJECT OR PHASE

WHAT IT IS:

One of the key attributes of a project is that it is temporary. This means that every project eventually comes to an end, and that is exactly where this integration process comes into play.

Close Project or Phase is all about shutting the project (or a particular phase, which is often like a mini-project) down properly.
This includes creating the necessary documentation and archives, capturing the lessons learned, and updating all organizational process assets.

Another important thing to note is that the team is released as part of this process.

Most of the tasks are administrative, financial, and legal. The exam may occasionally refer to these activities as Administrative Closure.

6th Edition PMBOK® Guide
Cross Ref. pg 121

Watch The Video
▶ http://**prep.pm**/4-8

WHY IT IS IMPORTANT:

Projects that skip this process often are left open, limping along for months without official closure. Taking the time to perform this step, and to do it properly, will ensure that the project is closed as neatly and as permanently as possible and that records are properly created and archived. These records become organizational process assets for use on future projects the organization undertakes.

Chapter Notes:

_____

_____

_____

_____

_____

_____

_____

Chapter Four

Chapter Notes:

_____

_____

_____

_____

_____

_____

_____

_____

_____

_____

_____

_____

_____

_____

WHEN IT IS PERFORMED:

By looking at the name of this process, you can probably deduce that it is performed at the very end of the project or at the end of each phase. Projects that have six phases would likely perform this process seven times (once after each phase, and once for the project as a whole). In real practice, you might well perform some of the activities in this process before the project or phase ends, but for the exam, think of it as the last process performed on a project or phase.

HOW IT WORKS / INPUTS:

Project Charter - The charter described why this project was being undertaken in the first place as well as the exit criteria.

It also has a place for someone to formally sign off on the project.

Project Management Plan — See Ch. 2, Common Inputs

Project Documents — See Ch. 2, Common Inputs

Accepted Deliverables - These flow out of the Validate Scope process. At this point, the deliverables will be complete, correct, and signed off.

Business Documents - This includes the business case and the benefits management plan. The business case provides an excellent yardstick to determine whether or not the project hit its targets and the benefits were realized as expected. These documents were brought into the process Develop Process Charter, and this process of Close Project or Phase is the corresponding project bookend.

Agreements - Remember to think of agreements as contracts when preparing for the exam. Any well-written agreements will specify exit criteria, so it is natural to bring them as inputs into this process.

Procurement Documentation — See Ch. 2, Common Inputs

Organizational Process Assets — See Ch. 2, Common Inputs

HOW IT WORKS / TOOLS:

Expert Judgment — See Ch. 2, Common Tools

Data Analysis — See Ch. 2, Common Tools

Meetings — See Ch. 2, Common Tools

HOW IT WORKS / OUTPUTS:

➜ **Project Documents Updates** - The lessons learned register is the main documented that would be updated here. Lessons learned are anything the team would do differently if they had the project to perform over again.

➜ **Final Product, Service, or Result Transition** - This output represents not so much the product itself, but the acceptance and handover of responsibility to the receiving party (e.g., the customer, operations, support group, or another company). The transition implies that the product has been accepted and is ready for this handover.

➜ **Final Report** - The final report is a summary of the project or phase. It will likely include information about scope, schedule performance, cost performance, benefits realization, and a summary of risks.

Organizational Process Assets Updates - In the course of a project, lessons will be learned, information will be gleaned, tools will be purchased or built, knowledge and experience will be gained, and documents (some of which may be reused one day) will be created. All of this should be updated as an organizational process asset and delivered to the appropriate group or individual(s) responsible for maintaining them. Often this will be the project management office.

Examples of organizational process assets that might be updated from this process include the customer's or sponsor's formal acceptance documentation, project closure documents, project files, and historical information. The lessons learned should be recorded as well.

Chapter Notes:

Close Project or Phase

Chapter Four

Chapter Notes:

_____

_____

_____

_____

_____

_____

_____

_____

_____

_____

_____

_____

_____

_____

_____

➔ The Agile Perspective on Integration Management

Projects that use adaptive methodologies such as Scrum, Lean, or others, rely more heavily upon the team than the project manager. In the preceding seven processes covered in this chapter, the project manager makes key decisions on integration activities, but on an agile project, it is the team that is empowered to make these decisions and to determine how the elements integrate. Agile teams favor "generalizing specialists" on the team over highly specialized individuals, so team members are generally aware of the needs of the project and are closely tied to the project, making it manageable to handle integration issues at the team level.

Chapter Notes:

INTEGRATION MANAGEMENT

QUESTIONS

1. **Producing a project plan may BEST be described as:**

    A. Creating a network logic diagram that identifies the critical path.

    B. Using a software tool to track schedule, cost, and resources.

    C. Creating a document that guides project plan execution.

    D. Creating a plan that contains the entire product scope.

2. **Project management plan updates are NOT an output of:**

    A. Perform Integrated Change Control.

    B. Develop Project Management Plan.

    C. Direct and Manage Project Work.

    D. Monitor and Control Project Work.

Chapter Notes:

_____

_____

_____

_____

_____

_____

_____

_____

_____

_____

_____

_____

_____

3. You are meeting with a new project manager who has taken over a project that is in the middle of executing. The previous project manager has left the company and the new project manager is concerned that change requests are streaming in from numerous sources including his boss, the customer, and various stakeholders. The project manager is not even aware of how to process all of these incoming change requests. Where would you refer him?

A. The project scope statement.

B. The project management plan.

C. The previous project manager.

D. The project charter.

4. Centurion Corporation has initiated a new project to modernize their human resources records and to bring them into compliance. A manager at Centurion is drafting the project charter for review. Which of the following would be the most important item that she would need in order to complete this task and why?

A. Managerial approval to proceed, because it may affect whether or not the project moves forward.

B. A scope statement, because it will set the parameters for the product scope.

C. A scope statement, because it will set the parameters for the project scope.

D. A business case, because it explains the justification for the project.

5. The project charter is:

A. Developed before the business case, and after the project management plan.

B. Developed after the business case, and before the project management plan.

C. Developed before the contract, and after the project management plan.

D. Developed before the contract, and before the project management plan.

6. The project management information system would likely include all of the following EXCEPT:

    A. A scheduling tool.

    B. An information distribution system.

    C. A system for collecting information from team members.

    D. A system for identifying stakeholders.

7. A defect in the product was brought to the project manager's attention, and now the project team is engaged in repairing it. Which project management process would be the most applicable to this?

    A. Perform Integrated Change Control.

    B. Monitor and Control Project Work.

    C. Direct and Manage Project Work.

    D. Close Project or Phase.

8. If you are creating a single document to guide project execution, monitoring and control, and closure, you are creating:

    A. The execution plan.

    B. The project management plan.

    C. The integration plan.

    D. The project framework.

9. Change control meetings are held as part of which process?

    A. Direct and Manage Project Work.

    B. Monitor and Control Project Work.

    C. Perform Integrated Change Control.

    D. Evaluate Requested Changes.

Chapter Notes:

_____
_____
_____
_____
_____
_____
_____
_____
_____
_____
_____
_____
_____
_____
_____

Integration Management Questions

Chapter Notes:

_____

_____

_____

_____

_____

_____

_____

_____

_____

_____

_____

_____

_____

_____

10. **Which of the following statements is NOT true regarding the project charter?**

A. The project charter justifies why the project is being undertaken.

B. The project charter assigns the project manager.

C. The project charter specifies any high-level schedule milestones.

D. The project charter specifies the types of contracts that will be used.

11. **Which of the following represents the project manager's responsibility regarding change on a project?**

A. To influence the factors that cause project change.

B. To ensure all changes are communicated to the change control board.

C. To reduce change wherever possible.

D. To prioritize change below results.

12. **The project management plan is made up of:**

A. The other planning outputs.

B. The other planning outputs, tools, and techniques.

C. The aggregate outputs of the PMIS.

D. The business case, key value justifications, and the GANTT chart.

13. **When changes are approved and made to the project, they should be:**

A. Tracked against the project baseline.

B. Incorporated into the project baseline.

C. Included as an addendum to the project plan.

D. Approved by someone other than the project manager.

14. **Which statement about project agreements is true?**

    A. Agreements are drafted between the project manager and the key stakeholders prior to resources being expended.

    B. Agreements are generally created only when one or more portions of the project are being procured from outside the organization.

    C. Agreements are inputs to create the project charter.

    D. Agreements are broadly considered to be an enterprise environmental factor.

15. **Work performance information is used for all of the following reasons EXCEPT:**

    A. It provides information on resource utilization.

    B. It provides information on which activities have started.

    C. It shows what costs have been incurred.

    D. It is used to help identify defects.

16. **You are a project manager, and your team is executing the work packages to produce a medical records archive and retrieval system. Two of the project's customers have just asked for changes that each says should be the number one priority. What would be the BEST thing to do?**

    A. Have the project team meet with the customers to decide which would be easiest and prioritize that one first.

    B. Assign someone from the team to prioritize the changes.

    C. Prioritize the changes without involving the team.

    D. Deny both changes since you are in project execution.

Chapter Notes:

Chapter Four

Chapter Notes:

_____

_____

_____

_____

_____

_____

_____

_____

_____

_____

_____

_____

_____

_____

17. The program manager is asking why your project is scheduled to take sixteen months. He claims that previous projects in the organization were able to be completed in less than half of that time. What would be the BEST thing to do?

    A. Look for historical information on the previous projects to understand them better.

    B. Refer the program manager to the schedule management plan.

    C. Refer the program manager to the project management plan.

    D. Explain to the program manager that estimates should always err on the side of being too large.

18. You work for a defense contractor on a project that is not considered to be strategic for the company. Although the project is not the company's top priority, you have managed to secure many of the company's top resources to work on your project. At today's company meeting, you find out that your organization has won a very large, strategic project. What should you do FIRST?

    A. Contact management to find out if you can be transferred to this project because it is strategic to the company.

    B. Contact management to find out how this new project will affect your project.

    C. Hold a team meeting and explain that since the resources have been allocated to your project, they are not eligible to go to the new project.

    D. Fast track your project to accelerate its completion date.

19. Each time that the project sponsor requests a change to the project, the project manager calls a meeting of the change control board. Which of the following is TRUE?

    A. This represents a collaborative style of management.

    B. This represents withdrawal by the project manager.

    C. This represents Perform Integrated Change Control.

    D. This represents the lack of an effective project management information system.

20&. Alex has received an inquiry from a functional manager about how the team is performing. In reality, the team's productivity has been lagging for the past two months, but Alex is confident that this problem can be resolved. Which process would most likely produce the information the functional manager has requested?

A. Direct and Manage Project Work.

B. Monitor and Control Project Work.

C. Report Performance.

D. Perform Integrated Change Control.

21. Your organization has a policy that any project changes that increase the project's budget by more than 1.5% must be signed off by the project office. You have a change that was requested by the customer that will increase the budget by 3%; however, the customer has offered to pay for all of this change and does not want to slow it down. Which option represents the BEST choice?

A. Approve the change yourself.

B. Ask the customer to take the change to the project office and explain the situation.

C. Do not allow the change since it increases the budget by over 1.5%.

D. Take the change to the project office.

22. The person or group responsible for evaluating change on a project is:

A. The change control board.

B. The sponsor.

C. The project team.

D. The program manager.

Chapter Notes:

Chapter Four

Chapter Notes:

_____

_____

_____

_____

_____

_____

_____

_____

_____

_____

_____

_____

_____

23. The output of the Direct and Manage Project Work process is:

   A. The work packages.

   B. The project management information system.

   C. The deliverables.

   D. The work breakdown structure.

24. Two projects are being considered by the project office: Project Clarity, and Project New Scale. The Chief Project Officer is planning to evaluate the projected Return On Investment Capital for both projects. In order to do that, what information would be most helpful?

   A. The total projected capital investment and net income.

   B. The total projected benefit and cost.

   C. The total projected capital expenditures and cost of capital.

   D. The total projected return on investment, the cost of capital, and the current interest rate.

25. Which component of the project management plan is created in Develop Project Management Plan?

   A. Change Management Plan.

   B. Requirements Management Plan.

   C. Process Improvement Plan.

   D. Stakeholder Engagement Plan.

INTEGRATION MANAGEMENT

ANSWERS

1. C. The project plan is a single, approved plan that drives execution, monitoring and control, and closure. Note that the definition in answer 'C' was not perfect, but it was the best choice. 'A' is incorrect since it is only a part of planning. 'B' is incorrect because that will not make up the entire project plan. 'D' is incorrect since scope may or may not be a part of the project plan, but it does not make up all of it.

2. B. The project management plan is created in Develop Project Management Plan. It, along with other plans, is updated in the other processes listed.

3. B. The project management plan would contain the methods for processing change requests to the project.

4. D. The business case is one of the business documents that is an input to the process of Develop Project Charter, where the charter is created, making this the best choice. The business case provides the reasons why the project needed to be initiated. 'A' is not a very good choice here because the charter, which is being created here, represents managerial approval, so that would not be needed to complete this task. Rather, that would be an outcome of this task. Both 'B' and 'C' are not good choices, because the scope statement is an output that is created later.

5. B. Questions like this will be on the exam, and in order to answer them, you have to understand the rough order in which the deliverables are produced and processes are conducted. In this case, the typical order among the items listed is the business case, contract, project charter, and project management plan. If you analyze the inputs and outputs used by the integration processes, you will gain a better understanding of this order.

Chapter Four

Chapter Notes:

_____

_____

_____

_____

_____

_____

_____

_____

_____

_____

_____

_____

_____

6. D. The project management information system (PMIS) is an automated system to support the project manager by optimizing the schedule and helping collect and distribute information. 'D' would not be a function of the PMIS. It is generally a manual process performed by the project manager and the team.

7. C. Direct and Manage Project Work is the only process in the list where defects are repaired. Approved change requests are an input, and deliverables are an output.

8. B. This is the definition of the project management plan.

9. C. As you think about this one, ask yourself which process group would use a tool like change control meetings. The answer to that question is "monitoring and controlling." Now, you can immediately narrow it down to two processes represented in answers 'B' and 'C'. Keep the flow of these processes in mind. Change requests flow out of Monitor and Control Project Work and into Perform Integrated Change Control, where they are evaluated in meetings. Answer 'D' may sound great, but it is not the name of a real process.

10. D. The project charter does not specify anything about contracts. A contract with your customer would have been an input into the Develop Project Charter process, and any contracts you may use during procurement won't be identified until later in the project. 'A' is incorrect because the project charter does specify why the project is being undertaken and often even includes a business case. 'B' is incorrect because the project charter is the place where the project manager is named. 'C' is incorrect because the project charter specifies any known schedule milestones and a summary level budget.

11. A. The project manager must be proactive and influence the factors that cause change. This is one of the key tenets of monitoring and controlling processes in general and Perform Integrated Change Control in particular.

12. A. The project management plan consists of many things, but the only one from this list that matches is the outputs from the other planning processes, such as risk, cost, time, quality, etc. 'C' is incorrect because the PMIS supports the project manager in carrying out the project management plan, but it does not generate it.

13. B. Did this one fool you? Approved changes that are made to the project get factored back into the baseline. Many people incorrectly choose 'A', but the purpose of the baseline is NOT to measure approved change, but to measure deviation.

14. C. Agreements are one of four inputs used to create the project charter. 'B' might look tempting, but agreements may be on any kind of project. 'D' is incorrect since you want to think of enterprise environmental factors as things within your organization that influence your project. An agreement is more binding than that.

15. D. The work performance information is all about how the work is being performed, but it is not used in identifying defects. 'A' is incorrect because it does provide detail on what resources have been used and when. 'B' is incorrect because it provides information on which activities have been started and what their status is. 'C' is incorrect because it provides information on what costs were authorized and what costs have been incurred.

16. C. Prioritizing the changes is the job of the project manager. 'A' is wrong because you do not want to distract the team at this point – they should be doing the work. 'B' is wrong because it is the project manager's responsibility to help prioritize competing demands. 'D' is incorrect, because changes cannot automatically be denied simply because you are in execution.

17. A. Historical information (an organizational process asset) was covered in Chapter 2 – Foundational Terms and Concepts, and it may provide an excellent justification for why your project is taking sixteen months, or perhaps it will show you how someone else accomplished the same type of work in less time. Either way, it provides a great benchmark for you to factor in to your project. 'B' is incorrect since the schedule management plan only tells how the schedule will be managed. 'C'

Chapter Notes:

_____

_____

_____

_____

_____

_____

_____

_____

_____

_____

_____

_____

_____

is incorrect because the project plan will not specifically address the program manager's concern about why the project is taking longer than he expects. 'D' is wrong because estimates should be accurate with a reserve added on top as may be appropriate.

18. B. Always evaluate things thoroughly before you act! You need to know if your project is going to be affected before taking action. Many people incorrectly choose 'D', but fast tracking the schedule increases risk, and that would not be necessary or appropriate until you fully understood the situation.

19. C. Change control boards meet to evaluate change requests. They do this during the process of Perform Integrated Change Control.

20. B. Monitor and Control Project work is the correct answer, since its main function is to produce the work performance reports, and these explain how the team is performing against the plan. 'C' is not a real process (interestingly, it used to be, but it is has been phased out).

21. D. As discussed in Chapter 2 – Foundational Terms and Concepts, organizational policies must be followed. None of the other options presents an acceptable alternative. 'A' would break company policy even though it looks harmless. Choice 'B' would be asking the customer to do the project manager's job.

22. A. The change control board is responsible for evaluating changes to the project.

23. C. The deliverables are the key output of Direct and Manage Project Work.

24. A. The formula for Return On Investment Capital (ROIC) is Net Income / the Total Capital Investment. This makes 'A' the best choice.

25. A. The change management plan, the configuration management plan, and the performance measurement baseline, are among the plans created in the process of Develop Project Management Plan. 'B' and 'D' are created elsewhere and are brought into this process to be compiled into the project management plan

Scope Management

Good news! Scope management is not a particularly difficult area to master, and it pays big dividends for the exam. It can be more intuitive than other areas, and there are no complex formulas to memorize and no particularly difficult theories. Instead, scope management is a logical group of processes to help you understand requirements, define, break down, and control the scope of the project, and verify that the product was completed correctly.

The term "scope" can be a bit tricky. It may refer to the scope of the entire project or just the scope of the product. The product scope is everything that must be completed in order to meet product requirements, while the project scope includes everything in the entire project plan. For example, you may document lessons learned at some point. That would be considered part of the project scope, because it does not really have anything to do with producing the product, but the lessons learned might be helpful for future projects.

Watch The Video
http://prep.pm/5-1

Difficulty:
MEDIUM
●●●●●●○○○○

Memorization:
MEDIUM
●●●●●○○○○○

Exam Importance:
HIGH
●●●●●●●●●○

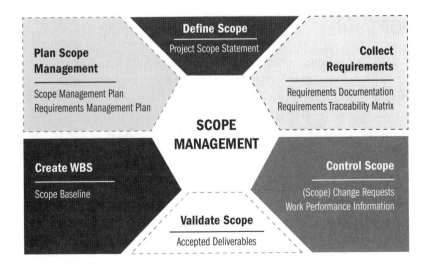

Plan Scope Management
Scope Management Plan
Requirements Management Plan

Define Scope
Project Scope Statement

Collect Requirements
Requirements Documentation
Requirements Traceability Matrix

Create WBS
Scope Baseline

SCOPE MANAGEMENT

Control Scope
(Scope) Change Requests
Work Performance Information

Validate Scope
Accepted Deliverables

Chapter Notes:

_____

_____

_____

_____

_____

_____

_____

_____

Chapter Five

Chapter Notes:

_____

_____

_____

_____

_____

_____

_____

_____

_____

_____

_____

_____

PHILOSOPHY:

The philosophy behind scope management can be condensed down to these two statements:

- The project manager should always be in control of the scope by thoroughly defining it and carefully managing the processes.

- Changes to the scope should be handled in a structured and controlled way.

It is important to begin with the end in mind when it comes to scope management so that each requirement and its acceptance criteria is documented. Good scope management makes sure that the scope is well defined and clearly communicated and that the project is carefully managed to limit unnecessary changes. The work is closely monitored so that when change does happen on the project, it is detected, evaluated, and documented. Project managers should work pro-actively to identify and influence the factors that cause change.

The overall goals of scope management are to define the need, to set stakeholder expectations, to deliver to the expectations, to manage changes, and to minimize surprises so that the product will ultimately gain approval.

IMPORTANCE:

The topic of scope is very important on the exam. When we refer to the project "scope," we are referring to the work needed to successfully complete the project and only that work. Many companies have a culture in which they try to exceed customer expectations by delivering more than was agreed upon; this practice, often referred to as "gold plating," increases risk and uncertainty and may add potential problems into the project. Given the choice, you always want to avoid gold plating.

PREPARATION:

While this section requires less actual memorization than some other knowledge areas, many of the test questions can be very tricky, requiring a solid and thorough understanding of the theories and practices of scope management.

SCOPE MANAGEMENT PROCESSES:

As a starting point, you should understand that the knowledge area of scope management consists of the following elements:

- Planning the overall scope-related efforts
- Gathering the requirements for the product and the project
- Defining and documenting the deliverables that are a part of the product and the project (the scope)
- Creating the work breakdown structure (WBS) and baselining the scope
- Checking the work being done against the scope to ensure that it is complete
- Ensuring that all of what is "in scope" and only what is "in scope" is completed and that changes are properly managed

There are six processes in the scope management knowledge area. These are Plan Scope Management, Collect Requirements, Define Scope, Create WBS, Validate Scope, and Control Scope.

Process Group	Scope Management Process
Initiating	(none)
Planning	Plan Scope Management, Collect Requirements, Define Scope, Create WBS
Executing	(none)
Monitoring & Controlling	Validate Scope, Control Scope
Closing	(none)

In the knowledge area of scope management, it is also essential that you know the main outputs that accompany each process. The different key outputs that are created are summarized in the chart below.

Process	Key Output(s)
Plan Scope Management	Scope Management Plan, Requirements Management Plan
Collect Requirements	Requirements Documentation, Requirements Traceability Matrix
Define Scope	Project Scope Statement
Create WBS	Scope Baseline
Validate Scope	Accepted Deliverables
Control Scope	(Scope) Change Requests, Work Performance Information

Chapter Notes:

_____
_____
_____
_____
_____
_____
_____
_____
_____
_____
_____
_____
_____
_____
_____
_____

113

Chapter Five

···· PLANNING

PLAN SCOPE MANAGEMENT

6th Edition PMBOK® Guide
Cross Ref. pg 134

WHAT IT IS:

Plan Scope Management is a process that looks at the other (subsequent) five scope processes and plans the overall approach as to how they will be carried out.

WHY IT IS IMPORTANT:

This process has a very significant impact on the success of the project since the requirements are the main means of understanding and managing stakeholder expectations. Also schedule, budget, quality specifications, risk factors, and resource planning will tie back to the work done here.

Watch The Video
▶ http://**prep.pm/5-2**

WHEN IT IS PERFORMED:

This process is a bit unusual in that it appears to be part of a loop. One of the outputs of Plan Scope Management is the Scope Management Plan, but the Scope Management Plan is part of the Project Management Plan, which is an input into Plan Scope Management. To understand this, consider that this process has several parts that are developed together. The unfinished Project Management Plan is brought in, and the Scope Management Plan is produced.

Chapter Notes:

_____

_____

_____

_____

_____

_____

_____

_____

HOW IT WORKS / INPUTS:

Project Charter — See Ch. 4, Develop Project Charter

Project Management Plan - The project management plan, although unfinished at this point, is brought in to help determine how the scope will be gathered, defined, broken down, validated, and managed.

Enterprise Environmental Factors — See Ch. 2, Common Inputs

Organizational Process Assets — See Ch. 2, Common Inputs

HOW IT WORKS / TOOLS:

Expert Judgment — See Ch. 2, Common Tools

Data Analysis — See Ch. 2, Common Tools

Meetings — See Ch. 2, Common Tools

HOW IT WORKS / OUTPUTS:

Scope Management Plan - The scope management plan is one of the 18 components of the project plan. It describes how the scope documents will be prepared and how the remaining five scope processes will be carried out.

Requirements Management Plan - The requirements management plan (another of the 18 components of the project plan) defines what activities the team will perform in order to gather and manage the project requirements. This document is only the plan for how the requirements will be managed and does not contain the requirements themselves.

The requirements management plan is important because it shows how requirements will be gathered, how decisions will be made, how changes to the requirements will be handled, and how the requirements will be documented.

Chapter Notes:

_____

_____

_____

_____

_____

_____

_____

_____

_____

_____

_____

_____

_____

Plan Scope Management

.... PLANNING

COLLECT REQUIREMENTS

6th Edition PMBOK® Guide
Cross Ref. pg 138

WHAT IT IS:

The process of Collect Requirements is about understanding what is needed to satisfy the stakeholders and then documenting that understanding. This is true for both the scope of the product and the scope of the entire project.

How much time and resource is invested in Collect Requirements will vary from project to project. Some projects do not need to invest significant time and resources in this process, and that is acceptable.

Watch The Video

http://prep.pm/5-3

WHY IT IS IMPORTANT:

Collect Requirements has a significant impact on the success of the project since documenting a common understanding of the project gives the project manager a great tool to set and manage stakeholder expectations. Also, schedule, budget, quality specifications, risk factors, and resource planning will tie back to these requirements.

Chapter Notes:

_____

_____

_____

_____

_____

_____

_____

_____

WHEN IT IS PERFORMED:

This process typically takes place quite early in the project because of the impact requirements have on the rest of the project. Some iterative methodologies repeat this process throughout much of the project.

The requirements will factor heavily into the project plan and should certainly be gathered and accurately documented before any execution takes place.

Develop Project Charter and Identify Stakeholders must be performed before it is possible to complete the Collect Requirements process since the charter gives the project manager authority to work on the project and the stakeholder register identifies the right people to involve in this process.

HOW IT WORKS / INPUTS:

Project Charter - The charter is brought into Collect Requirements because it provides a high-level description of the project's product, service, or result. This description is used as guidance to help define the requirements. It also gives the project manager formal organizational authority to carry out this work.

➔ Project Management Plan

> **Scope Management Plan** - Even though the requirements management plan is brought into this process, the scope management plan also brings clarity to the types of requirements that the team will gather.

> **Requirements Management Plan** - The requirements management plan describes how the requirements will be collected and documented.

> **Stakeholder Engagement Plan** - The stakeholder engagement plan informs how deeply the stakeholders should be involved in the requirements process and how this should be carried out.

Chapter Notes:

_____

_____

_____

_____

_____

_____

_____

_____

_____

_____

_____

_____

_____

_____

Project Documents

Assumption Log - The assumptions log lists the things you are treating as true for purposes of planning. For example, if you were managing the creation of a new type of medical device, you might have an assumption that the prototype passes clinical trials by a particular date. This documents the assumption and lets you proceed even though the prototype has not yet passed the trials.

Lessons Learned Register - This gives you information on best practices in your organization for gathering requirements. This particular input takes on greater importance with agile projects.

Stakeholder Register - The stakeholder register contains a list of all of the project stakeholders, and it is these stakeholders who can explain the requirements and the underlying needs. Since the requirements will be built to ultimately satisfy these stakeholders, it is important to involve the right people early in the project and to ensure that they have the appropriate voice from the start.

Business Documents - The business case could help direct the process of Collect Requirements since it explains the particular reasons this project is being undertaken.

Agreements — See Ch. 2, Common Inputs

Enterprise Environmental Factors — See Ch. 2, Common Inputs

Organizational Process Assets — See Ch. 2, Common Inputs

HOW IT WORKS / TOOLS:

Expert Judgment — See Ch. 2, Common Tools

➜ Data-Gathering

Brainstorming - These techniques are where ideas are shared in a rapid-fire setting and are not discussed or ranked until everyone is out of ideas. The goal is to gather numerous, creative responses.

Interviews - These are typically conducted by the project manager or business analyst with a subject matter expert. The subject matter expert can help explain what features or attributes the product should contain and why they matter.

Focus Groups - Whereas interviews are generally conducted one-on-one, focus groups are conducted by someone on the project team who meets with a group of stakeholders to discuss their needs and requirements. Focus groups are intended to create a safe environment for stakeholders to discuss their expectations of the project.

Questionnaires and Surveys - This technique works well with large groups of people, allowing the team to gather opinions and requirements rapidly. Because the questionnaire or survey is generally in a standard format, aggregation and analysis is easier than with some other forms.

Benchmarking - This technique is all about looking outside of the project to understand best practices and gain inspiration. It is generally best to look at organizations or projects that have something in common with this project.

Data Analysis - Do not worry about the list of different types of documents or data you might want to analyze. In this case, data analysis includes anything that might help you understand the requirements.

Collect Requirements

Chapter Five

Chapter Notes:

_____

_____

_____

_____

_____

_____

_____

_____

_____

_____

_____

_____

_____

➔ Decision Making

Voting - One of the more difficult aspects of a project manager's job can be to get various stakeholders to make a decision. There are numerous techniques that a project manager can use to help drive decisions forward. These techniques include Unanimity, Majority, Consensus, Plurality, and Autocratic Decision Making. Each of these techniques is explained further in the glossary. It would be a good idea to pause here and look up each of those five terms before going further.

Multicriteria Decision Analysis - A technique that uses a weighted matrix to assign values to each criterion and then rate them accordingly. This technique works well since some factors will almost always be more important than others. The multicriteria decision analysis yields a score that may be compared against other scores.

➔ Data Representation

Affinity Diagrams - An affinity diagram takes the ideas that came from brainstorming and organizes them into logical groups or categories.

Mind Mapping - A technique of diagramming ideas and creating meaningful associations in a graphical format. A mind map helps the team see relationships among ideas.

Interpersonal and Team Skills

Nominal Group Technique - A group technique where ideas are brainstormed and are voted on and sorted by priority.

Observation and Conversation - Also known as "job shadowing," observation is where a worker is studied as he performs his job. The goal is to understand how the worker performs and to capture any requirements that may not be evident through interviews or other methods. Conversation with the worker can also be an important component of this.

Facilitation - The goal behind facilitated workshops is to colocate all of the key stakeholders together and to elaborate the requirements. In order to have a successful facilitated workshop, it is essential to have a skilled facilitator. Problems can generally be dealt with in the sessions since all of the relevant people may already be there.

Examples of facilitated workshops are: Joint Application Development, Quality Function Deployment, and User Stories.

Context Diagram - A context diagram is the generic term for a use case diagram that shows systems and the "actors" that interact with each system. Each actor may be a user or another system.

Prototypes - These are an interactive model of the product. The advantage of a prototype is that the idea becomes tangible and can be used by people, allowing the project team to understand what works and does not work. Prototypes receive varying degrees of emphasis, depending on the end product and on the project methodologies. They are especially friendly to the project management idea of progressive elaboration, which stresses that a deliverable can be revisited repeatedly before it is finalized.

Another way of prototyping is to storyboard the flow of the product. This could be anything from wireframe screen mockups for a software application to the stages in a new robotic assembly line.

Chapter Notes:

Collect Requirements

Chapter Notes:

_____

_____

_____

_____

_____

_____

_____

_____

_____

_____

_____

_____

_____

_____

_____

HOW IT WORKS / OUTPUTS:

Requirements Documentation - This is simply a document that describes what needs to be performed and why each requirement is important on the project. The requirements documentation should include a description of:

- The root business problem being solved
- The source of the requirement
- The way each requirement addresses the problem
- How the business processes interact with the requirements
- Associated measurements for each requirement
- Business, legal, and ethical compliance
- Constraints and assumptions
- Anticipated impact of the requirement on others

Requirements Traceability Matrix - Once a requirement is collected, it is important to be able to identify the source. That is what this document does. The source could originate from a stakeholder or departmental request, a legal, contractual, or ethical need, an underlying requirement, or any number of other sources. The thing to remember here is that if a requirement is important enough to be documented, it is important to list the source here. The requirements traceability matrix can also include information about who owns the requirement, the status of the requirement, etc.

Req ID	Date	Description	Business Need	WBS Deliverables	Origin of Request	User Acceptance Test Case
11773	3/22/2018	Allow biometric login on approved supported devices	Ease of use	3.1.2.1.6	Tom G.	TS173
11810	3/23/2018	Support inapp PDF creation	Integration with document system	6.2.4.11.3	Support services -Kasim R	TS805
11811	3/23/2018	Integrate with mobile photo library	Requested feature	11.3.1.1.1	Customer request (see Database)	TS112
11822	3/26/2018	Configurable auto logout	Security	4.16.2.4.3.2	Mike T. (CSO)	TS32

···· PLANNING

DEFINE SCOPE

WHAT IT IS:

At some point, every successful project must develop a clear understanding of the requirements to be executed, verified, and delivered. The scope of the project must be understood and documented in detail.

6th Edition PMBOK® Guide
Cross Ref. pg 150

WHY IT IS IMPORTANT:

The scope of the project is what ultimately drives the execution of the project, and Define Scope is the process where the project's requirements are more thoroughly understood and documented. The importance of this process is directly related to how important the requirements are. A large, mission-critical project will perform this process very thoroughly, while a smaller project, or one that is highly similar to a project that has been performed previously, will probably be less formal and detailed. Likewise, a project that has extremely high material costs (e.g., an offshore drilling platform) will likely spend more time and effort on Define Scope than a project with less risk will.

Watch The Video

▶ http://**prep.pm/5-4**

Chapter Notes:

_____

_____

_____

_____

_____

_____

_____

Chapter Five

Chapter Notes:

_____

_____

_____

_____

_____

_____

_____

_____

_____

_____

_____

_____

_____

_____

_____

WHEN IT IS PERFORMED:

This process may be started as soon as the Collect Requirements process has been completed. Because projects are generally progressively elaborated, this process, along with the requirements, may be revisited many times throughout the life of the project; however, it is usually begun very early in the project life cycle.

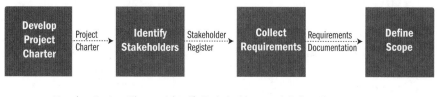

Develop Project Charter, Identify Stakeholders, and Collect Requirements
must be performed before it is possible to perform Define Scope.

HOW IT WORKS / INPUTS:

During the Define Scope process, the project manager refines the requirements collected earlier in the project by performing additional analysis, factoring in any approved changes, and adding detail. The project scope statement, which is the output of this process, has detailed information about the project scope and the requirements.

Project Charter - The project charter is the organization document formally creating the project and outlining its goals. Since this process will create a detailed view of the scope, the project charter is needed. If the project charter does not exist, then the project manager should still capture the project's overall goals, a brief description of the scope, and the known constraints and assumptions before performing Define Scope.

Project Management Plan - The scope management plan, one of the components of the project plan, is the part to focus on here. It describes how all of the scope activities will be managed, including this one.

124

Project Documents

Assumption Log - The assumption log is a list of everything that the team is treating as true even though it is uncertain at this point in the project.

 Requirements Documentation - The stakeholder requirements provide the primary fuel for this process. Requirements define what the project has to do and the degree to which it must perform. The process of Define Scope then turns those requirements into a more detailed project scope statement.

Risk Register - The risk register contains a list of all identified risks and planned responses that may influence the scope.

Enterprise Environmental Factors — See Ch. 2, Common Inputs

Organizational Process Assets — See Ch. 2, Common Inputs

HOW IT WORKS / TOOLS:

Expert Judgment - This tool involves having experts work with the project team to develop portions of the project scope statement. These are typically experts on the technical matters that need to be documented.

Data Analysis - Alternatives analysis is one means of data analysis where the requirements are reviewed to look at different ways of achieving the goals.

Decision Making — See Ch. 2, Common Tools

Interpersonal and Team Skills — See Ch. 2, Common Tools

Chapter Five

Chapter Notes:

_____

_____

_____

_____

_____

_____

_____

_____

_____

_____

_____

_____

_____

Product Analysis - Product analysis is a detailed analysis of the project's product, service, or result, with the intent of improving the project team's understanding of the product and helping to capture that understanding in the form of requirements. The tools that may be used in product analysis will vary among industries and organizations, but common ones include:

- Product breakdown
- Requirements analysis
- Systems analysis
- Systems engineering
- Value analysis
- Value engineering

HOW IT WORKS / OUTPUTS:

Project Scope Statement – The project scope statement is the document used to level-set among the project's stakeholders. The project scope statement contains many details pertaining to the project and product deliverables, including: the goals of the project, the product description, the requirements for the project, the constraints and assumptions, and the identified risks related to the scope. The objective criteria for accepting the product should also be included in the project scope statement.

Product Scope Description – this is a narrative description of the scope that is kept up to date throughout the project.

Deliverables – this includes a clear and measurable description of what the product is going to look and feel like. Every characteristic or attribute that matters should be documented here.

Acceptance Criteria – a checklist of the tests and measurements that will be performed before the product is accepted.

Project Exclusions – sometimes it is important to document what is out of scope with the project. For example, if a new car were being designed, and this car would specifically not be self-driving, that would be recorded here.

Project Documents Updates — See Ch. 2, Common Inputs

···· PLANNING

CREATE WBS

WHAT IT IS:

This process probably gets the award for the most confusing name. You would think that Create WBS would be all about producing the work breakdown structure, but the WBS is not listed as one of its outputs. Actually, this process does create the WBS, but at the same time it combines it with two other documents to create the Scope Baseline. While the main product of this process is the work breakdown structure, the main output will be the Scope Baseline. You will learn more about what a baseline is when we get to that output.

6th Edition PMBOK® Guide
Cross Ref. pg 156

WHY IT IS IMPORTANT:

The work breakdown structure, or WBS, is a very important topic for the exam. The reason for its importance is tied to how it is used. After its creation, the WBS becomes a hub of information for the project, and arguably becomes the most important component of the project plan. Risks, activities, costs, quality attributes, and procurement decisions all link back to the WBS, and it is a primary tool for verifying and controlling the project's scope.

Watch The Video

▶ http://**prep.pm**/5-5

Chapter Notes:

_____

_____

_____

WHEN IT IS PERFORMED:

Create WBS is typically performed early in the project, after the requirements have been collected and the scope has been defined, but before the bulk of the work is executed.

Develop Project Charter, Identify Stakeholders, Collect Requirements, and Define Scope must be performed before it is possible to perform Create WBS.

Chapter Notes:

_____

_____

_____

_____

_____

_____

_____

_____

_____

_____

_____

_____

_____

_____

HOW IT WORKS / INPUTS:

→ Project Management Plan - The important component of the project management plan is the Scope Management Plan. This is because there are multiple approaches a team can take to create the WBS and baseline the scope. The scope management plan describes which one the team will use on this project and how it will be carried out.

Project Documents

Project Scope Statement - The project scope statement describes the scope of the project. It will be used in this process as a primary starting point from which to create the WBS.

Requirements Documentation - This output of the Collect Requirements process ties each requirement back to a specific business need or benefit, and like all planning documents, this one is often progressively elaborated.

Enterprise Environmental Factors — See Ch. 2, Common Inputs

Organizational Process Assets — See Ch. 2, Common Inputs

Organizational process assets can take on different meanings in different contexts. In the case of Create WBS, the most common assets would consist of methodologies that spell out how to create the work breakdown structure, software tools to create the graphical chart, WBS templates, and completed WBS examples from previously performed projects.

HOW IT WORKS / TOOLS:

Expert Judgment — See Ch. 2, Common Tools

Decomposition - The main tool used in creating the WBS, decomposition, involves breaking down the project deliverables into progressively smaller components. In a WBS, the top layer is very general (perhaps as general as the deliverable or product name, or some even go so far as to make the top node the overall program), and each subsequent layer is more and more specific. The key to reading the WBS is to understand that every level is the detailed explanation of the level above it.

Decomposition may be thought of as being similar to the arcade game Asteroids™ from years ago. Large pieces are progressively broken down into smaller and smaller pieces.

So, how do you know when you have decomposed your work enough? As you have probably realized, the nodes could be decomposed to ridiculously low levels, wasting time and actually making the project difficult to understand, manage, and change. There are many things to consider when deciding how far to decompose work, but three of the best questions to ask are:

1. Are your work packages small enough to be estimated for time and cost?

2. Are the project manager and the project team satisfied that the current level of detail provides enough information to proceed with subsequent project activities?

3. Is each work package small enough to be able to be assigned to a single person or group that can be responsible for the results?

If you can answer "yes" to those three questions, your work packages are probably decomposed far enough.

Chapter Notes:

Create WBS

Chapter Notes:

_____

_____

_____

_____

_____

_____

_____

_____

_____

_____

_____

_____

_____

Many projects, including almost all agile projects, use a rolling wave technique to decompose requirements. This simply means that decomposition is not performed all at once. Instead, some of the WBS may be created and then that work may be carried out in the form of product development. Then more of the WBS is decomposed so that these activities repeat like rolling waves. The advantage to this approach is that it does not try to look too far into the future. Instead, it deals with things in the relatively short term and gets product into the hands of the users to make the creation of the WBS easier and more accurate.

HOW IT WORKS / OUTPUTS:

Scope Baseline - A baseline (whether for scope, schedule, cost, or quality) is the original plan plus all approved changes. In this instance, the scope baseline represents the combination of the project scope statement, the WBS, the WBS dictionary, work package, and planning package. When the scope baseline is created, it is placed under control, meaning that changes to the scope are made according to the scope management plan.

WBS

The writers of the current edition of the *PMBOK® Guide* currently advocate that the work breakdown structure always be based on the project deliverables, rather than the tasks needed to create those deliverables, and that it be built from the top down.

The WBS is primarily constructed through decomposition, the practice of breaking down deliverables (product features, characteristics, or attributes) into progressively smaller pieces. This process continues until the deliverables are small enough to be considered work packages. A node may be considered a work package when it meets the following criteria:

- The work package cannot be easily decomposed any further

- The work package is small enough to be estimated for time (effort)

- The work package is small enough to be estimated for cost

- The work package may be assigned to a single person

If the node is being subcontracted outside of the performing organization, that node, regardless of size, may be considered a work package, and the subcontracting organization builds a "sub-WBS" from that node.

The resulting WBS is a graphical, hierarchical chart, logically organized from top to bottom. Each node on the WBS has a unique number used to locate and identify it.

Each level of the WBS is mutually exclusive and cumulatively exhaustive. This means that there are no gaps and no overlap in the work packages. No piece of scope is eliminated, and nothing is duplicated.

Chapter Notes:

Create WBS

Chapter Notes:

_____

_____

_____

_____

_____

_____

_____

_____

_____

_____

_____

_____

_____

_____

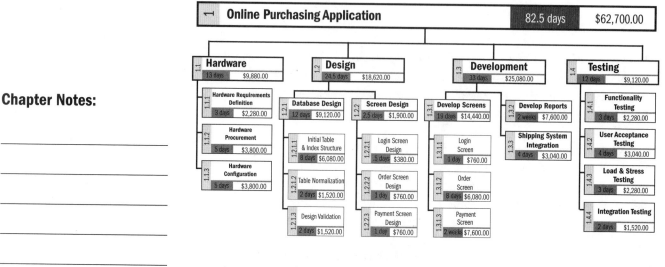

Elements of a Good Work Breakdown Structure (WBS):

- It must be detailed down to a low level. The lowest level consists of work packages that define every deliverable on the project.

- It is graphical, arranged like a pyramid, where each sub-level rolls up to the level above it.

- It numbers each element, and the numbering system should allow anyone who reads the WBS to find individual elements quickly and easily.

- It should provide sufficient detail to drive the subsequent phases of planning.

- It may often be borrowed from other projects in the organization as a starting point. These starting points are known as templates.

- It is thorough and complete. If an item is not in the WBS, it does not get delivered with the project.

- It is central to the project.

- The project team, and not just the project manager, creates the WBS. Developing the WBS can also be a means of team-building.

- It is an integration tool, allowing you to see where the individual pieces of work fit into the project as a whole.

- It helps define responsibilities for the team.

- It is a communication tool.

Work Package - Described in detail earlier in this chapter, the work packages are the lowest level of the work breakdown structure.

Planning Package - Planning packages are nodes on the WBS that are larger than work packages but that cannot be broken down into work packages at this time. Typically this would be true because not enough information is known at this time.

Control Account - Also known as a "cost account," a control account is a node on the WBS where the scope, time, and cost are measured. Control accounts contain usually contain several work packages and are used to measure earned value. A project may have numerous control accounts placed on the WBS at nodes where it would be particularly meaningful to measure the earned value of those parts of the project.

Chapter Notes:

_____

_____

_____

_____

_____

_____

_____

_____

_____

_____

_____

_____

_____

Create WBS

Chapter Five

Chapter Notes:

_____

_____

_____

_____

_____

_____

_____

_____

_____

_____

_____

_____

_____

_____

WBS Dictionary

The WBS dictionary is a document that details the contents of the WBS. Just as a language dictionary defines words, a WBS dictionary provides detailed information about the nodes on a WBS.

Because the WBS is graphical, there is a practical limit to how much information can be included in each node. The WBS dictionary solves this problem by capturing additional attributes about each work package in a different document that does not have the graphical constraints that the WBS does.

For each node in the WBS, the WBS dictionary might include the number of the node, the name of the node, the written requirements for the node, to whom it is assigned, and time, cost, and account information.

PROJECT : Online Ordering Application	
Work Package ID: 1.1.3	**Work Package Name: Configure New Hardware**
Work Package Description: All new hardware should be configured, including any hardware settings and preparation such as formatting of storage. The correct operating system should be loaded, and the appropriate patches should be applied. Any security settings, including virus scanning software, should be applied. The hardware should be added to the company domain and should be compliant with all company policy regarding hardware and security.	
Assigned to: Lee Abbott	**Department: I.T**
Date Assigned: 4/15/13	**Date Due:** 4/22/13
Estimated Cost: $3,800.00	**Accounting Code:** HMIT-0229

Sample WBS Dictionary Entry

Project Documents Updates - Through the process of creating the scope baseline and WBS, the understanding of the project often changes and improves. This change in understanding should be documented back in the appropriate place. For instance, if decomposition uncovered a missing requirement after validating that requirement with the stakeholders, the project manager should update the requirements documentation.

···· MONITORING & CONTROLLING

VALIDATE SCOPE

WHAT IT IS:

Validate Scope is easily confused with other processes. Many people fall into the trap of thinking that this process involves verifying that the scope is documented accurately; however, this is not correct. Validate Scope is the process of ensuring that the product, service, or result of the project matches the documented scope.

In general, controlling processes compare some plan with the results to see where they differ and take action if it is required. This fits Validate Scope very well since the product is compared with the scope to ensure the two match.

Validate Scope has quite a few similarities to the process of Control Quality (covered in Chapter 8, Quality Management) in that they both inspect the product against the scope; however, there are some key differences between them.

- Control Quality is performed before Validate Scope.

- Validate Scope is primarily concerned with completeness, while Control Quality is primarily concerned with correctness.

- Validate Scope is concerned with the acceptance of the product by the project manager, the sponsor, the customer, and others, while Control Quality is concerned with adherence to the quality specification.

One more important note about Validate Scope is that if the project is canceled before completion, Validate Scope should be performed to document where the product was in relation to the scope at the point when the project ended.

6th Edition PMBOK® Guide
Cross Ref. pg 163

Watch The Video
http://**prep.pm**/5-6

Chapter Notes:

_____

_____

_____

_____

_____

_____

_____

Chapter Notes:

_____

_____

_____

_____

_____

_____

_____

_____

_____

_____

_____

_____

_____

WHY IT IS IMPORTANT:

Once the process of Validate Scope is successfully completed, the product is accepted by the project manager, the customer, the sponsor, and sometimes by the functional managers and key stakeholders. This acceptance is a significant milestone in the life of the project.

WHEN IT IS PERFORMED:

This process would be performed after at least some of the product components have been delivered, although it may be performed several times throughout the life of the project. As mentioned previously, Validate Scope is performed after Control Quality. While it may be performed several times (iteratively), it would at least be performed once late in the project life cycle as the product is ready to be delivered.

HOW IT WORKS / INPUTS:

Project Management Plan — See Ch. 2, Common Inputs

Project Documents — See Ch. 2, Common Inputs

➡ **Verified Deliverables** - Verified deliverables flow out of the Control Quality process and into this one. Validate Scope is all about comparing the deliverables with the documented scope to ensure that everything was completed. This comparison may be performed several times during the life of the project.

Work Performance Data - Sometimes a team can achieve the right outcome, but the path to get there was unacceptable. For instance, if the team delivered a good product but individuals averaged 70-hour work weeks to accomplish the results, it is likely not acceptable. Work Performance Data tells more about "how" the deliverables were created, which needs to be considered along with the product itself.

HOW IT WORKS / TOOLS:

⊕ Inspection - Inspection involves a point-by-point review of the scope and the associated deliverable. For instance, a pre-occupancy walkthrough by a building inspector would be an example of the tool of inspection. User-acceptance testing of a software product could be another example where the tool of inspection was used to make sure the deliverables matched the documented scope.

Decision Making — See Ch. 2, Common Tools

HOW IT WORKS / OUTPUTS

⊕ Accepted Deliverables - Acceptance of the deliverables is the primary output of the process of Validate Scope and one of the most important in the project. This process is typically performed by the project manager, the sponsor, the customer, and the functional managers, and the result is a formal, written acceptance by the appropriate stakeholders

Work Performance Information - The work performance data flows into this process, and the more refined work performance information flows out. The WPI tells about how something was created, including whether it was on time, within budget, how the resources used compared with estimates, and other metrics of interest.

Change Requests — See Ch. 2, Common Outputs

Project Documents Updates — See Ch. 2, Common Outputs

Chapter Notes:

_____

_____

_____

_____

_____

_____

_____

_____

_____

_____

_____

_____

_____

Validate Scope

Chapter Five

···· MONITORING & CONTROLLING
CONTROL SCOPE

6th Edition PMBOK® Guide
Cross Ref. pg 167

WHAT IT IS:

Control Scope is a process that lives up to its name. This process is about maintaining control of the project by preventing scope change requests from overwhelming the project, and also about making certain that scope change requests are properly handled. This ensures that the scope baseline is always kept current (remember that the scope baseline will usually change over time on most projects).

One of the more challenging concepts behind Control Scope can be resolving disputes. Many disputes over project scope or product requirements are not simple, but the customer's interests should always be weighed heavily. That does not mean that the customer is always right. Instead, it means that the customer is one of the most important stakeholders. All other things being equal, disputes should be resolved in favor of the customer.

Watch The Video
▶ http://**prep.pm/5-7**

Chapter Notes:

WHY IT IS IMPORTANT:

Anyone who has managed a project where scope change was a problem knows the importance of Control Scope. This process makes certain all change requests are processed, and also that any of the underlying causes of scope change requests are understood and managed. It is important not only to manage scope change requests, but also to prevent unnecessary ones.

_____

_____

_____

_____

_____

_____

_____

_____

WHEN IT IS PERFORMED:

Control Scope is an ongoing process that begins as soon as the scope baseline is created. Until that point, the scope is not considered stable or complete enough to control; however, once the scope baseline is created, each scope change request must be carefully controlled and managed. Additionally, this process should be performed any time the work results are known to differ from the documented scope, whether or not the scope change was requested in advance.

HOW IT WORKS / INPUTS:

Project Management Plan - The project management plan contains the scope management plan and the scope baseline, and these are the most interesting components for Control Scope. Scope baseline consists of the WBS, the WBS dictionary and the project scope statement, and it is the documented source for what the project team is supposed to create. The scope baseline provides the baseline that the project manager will control.

Project Documents — See Ch. 2, Common Inputs

Work Performance Data - This input is very similar in nature to the performance reports (discussed in chapter 10, Communications Management). It provides information on all aspects of the work completed as it relates to the project plan. One example might be the volume of change requests flowing into the project. Note here how the raw work performance data is an input and the more refined work performance information is the output.

Organizational Process Assets — See Ch. 2, Common Inputs

Chapter Five

Chapter Notes:

_____

_____

_____

_____

_____

_____

_____

_____

_____

_____

_____

_____

_____

HOW IT WORKS / TOOLS:

➡ Data Analysis - Data analysis can cover a lot of ground, but in this case we are interested in variance analysis and trend analysis. Variance analysis measures differences between what was defined in the scope baseline and what was created and to investigate the root causes behind any differences. Trend analysis would help identify areas that are about to become problems.

HOW IT WORKS / OUTPUTS:

➡ Work Performance Information - Work performance information (WPI) is work performance data that has been processed and put into an actionable format.

Change Requests - As changes are made to the scope baseline, these must be factored into updates to the WBS. If the change represents a new piece of scope, the work must be decomposed in the WBS down to work package level and then brought into the other appropriate processes.

Project Management Plan Updates - The project management plan must be kept up to date throughout the life of the project. Any change in scope should be reflected in the project management plan, along with any other resulting changes in cost, schedule, risk, quality, procurement, etc.

Project Documents Updates — See Ch. 2, Common Outputs

The Agile Perspective on Scope Management

The six processes of scope management are handled very differently on projects that use agile or adaptive methodologies. These projects employ short "iterations" to prioritize the next sets of features to be developed. Backlogs of important features are "groomed" so that they are arranged by priority. This priority is dictated by what would give the stakeholders the highest value. The Stakeholders are very closely involved throughout each of these processes on an agile project.

Agile projects may also capture large usability scenarios, known as user stories, in the form of an agile epic story. These epic stories may even capture scenarios that span more than one project or product.

Prototypes can also play an important part in agile projects. A prototype allows a user to interact with the system without having to create the entire system to observe and understand how it might function.

The key differences are that agile projects do not try to define all of the functionality up front.

Chapter Notes:

Agile Perspective on Scope Management

Chapter Five

Chapter Notes:

_____

_____

_____

_____

_____

_____

_____

_____

_____

_____

_____

_____

SCOPE MANAGEMENT

QUESTIONS

1. Your project team is executing the work packages of your project when a significant disagreement regarding the interpretation of the scope is brought to your attention by two of your most trusted team members. How should this dispute be resolved?

    A. The project team should decide on the resolution.

    B. The dispute should be resolved in favor of the customer.

    C. The dispute should be resolved in favor of senior management.

    D. The project manager should consult the project charter for guidance.

2. Which of the following statements is FALSE regarding a work breakdown structure?

    A. Activities should be arranged in the sequence they will be performed.

    B. Every item should have a unique identifier.

    C. The work breakdown structure represents 100% of the work that will be done on the project.

    D. Each level of a work breakdown structure provides progressively smaller representations.

3. Mark has taken over a project that is beginning the construction phase of the product; however, he discovers that no work breakdown structure has been created. What choice represents the BEST course of action?

    A. He should not manage this project.

    B. He should stop construction until the work breakdown structure has been created.

    C. He should consult the WBS dictionary to determine whether sufficient detail exists to properly manage construction.

    D. He should document this to senior management and provide added oversight on the construction phase.

4. **The project has completed execution, and now it is time for the product of the project to be accepted. Who formally accepts the product?**

   A. The project team and the customer.

   B. The quality assurance team, senior management, and the project manager.

   C. The sponsor, key stakeholders, and the customer.

   D. The project manager, senior management, and the change control board.

5. **Creating the project scope statement is part of which process?**

   A. Project Scope Management.

   B. Collect Requirements.

   C. Define Scope.

   D. Validate Scope.

6. **The main point of Create WBS is to:**

   A. Decompose the scope of the product.

   B. Decompose the scope of the project.

   C. Create a baseline of the entire scope.

   D. Define all of the scope to be performed.

7. **The project scope statement should contain:**

   A. The work packages for the project.

   B. A high level description of the scope.

   C. The level of effort associated with each scope element.

   D. A detailed description of the scope.

Chapter Five

Chapter Notes:

———————————————
———————————————
———————————————
———————————————
———————————————
———————————————
———————————————
———————————————
———————————————
———————————————
———————————————
———————————————
———————————————

8. **The most important part of Validate Scope is:**

    A. Gaining formal acceptance of the project deliverables from the customer.

    B. Checking the scope of the project against stakeholder expectations.

    C. Verifying that the project came in on time and on budget.

    D. Verifying that the product met the quality specifications.

9. **The organizational process assets would include all of the following except:**

    A. Document templates.

    B. Financial control procedures.

    C. Standardization guidelines.

    D. The project management information system.

10. **Which of the following is NOT part of the scope baseline?**

    A. The requirements documentation.

    B. The project scope statement.

    C. The work breakdown structure.

    D. The WBS dictionary.

11. **You have taken over as project manager for a data warehousing project that is completing the design phase; however, change requests that affect the requirements are still pouring in from many sources, including your boss. Which of the following would have been MOST helpful in this situation?**

    A. A project sponsor who is involved in the project.

    B. A well-defined requirements management plan.

    C. A change control board.

    D. A change evaluation system.

12. **What is the function of the project sponsor?**

    A. To help manage senior management expectations.

    B. To be the primary interface with the customer.

    C. To fund the project and formally accept the product.

    D. To amplify influence with the functional managers.

13. **The project manager and the customer on a project are meeting together to review the product of the project against the documented scope. Which tool would be MOST appropriate to use during this meeting?**

    A. Verification analysis.

    B. Inspection.

    C. Gap analysis.

    D. Feature review.

14. **A project team has a dedicated scoping phase for their project where all subject matter experts are meeting together with a trained facilitator. They have interviewed each person in the room to gather ideas for functionality and are now voting on them to put them in order of priority. This list will be used to feed requirements to the project team. The group's activities are an example of:**

    A. The Nominal Group Technique.

    B. Brainstorming.

    C. The Borda Method.

    D. Tuckman's Model.

Chapter Notes:

Chapter Five

Scope Management: Questions

15. You have just assumed responsibility for a project that is in progress. While researching the project archives, you discover that the WBS dictionary was never created. Which of the following problems would LEAST likely be attributable to this?

A. Confusion about the meaning of specific work packages.

B. Confusion about who is responsible for a specific work package.

C. Confusion about which account to bill against for a specific work package.

D. Confusion about how to change a specific work package.

16. A team member makes a change to a software project without letting anyone else know. She assures you that it did not affect the schedule, and it significantly enhances the product. What should the project manager do FIRST?

A. Find out if the customer authorized this change.

B. Submit the change to the change control board.

C. Review the change to understand how it affects scope, cost, time, quality, risk, and customer satisfaction.

D. Make sure the change is reflected in the requirements management plan.

17. The product you have delivered has been reviewed carefully against the scope and is now being brought to the customer for formal acceptance. Which process is the project in?

A. Validate Scope.

B. Audit Scope.

C. Close Scope.

D. Control Scope.

18. You are working with stakeholders, using the Nominal Group Technique to help promote creativity. Which choice represents the MOST likely results of your work?

    A. The requirements documentation and the project scope statement.

    B. The requirements documentation and the requirements traceability matrix.

    C. The work breakdown structure and the WBS dictionary.

    D. Accepted deliverables and change requests.

19. Sara and Eric are two project managers having a discussion about which metrics to use to gauge project performance. They agree that benchmarking is a preferred approach, but Eric maintains that the best metrics should come from industry standards published by their industry group. Sara believes that they should benchmark within their own organization to see how well other departments are performing and base their own projections from those. In the context of their discussion, which of the following statements is true?

    A. Benchmarking is best performed against external companies to capture best practices from outside the organization.

    B. Benchmarking is best performed against departments within the organization to compare against similar entities.

    C. Benchmarking may look within the organization or outside the organization, based on the need.

    D. Benchmarking should be only be used once operations have stabilized in order to gather reliable metrics.

Chapter Notes:

_____
_____
_____
_____
_____
_____
_____
_____
_____
_____
_____
_____
_____
_____
_____
_____

Chapter Notes:

_____

_____

_____

_____

_____

_____

_____

_____

_____

_____

_____

_____

_____

_____

_____

20. **A large defense contractor to the government is facilitating an inspection of their project's product with their customer when the customer notices a feature that was not requested or documented. The project manager for the defense contractor points out that this feature adds value, but the customer is concerned that it may also introduce risk. Can the customer accept the product?**

    A. Only if the new feature passes inspection.

    B. No. The new feature has to be evaluated for its impact on the project.

    C. No. The new feature is outside of the documented scope, and that is unacceptable.

    D. Yes, as long as the product scope has been fulfilled.

21. **You are the project manager for a large construction project, and you identify two key areas where changing the scope of the product would deliver significantly higher value for the customer. Which of the following options is MOST correct?**

    A. Make the changes if they do not extend the cost and time line.

    B. Make the changes if they do not exceed the project charter.

    C. Discuss the changes with the customer.

    D. Complete the current project and create a new project for the changes.

22. **Which of the following activities is done FIRST?**

    A. Creation of the requirements documentation.

    B. Creation of the work breakdown structure.

    C. Creation of the activity list.

    D. Creation of the scope baseline.

23. Which of the following statements is TRUE concerning functionality that is over and above the documented scope?

    A. It should be channeled back through the change control board to ensure that it gets documented into the project scope.

    B. Additional functionality should be leveraged to meet or exceed customer expectations.

    C. The final product should include all the functionality and only the functionality documented in the scope baseline.

    D. Additional functionality should be reviewed by the project manager for conformity to the product description.

24. A project manager has been managing a project for six months and is nearing completion of the project; however, change requests are still pouring in. The project is ahead of schedule but over budget. Which of the following statements is TRUE?

    A. The project manager should influence the factors that cause change.

    B. Changes should only be evaluated after the original scope baseline has been delivered and accepted.

    C. Changes introduced at this point in the project represent an unacceptable level of risk.

    D. Changes should be evaluated primarily on the basis of how much value they deliver to the customer.

25. Complete the list of group decision-making techniques: Unanimity, Majority, Consensus, Plurality...

    A. Facilitated agreement.

    B. Autocratic.

    C. Solidarity.

    D. Coalition.

Chapter Five

SCOPE MANAGEMENT
ANSWERS

Chapter Notes:

_____

_____

_____

_____

_____

_____

_____

_____

_____

_____

_____

_____

_____

1. B. In general, disagreements should be resolved in favor of the customer. In this case, the customer is the best choice of the four presented. 'A' is not a good choice because it is your job to keep the team focused on doing the work and out of meetings where they are arguing about the scope. Besides, the team brought you this problem, so their ability to resolve it is already in question. 'C' is incorrect because all things being equal, project disputes should be resolved in favor of the customer and not in favor of senior management. Since you don't have enough information to steer you toward senior management, resolving it in favor of the customer was the right choice here. 'D' is incorrect because the project charter is a very general and high-level document. As it is issued before either the scope statement or the work breakdown structure is created, it would be of little use in resolving an issue of scope dispute that occurred during execution.

2. A. You don't tackle activity sequencing as part of the work breakdown structure. That part comes later. The WBS has no particular sequence to it, not to mention that it is not decomposed to activity level. 'B' is incorrect since every WBS element does have a unique identifier. 'C' is incorrect since the WBS is the definitive source for all of the work to be done. Remember – if it isn't in the WBS, it isn't part of the project. Choice 'D' is incorrect because the WBS is arranged as a pyramid with the top being the most general, and the bottom being the most specific. The lowest level of the WBS would also be the smallest representation of work.

3. B. In this situation, you cannot simply skip the WBS, as you may be tempted to do. Mark should take time to create the WBS, which is usually not a lengthy process. 'A' may sound good, but in reality a PMP needs to be ready to work to solve most problems. You might refuse to manage a project if there is an ethical dilemma or a conflict of interest, but not in other circumstances. 'C' is incorrect since the WBS dictionary cannot be created properly unless the WBS was created first. If there is a WBS dictionary and no WBS, that would be a big red flag. 'D' is incorrect since merely documenting that there is a serious problem is not a solution. Additionally, providing more oversight would not solve the problem here. The real problem is that the WBS has not been created, and that will trickle down to more serious problems in the future of the project.

4. C. The project manager verifies the product with the key stakeholders, the sponsor, and the customer.

5. C. The project scope statement is created as part of the Define Scope process. You should have narrowed your guesses down to 'B' and 'C' quickly, since the project scope statement is a planning output, and 'B' and 'C' are the only two planning processes. 'A' is incorrect because it is the name of a knowledge area and not a process, and 'D' represents a monitoring and controlling process, which usually results in outputs such as change requests but never planning documents.

6. C. The clue here is the words "main point" which would be found in the main output. The scope baseline represents three documents: the scope statement, the WBS, and the WBS dictionary, and this is the point of the process Create WBS. 'B' would be a better choice than 'A', but it is only a component of the scope baseline. 'D' would happen in the process Define Scope and not in Create WBS.

Chapter Notes:

_____

_____

_____

_____

_____

_____

_____

_____

_____

_____

_____

_____

_____

_____

Scope Management: Answers

Chapter Five

Chapter Notes:

_____

_____

_____

_____

_____

_____

_____

_____

_____

_____

_____

_____

_____

_____

_____

7. D. The project scope statement needs to include a detailed description of the scope of work to be performed. Choice 'A' is incorrect as the WBS is created later as part of the Create WBS process. 'B' is tricky, but it is incorrect. The project charter contains a very high level description of the scope, but the project scope statement is detailed. 'C' is incorrect, because the level of effort is estimated after the scope has been defined.

8. A. It is important to understand the processes and their inputs and outputs! Whereas all of these choices may be important, the only one that is listed as a part of Validate Scope is to get customer acceptance of the product. The other activities may be done during the project, but they aren't part of the Validate Scope process. 'D' is close, but that is formally part of the Control Quality process.

9. D. This question was not easy. Organizational process assets include things like templates, financial control procedures, and standardization guidelines; however, the PMIS (project management information system) is classified as an enterprise environmental factor since it is generally part of your environment.

10. A. This is the only choice that is not part of the scope baseline. It is used to help create the baseline, but it is not a part of it. 'B', 'C', and 'D' represent the three components of the scope baseline.

11. B. This one is tricky. If you missed it, don't feel bad, but it is important to know that questions like this are on the exam. The reason 'B' is correct is that the requirements management plan contains a plan for how changes will be handled. If too many changes are pouring in, it is likely that the requirements management plan was not well defined. 'A' is incorrect because it is not the sponsor's role to control change. He or she is paying you to handle that. 'C' is incorrect because if the change control board exists on your project, it only evaluates changes. The board is almost always reactive, not proactive. 'D' is incorrect since the change evaluation system is a made up term not found in PMI's processes.

12. C. It is the sponsor's job to pay for the project and to accept the product. Choice 'A' is really the project manager's job. 'B' is the project manager's job as well. It is not a clearly defined job for the sponsor. 'D' is not a function of the sponsor. If more influence were needed with the functional managers, that would be the role of senior management.

13. B. The project manager and customer are involved in the Validate Scope process, and the tool used here is inspection. The product is inspected to see if it matches the documented scope. 'A', 'C', and 'D' are not documented as part of the processes.

14. A. The Nominal Group Technique typically starts by gathering a large field of candidate items (in this case they are scope items) and voting on them to sort them from highest down to lowest in order of priority. It is designed to rapidly identify the scope items that would provide the highest value to the most people. 'B' is not a good choice since brainstorming doesn't involve interviews or voting. 'C' is a means of voting, but it is not a good fit for the scenario here since this also involved interviews. 'D' is a model of team building and performance and does match the question being asked.

15. D. This is the best choice here. The WBS dictionary contains attributes about each work package such as an explanation of the work package (which invalidates choice 'A'), who is assigned responsibility for the work package (which invalidates choice 'B'), and a cost account code (which invalidates choice 'C'). If a work package were changed, that would most likely alter the scope baseline, and information on how to go about this would be found in the scope management plan and not the WBS dictionary.

Chapter Notes:

_____

_____

_____

_____

_____

_____

_____

_____

_____

_____

_____

_____

_____

_____

Scope Management: Answers

Chapter Notes:

_____

_____

_____

_____

_____

_____

_____

_____

_____

_____

_____

_____

_____

_____

16. C. Notice the use of the word 'FIRST'. 'A' is wrong because the customer should never bypass the project manager to authorize changes directly. It is the project manager's job to authorize changes on the project. 'B' is incorrect since all changes might not go to the change control board. Even if a change control board exists on the project, the project manager doesn't automatically just send everything their way. The project manager should deal with it first. 'D' is incorrect because the requirements management plan is not even the place this would be reflected. The scope baseline would need to be updated, but only after the change had been properly evaluated to see if it even belonged.

17. A. The customer accepts the scope of the product in Validate Scope.

18. B. The Nominal Group Technique is a method used to promote creativity in the Collect Requirements process, and the two outputs that match that process are the requirements documentation and the requirements traceability matrix.

19. C. It may make sense to benchmark against other internal projects or departments or against external organizations. Either one is acceptable, which eliminates 'A' and 'B' as good choices. 'D' is not a good choice since metrics may be used at any time to provide good working targets. Waiting until operations have stabilized would likely miss out on many of the benefits of benchmarking.

20. B. This can be a tough scenario and a tough question. On the exam, gravitate toward answers that have words like "understand" and "evaluate" in them. The product cannot be formally accepted without understanding its impact on the entire project. There is a bias on the exam against the practice of adding extra scope to the project, known as gold plating. Wherever you see this, your first instinct should be against doing it or accepting it.

21. C. Choices 'A' and 'B' are no-nos on the exam. You don't just make changes because they "add value." Does the customer want the change? Does the change increase the project risk or put the quality in jeopardy? Between 'C' and 'D', the best answer is 'C'. The reason is that just because the project manager thinks this is a good piece of functionality doesn't mean that he should automatically add it. The customer should have input into this decision as well. Choice 'D' might be correct in limited circumstances if you knew that you were at or near the end of the project, but changes on a project rarely require the automatic initiation of a new project.

22. A. The requirements documentation is typically created quite early on the project. In this case, it would be created well before the work breakdown structure and the scope baseline (which is made up of the scope statement, the WBS, and the WBS dictionary). The activity list would be created last in this list, so the order of creation of the documents listed would be A, B, D, and C.

23. C. Answers 'A', 'B', and 'D' are all incorrect, since they encourage adding or keeping the additional functionality. It is important not to add extras to the project for many reasons. The final product should be true to the scope. If you missed this, reread the section on scope management and gold plating.

24. A. The project manager needs to be proactive and influence the root causes of change. 'B' would be ridiculous in the real world. Imagine getting a change request near the end of the project that is good for the project and refusing to do it until you completed the original scope. Some change is good! 'C' is incorrect because although some change may introduce an unacceptable level of risk, all change certainly does not. Some changes could dramatically reduce the project risk and help the project. 'D' is incorrect, because value is not the primary criterion for evaluating change. A change may deliver high value, but also introduce too much risk or cost, or delay the project unacceptably.

25. B. These are all group decision-making techniques. Although 'A', 'C', and 'D' may sound like good choices, you need to know these five (Unanimity, Majority, Consensus, Plurality, and Autocratic, and Multicriteria Decision Analysis) before sitting for the exam.

Chapter Five

Chapter Notes:

_____

_____

_____

_____

_____

_____

_____

_____

_____

_____

_____

_____

_____

Schedule Management

From the indicators at the right of the page, you can tell that you may find this chapter to be more difficult than the previous chapter on scope management. In order to help you prepare for this topic, this book has clearly broken down the practices and outlined the techniques and formulas you will need to know in order to ace the questions on the exam. By the time you have completed this chapter, you may well have a higher level of confidence here than on any other section of the test.

Spending extra time here will yield direct dividends on the exam! Make sure that you learn both the processes and the techniques so that you can approach these questions with confidence.

PHILOSOPHY:

Project Schedule Management is concerned primarily with activities, scheduling, and schedule management. The philosophy here, as elsewhere, is that the project manager should be in control of the schedule, and not vice versa. The schedule is built from the ground up, derived from the scope baseline and other information, and rigorously managed throughout the life of the project. At the same time, the schedule should be as flexible as possible to accommodate the reality of planned and unplanned schedule changes.

Watch The Video
http://prep.pm/6-1

Difficulty:
HIGH
●●●●●●●●○○

Memorization:
HIGH
●●●●●●●●●○

Exam Importance:
MEDIUM
●●●●●●○○○○

Chapter Notes:

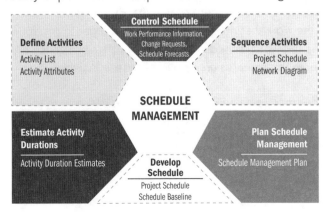

157

Chapter Six

Chapter Notes:

_____

_____

_____

_____

_____

_____

_____

_____

_____

_____

_____

_____

There are six processes related to schedule management that you should understand. They are:

1. Plan Schedule Management (planning out the next five processes)

2. Define Activities (list the project activities)

3. Sequence Activities (order the activities and create the project network diagram)

4. Estimate Activity Durations (determine time estimates for each activity)

5. Develop Schedule (create the schedule)

6. Control Schedule (monitor and adjust schedule performance)

You will see from reading this chapter that the driving philosophy behind schedule management is mathematical; it is primarily cold, hard analysis. The project manager does not merely accept whatever schedule goals are handed down or suggested. Instead, the schedule is based on the work to be done and it needs to conform to other calendar requirements, constraints, and strategic goals.

Additionally, while most of the topics within this book are integrated and related, the topics of scope, schedule, and cost are particularly tightly linked. Changes made to one area will almost certainly have direct impacts on the other two.

As in other areas, it is best that project managers begin from the bottom up. The WBS, which was covered in the previous chapter, is used heavily in several of the schedule management processes. By starting with the WBS, you can define the work that must be carried out in order to produce these deliverables. The individual schedule activities are then sequenced, and the resource and duration estimates are applied to these activities.

This approach has many similarities to the practices in scope management. Most similar is that your analysis and the resulting deliverables are comprehensive and complete.

IMPORTANCE:

Schedule management has traditionally been a favorite area to exploit for the exam.

PREPARATION:

Modern project managers typically rely on software to perform complex schedule and time calculations, but for the exam, you will need to understand the theories and practices for schedule management that underlie the software.

Some people are intimidated by the mathematical and logical aspects of this section because they do not understand the diagramming techniques and processes. A reliance on intuition will not get you very far on these questions. You either know how to calculate them or you do not. It is far better to spend time learning the techniques than to try to fumble your way through them on the exam. Most people who do not pass the exam fail by a handful of questions, so this section is not optional. You will need to memorize and understand the concepts presented in this chapter.

This book's approach to these exam questions falls into two categories:

1. There are several key terms that may be new to you, or they may have slightly different meanings than you are used to. Many of the questions on the exam will test your knowledge of specific terms and nuances, so it is important to be able to recognize and clearly understand them even if you do not memorize the definitions word for word.

2. There are formulas and techniques for estimating and diagramming. Memorization alone is not sufficient here. You must be able to calculate estimates, float, and critical path, among others.

Although the logic and math portions can be daunting to some people as they approach the exam, the right answer is often much easier to determine than with the situational questions. Once you master the techniques presented in this chapter, you can work out the right answer on your own

Chapter Notes:

Chapter Notes:

_____

_____

_____

_____

_____

_____

_____

_____

_____

_____

_____

_____

_____

and simply match it to the list of choices. For many, these questions become favorites on the exam.

Schedule Management Processes

There are six processes in the schedule management knowledge area. Following are the break-outs that show to which process group each item belongs:

Process Group	Schedule Management Process
Initiating	(none)
Planning	Plan Schedule Management, Define Activities, Sequence Activities, Estimate Activity Durations, Develop Schedule
Executing	(none)
Monitoring & Controlling	Control Schedule
Closing	(none)

In the knowledge area of schedule management, it is also essential that you know the main outputs that are produced during each process. The different key outputs that are created in each process are summarized in the following chart.

Process	Key Output(s)
Plan Schedule Management	Schedule Management Plan
Define Activities	Activity List, Activity Attributes
Sequence Activities	Project Schedule Network Diagrams
Estimate Activity Durations	Activity Duration Estimates
Develop Schedule	Project Schedule, Schedule Baseline
Control Schedule	Work Performance Information, Change Requests, Schedule Forecasts

.... PLANNING

PLAN SCHEDULE MANAGEMENT

WHAT IT IS:

Schedule management has a total of six processes, and Plan Schedule Management is the one that defines how the other five will be carried out.

6th Edition PMBOK® Guide
Cross Ref. pg 179

WHY IT IS IMPORTANT:

Schedule management follows the same pattern you observed in scope management, with a process at the beginning (Plan Schedule Management) to define how all of the related activities will be performed and one process at the end (Control Schedule) to review how it all went and to make any necessary adjustments. We will define the plan and the work up front so that we can have a way to measure performance and make any needed adjustments.

Watch The Video

http://**prep.pm/6-2**

WHEN IT IS PERFORMED:

The process of Plan Schedule Management may be performed early in the project since the schedule is usually a key component of the project plan. At a minimum, it should be performed before the other five schedule management processes are carried out.

HOW IT WORKS:

Plan Schedule Management is a relatively streamlined process with a few common inputs and tools and a single, important output.

Chapter Notes:

_____

_____

_____

_____

_____

_____

_____

_____

Chapter Six

Chapter Notes:

_____

_____

_____

_____

_____

_____

_____

_____

_____

_____

_____

_____

_____

HOW IT WORKS / INPUTS:

Project Charter — See Ch. 2, Common Inputs, Develop Project Charter

Project Management Plan — See Ch. 2, Common Inputs

Enterprise Environmental Factors — See Ch. 2, Common Inputs

Organizational Process Assets — See Ch. 2, Common Inputs

HOW IT WORKS / TOOLS:

Expert Judgment — See Ch. 2, Common Tools

Data Analysis — See Ch. 2, Common Tools

Meetings — See Ch. 2, Common Tools

HOW IT WORKS / OUTPUTS:

Schedule Management Plan - As you can see, the inputs and tools are predictable and provide unlikely exploits for the exam. The schedule management plan is really the whole point of this process. The schedule management plan will become part of the project plan, and it defines how the schedule will be defined, how it will be measured, how and how often the team will track progress, and what will happen if the project veers away from the plan. It also describes how progress will be reported and any other relevant details on how the remaining five schedule management processes will be carried out.

···· PLANNING

DEFINE ACTIVITIES

WHAT IT IS:

Once the scope baseline has been created, it can be used to break down (decompose) the work into the activities it will take to turn it into a reality. The main result of this planning process is the activity list. This list represents all of the schedule activities that will need to take place for the project to be completed. This is primarily accomplished by taking the WBS and decomposing the work packages even further until they represent schedule activities. The difference between work packages in a WBS and an activity list is that the activity list is more granular and is decomposed into individual schedule activities. Work packages will often contain bundles of related activities that may involve multiple groups of people. It is these activities that comprise the activity list. The activity list is used as the basis for the next four schedule management processes: Sequence Activities, Estimate Activity Durations, Develop Schedule, and Control Schedule.

If the project is being performed under procurement, this planning process will most likely be performed by the subcontracting organization, with the results being provided to the organization that is responsible for the management of the overall project.

WHY IT IS IMPORTANT:

In project scope management, we focused on the work that we needed to perform on the project. Now, in this chapter we are looking at *how* and *when* it will be accomplished. The activity list will be an essential input into building the schedule, so it is important that it be both complete and correct.

6th Edition PMBOK® Guide
Cross Ref. pg 183

Watch The Video

▶ http://**prep.pm/6-3**

Chapter Notes:

_____

_____

_____

_____

_____

_____

_____

Chapter Notes:

_____

_____

_____

_____

_____

_____

_____

_____

_____

_____

_____

_____

_____

WHEN IT IS PERFORMED:

The process of Define Activities is often performed as soon as the scope has been baselined. In other words, it is common to create the activity list after the requirements documentation, project scope statement, work breakdown structure, and the WBS dictionary have been created and are in a stable form (i.e., they are under control).

HOW IT WORKS / INPUTS:

Project Management Plan

The two key components here are the schedule management plan and the scope baseline.

⊙→ Schedule Management Plan - The schedule management plan specifies how Define Activities (and the other schedule management processes) will be carried out. It may cover details like how granular you want your schedule activities to be, what methods you will use to do this, and what kinds of activity attributes you will record.

⊙→ Scope Baseline -The scope baseline is made up of the approved project scope statement, the WBS, and the WBS dictionary. The scope baseline provides the primary input into this process. Each schedule activity that is defined in this process should tie back to a specific deliverable in the scope baseline.

Enterprise Environmental Factors — See Ch. 2, Common Inputs

Organizational Process Assets — See Ch. 2, Common Inputs

HOW IT WORKS / TOOLS:

Expert Judgment - Expert judgment in decomposing activities may come from numerous sources, including team members, consultants, and functional managers. One of the best sources for expertise in decomposing a work package into an activity may be the person who will ultimately be responsible for executing the work package or the schedule activity, or someone who has performed something similar in the past.

Decomposition - If you understood decomposition as it was used in the Create WBS process, you will have no trouble here. Each work package at the bottom of the WBS is simply decomposed into smaller pieces, known as schedule activities. The project manager should solicit heavy involvement from the project team or the functional managers to leverage their expertise when performing this process.

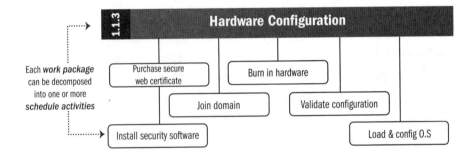

1.1.3 **Hardware Configuration**

Each *work package* can be decomposed into one or more *schedule activities*

- Purchase secure web certificate
- Join domain
- Install security software
- Burn in hardware
- Validate configuration
- Load & config O.S

Rolling Wave Planning - The concept of rolling wave planning is a form of progressive elaboration that models project planning the way we see things in the real world.

Suppose, for example, that you are standing at the edge of a field. You may be able to see some things in great detail, even counting individual blades of grass at your feet. The further off you look, however, the less detail you will be able to perceive. Distant objects, such as a mountain range several miles away, would appear general and hazy.

Rolling wave planning mirrors this construct by assuming that things in the near future should be relatively clear, while project activities in the distant

Chapter Notes:

Chapter Notes:

_____

_____

_____

_____

_____

_____

_____

_____

_____

_____

_____

_____

_____

_____

future may not be as detailed or as easily understood. Armed with that perspective, a project manager may choose to carefully decompose certain work packages, with anticipated execution in the near term, in great detail, while delaying analysis on work packages that will not be accomplished until later in the project.

This type of planning must be revisited throughout the project, much as waves continually roll onto the shore.

Rolling wave planning is a popular concept with agile projects, and it is used more frequently on projects like the creation of an information technology system, and less often on projects within the construction industry where unknowns may cost millions of dollars.

Meetings — See Ch. 2, Common Tools

HOW IT WORKS / OUTPUTS:

Activity List - All of the schedule activities that need to be performed in order to complete the project are compiled into the activity list. Each activity in the list should map back to one and only one work package (a work package, however, typically has more than one activity belonging to it). One major difference between a work package and a schedule activity is that the work packages are deliverables-based, focusing on the scope of the project, while the activities are focused on the work that needs to be done in order to execute the work packages. The activities should include enough information to transition them to the project team so that the work may be performed.

The activity list's usefulness is tied to its completeness and accuracy. It is important to identify and document each activity that must be performed in order to complete the project.

It is important to note that a line exists between the work breakdown structure and the activity list. Although the activity list is an extension of the work breakdown structure, it is not a part of the work breakdown structure. The WBS belongs to the scope baseline, while the activity list is more closely related to the project's schedule.

The activity list by itself is generally limited only to an identifier, such as an activity name or a unique numeric identifier, and a description.

The following table will help you understand the difference between the two.

Work Breakdown Structure	Activity List
Deliverable-based	Effort based; focused on effort required to complete work packages
Used as a central tool to manage the project	Used to build the schedule
Contains information on deliverables, resources, schedule, and cost	Contains activity name, description, and an estimated duration
One work package maps to one or many schedule activities	Each schedule activity maps back to a single work package

 Activity Attributes - As planning progresses, there will be a need to store additional information about activities. For example, the person responsible for this activity, the parts that need to be procured before this activity may be started, and the location at which the work will be performed could be highly important.

Activity attributes may be stored with the activity list or in a separate document and are typically added after the initial activity list has been created.

Note that any time you see the activity list, you will also see the activity attributes. The activity attributes may be thought of as an expansion of the activity list.

Milestone List - The key project milestones are produced as a part of this process. These milestones may be related to imposed dates (such as a contractual obligation), schedule constraints, or projected dates based on historical information. Milestones are always significant dates or events and have zero duration.

Change Requests — See Ch. 2, Common Outputs

Project Management Plan Updates —
See Ch. 2, Common Outputs

Chapter Notes:

_____

_____

_____

_____

_____

_____

_____

_____

_____

_____

_____

Define Activities

Chapter Six

SEQUENCE ACTIVITIES

6th Edition PMBOK® Guide
Cross Ref. pg 187

WHAT IT IS:

The Sequence Activities process is primarily concerned with taking the activity list that we created in the previous process of Define Activities and arranging those activities in the order they must be performed.

This process is all about understanding and diagramming the relationships that schedule activities have with each other.

Watch The Video

http://**prep.pm/6-4**

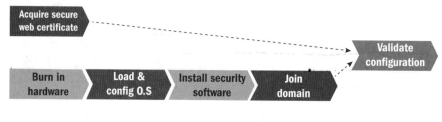

Schedule activities logically sequenced

Chapter Notes:

_____

_____

_____

_____

_____

_____

_____

_____

WHY IT IS IMPORTANT:

A network logic diagram is a picture in which each activity is drawn and placed in the order it must be performed, and the amount of time each activity takes is represented with a number. Sequence Activities is the planning process in which these network diagrams are produced.

Network diagramming is the preferred method for representing activities, their dependencies, and sequences. The precedence diagramming method (also known as an activity-on-node diagram) is discussed later in this chapter.

WHEN IT IS PERFORMED:

Because of the flow of inputs and outputs between other processes, the process of Sequence Activities must be performed after Define Activities and before Develop Schedule.

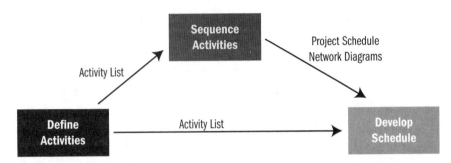

Define Activities must be performed before Sequence Activities or Develop Schedule

HOW IT WORKS / INPUTS:

Project Management Plan

Schedule Management Plan - The schedule management plan will be an important input here, because it defines how this process will be carried out.

Scope Baseline - The scope baseline contains the WBS, constraints, and assumptions among other things, which may be helpful in sequencing activities.

Sequence Activities

Chapter Notes:

_____

_____

_____

_____

_____

_____

_____

_____

_____

_____

_____

_____

_____

_____

_____

Project Documents

 Activity List - The activity list is the most important input into Sequence Activities. It is in this process that the schedule activities from the activity list will be arranged, or sequenced, into a diagram that represents the order in which they must be performed.

Activity Attributes - The activity attributes, produced in Define Activities, are brought into this process since they contain additional information about each activity that may influence how it is sequenced.

Assumption Log - Assumptions are anything we treat as true for the purposes of planning. For example, on a construction project, you might assume you will have at least a certain number of days where the weather permits outdoor work, or on an information technology project, you might assume that you will be able to recruit a number of developers for a particular computer language by a given date. These assumptions should be documented in the assumption log and brought into this process.

Milestone List - Milestones are events that must be considered in the life of the project.

There is an interesting relationship between milestones and the process of Sequence Activities. Milestones are often imposed from outside the project (e.g., the project sponsor indicates an overall deliverable date), and activities typically come from within the project (e.g., the decomposition of work packages). Because of this, activities will often need to be arranged in a specific way in order to meet key milestones. For instance, if the customer specified a milestone of a pre-construction walkthrough at a certain point in time, then the activity of cleaning up the work site may need to be sequenced in earlier than would otherwise be necessary.

Enterprise Environmental Factors — See Ch. 2, Common Inputs

Organizational Process Assets — See Ch. 2, Common Inputs

HOW IT WORKS / TOOLS:

Precedence Diagramming Method (PDM) - The precedence diagramming method creates a graphical representation of the schedule activities in the order in which they must be performed on the project.

Activities are represented by the nodes (rectangles), with arrows representing the dependencies that exist between the activities.

The project network diagram illustrated uses the activity on node convention to represent the activities. In this case, the nodes are shown as rectangles, and the activities are represented inside the node, usually by letters of the alphabet. Units of duration are shown above the nodes.

The second half of this chapter has a special focus on project network diagramming including the precedence diagramming method.

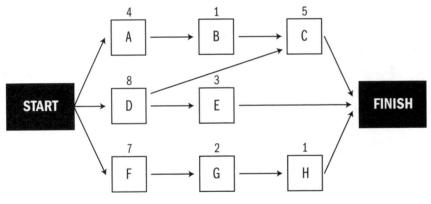

An example of an Activity on Node diagram created using PDM

Chapter Notes:

_____
_____
_____
_____
_____
_____
_____
_____
_____
_____
_____
_____
_____
_____
_____
_____
_____

Sequence Activities

Chapter Six

Chapter Notes:

_____

_____

_____

_____

_____

_____

_____

_____

_____

_____

_____

_____

_____

➔ **Dependency Determination and Integration** - Dependencies are those things that influence which activities must be performed first. For example, a road must be graded before it can be paved. If grading and paving the road were two activities on the project, then we would say that the start of the activity of paving the road is dependent upon the finish of the activity of grading the road, thus these two activities have a finish-to-start relationship.

Two activities with a dependency, creating a finish-to-start relationship

There are four main kinds of dependencies that may exist among activities.

Mandatory Dependencies

A mandatory dependency is one that cannot be broken. Given the example where paving the road is dependent upon grading it, the dependency is unavoidable, or mandatory. Mandatory dependencies are also known as hard logic, since a mandatory dependency is considered unmovable and always true.

Discretionary Dependencies

Discretionary dependencies, unlike the preceding example, are not always true. These would often be the result of best practices, and may vary organization to organization and even project to project. For instance, the project of managing the remodeling of a house may have a discretionary dependency between painting the walls and carpeting the floors, where painting must be completed before carpeting could be installed. There is no absolute rule that says the carpet could not be installed before the painting begins.

Discretionary dependencies are also known as soft logic or preferred logic and are typically based on historical information, expert judgment, and best practices.

External Dependencies

External dependencies are those dependencies that must be considered but are outside of the project's control and scope. For instance, if an automobile is being developed to use alternative technology, there may be an external dependency on a supplier providing a battery that meets certain specifications before the project can meet its schedule. Because these are dependencies, they must be identified and documented as part of this process.

Internal Dependencies

Internal dependencies are those dependencies that the team can control. For example, a dependency that shows that the marketing department has to finish creating logos and web pages before an application can be released would probably be categorized as an internal dependency since both of these are within the control of the project team.

Chapter Notes:

_____

_____

_____

_____

_____

_____

_____

_____

_____

_____

_____

_____

_____

Sequence Activities

Chapter Notes:

_____

_____

_____

_____

_____

_____

_____

_____

_____

_____

_____

_____

_____

Leads and Lags - A lead is simply one activity getting a jump-start on another. Consider, for instance, a software project that has a dependency between finishing the development of a section of code and beginning the quality inspection. Since the development has to finish before the testing begins, we would say that a mandatory finish-to-start dependency exists between the two activities.

An example of a lead would be if the individual or group performing the quality inspection gets an unfinished beta copy of the software in order to get a head start. Note that leads do not do away with the finish-to-start relationship that exists. Instead, it simply "cheats" that relationship.

Leads increase risk, and the rationale behind them should be clearly explained and documented.

Think of a lag as a waiting period that exists between two activities. A lag is a situation where a waiting period must occur between one activity and another dependent activity. An example of a lag would be if one activity was to order a computer server and another activity was to configure the server, then a lag might exist between the time the server is ordered and the time it arrives and can be configured. During a lag, there is no work being performed by the organization against this activity; no resources are being expended. They are simply waiting.

Project Management Information System —
See Ch. 2, Common Tools

HOW IT WORKS / OUTPUTS:

Project Schedule Network Diagrams - The project Schedule network diagrams are covered in depth in the Critical Path Method section later in this chapter. These diagrams are a graphical way of depicting schedule activities, their dependencies, and their sequence.

Project Documents Updates — See Ch. 2, Common Outputs

···· PLANNING

ESTIMATE ACTIVITY DURATIONS

WHAT IT IS:

This process is exactly what it sounds like. Each activity in the activity list is analyzed to estimate how long it will take.

There is an important difference between duration and level of effort, and this process focuses on determining duration.

The duration of an activity is a function of many factors, including who will be doing the work, when they are available, how many resources will be assigned to this activity, and the amount of work contained in the activity.

6th Edition PMBOK® Guide
Cross Ref. pg 195

WHY IS IT IMPORTANT:

These activity duration estimates will become a primary input into creating the schedule when the overall project time line has been created.

Watch The Video
http://prep.pm/6-5

Chapter Notes:

WHEN IT IS PERFORMED:

Estimate Activity Durations is performed after the activity resource requirements have been gathered and before the schedule is developed.

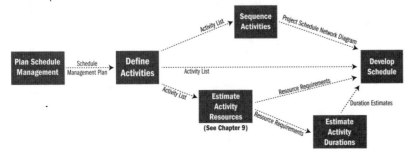

Chapter Six

Chapter Notes:

_____

_____

_____

_____

_____

_____

_____

_____

_____

_____

_____

HOW IT WORKS / INPUTS:

Project Management Plan

Schedule Management Plan - The schedule management plan is one of the key components of the project management plan used as an input here, because it defines how this process will be carried out. For Estimate Activity Durations, it would describe how the activity duration estimates will be derived and how accurate and precise they will need to be.

Scope Baseline - The main part of the scope baseline we are concerned with here is the WBS, since all activity estimates should eventually be mapped back to the work packages.

Project Documents

There is no need to memorize the full list of project documents used as inputs. They are activity attributes, activity list, assumption log, lessons learned register, milestone list, project team assignments, resource breakdown structure, resource calendars, resource requirements, and the risk register. The most important ones are discussed here:

 Activity List - The activity list is a primary input for this process. Every activity in the list should be estimated to determine its duration.

Activity Attributes - The activity attributes always accompany the activity list. These attributes provide additional information about each activity in the list.

Resource Requirements - Since the duration is a function of the amount of work associated with an activity and the resources assigned to perform that work, the activity resource requirements need to be brought into this process.

→ **Resource Calendars** - These resource calendars are updated in the Estimate Activity Resources process (See Ch. 9). These calendars show physical and human resource usage across the entire project and sometimes the entire enterprise.

Resource Breakdown Structure - The resource breakdown structure provides an organized chart of resources by category or type.

Enterprise Environmental Factors - Things that influence your project such as what records an organization requires, safety standards, and regulations can all affect how long an activity takes. For instance, it may take far longer to perform an activity in a nuclear power plant than it does in a conventional power plant due to enterprise environmental factors, and these must be considered in order to accurately estimate the duration of activities.

Organizational Process Assets - These could take the form of a rich database of historical information that shows the estimated and actual durations for activities for a previous project, while another organization may have specific calendar requirements when resources are available. Anything that gives structure or guidance to your activity duration estimates would be considered an organizational process asset.

HOW IT WORKS / TOOLS:

Expert Judgment - Anyone who has managed a project will attest that the duration of an activity can be notoriously hard to estimate in advance. The expert providing the judgment should follow some basis, such as analysis or historical information, whether documented or experiential.

→ **Analogous Estimating** - Analogous estimating, also known as top-down estimating, is where an activity from a project previously performed within the organization is used to help estimate another activity's duration.

Typically, the previous actual time spent on the similar activity is used as the estimate for another similar activity. The technique is combined with expert judgment to determine if the two activities are truly alike.

Chapter Notes:

_____

_____

_____

_____

_____

_____

_____

_____

_____

_____

_____

_____

_____

_____

_____

Estimate Activity Durations

Chapter Notes:

_____

_____

_____

_____

_____

_____

_____

_____

_____

_____

_____

_____

_____

→ **Parametric Estimating** - If one team can install 100 feet of fence in one day, then it would take 10 teams to install 1,000 feet of fence in one day. This kind of linear extrapolation is an example of parametric estimating.

Parametric estimating can work well for activities that are either linear or easily scaled. It is not as effective for activities that have not been performed before or those for which little or no historical information has been gathered.

→ **Three-Point Estimating** - Three-point estimating, also called PERT estimates (for Program Evaluation and Review Technique), use three data points for the duration instead of simply one. These are pessimistic, most likely (also known as realistic), and optimistic estimates.

There are two primary ways of calculating a three-point estimate: beta distribution and triangular distribution.

Beta Distribution

We will begin by looking at beta distribution. As an example of how this is used, suppose a developer estimates that it will most likely take 9 days to write a module of code; however, she also supplies an optimistic estimate of 7 days and a pessimistic estimate of 17 days.

She then applies a formula, usually in the form of a weighted average, to these estimates to distill them down to a single estimate. The traditional formula is:

(Pessimistic + 4 × Realistic + Optimistic) ÷ 6

In the example above, the numbers would be substituted as (17 + 4 × 9 + 7) ÷ 6 = 10 days. This number is used as the activity duration estimate for this schedule activity.

When considering beta distribution, another important formula to memorize for the exam is one used to calculate the standard deviation (expressed as σ) for an estimate.

(Pessimistic - Optimistic) ÷ 6

This formula is not the actual standard deviation, but a shortcut that makes quite a few assumptions about the data. It's a good idea to know for the exam, but be careful before using this in actual practice.

Given these formulas, let us consider the following estimates for activities A, B, and C.

ACTIVITY	Optimistic	Pessimistic	Most Likely
A	22	35	25
B	60	77	70
C	12	40	20

Now, using the formulas above, we will calculate the three point estimate for each of these activities.

ACTIVITY	Optimistic	Pessimistic	Most Likely	3 Point Estimate
A	22	35	25	26.17
B	60	77	70	69.5
C	12	40	20	22

Triangular Distribution

The technique of triangular distribution is very similar to beta distribution; however, it is a bit easier. For our purposes in estimating, triangular distribution is a simple average of the values of the pessimistic, optimist, and most likely estimates.

(Pessimistic + Realistic + Optimistic) ÷ 3

You also need to be prepared to recognize beta and triangular distribution graphs for the exam. Simply being able to identify which one is beta and which one is triangular should be sufficient. The triangular shape associated with triangular distribution makes that a snap.

Estimate Activity Durations

Chapter Six

Chapter Notes:

_____

_____

_____

_____

_____

_____

_____

_____

_____

_____

_____

_____

_____

_____

_____

If you encounter three-point estimating on the exam, use the formula for triangular distribution by default.

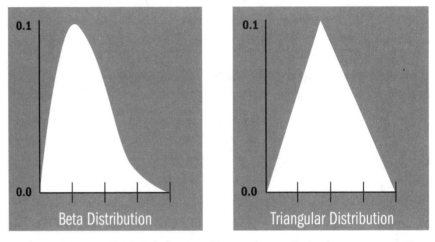

A graphical representation of beta and triangular distribution

Bottom-Up Estimating - Bottom-up estimating is essentially the opposite of analogous estimating. Using this technique, each step needed to complete an activity is estimated, and those estimates are added together to get the activity's duration estimate. This works well when the activity is understood very well and the organization has experience with this type of activity. Bottom-up estimating can be a very powerful and accurate technique to use when there are few unknowns.

Data Analysis

Alternatives Analysis - The most common alternatives analysis performed is "make or buy" analysis to determine whether to perform an activity in house or to outsource it; however, there are other types where you might look at whether to use one highly-skilled individual or two or more people with a lower skill level, whether to invest in automation and at what level, etc. The point of this is to make optimal decisions for the project and the organization.

Reserve Analysis - Reserve time, also called contingency, is extra time added to an activity duration estimate.

Reserve time estimates are revisited throughout the life of the project, being revised up or down as more information on schedule risk becomes available.

Decision Making — See Ch. 2, Common Tools

Meetings — See Ch. 2, Common Tools

HOW IT WORKS / OUTPUTS:

Duration Estimates - All of the preceding inputs and tools for this process are used together to produce this key output: the duration estimates for the activities.

The duration estimates contain an estimated amount of time for each activity in the activity list. Ideally, these estimates represent a range such as the optimistic-pessimistic-realistic ones covered in the three-point estimate technique discussed earlier in this process.

Basis of Estimates - This is the supporting detail that shows how the activity duration estimates were derived and what tradeoffs and alternatives were considered.

Project Documents Updates - As each activity is being estimated at a low level, updates to the activity attributes are a normal by-product of this process. Additionally, any assumptions made as part of the estimates as well as any lessons learned should be documented.

Chapter Notes:

Estimate Activity Durations

Chapter Six

···· PLANNING

DEVELOP SCHEDULE

6th Edition PMBOK® Guide
Cross Ref. pg 205

WHAT IT IS:

The process of Develop Schedule is one of the largest of the 49 processes, containing 20 combined inputs, tools, and outputs.

As anyone who has managed a complex project will attest, developing the schedule can be one of the most daunting parts of the project.

Watch The Video
http://**prep.pm/6-6**

WHY IT IS IMPORTANT:

The schedule is usually one of the most visible and important parts of the project plan. In fact, many inexperienced project managers often mistakenly refer to the depictions of the schedule as the project plan or use the two terms interchangeably.

As you can tell by the name, this process is the one where the project's schedule is created.

Chapter Notes:

_____

_____

_____

_____

_____

_____

_____

_____

WHEN IT IS PERFORMED:

The process of Develop Schedule is typically performed after the processes of Estimate Activity Resources (See Ch. 9), Estimate Activity Durations, and Sequence Activities have been performed and before Determine Budget (See Ch. 7) is performed.

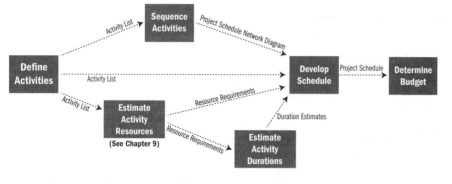

A diagram showing the order of Schedule Management's planning processes and the integration with Cost Management

HOW IT WORKS / INPUTS:

Project Management Plan

Schedule Management Plan - The schedule management plan is the part of the project plan that specifies how the schedule will be calculated, and developed, and what forms it will ultimately take.

Scope Baseline -The scope baseline is an input to most of the schedule management processes. This is because the scope and the schedule are closely intertwined. The deliverables described in the scope baseline will drive much of the schedule development.

Project Documents

Activity Attributes - The activity attributes always accompany the activity list. They provide expanded information on each activity in the list, and these details may be important when scheduling the activity.

Activity List - The activity list is the list of all activities that need to be scheduled and performed on the project. It is a bit redundant here as an input since the project schedule network diagrams (covered later in the list of inputs to this process) implicitly contain the activity list.

Chapter Notes:

Develop Schedule

Chapter Notes:

_____

_____

_____

_____

_____

_____

_____

_____

_____

_____

_____

_____

_____

_____

Assumption Log - Any assumptions that relate to the schedule should be brought into this process. These are things that you will treat as true while developing the schedule (e.g. weather or availability of resources).

Basis of Estimates — See Estimate Activity Durations, Outputs

Duration Estimates — See Estimate Activity Durations, Outputs

Lessons Learned - This refers to lessons learned in this project that might help with schedule development. Considering that the Develop Schedule process will often be revisited multiple times throughout the life of the project, lessons learned from previous activities or phases can be very valuable.

Milestone List - Milestones are significant events in the life of the project, and they often play a role in schedule development. Consider that some milestones are imposed from the start of the project (e.g., the new stadium has to be ready for opening day), so it is not unusual for the schedule to have to be built around one or more milestones.

Project Schedule Network Diagrams - The project schedule network diagrams were created earlier in Sequence Activities, and they now become a primary input into Develop Schedule. The project schedule network diagrams show the order in which activities must be completed, while the schedule assigns dates to each of these activities.

Project Team Assignments - The schedule is ultimately a function of how long activities will take to complete using the available resources, and team assignments can have a major impact on the actual schedule. Project team assignments are produced as an output of Acquire Resources.

Resource Calendars - The resource calendars show availability of resources, which can strongly influence scheduling.

Develop Schedule

Resource Requirements - This is used hand-in-hand with the previous document of resource calendars to help create the schedule.

Risk Register - The risk register lists all identified project risks, and many of these risks may relate to the schedule.

Agreements — See Ch. 2, Common Inputs

Enterprise Environmental Factors — See Ch. 2, Common Inputs

Organizational Process Assets — See Ch. 2, Common Inputs

HOW IT WORKS / TOOLS:

Schedule Network Analysis - This technique actually refers to a group of techniques used to create the schedule. Any of the other specific tools or techniques that are part of the process of Develop Schedule may be used as part of this general tool.

Critical Path Method (CPM) - Before trying to understand the critical path method, it is important to understand what the critical path is. A project's critical path is the combination of activities that, if any are delayed, will delay the project's finish.

The critical path method is an analysis technique with three main purposes:

1. To calculate the project's finish date.

2. To identify how much individual activities in the schedule can slip (or "float") without delaying the project.

3. To identify the activities with the highest risk that cannot slip without changing the project finish date.

A more detailed explanation of the critical path method appears later in this chapter under the heading, "Special Focus: Critical Path Method." The section shows specific techniques and provides exercises that you will need to be able to perform.

Chapter Notes:

_____
_____
_____
_____
_____
_____
_____
_____
_____
_____
_____
_____
_____
_____

Develop Schedule

Chapter Notes:

———————————

———————————

———————————

———————————

———————————

———————————

———————————

———————————

———————————

———————————

———————————

———————————

———————————

———————————

Critical Chain Method - Based on the theories of Eliyahu Goldratt, critical chain provides a way to view and manage uncertainty when building the project schedule.

The traditional way of building the schedule, using the critical path method, gathers realistic activity duration estimates and assembles the schedule, identifying the longest (critical) path through the network. Buffers may be added to certain high-risk activities in order to ensure that their uncertainty is managed.

The critical chain method modifies this technique by estimating each activity as aggressively as possible, building the schedule network, and then adding one lump-sum buffer to the end of the network before the finish date. This lump-sum buffer is then used to manage any individual activity that might be in danger of slipping, whether it is on the critical path or in danger of affecting the critical path. One advantage of this approach is that the team is not made aware of the buffers and therefore they are kept on an aggressive schedule. A buffer, however, does exist, and it is under the control of the project manager.

Resource Optimization - These two techniques seek to use resources in the most efficient ways, and they are important to know for the exam.

Resource Leveling

When many people think about the technique of resource leveling, they may mistakenly consider only what their project management software does to level resources. Resource leveling is when your resource needs meet up with the organization's ability to supply resources.

In order to resource-level the project, you first use the critical path method to calculate and analyze all of the network paths for the project. Then you apply resources to that analysis to see what effect it has on schedule outcome. This technique often results in a change to the critical path and the project's completion date.

Consider the following scenario. After performing the processes of Estimate Activity Durations and Estimate Activity Resources (See Ch. 9), you end up with the following project schedule network diagram.

ACTIVITY ID	ACTIVITY	Preceding Activity	Resources Needed	Quantity of Resource Required	Estimated Durations (in days)
A	Database Design	Start	Database Administrator	2	8
B	Data Entry	A	Data Entry Clerk	10	5
C	Write stored procedures	A	Programmer	8	5
D	Test stored procedures	B,C	Quality Control Engineer	1	2

Chapter Notes:

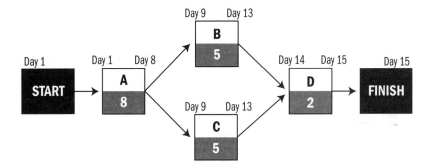

The project network diagram above was created from the preceding table using the critical path method. Now, however, consider what would happen if the organization could not provide eight programmer resources as reflected in this scenario. Instead, they can only supply two. The scenario must be resource leveled, resulting in a longer overall network diagram as follows:

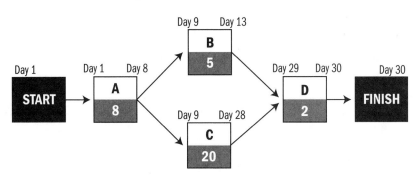

Chapter Notes:

_____

_____

_____

_____

_____

_____

_____

_____

_____

_____

_____

_____

_____

_____

After the resource calendar has been applied and the schedule has been leveled, a schedule is created based on the resources applied, where each activity is assigned a projected start and finish date.

Resource Smoothing

Resource smoothing looks at the schedule in light of resource constraints. When resource smoothing is used, the critical path and the completion date do not change. The activities may change within their float, but that is all. Resource smoothing is usually less disruptive to the schedule than resource leveling.

Data Analysis

What-if scenario analysis

This is essentially a way of looking at risk to determine how certain events or scenarios would impact the schedule. The goal is to determine whether or not the schedule is practical and whether reserves and buffers are appropriate.

Simulation

Simulation applies a number of scenarios against the project schedule to determine the probabilities that it will finish on time.

You should expect questions on the exam to refer to Monte Carlo analysis for this. Monte Carlo analysis is performed by computer and evaluates probabilities by considering a huge number of simulated scheduling possibilities or a few selected likely scenarios. A computer employing Monte Carlo analysis can perform this analysis and identify the highest risk activities that may not otherwise be apparent, showing the impact of these changes on the schedule.

 Leads and Lags - This technique, mirroring the one in the Sequence Activities process, ensures that the leads and lags are accurately applied to the schedule and adjusted appropriately.

➔ **Schedule Compression** - On many projects, there are ways to complete the project schedule earlier without cutting the project's scope. That is the purpose of schedule compression.

Two types of questions that you will probably encounter on the exam involving schedule compression are related to crashing and fast tracking. Crashing involves adding resources to a project activity so that it will be completed more quickly. Crashing almost always increases costs.

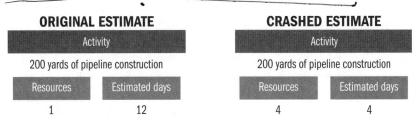

ORIGINAL ESTIMATE

Activity
200 yards of pipeline construction

Resources	Estimated days
1	12

CRASHED ESTIMATE

Activity
200 yards of pipeline construction

Resources	Estimated days
4	4

An example of crashing the schedule by adding more resources to an activity

Note that in the preceding example, increasing the number of resources does decrease the time but not by a linear amount. This is because activities will often encounter the law of diminishing returns when adding resources to an activity. The old saying "too many cooks spoil the broth" applies to projects as well as cooking.

Fast tracking means that you re-order the sequence of activities so that some of the activities are performed at the same time. Fast tracking does not necessarily increase costs, but it almost always increases risk to the project since discretionary dependencies are being ignored and additional activities are happening simultaneously. (Discretionary dependencies were discussed under the process of Sequence Activities.)

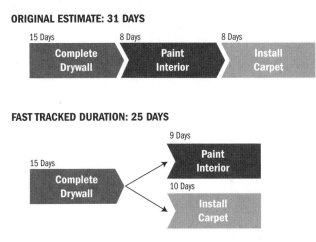

ORIGINAL ESTIMATE: 31 DAYS

15 Days — Complete Drywall | 8 Days — Paint Interior | 8 Days — Install Carpet

FAST TRACKED DURATION: 25 DAYS

15 Days — Complete Drywall
9 Days — Paint Interior
10 Days — Install Carpet

Chapter Notes:

Develop Schedule

Note that fast tracking often results in some individual activities taking longer, and it increases the risk. In the example above, the workers may have a harder time moving around each other, thus increasing the time to paint and install carpet. Also, there is an increased risk associated with these activities. For example, the painters could damage the carpet, or the carpet installers could be hampered by the fresh paint.

Develop Schedule

Chapter Notes:

_____

_____

_____

_____

_____

_____

_____

_____

_____

_____

_____

_____

_____

_____

Project Management Information System —
See Ch. 2, Common Tools

 Agile Release Planning - Adaptive projects use the product backlog to create an overall release plan. The backlog contains the user stories that the team has identified. These stories are prioritized by value to the customer and are then estimated by the team as to difficulty. Then the team selects which features and user stories will be included in planned releases.

HOW IT WORKS / OUTPUTS:

 Schedule Baseline - The schedule baseline is the approved schedule that has been placed under control. Keep in mind that a baseline is the original plan plus all approved changes, so it may be changed, but only through a formal process. If the schedule slips, that delay would not become incorporated into the baseline since it was not approved in advance.

 Project Schedule - The project schedule shows when each activity is scheduled to begin and end; it also shows a planned start and finish date for the overall project. The schedule is typically represented graphically, and there are different forms it may take. The most common forms are covered as follows:

Bar Charts (also called Gantt Charts) - Bar charts, or Gantt charts, show activities represented as horizontal bars and typically have a calendar along the horizontal axis. The length of the bar corresponds to the length of time the activity should require.

Activity Name	Duration	Start	Finish	Jan 15, '17	Jan 22, '17	Jan 29, '17	Feb 05, '17
Start	0 days	Thu 1/18/17	Thu 1/18/17				
Activity A	7 days	Thu 1/18/17	Wed 1/25/17				
Activity B	5 days	Thu 1/26/17	Mon 1/30/17				
Activity C	4 days	Tue 1/31/17	Fri 2/03/17				
Activity D	2 days	Thu 1/18/04	Fri 1/19/17				
Activity E	9 days	Sat 1/21/17	Sun 1/29/17				
Finish	0 days	Fri 2/03/17	Fri 2/03/17				

Project: Sandstorm — Activity / Progress / Milestone

A bar chart, or Gantt chart, can be easily modified to show percentage complete (usually by shading all or part of the horizontal bar). It is considered to be a good tool to use to communicate with management, because unlike the project network diagram, it is easy to understand at a glance.

Milestone Charts - A milestone chart, as the name implies, only represents key events (milestones) for the project. Milestones may be significant events or deliverables that are the responsibility of the project team or external parties.

Milestone charts, because of the general level of information they provide, should be reserved for brief, high-level project presentations where a lot of schedule detail would be undesirable or even distracting.

Activity Name	Duration	Jan 15, '17	Jan 22, '17	Jan 29, '17	Feb 05, '17	Feb 12, '17	Feb 19, '17
Marketing Studies Complete	0 days	1/18					
Requirements Gathered	0 days		1/27				
High level design	0 days			2/3			
Prototype ready	0 days					2/13	
Detailed design	0 days						2/20

Project: Firestorm — Milestone

Chapter Six

Chapter Notes:

_____

_____

_____

_____

_____

_____

_____

_____

_____

_____

_____

_____

_____

Project Schedule Network Diagram - The project schedule network diagram is a useful detail-driven tool that provides a powerful view of the dependencies and sequences of each activity. It is the best representation for calculating the critical path and showing dependencies on the project.

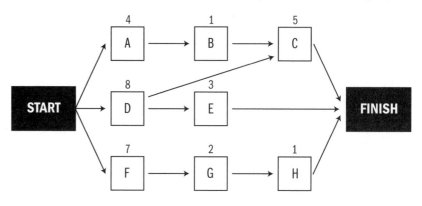

Schedule Data - Schedule data refers to the information the project team used to model and create the project schedule. It would include schedule templates that were used, the activities and their attributes, estimated durations, and any constraints and assumptions. This output is simply the data which supports how this schedule was developed.

Project Calendars - A project calendar shows the schedules, hours, and shifts for all of the activities.

Change Requests — See Ch. 2, Common Outputs

Project Management Plan Updates —
See Ch. 2, Common Outputs

Project Documents Updates - These updates to the resource requirements are a very common output in Develop Schedule, especially in the case of the tool of resource leveling, which adjusts the resources that are required in light of the organization's ability to supply them. Updates to activity attributes, assumption logs, risk registers, duration estimates, and calendars are also common.

···· MONITORING & CONTROLLING

CONTROL SCHEDULE

WHAT IT IS:

As you can tell from its name, Control Schedule is a monitoring and controlling process. The concept behind monitoring and controlling processes in general is to compare the work results to the plan and ensure that they line up. In this process, the schedule is controlled to make sure that time-related performance on the project is in line with the plan.

One of the more important concepts to master with Control Schedule (and most monitoring and controlling processes in general) is that schedule changes are not only reacted to, but the schedule is reviewed and adjusted proactively. That is, the project manager should be out in front of the project, influencing changes before they affect the project. Of course, at times, changes to the schedule may occur and the project manager will have to react to them, but the project manager should be proactive whenever possible.

WHY IT IS IMPORTANT:

Any time the schedule changes or a change request that affects the schedule occurs, the change should be evaluated and planned. The schedule should be monitored continuously against the actual work performed to ensure that things stay on target.

WHEN IT IS PERFORMED:

The process of Control Schedule is performed throughout the life of the project from the moment the schedule is developed until all scheduled activities have been completed. This ensures that the schedule is always up to date.

6th Edition PMBOK® Guide
Cross Ref. pg 222

Watch The Video

http://prep.pm/6-7

Chapter Notes:

_____

_____

_____

_____

_____

_____

_____

_____

Chapter Six

Chapter Notes:

———————————————
———————————————
———————————————
———————————————
———————————————
———————————————
———————————————
———————————————
———————————————
———————————————
———————————————
———————————————
———————————————

HOW IT WORKS / INPUTS:

Project Management Plan - The project management plan contains the schedule management plan and the schedule baseline, both of which are essential components for this process. The schedule management plan is important since it defines how the schedule will be managed and changed, and Control Schedule is the process that reviews and manages those changes, while the schedule baseline provides the latest approved version of the project schedule. As changes are made or change requests are approved, the schedule baseline is updated to reflect those changes. Both of these components have been officially melded into the project management plan by this time.

Project Documents — See Ch. 2, Common Inputs

Lessons Learned Register - Because many lessons learned relate to schedule and cost, it is an input here, and the updated version will flow out of this process.

Project Calendars - Projects may have multiple calendars, possibly spanning multiple organizations. For example, if components of a project were being developed in both China and France, the holidays and working periods would differ significantly. These calendars will be necessary when controlling (and likely adjusting) the schedule.

Project Schedule - This is the documented version of what is being controlled in this process.

Resource Calendars - As this process will likely make adjustments to the schedule, the availability of resource, contained in the resource calendars, is important.

Schedule Data - Supporting information is almost always a good thing to have, and the schedule data is the supporting information that may contain explanations of why certain scheduling decisions were made and the factors that went into those decisions.

Work Performance Data - Work performance data gives information on how the work is being performed. In this case, it will tell us how particular schedule activities are being completed. This can help identify trends and provide useful information to compare against the schedule.

Organizational Process Assets - Anything that the organization has that can make this process run more smoothly could be considered an organizational process asset. For example, a system for formally evaluating schedule change or a software system to help detect changes or measure variances would be an organizational process asset.

HOW IT WORKS / TOOLS:

Data Analysis - Six forms of data analysis are used here:

Earned Value Analysis — (Discussed in Chapter 7)

→ **Iteration Burndown Chart** - An iteration burndown chart is an agile tool used to display the team's progress of completing the work in the backlog. Agile teams generally post this in a very visible space so that progress is transparent and easily viewed by stakeholders.

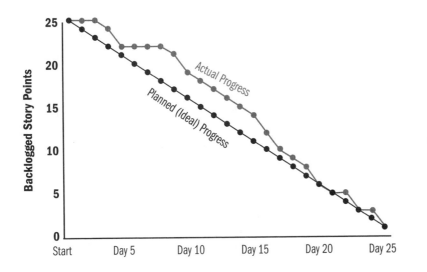

Chapter Notes:

_____

_____

_____

_____

_____

_____

_____

_____

_____

_____

_____

_____

Performance Reviews - Team performance needs to be considered if the schedule performance is deviating from the plan.

Trend Analysis - Trends can alert to positive or negative outcomes before they happen. For example, if your schedule performance is trending in a progressively worsening direction, it may require corrective action before a date is actually missed.

Variance Analysis - This compares the schedule baseline with reality to understand what variances are occurring.

What-if Scenario Analysis - This is a powerful tool that looks at possible scenarios to get the project back on schedule.

Critical Path Method - The critical path method is covered in detail later in this chapter. It is used to calculate the duration of the project and the activities that represent the highest risk to on-time completion.

Project Management Information System —
See Ch. 2, Common Tools

Resource Optimization - When the schedule changes, whether or not those changes were anticipated, it can cause a ripple effect throughout the whole project. In this case, the resources that had been carefully allocated across the project may need to be leveled or smoothed again to ensure they match the changed schedule. This technique was described in detail under the Develop Schedule process.

Leads and Lags - Leads and lags will always have some effect on the schedule, even if they do not affect the delivery date. As the project management plan is executed, the leads and lags need to be adjusted to reflect reality so as to provide the most realistic view of the schedule possible.

Schedule Compression - These techniques, covered under Develop Schedule, are used to search for ways to shorten the plan in order to make it match reality or meet commitments.

HOW IT WORKS / OUTPUTS:

➔ Work Performance Information - The updated schedule performance index (SPI), schedule variance (SV) and other earned value measurements relevant to the schedule need to be calculated and communicated out. These concepts are covered in the next chapter on Cost Management.

➔ Schedule Forecasts - The schedule is only a plan, but when it is compared against actual performance data, meaningful forecasts can be made. The most common forecasts are the Estimate At Completion (EAC) and Estimate To Completion (ETC), covered in the next chapter under the topic of Earned Value Management.

➔ Change Requests - Change requests are a normal byproduct of Control Schedule. For instance, if actual performance is far ahead of schedule, a change request may be introduced to consider a new piece of functionality previously considered impossible to deliver on time. Conversely, if the project is running behind schedule, a change request to outsource key components may be introduced.

Project Management Plan Updates - As the schedule changes, impact to the project's scope and budget are to be expected. As components of the project management plan change, they need to be captured as updates.

Project Documents Updates — See Ch. 2, Common Outputs

Chapter Notes:

Control Schedule

Chapter Notes:

_____

_____

_____

_____

_____

_____

_____

_____

_____

_____

_____

_____

_____

_____

➔ The Agile Perspective on Schedule Management

Agile projects do not try to define the entire scope up front, so it stands to reason that it is impossible to plan the whole project schedule. The reason for this is that when the team delivers some functionality to the customer, it is expected that the scope will change.

The agile approach is to plan in much smaller, more flexible increments, prioritized by what is most valuable to the customer.

Another agile approach is on-demand scheduling. In this approach, Agile teams use a Kanban board showing work in progress. Technically, work is not scheduled in advance. Instead, work is "pulled" from the board when resources become available. This approach works best when the backlog of work to be performed is well groomed (i.e. it is up to date, the effort is estimated, and each item accurately reflects the priority it would deliver to the customer).

SPECIAL FOCUS: CRITICAL PATH METHOD

The following section is of key importance

One very important tool used in Develop Schedule is a mathematical analysis technique called critical path method. You should be very comfortable with this technique, so a good portion of the rest of this chapter is dedicated to the subject.

Network Paths

The term "network path" refers to a sequence of events that affect each other on the project from start to finish. These activities form a path through the project. Paths are important because they illustrate the different sets of sequences in which activities must be performed, and they are used to identify areas of high risk on the project. In a real project, there will usually be numerous paths through the network diagram, and software is typically used to represent and calculate them.

To understand the paths, refer to the network diagram and corresponding tables that follow.

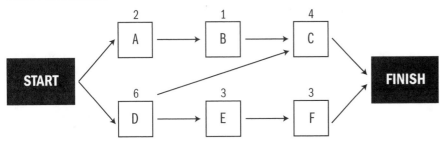

Figure 6-1: Network Logic Diagram – Activity on Node

Duration units shown in weeks

Activity	Duration (weeks)
A	2
B	1
C	4

Activity	Duration (weeks)
D	6
E	3
F	3

Table 6-2: Individual activities

Chapter Six

Chapter Notes:

———————————————

———————————————

———————————————

———————————————

———————————————

———————————————

———————————————

———————————————

———————————————

———————————————

———————————————

———————————————

———————————————

In the preceding diagram and tables, each node has a corresponding duration as listed in Table 6-2. Each possible path through the network is determined by following the arrows in the diagram in Figure 6-1.

Critical Paths

Determining the critical path through the network is a tool used heavily in creating the schedule. Critical path calculations show you where most of the schedule risk exists.

The critical path is made up of activities that cannot be delayed without delaying the finish of the project. By following the steps taken in creating the network diagram, the critical path is determined simply by identifying the longest path through the system. In the previous example, it is Start-D-E-F-Finish, because activities D (6) + E (3) + F (3) will take 12 weeks, and this is the longest path through the system.

Keep in mind that it is not unusual to have more than one critical path on a project. This occurs when two or more paths tie for the longest path. In this event, schedule risk is increased because there are an increased number of ways the project could be delayed.

Float

After you have mastered the concepts for activity on node, calculating float (sometimes referred to as "slack") is also easy. Before attempting any exercises, it is critical to understand the following:

1. Float is simply how much time an activity can slip before it changes the critical path. Another way of thinking about float is that it is the maximum amount of time an activity can slip without pushing out the finish date of the project.

2. If an item is on the critical path, it has zero float. Although there are technical cases where this might not be true, you should not encounter any such examples on the exam.

Keeping the preceding two items in mind, let us revisit the activity on node network diagram in figure 6-1 using this example:

Question: What is the float for Activity D?

Answer: 0 weeks. Activity D cannot slip without affecting the finish date because it is on the critical path.

Question: What is the slack for Activity C?

Answer: 2 weeks. If activity C slips by more than 2 weeks, then the path Start-D-C-Finish would delay the finish of the project.

There is a simple way to do this that will allow you to breeze through the questions on the exam. The method is a brute force approach. If the exam asks you to calculate the slack for an activity, simply look at the project network diagram and find the duration you can substitute for that activity that will put it on the critical path. You should be able to zero in on the float right away. If you have created a path chart, such as the one shown here, this method is a snap.

PATH	Activities	Path Duration (weeks)
Start - A - B - C - Finish	2+1+4	7
Start - D - C - Finish	6+4	10
Start - D - E - F - Finish	6+3+3	12

In this example:

- Activity A has float of 5 weeks, because this activity may be delayed up to 5 weeks without delaying the finish of the project

- Activity B also has float of 5 weeks, because paths with Activity B could slip up to 5 weeks without changing the project's finish date.

- Activity C is slightly trickier. It has a float of only 2 weeks. Even though it could slip 5 weeks in the first path listed in Table 6-3, if it slipped from 4 weeks to 6 weeks, then path Start-D-C-Finish would be on the critical path. Therefore, we take the smallest slippage possible, and that becomes the float for this activity.

Chapter Notes:

_____

_____

_____

_____

_____

_____

_____

_____

_____

_____

_____

_____

_____

After a little practice, this will become the easiest and quickest way to calculate float. There are detailed exercises at the end of this chapter to help cement your understanding of this.

Note that on the exam you may see the terms forward pass or backward pass related to the critical path. These methods of determining early or late start or early or late finish are presented below.

Early Start

The early start date for an activity is simply the earliest date it can start when you factor in the other dependencies. This is the date the activity will start if everything takes as long as it was estimated. Consider the figure that follows (this diagram is the same as Figure 6-1, referenced earlier).

Question: *Given the following diagram, what is the early start for Activity B?*

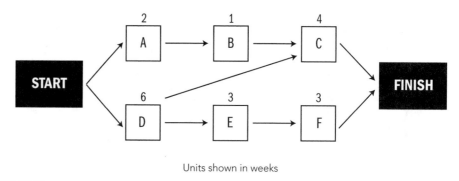

Units shown in weeks

The answer is week 3. The reason is that Activity A is scheduled to take 2 weeks. It begins on week 1, and finishes on week 2. Activity B could then begin on the first day of week 3.

This technique is called a "forward pass" because we have moved "forward" through the diagram, starting from the start date to perform our calculations.

Early Finish

The early finish date is the early start date plus the duration estimate minus 1 unit. In the example above, the early finish date for Activity 'A' would be 2 weeks after the early start date. Since the early start date is week 1, the early finish would be week 2. This makes sense since the activity takes all of week 1 and all of week 2, finishing at the end of week 2.

Here we also performed a "forward pass," as again we based our calculations on the start date and worked forward through the network.

Late Start

The late start date for an activity turns the problem around and looks at it from the other end of the network diagram. It asks, "What is the latest this activity could start and not delay the project's finish date?" Although there are many methods that may be used to calculate late start, the easiest way is to simply add the float to the early start. This will give us the absolute latest date that the activity can start and not impact the finish date, assuming that the activity takes as long as was estimated.

> *Question: Given the example in the previous table, what is the late start for Activity 'B'?*
>
> Answer: Week 8. The reason is that this activity has 5 weeks of float, and if the early start is week 3, the late start would be week 3 + 5 weeks of float = week 8.

Remember that for activities with zero float or slack, the late start and the early start will be the same.

This technique is called a "backward pass." The reason is that you must begin at the end of the network diagram and work your way backward, evaluating how close activities may slide toward the finish without moving the finish.

Chapter Six

Chapter Notes:

_____

_____

_____

_____

_____

_____

_____

_____

_____

_____

_____

_____

_____

_____

Late Finish

An activity's late finish will be the late start plus the activity's duration estimate minus 1 unit.

In the example above, the late start for Activity B is week 8, and the duration is 1 week, so the late finish date would also be week 8. If the fact that both the start and finish are shown as week 8 confuses you, keep in mind that the start represents the first day of week 8, and the finish represents the last day of week 8.

Remember that for activities with zero float or slack, the late finish and the early finish will be the same.

Calculating the late finish date by adding the activity's duration to the late start date is another example of a "backward pass."

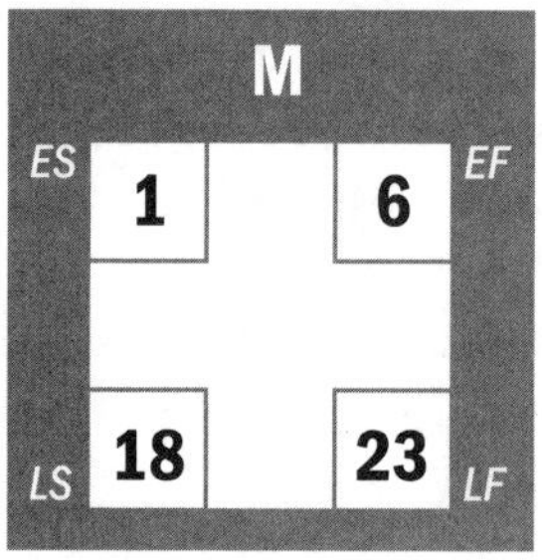

Project Network Node

ES, EF, LS, and LF

Often a node on the project network diagram may be represented as in the preceding diagram, with the early start in the upper left corner (represented by ES), the early finish in the upper right (EF), the late start in the bottom left (LS) and the late finish in the bottom right (LF). By dividing each node on a project network diagram into quadrants, all four of these may be represented for every node in the diagram.

Free Float

Also known as "free slack," free float is the amount of time an activity can be delayed without affecting the early start date of subsequent dependent activities. If this leaves you scratching your head, consider the following diagram:

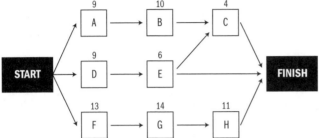

The free float of activity E would be determined by calculating how long it could slip before it impacted the early start of activity C. In this example, activity E has 4 units of free float. Note that this is different from its float, which is 19 units.

Negative Float

Negative float is a situation that occurs when an activity's start date occurs before a preceding activity's finish date. For instance, suppose that there is a constraint for an activity (Activity D) that involves a 1 day final inspection of a building that is to begin and be completed on July 15th; however, a preceding activity (Activity C) that encompasses testing the electrical components of the project does not finish until July 25th. If work is scheduled 7 days per week, then it could be stated that Activity D has a negative float of 10 days.

Technically, negative float exists when an activity's finish date happens before its scheduled start date. In the example above, Activity D is supposed to finish at the end of the 15th; however, it cannot even begin until 10 days later. There Activity D has 10 days of negative float.

Negative float for an activity tells you that your schedule has problems. It most often occurs when immovable constraints or milestones are imposed by forces outside the project, causing an impossible situation. Negative float may be resolved by several methods, such as reworking the logic of the schedule, crashing, or fast-tracking.

Chapter Six

Chapter Notes:

_____

_____

_____

_____

_____

_____

_____

_____

_____

_____

_____

_____

_____

_____

Schedule Management: Key Terms

SUMMARY OF KEY TERMS:

You need to understand each of the following key terms. You do not have to memorize every term word for word, but you should be able to recall the general definition and apply them on the exam.

Activity Decomposition – Similar to scope decomposition (remember the asteroids metaphor), except that the final result here is an activity list instead of the WBS.

Activity Duration Estimates – Probable number of periods (weeks, hours, days, months, etc.) this activity should take with the probable range of results. Example:

Activity Duration Estimate	Explanation
1 Week +/- 3 days	The activity should take between 2 and 8 days, assuming a 5 day work week.
1 Month + 20% probability it will be accomplished later	There is an 80% likelihood that the activity will be completed within the month and a 20% chance that it will exceed a month.

Activity List – A list of every activity that will be performed on the project.

Activity on Arrow Diagram – A rarely used type of network diagram where activities are represented by the arrows connecting the nodes. Nodes are typically represented by circles in this type of project network diagram.

Activity on Node Diagram – A type of network diagram where activities are represented on rectangular nodes with arrows representing the dependencies.

Analogous Estimating – A form of expert judgment often used early on when there is little information available. Example: "This project is similar to one we did last year, and that one took three months, so we will estimate three months for this project." It is performed from the top down, focusing on the big picture.

Backward Pass – The method for calculating late start and late finish dates for an activity (see explanation of float, early and late starts and finishes earlier in this chapter for a detailed explanation).

Beta Distribution – a method of estimating activity duration using the formula: (Pessimistic + 4 × Realistic + Optimistic) ÷ 6.

Critical Path – The paths through the network diagram that show which activities, if delayed, will affect the project finish date. For schedule, the critical path represents the highest risk path in the project.

Dependencies – Activities that must be completed before other activities are either started or completed.

Dependencies	Description	Example
Mandatory	Also called "hard logic," these activities must be followed in sequence.	Clearing the lot on a construction site before pouring the foundation.
Discretionary	Also called "soft logic." Expert judgment and best practices often dictate that particular activities are performed in a particular order. The dependencies are discretionary because they are based on expert opinion rather than mandatory or hard logic.	Painting the interior before putting down carpet.
Internal	Dependencies relying on factors within control of the performing organization.	Availability of funding and resources.
External	Dependencies relying on factors outside of the project	Zoning approval for a new building. Weather for a rocket launch.

Dummy Activity – An activity in a network diagram that does not have any time associated with it. It is only included to show a relationship, and is usually represented as a dotted or dashed line. Dummy activities only exist in activity on arrow diagrams.

Chapter Notes:

_____

_____

_____

_____

_____

_____

_____

_____

_____

_____

_____

_____

_____

Schedule Management: Key Terms

Chapter Six

Chapter Notes:

_____

_____

_____

_____

_____

_____

_____

_____

_____

_____

_____

_____

_____

_____

Duration Compression – A technique primarily made up of two means of compressing the schedule: crashing and fast-tracking, described in the following table:

Techniques	Description	Example
Crashing	Applying more resources to reduce duration. Crashing the schedule usually increases cost.	If setting up a computer network takes one person 6 weeks, three resources may be able to do it in two weeks. Note - Crashing usually does not reduce the schedule by a linear amount.
Fast Tracking	Performing activities in parallel that would normally be done in sequence. Fast tracking activities usually increases project risk, and these activities have a higher probability of rework.	Example: In XYX Corp, no coding on software modules is allowed until after the database design in complete, but when fast tracking, the activitites could be done in parallel if it is not a mandatory dependency.

Delphi Technique – A means of gathering expert judgment where the participants do not know who the others are and therefore are not able to influence each other's opinion. The Delphi technique is designed to prevent groupthink and to find out a participant's real opinion.

Expert Judgment – A method of estimating in which experts are asked to provide input into the schedule. Combining expert judgment with other tools and methods can significantly improve the accuracy of time estimates and reduce risk.

Float – How much time an activity can be delayed without affecting the project's finish date. Also known as "slack."

Forward Pass – The method for calculating early start and early finish dates for an activity (see explanation of float and early and late starts and finishes earlier in this chapter).

Free float – Also known as "free slack." How much time an activity can be delayed without affecting the early start date of subsequent dependent activities.

Heuristics – Rules for which no formula exists. Usually derived through trial and error.

Lag – The delay between an activity and the subsequent one dependent upon it. For example, if you are pouring concrete, you may have a 3 day lag after you have poured the concrete before your subsequent activities of building upon it can begin. Since no work is taking place during that 3 day period, it is considered to be a lag and not part of the actual activity.

Lead – Activities with finish-to-start relationships cannot start until their predecessors have been finished; however, if you have 5 days of lead time on an activity, it may begin 5 days before its predecessor activity has finished. Think of it as getting a head start, like runners in a relay race. Lead time lets the subsequent task begin before its predecessor has finished.

Mathematical Analysis – A technique to show scheduling possibilities where early and late start and finish dates are calculated for every activity without looking at resource estimates.

Milestones – High level points in the schedule used to track and report progress. Milestones usually have no time associated with them.

Monte Carlo Analysis – Computer simulation that throws a high number of "what if" scenarios at the project schedule to determine probable results.

Network Diagram – (Also called network logic diagram or project network diagram.) A method of diagramming project activities to show sequence and dependencies.

Negative Float – A situation that occurs when an activity's start date comes before a preceding activity's finish date. Technically, negative float exists when an activity's finish date happens before its scheduled start date. Negative float for an activity indicates a schedule with problems. Reworking the logic of the schedule, crashing, or fast-tracking are potential solutions.

Precedence Diagramming Method – (Also called Activity on Node.) A type of network diagram where the boxes are activities, and the arrows are used to show dependencies between the activities.

Chapter Six

Chapter Notes:

_____

_____

_____

_____

_____

_____

_____

_____

_____

_____

_____

_____

_____

Reserve Time (Contingency) – A schedule buffer used to reduce schedule risk. The chart below represents the most common types of reserve for a project.

Contingency	Example
Project %	Add 15% to the entire project schedule
Project lump sum	Add 2 months calendar schedule to the project
Activity %	Add 10% to each activity (or to key, high-risk activities)
Activity lump sum	Add 1 week to each activity (or to key, high-risk activities)

Schedule Baseline – The approved schedule that is used as a basis for measuring and reporting. It includes the original project schedule plus all approved updates.

Slack – See "Float."

Triangular Distribution – a method of estimating activity duration using the formula: (Pessimistic + Realistic + Optimistic) ÷ 3.

Variance Analysis – Comparing planned versus actual schedule dates.

EXERCISES

In order to test yourself on schedule management,
complete the following questions based on Figure 6-7 below.

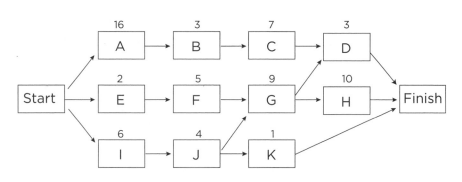

Figure 6-7: Project Network Diagram.

Durations shown in days

1. List all the paths through the network logic diagram
   as illustrated in Figure 6-7.

2. What is the critical path through the network diagram
   shown in Figure 6-7?

3. List the slack for each activity in the network diagram
   shown in Figure 6-7.

Chapter Six

Chapter Notes:

_____

_____

_____

_____

_____

_____

_____

_____

_____

_____

_____

_____

_____

_____

4. Provided the following table, how many weeks long is the critical path?

Activity	Preceding Activity	Duration (in weeks)
Start		0
A	Start	6
B	A, E	2
C	B	2
D	C	3
E	Start	1
F	A, E	1
G	F, B	7
Finish	D, G	0

5. Given the table in question 4 above, describe the effect of Activity D taking twice as long as planned.

6. An activity has 3 estimates, provided below:

    Optimistic   =   10 days

    Pessimistic   =   25 days

    Realistic   =   15 days

    What is the beta distribution estimate for this activity?

7. Given the project network node depicted below, fill in the value in the missing quadrant, and calculate the duration and the float for the activity.

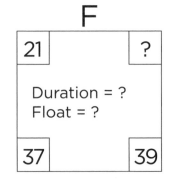

ANSWERS TO EXERCISES

1. There are six possible paths through the system, listed in the table below:

Path
Start-A-B-C-D-Finish
Start-E-F-G-D-Finish
Start-E-F-G-H-Finish
Start-I-J-G-D-Finish
Start-I-J-G-H-Finish
Start-I-J-K-Finish

Chapter Notes:

2. Because two paths tie for the longest duration, there are two critical paths:

Start-A-B-C-D-Finish – duration 29 days

Start-I-J-G-H-Finish – duration 29 days

Path	Durations	Total
Start-A-B-C-D-Finish	16+3+7+3	29 days
Start-E-F-G-D-Finish	2+5+9+3	19 days
Start-E-F-G-H-Finish	2+5+9+10	26 days
Start-I-J-G-D-Finish	6+4+9+3	22 days
Start-I-J-G-H-Finish	6+4+9+10	29 days
Start-I-J-K-Finish	6+4+1	11 days

Chapter Notes:

_____

_____

_____

_____

_____

_____

_____

_____

_____

_____

_____

_____

3. This task is easier than it first appears since over 70% of the activities were on the critical path. Those activities automatically have zero slack; thus, no calculations are necessary for most of the activities.

    The way to solve for these is to take each path listed above and go through them one at a time. If the path is a critical path, or if the activity is found on the critical path, simply skip it. If the path is not the critical path, then take the sum of the items on that path and subtract it from the total critical path. For activity E, it is found on 2 paths above. One of them totals 19, and the other 26. We always use the larger one and subtract it from the critical path total of 29. That leaves a slack of 29-26, or 3 for activity E.

Activity	On Critical Path?	Slack (Float) in days
A	Y	0
B	Y	0
C	Y	0
D	Y	0
E	N	3
F	N	3
G	Y	0
H	Y	0
I	Y	0
J	Y	0
K	N	18

4. Your first step in solving this problem is to draw out a network logic diagram. Your diagram should look similar to the one shown below:

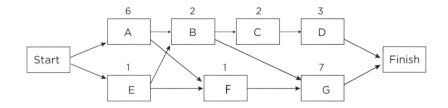

The next step is to list out all paths through the network:

Path	Durations	Total
Start-A-B-C-D-Finish	6+2+2+3	13
Start-A-B-G-Finish	6+2+7	15
Start-A-F-G-Finish	6+1+7	14
Start-E-B-C-D-Finish	1+2+2+3	8
Start-E-B-G-Finish	1+2+7	10
Start-E-F-G-Finish	1+1+7	9

The answer is 15 weeks, based on the fact that Start-A-B-G-Finish has a duration of 15 weeks, and that is the longest duration of any path.

5. If Activity D were to take twice as long as planned, that would change its duration from 3 to 6 weeks. This would have two effects:

    •   The critical path would change. The new critical path would be Start-A-B-C-D-Finish.

    •   The project finish date would be extended by 1 additional week, meaning the overall project would take 16 weeks.

To arrive at this solution, reconstruct the table as follows:

Path	Durations	Total
Start-A-B-C-D-Finish	6+2+2+6	16
Start-A-B-G-Finish	6+2+7	15
Start-A-F-G-Finish	6+1+7	14
Start-E-B-C-D-Finish	1+2+2+6	11
Start-E-B-G-Finish	1+2+7	10
Start-E-F-G-Finish	1+1+7	9

Note how the longest path has changed to the first one in the table above.

Chapter Six

Chapter Notes:

_____

_____

_____

_____

_____

_____

_____

_____

_____

_____

_____

_____

_____

_____

6. The formula for beta distribution estimates is:

    (Pessimistic + 4 × Realistic + Optimistic) ÷ 6

    Which is equivalent to...

    (25 + (4 × 15) +10) ÷ 6

    This yields a duration estimate of 15.83.

7. For this exercise, the early finish (top right quadrant), the duration, and the float were in question.

    Given the example, it is easiest to begin with the duration. This may be calculated easily by subtracting the late start (bottom left) from the late finish (bottom right) and adding one. 39-37+1 yields an activity duration of 3 (if this confuses you, consider that days 37, 38, and 39 are all working days). Now, simply count 3 days from the early start (top left), using day 21 as a working day, and it gets you to an early finish of day 23 (day 21, 22, and 23). The float is the late start - the early start, represented as 37 - 21 = 16. Even though this is the only node we have, we could further deduce that the early start or early finish date could slip 16 days without affecting the critical path and endangering the finish date.

    F

21		23
	Duration = 3 days Float = 16 days	
37		39

SCHEDULE MANAGEMENT

QUESTIONS

1. You are the project manager for the construction of a commercial office building that has very similar characteristics to a construction project performed by your company two years ago. As you perform Define Activities, what is the BEST approach?

   A. Use the activity list from the previous project as your activity list.

   B. Generate your activity list without looking at the previous project's list and compare when your project's list is complete.

   C. Use the gap analysis technique to identify any differences between your project and the previous project.

   D. Use the previous activity list to help construct your list.

2. The customer has called a project team member to request a change in the project's schedule. The team member asks you what the procedure is for handling schedule changes. Where should you refer the team member to help him understand the procedure?

   A. The project office.

   B. The integration management plan.

   C. The schedule management plan.

   D. Inform the team member that the customer has the ultimate decision.

3. If you were creating duration estimates for a schedule activity, which of the following tools or techniques would NOT be appropriate to use?

   A. Expert judgment.

   B. Data analysis.

   C. Three-point estimating.

   D. Least-squares estimating.

Chapter Notes:

_____

_____

_____

_____

_____

_____

_____

_____

_____

_____

_____

_____

_____

_____

_____

_____

_____

_____

Chapter Notes:

_____

_____

_____

_____

_____

_____

_____

_____

_____

_____

_____

_____

_____

4. Senior management has called you in for a meeting to review the progress of your project. You have been allocated 15 minutes to report progress and discuss critical issues. Which of the following would be BEST to carry with you in this case?

   A. A milestone chart.

   B. The project network diagram.

   C. The project management plan.

   D. The recent project status reports from your team members.

5. Which of the following is FALSE concerning an activity's early finish and/or late finish?

   A. Early finish represents the earliest possible date an activity could finish.

   B. Late finish represents the latest possible date an activity could finish without lengthening the critical path.

   C. The difference between an activity's early finish and late finish is the same as the difference between the early start and late start.

   D. Early finish is typically depicted in the node's lower left quadrant, and late finish is depicted in the lower right quadrant.

6. The amount of time that an activity may be delayed without extending the critical path is:

   A. Lag.

   B. Grace period.

   C. Free factor.

   D. Slack.

7. **Crashing differs from fast tracking because crashing:**

   A. Usually decreases value.

   B. Usually increases the cost.

   C. Usually takes more time.

   D. Usually saves more money.

8. **If senior management tells you "The last project we did like this took us 15 months," what estimating method is being used?**

   A. Delphi technique.

   B. Principle of activity equivalence.

   C. Analogous estimating.

   D. Bottom-up estimating.

9. **You are advising a project manager who is behind schedule on his project. The sponsor on his project is very unhappy with the way things have progressed and is threatening to cancel it. The sponsor has accepted a revised due date from the project manager but did not allow any increased spending. Which of the following would represent the BEST advice for the project manager in this case?**

   A. Fast track the schedule.

   B. Request a new sponsor from senior management.

   C. Crash the schedule.

   D. Talk with the customer to see if budget may be increased without the sponsor's involvement.

Chapter Notes:

_____

_____

_____

_____

_____

_____

_____

_____

_____

_____

_____

_____

_____

_____

Schedule Management: Questions

Chapter Notes:

_____

_____

_____

_____

_____

_____

_____

_____

_____

_____

_____

_____

10. **Based on the diagram in question 14, which is the correct match?**

    A. ES = 16, Float = 19.

    B. EF = 40, LS = 21.

    C. Float = 5, Duration = 19.

    D. Float = 5, LF = 40.

11. **Which scheduling approach inserts non-working buffer time to be managed by the project manager?**

    A. Critical chain method.

    B. Critical path method.

    C. Resource leveling.

    D. Schedule modeling.

12. **What is the BEST tool to use to calculate the critical path on a project?**

    A. Work breakdown structure.

    B. GERT diagram.

    C. Gantt chart.

    D. Project network diagram.

13. **Consider the table at right: What is the critical path?**

    A. Start-A-E-H-Finish.

    B. Start-C-E-H-Finish.

    C. Start-B-D-I-Finish.

    D. Start-B-D-G-Finish.

Activity	Duration	Dependent on
Start	0	
A	3	Start
B	4	Start
C	2	Start
D	2	B
E	5	A,C
F	1	B
G	6	D, F
H	11	E
I	8	D, F
Finish	0	G, H, I

14. **Based on the diagram to the right, which of the following statements is true?**

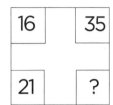

   A. This activity is on the critical path.

   B. This activity is not on the critical path.

   C. The activity shown should be decomposed further.

   D. In order for the project to stay on schedule, the activity needs to finish on day 35 or earlier.

15. **Referring to the table in question 13, what is the float for Activity D?**

   A. 0 days.

   B. 3 days.

   C. 5 days.

   D. 7 days.

16. **An activity has a duration estimate that is best case = 30 days, most likely = 44 days, and worst case = 62 days. What is the weighted three-point estimate for this activity?**

   A. 44.67 days

   B. 34.67 days

   C. 5.33 days

   D. 59.33 days

Chapter Six

Chapter Notes:

_____

_____

_____

_____

_____

_____

_____

_____

_____

_____

_____

_____

_____

_____

17. A government contracting firm that builds large infrastructure projects is analyzing the time it will take to plan phase one of a bridge renovation. The program manager's opinion is that approximately 24% of the time should be added to the beginning of the schedule for planning; however, the project manager states that her experience is that when the existing infrastructure is already in place, the general rule is that planning should take about half this much time. The project manager's beliefs are an example of:

A. An heuristic.

B. An organizational process asset.

C. An attribute.

D. Value engineering.

18. Which of the following choices best fits the description of a project manager applying the technique of what-if scenario analysis?

A. Using project management software to build three versions of the project schedule.

B. Using Monte Carlo analysis to identify what would happen if schedule delays occurred.

C. Using critical path method to analyze what would happen if the critical path actually occurred.

D. Discussing with the functional managers what they would do if certain project team members quit the project early.

19. How do the activity list and activity attributes relate to each other?

A. The activity list focuses on schedule activities, while the activity attributes apply to WBS activities.

B. The activity attributes are created prior to the activity list.

C. The activity list may be substituted for the activity attributes in most processes.

D. Activity attributes provide additional information for each activity on the activity list.

20. You are discussing the schedule with members of your team when one of them describes a group of activities that can start at any time but must finish in a specific order. You decide to investigate this further. What would be the best way to recognize these activities?

    A. Look for a Gantt chart with a group of activities that have staggered or stair-stepped finish dates.

    B. Look for a group of activities with a start-to-finish relationship.

    C. Look for a group of activities with a finish-to-finish relationship.

    D. Look for this information on the activity attributes.

21. Which of the following is the BEST description of the critical path?

    A. The activities that represent critical functionality.

    B. The activities that represent the largest portions of the work packages.

    C. The activities that represent the highest schedule risk on the project.

    D. The activities that represent the optimal path through the network.

22. Which of the following is TRUE about Estimate Activity Durations?

    A. It must be performed after Sequence Activities.

    B. It must be performed after Develop Schedule.

    C. Parametric estimates may be used to derive the durations.

    D. The activity duration estimates must be validated during Develop Schedule.

23. If schedule activities are not properly decomposed, which of the following would NOT be an expected outcome?

    A. The team encounters difficulty estimating cost and time.

    B. The team encounters difficulty in building the schedule.

    C. The team encounters difficulty in calculating earned value.

    D. The team encounters difficulty in creating the responsibility assignment matrix.

Chapter Notes:

_____
_____
_____
_____
_____
_____
_____
_____
_____
_____
_____
_____
_____
_____
_____
_____

Schedule Management: Questions

Chapter Six

Chapter Notes:

24. Your project schedule has just been developed, approved, and distributed to the stakeholders and presented to senior management when one of the resources assigned to an activity approaches you and tells you that her activity cannot be performed within the allotted time due to several necessary pieces that were overlooked during planning. Her revised estimate would change the schedule but would not affect the critical path. What would be the BEST way for the project manager to handle this situation?

A. Adhere to the published schedule and allow for any deviation by using schedule reserve.

B. Go back to Estimate Activity Durations and update the schedule and other plans to reflect the new estimate.

C. Use an independent party to validate her claim.

D. Replace the resource with someone who says they can meet the published schedule.

25. Jan is working with the project team to produce an estimate for a particular activity. They have gathered expert opinions and have determined that the optimistic estimate is 4.5 days, and the pessimistic estimate is 13 days. The most likely estimate is 7 working days. Given the team's preference for triangular distribution, what estimate should they use?

A. 7 days.

B. 7.6 days.

C. 8.2 days.

D. 11 days.

SCHEDULE MANAGEMENT
ANSWERS

1. D. The previous activity list would make an excellent tool to help you ensure that you are considering all activities. Any historical information such as this is thought of as an organizational process asset. 'A' is incorrect because you cannot simply substitute something as intricate as a complete activity list. 'B' is incorrect because the other activity list would provide a good starting point and should be considered before you create your activity list. 'C' (gap analysis) is a tool that is used in the real world that is not defined by PMI, nor is it used in activity list definition.

2. C. The schedule management plan, discussed in chapter 4, is part of the project plan. This is the best source of information on how changes to the schedule are to be handled. 'A' is incorrect because the project office's job is to define standards – not to make decisions on tactical items such as this. 'B' may sound like a real plan, but there is no such thing. Answer 'D' would be the worst choice. The customer is not always right when it comes to requesting changes. Procedures should be defined and followed in order to improve the project's chances of success.

3. D. Since we are creating activity duration estimates, we are performing the process of Estimate Activity Durations. Answers 'A', 'B', and 'C' are all tools used in Estimate Activity Durations, but 'D' is a made up term.

4. A. Milestone charts show the high level status, which would be appropriate given the audience and time allocated for this update.

Chapter Six

Chapter Notes:

_____

_____

_____

_____

_____

_____

_____

_____

_____

_____

_____

_____

5. D. The early finish is typically depicted in a node's upper right quadrant, while the late finish is in the lower right. 'A' was not a good choice because that accurately defines the early finish, given the activity's estimated duration. 'B' is not correct because that is the definition of the late finish. 'C' is not a good choice, because the float (or slack) determines the gap between early finish and late finish and between the early start and late start. Since the float is the same, the difference between those dates should also be the same.

6. D. The slack (or float) is the amount of time an activity may be delayed without affecting the critical path.

7. B. Crashing adds more resources to an activity. This usually increases the cost due to the law of diminishing returns which predicts that 10 people usually cannot complete an activity in half the time that 5 people can. The savings from crashing are rarely linear. 'A' is incorrect because crashing does not directly affect the project's value. 'C' is incorrect because crashing may or may not require more time than fast tracking – depending on the situation. 'D' is incorrect because crashing usually costs more money than fast tracking.

8. C. In this example management is providing you with analogous estimates. These estimates use actual durations from previous projects (historical information or organizational process assets) to produce estimates for a similar project.

9. A. In this case, you must compress the schedule without increasing the costs. Fast tracking does not directly add cost to the project and is the best choice in this case. 'B' is incorrect. The sponsor is paying for the project. Do this, and your sponsor will probably be asking for a new project manager instead. 'C' is incorrect because crashing usually adds cost to the project, and that is not allowed in this scenario. 'D' is incorrect because the sponsor authorizes budget. Doing an end-run around the sponsor and going to the customer would be very inappropriate.

10. D. In order to answer this question, you'll need to calculate the duration, the float, and the late finish. The early finish is given to us as 35 (eliminating 'B' as a potential correct answer). To calculate the duration, subtract the early start (top left) from the early finish (top right) and add one. This works out to 35 − 16 + 1 = 20, eliminating 'C' as a possible answer. To calculate the float, subtract the early start from the late start. This is 21 − 16 = 5. Now we can also eliminate 'A' as a possibility, so we actually have enough information to guess 'D' as the correct answer. To confirm it, we need to calculate the late finish (LF). Late Finish = Late Start + duration − 1, or LF = 21 + 20 - 1 = 40.

11. A. The critical chain method provides a buffer to be used by the project manager to protect the critical path. Typically, the team is not aware of this buffer.

12. D. The project network diagram shows duration and dependencies which would help you calculate the critical path. 'A' is incorrect because the WBS does not show durations or activity dependencies. 'B' is incorrect because GERT is most helpful for showing conditions and branches. 'C' is incorrect because a Gantt chart is very useful for showing percentage complete on activities but is not the best tool for showing activity dependencies or calculating the critical path.

Chapter Notes:

_____

_____

_____

_____

_____

_____

_____

_____

_____

_____

_____

_____

Chapter Notes:

13. A. The critical path is determined in 3 steps. The first step is to draw out the project network diagram. Yours should look similar to the one depicted as follows (note that activities B and C were moved to make the diagram neater – don't worry if your diagram does not look this neat):

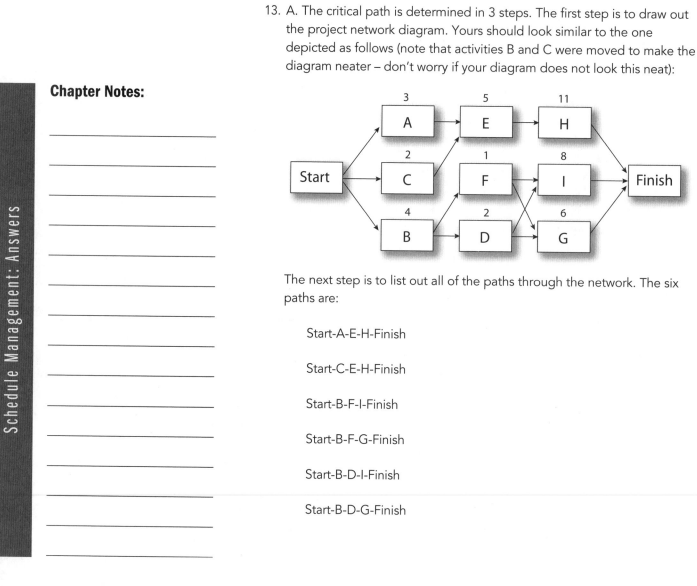

The next step is to list out all of the paths through the network. The six paths are:

Start-A-E-H-Finish

Start-C-E-H-Finish

Start-B-F-I-Finish

Start-B-F-G-Finish

Start-B-D-I-Finish

Start-B-D-G-Finish

The last step is to add up all of the values associated with each path as is done below:

Start-A-E-H-Finish = 0+3+5+11+0 = 19

Start-C-E-H-Finish = 0+2+5+11+0 = 18

Start-B-F-I-Finish = 0+4+1+8+0 = 13

Start-B-F-G-Finish = 0+4+1+6+0 = 11

Start-B-D-I-Finish = 0+4+2+8+0 = 14

Start-B-D-G-Finish = 0+4+2+6+0 = 12

The critical path emerges as Start-A-E-H-Finish because the path adds up to 19, which is longer than any of the other paths. If any of the activities in this path are delayed, the finish of the project will be delayed.

14. B. This diagram was used elsewhere in this quiz in a different way. That is common to see on the exam as well. This activity has 5 days of float (slack). To calculate the float, subtract the early start from the late start. This is 21 – 16 = 5. You should assume that any activity with a positive float (>0) is not on the critical path. 'C' does not work since there is not nearly enough information to point you toward further decomposition. 'D' might have fooled you, but 35 is the early finish. The late finish is actually 40 (Late Finish = Late Start + duration – 1, or LF = 21 + 20 - 1 = 40). This means that this activity needs to be complete by day 40 in order for the project to stay on schedule.

Chapter Notes:

_____

_____

_____

_____

_____

_____

_____

_____

_____

_____

_____

_____

_____

Schedule Management: Answers

Chapter Notes:

_____

_____

_____

_____

_____

_____

_____

_____

_____

_____

_____

_____

_____

15. C. The float (or slack) of an activity is the amount of time it can slip without moving the critical path. In this case, we must calculate the float of Activity D. If Activity D was on the critical path, we would immediately know that the float was 0, but in this case it is not.

   To solve this problem, we must first list out all of the paths. We will use the list from the previous question.

   Start-A-E-H-Finish = 0+3+5+11+0 = 19

   Start-C-E-H-Finish = 0+2+5+11+0 = 18

   Start-B-F-I-Finish = 0+4+1+8+0 = 13

   Start-B-F-G-Finish = 0+4+1+6+0 = 11

   Start-B-D-I-Finish = 0+4+2+8+0 = 14

   Start-B-D-G-Finish = 0+4+2+6+0 = 12

   The next step is to identify the ones that have Activity D in them. They are:

   Start-B-D-I-Finish = 0+4+2+8+0 = 14

   Start-B-D-G-Finish = 0+4+2+6+0 = 12

   Now the task is simple. We simply subtract the path sums from the length of the critical path for each (19-14 = 5, and 19-12 = 7), and finally we take the smaller of those two values which is 5. Therefore, the float for Activity D is 5.

16. A. The formula for a weighted three-point estimate is (Pessimistic + 4 × Realistic + Optimistic) ÷ 6. In this example, the terms were switched around slightly, but it equates to (62 + 4 × 44 + 30) ÷ 6 = 268 ÷ 6 = 44.67.

17. A. An heuristic is a process or method that exists when the rules are loosely defined or when there are no rules at all. The question asked what do the project manager's beliefs exemplify. Since the project manager has a "general rule" that the planning should take less time but it is only based on experience and not a firm rule, it fits the definition well. 'B' is not a good answer since there are opinions and general rules at work here but no real assets. 'C' is not a good answer since you would have to ask "an attribute of what?" It simply doesn't fit well in this context. 'D' does not work because value engineering (discussed more in the next chapter) is all about trying to squeeze the most value out of a deliverable without affecting the cost. Cutting planning is not a good example of this.

18. B. What-if analysis can take on many forms, but the form you are most likely to see on the exam is Monte Carlo analysis, which throws a large number of scenarios at the schedule to see what would happen if one or more scenarios occurred.

19. D. The activity attributes simply expand on the information for each activity. 'A' is incorrect since the activity attributes tie back to the activity list and not the WBS. 'B' is incorrect since the activity attributes may be created at the same time or after the activity list, but not before. 'C' is incorrect since the activity attributes may never be substituted for the activity list. Instead the activity attributes accompany the activity list, providing additional information on each activity.

20. C. This scenario describes tasks that have finish dates linked in finish-to-finish order.

21. C. This one may have been difficult for you, because it is a non-traditional definition of the critical path. The critical path is the series of activities, which if delayed, will delay the project. This makes these activities the highest schedule risk on the project. 'A' is incorrect because the critical path has no relationship with functionality. 'B' is incorrect because the size of the work packages does not directly correlate to the critical path. 'D' is incorrect because the critical path does not represent the optimal path through the network.

Chapter Notes:

Schedule Management: Answers

Chapter Six

Chapter Notes:

_____

_____

_____

_____

_____

_____

_____

_____

_____

_____

_____

_____

_____

_____

_____

22. C. One of the important tools used in Estimate Activity Durations is parametric estimates. 'A' was incorrect because none of the outputs of Sequence Activities is an input into Estimate Activity Durations, meaning that there is no reason one has to be performed before the other. 'B' is incorrect because Develop Schedule should always be performed after Estimate Activity Durations (how will you be able to create the schedule if you don't know how long the component activities will take?). 'D' is incorrect because validation of the activity durations sounds like a great thing to do, but it is not a part of the Develop Schedule process.

23. D. This is a problem many project managers have faced. As you answer this question, keep in mind that WBS nodes are decomposed into work packages first. Then schedule activities are decomposed from the work packages. 'A', 'B', and 'C' all relate to problems you would have if the schedule activities are not properly decomposed, but 'D' is related to the work packages, and you are not given anything in the question that suggests there is a problem with the way they were decomposed.

24. B. Changes happen. Some of them are submitted as change requests, and some of them come out of nowhere. In this case, you would want to return to planning and update the plans. The project will not be delayed, and the resource has given a good reason why the dates need to be revisited (a common occurrence in the real world). 'A' is incorrect, because the plan should reflect reality – not an unrealistic estimate. 'C' is incorrect, because you cannot possibly get an outside opinion every time a resource needs to change a date. 'D' is incorrect, because the resource gave a good reason for the adjustment. It was not that she was lacking in training or ability, but that pieces were left out of planning. Therefore, 'B' represents the all-around best answer.

25. C. Triangular distribution for these purposes is really nothing more than a simple average, which is $(4.5 + 13 + 7) \div 3 = 8.16$ (rounded to 8.2). 'A' was a trap for someone who simply saw the most likely estimate of 7 days and wanted to avoid doing any math. 'B' worked out for beta distribution $(P + 4R + O) \div 6$, but that was not what was asked here. 'D' was a random number.

Cost Management

The topic of cost management, like schedule management, has formulas that you will need to master. This chapter will explain these formulas clearly and provide methods and exercises for quick retention. You will need to memorize some of these formulas, but understanding them is just as important.

The reality is, if you enjoy math, you will probably like this chapter. But if math is not your strong suit, take the time to work through these problems anyway. Do not give in to the temptation to skip the formulas. The majority of people who do not pass the exam fall short by a small handful of questions, so take the attitude that every single question counts.

Most of the principles and techniques explained here, such as earned value, come from well-established practices in the fields of cost accounting, managerial accounting, and finance.

From the indicators on this page, you can tell that most people find this chapter to be one of the more difficult ones. In order to help you prepare for this topic, this book has clearly broken down the practices and outlined the techniques and formulas needed to ace the questions on the exam.

It is also essential that you know the main outputs that are produced during each of the four processes. The different tasks that are performed in each process are summarized in the following chart:

Watch The Video
http://**prep.pm/7-1**

Difficulty:
HIGH
●●●●●●●●●○

Memorization:
HIGH
●●●●●●●●●○

Exam Importance:
HIGH
●●●●●●●●○○

Chapter Notes:

_____

_____

_____

_____

_____

_____

_____

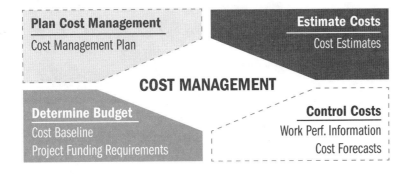

Plan Cost Management
Cost Management Plan

Estimate Costs
Cost Estimates

COST MANAGEMENT

Determine Budget
Cost Baseline
Project Funding Requirements

Control Costs
Work Perf. Information
Cost Forecasts

Chapter Notes:

_____

_____

_____

_____

_____

_____

_____

_____

_____

_____

_____

_____

PHILOSOPHY:

This knowledge area looks at the costs of the human and physical resources and when those costs will be incurred. While the actual tools and techniques behind cost management may be different from schedule management, the driving philosophy has many similarities. Favor a detail-oriented approach. All costs should be planned and carefully tracked. The project manager should tie costs to activities and resources and build the estimates from the bottom up.

If you are trying to build a budget, it can seem a little counter intuitive that the overall budget total is usually determined prior to knowing costs, but this is reality. The reason is that many companies use fiscal year planning cycles that must be completed far in advance of their project planning. That is why the budget total may be determined before the project is really understood. Budgetary constraints are a fact of life, but instead of blindly accepting whatever budget the organization comes up with, the project manager should carefully review the scope of work and the duration estimates and then reconcile them to the scope and projected costs. Adjustments to the project scope, the budget, or the schedule are much easier to justify by working up from a detailed level instead of from the top down. Although summary budgets are often the first thing created in the real world, when it comes to detailed planning, the overall approach advocated here is scope first, schedule second, and budget third.

Throughout this book, you will see that estimates should be built from the bottom up. At the point in the process where budgets are created, you should have a well-defined work breakdown structure, an activity list with resource and duration estimates for each activity, and a schedule.

The budget is then constructed by applying rates and dates against those resources and activities to create activity cost estimates and a cost baseline, as prescribed in the cost management plan.

It is the project manager's job to constantly monitor and control costs against schedule, scope, quality, and risk to ensure that all projections remain realistic and clearly defined.

IMPORTANCE:

The topic of cost management is very important. You will want to have a solid understanding of the four processes presented in this chapter and be able to apply the key formulas as well.

PREPARATION:

Learning the key formulas for Cost Management is a must. Learning to apply them is equally as important. The good news is that the formulas are not overly difficult, and there are plenty of explanations and examples in this book to help cement the concepts.

Memorization is important; however, understanding the formulas is more important. Once you grasp the formulas and concepts, the memorization will be a snap. In fact, some people studying for the exam only memorize the concepts and reconstruct the formulas as needed. This is possible because each formula has a purpose, so read and reread this chapter until it is clear to you.

Process Group	Cost Management Process
Initiating	(none)
Planning	Plan Cost Management, Estimate Costs, Determine Budget
Executing	(none)
Monitoring & Controlling	Control Costs
Closing	(none)

Process	Primary Outputs
Plan Cost Management	Cost Management Plan
Estimate Costs	Cost Estimates
Determine Budget	Cost Baseline, Project Funding Requirements
Control Costs	Work Performance Information, Cost Forecasts

Chapter Seven

Chapter Notes:

_____

_____

_____

_____

_____

_____

_____

_____

_____

_____

_____

_____

_____

_____

IMPORTANT CONCEPTS

Before you begin to explore the four processes that make up this knowledge area, take a moment to familiarize yourself with the following two important terms. While these do not fit within any particular process, the concepts underpin this chapter.

Life-Cycle Costing - Instead of simply asking "how much will this product cost to develop?", life-cycle costing looks at the total cost of ownership from purchase or creation, through operations, and finally to disposal. It is a practice that encourages making decisions based on the bigger picture of ownership costs.

For instance, it may be less expensive for the project to use generic computer servers to develop a software product; however, if the organization will have to maintain those servers, and if that organization has expertise and existing service contracts with IBM, then the project may be making a shortsighted decision that will have adverse effects downstream.

Value Engineering - Value engineering is the practice of trying to get more out of the project in every possible way. It is a way of working to increase the bottom line, decrease costs, improve quality, shorten the schedule, and generally squeeze more benefit and value out of each aspect of the project. The key to value engineering is that the scope of work is not reduced by these other efforts.

···· PLANNING

PLAN COST MANAGEMENT

WHAT IT IS:

This process follows the same pattern as the Plan Scope Management and Plan Schedule Management processes. It is the process that creates the plan that will guide and direct the activities in the other three cost management processes.

6th Edition *PMBOK® Guide*
Cross Ref. pg 235

WHY IT IS IMPORTANT:

This process gives guidance to the other cost management processes, and cost is an important area, both in actual projects and on the exam.

Watch The Video
http://**prep.pm/7-2**

WHEN IT IS PERFORMED:

The general rule (and one that will help you on the exam) is that scope activities are performed first, schedule activities second, and cost and budget activities third, but as is true with most rules, there are exceptions to this one. The exception is that overall budgets or budgetary constraints may be determined before the project is initiated, so while the cost details will not be understood until after the scope has been planned and resources have been assigned and activity durations have been determined, the high-level constraints and perhaps even the funding schedules will often be specified in the project charter.

Chapter Notes:

_____

_____

_____

_____

_____

_____

_____

HOW IT WORKS:

Plan Cost Management is a relatively streamlined process with a few common inputs and tools and a single, important output.

Chapter Seven

Chapter Notes:

_____

_____

_____

_____

_____

_____

_____

_____

_____

_____

_____

_____

_____

HOW IT WORKS / INPUTS:

Project Charter — See Ch. 4, Develop Project Charter

Project Management Plan — See Ch. 2, Common Inputs

Enterprise Environmental Factors — See Ch. 2, Common Inputs

Organizational Process Assets — See Ch. 2, Common Inputs

HOW IT WORKS / TOOLS:

Expert Judgment — See Ch. 2, Common Tools

Data Analysis — See Ch. 2, Common Tools

Meetings — See Ch. 2, Common Tools

HOW IT WORKS / OUTPUTS:

Cost Management Plan - The cost management plan is the only significant part of this process. It is the plan that describes how the processes of Estimate Costs, Determine Budget, and Control Costs will be carried out. The cost management plan will ultimately become an important component of the project management plan.

The cost management plan also specifies things like units of measure (dollars, pesos, or yen), levels of precision (we are going to report costs to the nearest thousand dollars), and levels of accuracy (we are targeting to have estimates fall within +/- 8% of actual costs). It will specify approval thresholds, how those approvals are carried out, and it will define how cost performance is to be measured.

.... PLANNING

ESTIMATE COSTS

WHAT IT IS:

Most of the processes in this book are intuitively named, making it that much easier to understand them. Estimate Costs is a good example of that. Its name indicates exactly what it does.

In Estimate Costs, each schedule activity is analyzed to evaluate the activity time estimates and the resource estimates associated with them, and a cost estimate is produced.

6th Edition *PMBOK® Guide*
Cross Ref. pg 240

WHY IT IS IMPORTANT:

If you've heard the old saying that "the devil is in the details," then you know why Estimate Costs is important. In this process, you gain a detailed understanding of the costs involved in performing a project.

Watch The Video
http://**prep.pm**/7-3

WHEN IT IS PERFORMED:

Estimate Costs, like many other processes, may be conducted over and again throughout the project; however, there are a few essential predecessor processes that must be completed before it can be performed adequately. Costs are estimated against schedule activities, so the project's schedule has to be created first.

Chapter Notes:

Define Scope → Create WBS → Define Activities → Estimate Activity Resources

Estimate Activity Durations → Develop Schedule → Estimate Costs

The order of certain processes from Define Scope to Estimate Costs

_____

_____

_____

_____

_____

_____

_____

Chapter Seven

Chapter Notes:

_____

_____

_____

_____

_____

_____

_____

_____

_____

_____

_____

_____

_____

HOW IT WORKS:

Cost estimates, prepared for each activity, are categorized in terms of their accuracy. In other words, how much leeway are you giving yourself with your estimating?

When it comes to estimates that result from this process, there are many options. Consider the table that follows:

Estimate Type	Range
Rough Order of Magnitude Estimate	-25% to +75%
Preliminary Estimate	-20% to +30%
Definitive Estimate	-5% to +10%

Which of these different types of estimating approaches are used, depends on how much of the project is understood at this point. For instance, during the initiation of a project where very little has been defined, a rough order of magnitude estimate may suffice, while later in the project, a definitive estimate may be in order. Typically, the more you understand about an activity and the closer in time you get to actually spending money for it, the more precise you want that activity's estimate to be.

HOW IT WORKS / INPUTS:

Project Management Plan - By this time, it should be a familiar pattern that a management plan is created at the beginning of a knowledge area, and that management plan guides the other processes in that knowledge area. In this case, the cost management plan, the quality management plan, and the scope baseline are the three important components that will guide the process of Estimate Costs. The cost management plan specifies how costs estimates will be derived and how accurate and precise they are expected to be.

The scope baseline, created earlier in Create WBS, ties each element of the scope back to the underlying need it was designed to address. Also, the project scope statement provides information on constraints and assumptions related to the scope, and these can dramatically affect the cost estimates.

Project Documents
There are four key documents brought into this process.

Lessons Learned Register – This is a common sense input to an estimating process.

Project Schedule – Cost estimates are largely a function of the activity's duration and the resources required. The schedule contains all of the activities, and costs are estimated at a schedule activity level, but there may be additional ways in which the schedule can affect the cost estimates. For example, certain types of seasonal materials or labor may be more expensive at some times than others, and the schedule can help the project team anticipate that impact.

Resource Requirements – This document identifies the types and quantities of resources needed to get the work done.

Risk Register – The risk register may have specific information on identified risks related to costs. Any such information should be factored in to this estimating process.

Enterprise Environmental Factors — See Ch. 2, Common Inputs

Organizational Process Assets — See Ch. 2, Common Inputs

Estimate Costs

Chapter Seven

Chapter Notes:

_____

_____

_____

_____

_____

_____

_____

_____

_____

_____

_____

_____

HOW IT WORKS / TOOLS:

Expert Judgment — See Ch. 2, Common Tool

 Analogous Estimating - The tool of analogous estimating uses the actual results of projects that have been performed by your organization as the estimates for your activities. Analogous estimates are typically easier to use, and their accuracy depends on how similar the two projects actually are.

 Parametric Estimating - Parametric estimating is a tool often used on projects that have access to good historical information, and it works best for linear, scalable projects. For instance, if you knew that it cost $9,000,000 to build a mile of roadway, then you could estimate that it would cost $72,000,000 to build 8 miles of road.

 Bottom-Up Estimating - The technique of bottom-up estimating produces a separate estimate for each schedule activity. These individual estimates are then aggregated up to summary nodes on the WBS.

Bottom-up estimating is considered to be highly accurate; however, it can also be time-consuming and labor-intensive.

Three-Point Estimating — See Ch. 6, Estimate Activity Durations, Tools page 178. The same math and principles apply here for beta and triangular distributions.

Data Analysis

Alternatives Analysis - The reality of hard costs frequently motivates teams to investigate other ways of accomplishing a goal or completing an activity. This involves reviewing options for changing scope, schedule, size, quantities, or other creative ways to bring costs in line with the goals of the project.

Reserve Analysis - It is normal for the cost estimates to include reserve amounts, also called contingencies. This is simply a buffer against slippage on the project.

The reserve amounts should be analyzed as part of the Estimate Costs process simply to ensure that the amount of reserve being planned properly reflects the risk associated with the project.

Cost of Quality - The technique of evaluating the cost of quality, often abbreviated as COQ, looks at all of the costs that will be realized in order to achieve quality. This tool is also used in the Plan Quality Management process. The costs of items that are not conformant to quality standards are known as cost of poor quality, often abbreviated as CoPQ.

Project Management Information System —
  See Ch. 2, Common Tools

Decision Making — See Ch. 2, Common Tools

HOW IT WORKS / OUTPUTS:

Cost Estimates - The cost estimates are the primary output of this process. These estimates address how much it would cost to complete each schedule activity on the project along with a contingency or reserve amount.

Cost estimates might include things like labor, materials, taxes and fees, direct, and indirect costs. Even things like currency exchange rates and inflation would be included here. The basic rule is if there is a cost anticipated to complete something, it should be reflected right here.

Basis of Estimates - Embrace the mind-set that you can never have too much supporting detail. Here, especially, it is important to include enough information on how you derived the activity cost estimates.

Project Documents Updates - As the activity cost estimates are created, it is normal for the assumptions log, the lessons learned register, and the risk register to be updated.

Chapter Notes:

Estimate Costs

···· PLANNING

DETERMINE BUDGET

6th Edition *PMBOK® Guide*
Cross Ref. pg 248

WHAT IT IS:

In order to understand this process, you need to understand what a budget is. A budget takes the estimated project expenditures and maps them back to dates on the calendar. In other words, the Determine Budget process time-phases the cost estimates so that the performing organization will know how to plan for cash flow and likely expenditures.

WHY IT IS IMPORTANT:

A good budget will help the organization plan its expenditures appropriately and will prevent them from tying up too much money throughout the life of the project. For example, a construction project may have relatively low costs early on, but these costs usually rise dramatically in the construction phase. The cost baseline will reflect this, helping the organization to plan accordingly.

Although a high-level budget, similar to a cost constraint, may be provided by the organization when the project is created, a detailed budget shows costs and timelines for each work package or schedule activity.

Watch The Video

▶ http://**prep.pm/7-4**

Chapter Notes:

_____

_____

_____

_____

_____

_____

_____

WHEN IT IS PERFORMED:

A lot has to take place before you can carry out this process. Because the budget typically maps back to the schedule activities, it should be performed after Define Activities, Estimate Activity Durations, and Estimate Activity Resources have been performed. Additionally, because the budget is time-phased, it should be performed after Develop Schedule since that is where the project's time line is determined, also since it is based on the activity cost estimates, it should be performed after the process of Estimate Costs.

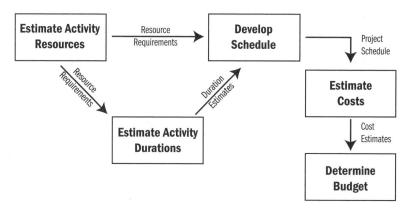

A diagram showing the order of Cost Management's planning processes and the integration with Schedule Management

HOW IT WORKS / INPUTS:

Project Management Plan

Cost Management Plan - The cost management plan specifies how the budget will be created, as well as the role the budget will play in the management of the project.

Resource Management Plan - The resource management plan will have information about labor rates, material costs, and other information that will be used to create the cost baseline.

Scope Baseline - The scope baseline contains the project scope statement, the WBS, and the WBS dictionary. All of these will give us the information on why the scope was set where it was, what its limits are, and what other scope-related constraints exist. For instance, certain elements of scope may be non-negotiable since they are required by contract, while other requirements may be easily changed. As the project's budget is being created, the scope should be carefully considered.

Also, the budget is not only mapped back to the schedule (that is, time-phased), but costs are also tied back to nodes on the work breakdown structure, and the WBS dictionary will provide expanded attributes, information, and details on each of the work packages.

Chapter Seven

Chapter Notes:

_____

_____

_____

_____

_____

_____

_____

_____

_____

_____

_____

_____

_____

Project Documents

Basis of Estimates - The basis for estimates describes how you derived the cost estimates you are using here.

Cost Estimates - The activity cost estimates are a primary input into this process. They provide details on what each schedule activity is estimated to cost. Because every schedule activity maps back to a single work package, these activity cost estimates are added together to get the cost for their parent work package.

Project Schedule - The cost baseline is time-phased, meaning that it shows what costs will be incurred and when they will be incurred. The schedule helps tie these costs back to periods of time for planning purposes.

Risk Register - The risk register contains all of the identified risks on the project. These risks need to be carefully considered as the budget and funding requirements are developed.

Business Documents

Business Case - How much you spend on an activity or a resource may be influenced by how important it is. The business case gives you an idea of why the project is being undertaken, which can give you an idea as to whether this particular activity gets premium resources or may be performed at a standard level.

Benefits Management Plan - This plan will indicate when, how, and the expected size of benefits to be realized by the project, and this information can influence when project expenditures are made.

Agreements - Agreements and contracts may provide information on what costs the project is contractually obliged to incur as well as when. For instance, the contract may specify that only one specific brand of computer server may be used in a data center or that the project is obligated to use at least five of these servers and that they must be procured in the current fiscal year. Any contractual information that affects the cost or expenditures should be factored into the Determine Budget process.

Enterprise Environmental Factors — See Ch. 2, Common Inputs

Organizational Process Assets — See Ch. 2, Common Inputs

HOW IT WORKS / TOOLS:

Expert Judgment - This is, perhaps, the most important tool used in the Determine Budget process. Good estimates (whether they are for cost, time, or another resource) should almost always have some expert judgment applied. In most scenarios, the person doing the work or responsible for the activity should be consulted for input.

Cost Aggregation - Even though costs are estimated at an activity level, these cost estimates should be rolled up to the work package level where they will be measured, managed, and controlled during the project.

Some organizations aggregate costs higher up on the WBS. These nodes, above the work packages, are control accounts for tracking performance.

Data Analysis - Data analysis primarily looks at management reserve. Almost all projects maintain some financial reserve to protect them against cost overrun. How much they keep and how they track it will vary from project to project. Contingency reserves are risk amounts for activity overrun, while management reserve is an amount controlled by the project manager for complete unknowns or similar risks. .

There is no one prescribed way to perform this data analysis; however, the contingency amount should be in keeping with the risk levels and tolerances on the project.

Chapter Notes:

_____

_____

_____

_____

_____

_____

_____

_____

_____

_____

_____

_____

_____

_____

Determine Budget

Chapter Seven

Chapter Notes:

_____

_____

_____

_____

_____

_____

_____

_____

_____

_____

_____

_____

_____

_____

Historical Information Review - Historical information review means either an analogous or a parametric estimating model based on historical data. An example of parametric estimating would be basing the cost of the development of a software application on the estimated number of lines of code or screens involved, or basing the cost of an airport runway on its planned length.

Parametric estimates work best when the project being undertaken is highly similar to previous projects and there is significant historical information available within your organization or industry.

Funding Limit Reconciliation - Many companies are required to budget for projects months or years before the actual scope is known, and a single project may span several fiscal years. Because of that, it is normal for a project to receive a funding limit or constraint when the project is begun.

It is important for the project to reconcile planned spending with these funding limits. For instance, the organization may specify that they will only be able to provide $200,000 in the first month of a project, but $450,000 in the second month. The project's cost baseline ultimately needs to be compatible with these limitations.

Financing - Acquiring capital from outside sources may be necessary in order to meet the funding requirements.

HOW IT WORKS / OUTPUTS:

Cost Baseline - The cost baseline plus management reserve makes up the project's budget, and you should expect to see questions related to it on the exam. This baseline includes cost estimates for all activities along with contingency reserves. The cost baseline specifies what costs will be incurred and when they are anticipated. Larger projects may be divided into multiple cost baselines. For instance, one cost baseline may track domestic labor costs, while a second cost baseline is used to track international labor costs. In traditional projects, the funding forms an S curve, meaning that the costs start off slowly, accelerate throughout construction phase of the project, and begin to slow down during testing and closure. When analyzed cumulatively, these planned expenditures form a characteristic S pattern as is shown in the following illustration.

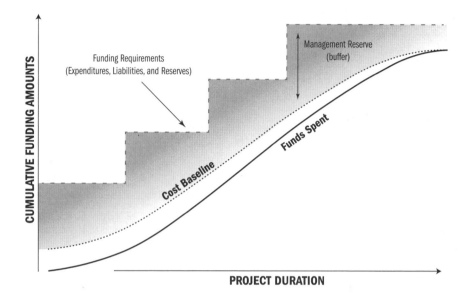

S-Curve diagram showing the relationship of cost and time

Project Funding Requirements - The project funding requirements are made of up the cost baseline plus management reserves. It would be impractical for most projects to petition management for authorization on each individual cost, so instead, the project determines funding requirements using the cost baseline. The funding requirements are almost always related to the planned expenditures, but they are not identical to them. For instance, a project may request $20,000 per month throughout the life of the project, or they may require a larger portion early on in order to purchase equipment or incur other fixed costs.

Project Documents Updates - Oftentimes performing the process of Determine Budget results in changes to the project's scope, schedule, risks, or costs. If any of these changes affect the way in which costs are managed (or the way change requests to the costs are managed), then the corresponding plan or document should be updated to reflect this.

Determine Budget

MONITORING & CONTROLLING

CONTROL COSTS

6th Edition *PMBOK® Guide*
Cross Ref. pg 257

WHAT IT IS:

Control Costs, in many ways, is a classic monitoring and controlling process. There are two important things to keep in mind about controlling processes:

1. They are proactive. They do not wait for changes to occur. Instead, they try to influence the factors that lead to change.

2. Controlling processes measure what was executed against what was planned. If the results of what was executed do not match the cost baseline, then appropriate steps are taken to bring the two back in line. This could either mean changing future plans or changing the way the work is being executed.

Control Costs is concerned with cost variance. In project management, cost variances are described as either being positive (good) or negative (bad), but even positive cost variances need to be understood and the plan must be adjusted. Accurate planning is the goal here.

Watch The Video
http://**prep.pm/7-5**

WHY IS IT IMPORTANT:

Control Costs is an essential process for ensuring that costs are carefully monitored and controlled. It ensures that the costs stay on track and that change is detected whenever it occurs.

Chapter Notes:

_____

_____

_____

_____

_____

_____

_____

_____

WHEN IT IS PERFORMED:

Control Costs is not a process that is performed only once. Instead, it is performed regularly throughout the project, typically beginning as soon as the project incurs costs. The activities associated with Control Costs are usually performed with more frequency as project costs increase. For example, many projects will perform Control Costs monthly during planning phases and weekly (or even more frequently) during construction phases, where costs would probably peak.

HOW IT WORKS / INPUTS:

Project Management Plan - The cost baseline is the most important component of the project management plan used in Control Costs. A baseline is the original plan plus all approved changes. The cost baseline (also known as the budget) shows what costs are projected and when they are projected to occur. The cost baseline is the plan against which the actual costs are measured. Projects that use earned value refer to the cost baseline as the performance measurement baseline.

Another important component of the project management plan for this process is the cost management plan. This plan lays out how costs will be managed throughout the life of the project.

Project Documents — See Ch. 2, Common Inputs

Project Funding Requirements - The project funding requirements, like the cost baseline, are part of the plan against which the actual funding is measured. In this case, positive or negative variances from the planned funding requirements will be evaluated so that corrective action may be taken if necessary.

Work Performance Data — See Ch. 2, Common Inputs

Organizational Process Assets — See Ch. 2, Common Inputs

Chapter Notes:

Control Costs

Chapter Seven

Chapter Notes:

_____

_____

_____

_____

_____

_____

_____

_____

_____

_____

_____

_____

_____

HOW IT WORKS / TOOLS:

Expert Judgment — See Ch. 2, Common Tools

Data Analysis

→ Earned Value Analysis - Earned Value, covered in the next section of this chapter, is a method of measuring actual performance against the original plan. Earned value measurement can help identify areas where the project is performing differently than the plan. Earned value measurement would identify variances (such as Cost Variance) as well as trends (such as Cost Performance Index) that directly influence the Control Costs process.

Variance Analysis - Project managers do not like variance from the plan. Positive variance is better than negative variance, but it still reflects inaccurate planning. All variances should be analyzed and understood.

Trend Analysis - Trends can alert you to problems before they manifest. For example, suppose your project is currently within budget but the past three months have been trending in the wrong direction. It gives you a way to proactively identify a developing situation.

Reserve Analysis - Reserves are pools of money set aside to keep the project running smoothly in case a risk event occurs. Periodic analysis is needed in order to ensure that the project still has the right amount set aside. It does not serve the performing organization well if there is too much reserve set aside, and it puts the project at risk if there is too little. Reserve Analysis is the technique used to evaluate and adjust this as needed.

→ TCPI - The concept of the To-Complete Performance Index is an earned value technique that focuses on the performance needed in order to achieve your earned value targets. TCPI is covered in more detail in the special focus section on earned value later in this chapter.

Project Management Information System (PMIS) - Because the calculations involved in Control Costs (especially the earned value calculations) can be tedious and complex, project management software is typically used to calculate actual values and assist with what if analysis.

HOW IT WORKS / OUTPUTS:

➔ **Work Performance Information** - Work performance information shows how the project is performing against the plan. For the process of Control Costs, the performance measurements of CV, SV, CPI, SPI, TCPI, and VAC (all covered later in this chapter) are especially helpful, since they help show variances and trends on how the project is performing.

➔ **Cost Forecasts** - Budget forecasts are your projections for how much funding will be needed and when it will be needed from this point forward.

The two values that relate most closely to completion are Estimate At Completion (EAC) and Estimate To Complete (ETC). These numbers are used to help forecast a likely completion for the project. Both EAC and ETC are covered in more detail later in this chapter.

Change Requests - As Control Costs is performed, requested changes are a normal output. For instance, if the process of Control Costs showed that the project was going to cost significantly less or more than the cost baseline, then certain changes would likely result to bring the project back in line. These changes could take the form of reducing the scope, increasing the budget, or changing factors related to execution.

Project Management Plan Updates —
        See Ch. 2, Common Outputs

Project Documents Updates — See Ch. 2, Common Outputs

Chapter Seven

Chapter Notes:

_____

_____

_____

_____

_____

_____

_____

_____

_____

_____

_____

_____

→ The Agile Perspective on Cost Management

In order to create a detailed, time-phased budget, the scope and schedule need to be known in detail. On projects that adopt an agile approach, flexibility and adaptability are favored over long range detailed planning, and that includes budgeting. This means that agile projects may estimate costs for the next iteration in detail but would not try to create an accurate, long term plan. Some budget estimates could be extrapolated by calculating the team "burn rate," but they would not be detailed or necessarily accurate.

On an agile project where the budget was not flexible, the scope and schedule would need to be (the triple constraint exists on agile and traditional waterfall projects). For example, if an organization was willing to fund up to $68,000 per month for a project's development but could not exceed that amount, it would constrain the size of the team and possibly the hours they could work. The project team would need to adapt the scope and schedule to fit that funding constraint.

SPECIAL FOCUS: EARNED VALUE

➔ The following section is of key importance

If you are wrestling with your understanding of earned value, think about the concept of debits and credits. In a double entry accounting system, for every debit to one account, there is a corresponding credit to another account. Earned value is similar in that if you spend a dollar on labor for your project, that dollar doesn't just evaporate into thin air. You are "earning" a dollar's value back into your project. If you buy bricks or computers, write code or documentation, or perform any work on the project, those activities earn value for your project.

There are several key formulas associated with earned value management that often appear on the test, and they require both memorization and understanding. Following is a chart that presents a summary of the key terms used in earned value calculations.

Note that for Planned Value, Earned Value, and Actual Cost, there are older, equivalent terms that still show up on the exam. These older terms and their associated abbreviations are shown along with the current terms on the chart on the following page, and you must be able to recognize and apply either one on the exam.

Chapter Notes:

_____

_____

_____

_____

_____

_____

_____

_____

_____

_____

_____

_____

_____

_____

Chapter Seven

TERM	ABBREV.	DESCRIPTION	FORMULA
Budgeted At Completion	BAC	How much was originally planned for this project to cost.	No one formula exists. BAC is derived by looking at the total budgeted cost for the project.
Planned Value (also known as Budgeted Cost of Work Scheduled)	PV (or BCWS)	How much work should have been completed at a point in time based on the plan. Derived by measuring planned work completed at a point in time.	$PV =$ Planned % Complete X BAC
Earned Value (also known as Budgeted Cost of Work Performed)	EV (or BCWP)	How much work was actually completed during a given period of time. Derived by measuring actual work completed at a point in the schedule.	EV = Actual % Complete X BAC
Actual Cost (also known as Actual Cost of Work Performed)	AC (or ACWP)	The money spent during a given period of time.	Sum of the costs for the given period of time.
Cost Variance	CV	The difference between what we expected to spend and what was actually spent.	$CV = EV - AC$
Schedule Variance	SV	The difference between where we planned to be in the schedule and where we are in the schedule.	$SV = EV - PV$
Cost Performance Index	CPI	The rate at which the project performance is meeting cost expectations during a given period of time.	$CPI = EV \div AC$
Cumulative CPI	CPI^c	The rate at which the project performance is meeting cost expectations from the beginning up to a point in time. CPI^c is also used to forecast the project's costs at completion.	$CPI^c = EV^c \div AC^c$
Schedule Performance Index	SPI	The rate at which the project performance is meeting schedule expectations up to a point in time.	$SPI = EV \div PV$
Estimate At Completion	EAC	Projecting the total cost at completion based on project performance up to a point in time.	$EAC = BAC \div CPI^c$
Estimate To Completion	ETC	Projecting how much more will be spent on the project, based on past performance.	$ETC = EAC - AC$
Variance At Completion	VAC	The difference between what was budgeted and what will actually be spent.	$VAC = BAC - EAC$
To-Complete Performance Index	$TCPI_c$	Performance that must be achieved in order to meet financial or schedule goals.	$TCPI_c = (BAC - EV) \div$ Remaining Funds

EVM Example

Consider the following example:

You are the project manager for the construction of 20 miles of sidewalk. According to your plan, the cost of construction will be $15,000 per mile and will take 8 weeks to complete.

2 weeks into the project, you have spent $55,000 and completed 4 miles of sidewalk, and you want to report performance and determine how much time and cost remain.

Below, we will walk through each calculation to show how we arrive at the correct answers.

Budget at Completion

In the approach outlined by this book, you always begin by calculating BAC. Budget at completion simply means, "how much we originally expected this project to cost." It is typically very easy to calculate. In our example, we take 20 miles of sidewalk X $15,000 per mile. That equates to a BAC of $300,000.

BAC = $300,000

Planned Value

The planned value is how much work was planned for this point in time. The value is expressed in dollars.

Planned Value = Planned % complete X BAC

We do this by taking the BAC ($300,000) and multiplying it by our % complete. In this case, we are 2 weeks complete on an 8 week schedule, which equates to 25%. $300,000 X .25 = $75,000. Therefore, we had planned to spend $75,000 after two weeks.

PV = $75,000

Earned Value

Chapter Notes:

_____

_____

_____

_____

_____

_____

_____

_____

_____

_____

_____

_____

_____

_____

_____

If you have been intimidated by the concept of earned value, relax. Earned value is based on the assumption that as you complete work on the project, you are adding value to the project. Therefore, it is simply a matter of calculating how much value you have "earned" on the project.

Planned value is what was planned, but earned value is what actually happened.

EV = Actual % Complete X BAC

In this case, we have completed 4 miles of the 20 mile project, which equates to 20%. We multiply that percentage by the BAC to get EV. It is $300,000 × 20% = $60,000. This tells us that we have completed $60,000 worth of work, or more accurately, we have earned $60,000 of value for the project.

EV = $60,000

Actual Cost

Building on the above illustration, we will calculate our actual costs. Actual cost is the amount of cost you have incurred at this point, and we are told in the example that we have spent $55,000 to date. In this example, no calculation is needed.

AC = Actual Cost

AC = $55,000

Cost Variance

Cost variance (CV) is how much actual costs differ from planned costs. We derive this by calculating the difference between EV and AC. In this example, it is EV of $60,000 – AC of $55,000. A positive variance (as in this case) reflects that the project is doing better on cost than expected.

For those who are curious, the reason we use EV in this formula instead of PV is that we are calculating how much the actual costs have varied. If we used PV, it would give us the variance from our plan, but the cost variance measures actual cost variance, EV is based on actual performance, whereas PV is based on planned performance.

A positive CV is a good thing. It indicates that we are doing better on costs than we had planned. Conversely, a negative CV indicates that costs are running higher than planned.

CV = EV−AC

CV = $5,000

Schedule Variance

Schedule variance (SV) is how much our schedule differs from our plan. Where people often get confused here is that this concept is expressed in dollars. SV is derived by calculating the difference between EV and PV. In this example, the schedule variance is EV of $60,000 − PV of $75,000. A negative variance (as in this case) reflects that we are not performing as well as we had hoped in terms of schedule. A positive SV would indicate that the project is ahead of schedule.

SV = EV−PV

SV = −$15,000

Chapter Seven

Chapter Notes:

_____

_____

_____

_____

_____

_____

_____

_____

_____

_____

_____

_____

_____

Cost Performance Index

The cost performance index gives us an indicator as to how much we are getting for every dollar we spend. It is derived by dividing Earned Value by the Actual Cost. In this example, Earned Value = $60,000, and our Actual Cost = $55,000. $60,000 ÷ $55,000 = 1.09.

This figure tells us that we are getting $1.09 worth of performance for every $1.00 we spent. A CPI of 1 indicates that the project is exactly on track. A closer look at the formula reveals that values of 1 or greater are good, and values less than 1 are undesirable.

CPI = EV ÷ AC

CPI = 1.09

Schedule Performance Index

A corollary to the cost performance index is the schedule performance index, or SPI. The schedule performance index tells us how fast the project is progressing compared to the project plan. It is calculated by dividing earned value by the planned value. In this example, earned value = $60,000, and our planned value = $75,000. $60,000 ÷ $75,000 = 0.8. This tells us that the project is progressing at 80% of the pace that we expected it to, and when we look at the example, this conclusion makes sense. We had expected to lay 20 miles of sidewalk in 8 weeks. At that rate, after 2 weeks, we should have constructed 5 miles, but instead the example tells us that we had only constructed 4 miles. That equates to 4÷5 performance, which is 80%. Like the cost performance index, values of 1 or greater are good, and values that are less than 1 are undesirable.

SPI = EV ÷ PV

SPI = 0.8

A common way for the cost performance and schedule performance index to be used is to track them over time. This is often displayed in the form of a graph, as illustrated below. This graph may be easily interpreted if you consider that a value of 1 indicates that the index is exactly on plan.

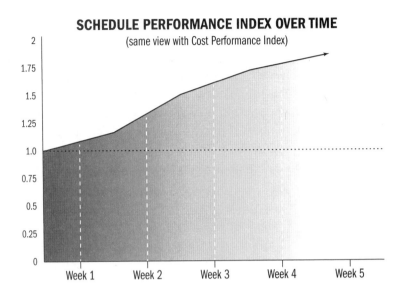

SCHEDULE PERFORMANCE INDEX OVER TIME
(same view with Cost Performance Index)

Estimate At Completion

Estimate at completion is the amount we expect the project to cost when it is finished, based on where we are today. Think of it as if you know you are half way through the project, and you are currently 20% over budget. Then the estimate at completion projects that variance out to the end of the project. There are many ways to calculate EAC, but for the exam, the most straightforward way is to take the BAC and divide it by our CPI. In this example, we expected to spend (BAC) $300,000 and our CPI is 1.09. $300,000 ÷ 1.09 = $275,229.36. This should make sense. We are doing better on costs than we had originally planned, and this value reflects that.

$$EAC = BAC \div CPI^c$$

EAC = $275,229.36

Chapter Seven

Chapter Notes:

_____

_____

_____

_____

_____

_____

_____

_____

_____

_____

_____

_____

_____

_____

Estimate To Complete

Estimate to completion is simply how much more we expect to spend from this point forward based on what we've done so far. It can be easily backed into by taking our estimate at complete (what we expect to spend) and subtracting what we have spent so far (Actual Cost). Given the numbers above, it would be EAC of $275,229.36 - AC of $55,000 = $220,229.36. This tells us that we expect to spend $220,229.36 more, given our performance thus far.

ETC = EAC − AC

ETC = $220,229.36

Variance at Completion

Variance at completion is the difference between what we originally budgeted and what we expect to spend. A positive variance indicates that we are doing better than projected, and a negative variance indicates that we expect the project to run over on costs.

In this example, our BAC was $300,000; however, our EAC is now $275,229.36. $300,000 − $275,229.36 = $24,770.64.

VAC = BAC - EAC

VAC = $24,770.64

Cumulative CPI (CPI^c)

Once you understand the concept of earned value, the cumulative cost performance index (expressed as CPI^c) is not as intimidating as it may first look. Recall that the regular CPI is simply EV÷AC, the efficiency indicator of performance during a given period of time. The CPI^c is simply all of the periodic earned value calculations added together (EV^c) and divided by all of the periodic actual cost calculations added together (AC^c).

Consider a company that took earned value measurements at monthly intervals for the past three months, as summarized in the table below.

	EV	AC
Month 1	$22,000	$13,700
Month 2	$151,000	$137,900
Month 3	$107,000	$98,400

The following table, using the same example, conveys the usefulness of CPI and CPI^c.

	EV	EV^c	AC	AC^c	CPI	CPI^c
Month 1	$22,000	$22,000	$13,700	$13,700	1.61	1.61
Month 2	$151,000	$173,000	$137,900	$151,600	1.09	1.14
Month 3	$107,000	$280,000	$98,400	$250,000	1.09	1.12

Given this information, the CPI^c would be calculated by adding up all of the earned value figures ($280,000) and dividing by the sum of the actual costs ($250,000). This yields a cumulative CPI of 1.12.

Cost Performance Index (CPI) was calculated by applying the formula CPI = EV÷AC, which gave us a calculation of the monthly performance. For the Cumulative Cost Performance Index (CPI^c), we applied the formula CPI^c = EV^c÷ AC^c, which calculates the project's performance up to a point in time.

These values are useful, because the monthly CPI only provided a snapshot of your earned value performance during a certain period of time, but the cumulative CPI can show a number that factors in performance efficiency in all months up to a point in time. The cumulative CPI has been shown to be a good predictor of performance at completion, even when used very early in the project.

Chapter Notes:

Earned Value

Chapter Notes:

———————————————

———————————————

———————————————

———————————————

———————————————

———————————————

———————————————

———————————————

———————————————

———————————————

———————————————

———————————————

———————————————

TCPI (also expressed as $TCPI_c$)

The To-Complete Performance Index is the performance which must be achieved on all remaining work in order to meet either financial or schedule goals. TCPI can come in two varieties: $TCPI_c$ for cost, and $TCPI_s$ for schedule. Since the PMBOK Guide only mentions the cost version, this book will focus on that index. It is calculated as follows:

$TCPI_c$ = (BAC - EV) ÷ Remaining funds. Remaining funds = BAC - AC if targeting original budget, or EAC - AC if targeting the current forecast.

As an important note, this breaks the general rule that an index of 1 or greater is good, and less than one is undesirable. Since this is looking at the performance the project would need to achieve to end on target, a lower index is good, since it means that you could underperform and still meet your target, while an index of greater than one is bad since you are essentially saying that you would need to overperform against the plan in order to meet your estimates.

Types of Cost

Several types of questions regarding cost may appear on the exam. It is important to understand the difference between the different types of cost presented as follows:

COST TYPE	EXPLANATION
Fixed	Costs that stay the same throughout the life of the project. An example is a piece of heavy equipment, such as renting a bulldozer.
Variable	Costs that may vary on a project. Examples are hourly labor, and fuel for the bulldozer.
Direct	Expenses that are billed directly to the project. An example is the materials used to construct a building.
Indirect	Costs that are shared and allocated among several or all projects. An example could be a manager's salary. The team might be direct costs on a project, but the manager's salary is overhead and would be considered an indirect cost.
Sunk	Costs that have been invested into or expended upon the project. Sunk costs are like spilt milk. If they are unrecoverable, they are to be treated as if they are irrelevant! This is difficult for many people to understand, but the statement "we've spent over 10 million dollars on this project, and we're not turning back now" is not good decision-making if the costs are unrecoverable, or "sunk."
Opportunity	The cost of the loss of potential benefit from the alternatives when a choice is made that excludes those alternatives. Opportunity cost most often is associated with project selection.

Chapter Seven

Chapter Notes:

_____

_____

_____

_____

_____

_____

_____

_____

_____

_____

_____

_____

_____

EXERCISES

Example 1

You are constructing 6 additional rooms on an office building. Each of the six rooms is identical, the projected cost for the project is $100,000, and construction is expected to take 5 weeks.

At the end of the 2nd week, you have spent $17,500 per room and have finished 2 rooms; you are ready to begin on the 3rd.

1. **Based on the information provided in the example above, fill in the values for the following table:**

	VALUE
Budget at Completion	
Planned Value	
Earned Value	
Actual Cost	
Cost Variance	
Schedule Variance	
Cost Performance Index	
Schedule Performance Index	
Estimate At Completion	
Estimate To Complete	
Variance At Completion	
To-Complete Performance Index (cost)	

2. **Is the project ahead of or behind schedule?**

3. **Is the project going to be completed over or under budget?**

Example 2

Here is another example to test your understanding of these concepts.

You have planned for a project to write a software application to take 1 year. The costs on this project are budgeted at $12,500 per month.

Six months into the project, you find that the software application is 50% completed, and you have spent $70,000.

4. **Based on the information provided, fill in the values for the following table:**

	VALUE
Budget at Completion	
Planned Value	
Earned Value	
Actual Cost	
Cost Variance	
Schedule Variance	
Cost Performance Index	
Schedule Performance Index	
Estimate At Completion	
Estimate To Complete	
Variance At Completion	
To-Complete Performance Index (cost)	

5. **Is the project ahead of or behind schedule?**

6. **Is the project going to be completed over or under budget?**

Chapter Seven

Earned Value: Exercises

7. **For each column, circle the one cell that shows the most desirable value in that column.** (Note that some of these attributes are covered in Chapter 4- Integration Management)

IRR	SPI	CPI	NPV	Payback Period	BCR	ROI	TCPI$_c$
22%	1	.5	$25,000	16 mos	2	9%	.5
0%	0	1	$95,000	2 yrs	1.5	12%	.9
12%	.8	1.2	$50,000	16 wks	1	-2%	1
-3%	1.2	1.15	$71,000	25 mos	.2	3%	2

8. **Project X was expected to take four months and cost $70,000 per month. At the end of month one, the project was 20% complete, and had spent $89,000. At the end of month two, it was 40% complete and had spent $151,000. What is the cumulative CPI for Project X at the end of month two?**

ANSWERS TO EXERCISES

1. Your answers should look like these:

	VALUE
Budget at Completion	$ 100,000
Planned Value	$ 40,000.00
Earned Value	$ 33,333.33
Actual Cost	$ 35,000.00
Cost Variance	- $ 1,666.67
Schedule Variance	- $ 6,666.67
Cost Performance Index	0.95
Schedule Performance Index	0.83
Estimate At Completion	$ 105,263.15
Estimate To Complete	$ 70,263.15
Variance At Completion	- $5,263.15
To-Complete Performance Index (cost)	1.03

- BAC = $100,000.00

- PV = 2 weeks ÷ 5 weeks = 40% complete X 100,000 = $40,000

- EV = 2 rooms ÷ 6 rooms = 33.3% complete X 100,000 = $33,333.33

- AC = $17,500 per room X 2 rooms = $35,000

- CV = (EV) $33,333.33 – (AC) $35,000.00 = -$1,666.67

- SV = (EV) $33,333.33 – (PV) $40,000.00 = -$6,666.67

- CPI = (EV) $33,333.33 ÷ (AC) $35,000.00 = 0.95

- SPI = (EV) $33,333.33 ÷ (PV) $40,000.00 = 0.83

Chapter Seven

Chapter Notes:

_____

_____

_____

_____

_____

_____

_____

_____

_____

_____

_____

_____

- EAC = (BAC) $100,000.00 ÷ (CPI) 0.95 = $105,263.15

- ETC = (EAC) $105,263.15 – (AC) $35,000.00 = $70,263.15

- VAC = (BAC) $100,000.00 – (EAC) $105,263.15 = –$5,263.15

- TCPIc = ((BAC) $100,000.00 – (EV) $33,333.33) ÷ ((BAC) $100,000.00 – (AC) $35,000) = 1.03

2. Is the project ahead of or behind schedule?
   The project is behind schedule. The easiest way to determine this is by looking at the SPI. Since it is less than 1, we can determine that the project is not doing well in terms of the schedule.

3. Is the project going to be completed over or under budget?
   There are two ways to see that the project is going to run over budget. First, the CPI is less than 1. Second, the VAC is negative.

4. Check your answers against the values in the following table:

	VALUE
Budget at Completion	$ 150,000
Planned Value	$ 75,000.00
Earned Value	$ 75,000.00
Actual Cost	$ 70,000.00
Cost Variance	$ 5,000.00
Schedule Variance	$ 0
Cost Performance Index	1.07
Schedule Performance Index	1
Estimate At Completion	$ 140,186.91
Estimate To Complete	$ 70,186.91
Variance At Completion	$ 9,813.09
To-Complete Performance Index (cost)	0.94

- BAC = $150,000.00

- PV = 6 months ÷ 12 months = 50% complete X 150,000 = $75,000

- EV = Project is 50% complete X 150,000.00 = $75,000.00

- AC = $70,000 .00

- CV = (EV) $75,000.00 – (AC) $70,000.00 = $5,000.00

- SV = (EV) $75,000.00 – (PV) $75,000.00 = $0

- CPI = (EV) $75,000.00 ÷ (AC) $70,000.00 = 1.07

- SPI = (EV) $75,000.00 ÷ (PV) $75,000.00 = 1

- EAC = (BAC) $150,000.00 ÷ (CPI) 1.07 = $140,186.91

- ETC = (EAC) $140,186.91 – (AC) $70,000.00 = $70,186.91

- VAC = (BAC) $150,000.00 – (EAC) $140,186.91 = $9,813.09

- TCPIc = ((BAC) $150,000.00 – (EV) $75,000) ÷ (BAC) $150,000 – (AC) $70,000) = 0.94

5. Is the project ahead of or behind schedule?
   This would be classified as a "trick" question, as neither answer is correct. Since the SPI is 1, we can see that the project is exactly on schedule.

6. Is the project going to be completed over or under budget?
   The project is projected to finish ahead of (under) budget, due to the cost performance index being greater than 1.

Chapter Notes:

_____

_____

_____

_____

_____

_____

_____

_____

_____

_____

_____

_____

_____

Earned Value: Answers to Exercises

Chapter Seven

Chapter Notes:

_____

_____

_____

_____

_____

_____

_____

_____

_____

_____

_____

_____

_____

7. The most desirable project attributes for each column are shaded in the chart below. Note that some of these formulas came from Chapter 4, Integration Management. If you found the TCPIc answer confusing, remember that TCPI breaks the index rule where the larger number is usually more desirable. TCPI looks forward, so with a TCPIc of .5, we are saying that the project could spend at twice the projected rate from this point until the end and still end on budget.

IRR	SPI	CPI	NPV	Payback Period	BCR	ROI	TCPI$_c$
22%	1	.5	$25,000	16 mos	2	9%	.5
0%	0	1	$95,000	2 yrs	1.5	12%	.9
12%	.8	1.2	$50,000	16 wks	1	-2%	1
-3%	1.2	1.15	$71,000	25 mos	.2	3%	2

Did you notice that for most of these measurements, the bigger value is the best one? That is true for all except for the payback period, where you want the shortest time to recoup project costs, and for TCPIc where smaller numbers are better.

8. If you got this one, give yourself a big pat on the back! In order to answer it, you first had to calculate the earned value for months one and two.

    Month 1 EV = 0.2 × $280,000 = $56,000
    Month 2 EV = 0.2 × $280,000 = $56,000
    Month 2 AC = $151,000

    After getting these values, the CPIC is a snap. It is simply the sum of the earned value numbers divided by the sum of the actual costs. Since you already know the sum of the actual costs is $151,000, all you have to do is add the earned values together and divide. This yields $112,000 ÷ $151,000 = a cumulative CPI (CPIc) of 0.74.

COST MANAGEMENT

QUESTIONS

Note: Some of these questions are based on material covered in previous chapters as well as this chapter.

Chapter Notes:

1. Your schedule projected that you would reach 50% completion today on a road construction project that is paving 32 miles of new highway. Every 4 miles is scheduled to cost $5,000,000. Today, in your status meeting, you announced that you had completed 20 miles of the highway at a cost of $18,000,000. What is your Planned Value?

    A. $12,800,000.

    B. $18,000,000.

    C. $20,000,000.

    D. $40,000,000.

2. If the CPI is 0.1, this indicates:

    A. The project is performing extremely poorly on cost.

    B. The project is costing 10% over what was expected.

    C. The project is only costing 90% of what was expected.

    D. The project is performing extremely well on cost.

3. Activity cost estimates are used as an input into which process?

    A. Estimate Costs.

    B. Determine Budget.

    C. Analyze Costs.

    D. Control Costs.

Chapter Notes:

_____

_____

_____

_____

_____

_____

_____

_____

_____

_____

_____

_____

_____

_____

4. Based on the following Benefit Cost Ratios, which project would be the best one to select?

   A. BCR = −1.

   B. BCR = 0.

   C. BCR = 1.

   D. BCR = 2.

5. The difference between present value and net present value is:

   A. Present value is expressed as an interest rate, while net present value is expressed as a dollar figure.

   B. Present value is a measure of the actual present value, while net present value measures expected present value.

   C. Present value does not factor in costs.

   D. Present value is more accurate.

6. Kayla is reviewing the budget and spending to ensure that she has enough money to pay vendors for the next projected phase. The CFO of the company has provided extra funds to allow for contingencies, but Kayla is not yet confident that it is enough. Which process is Kayla most likely performing?

   A. Plan Cost Management.

   B. Estimate Costs.

   C. Analyze Budget.

   D. Control Costs.

7. Your best cost estimate for an activity is $200,000, but the estimate you document has a range of $150,000 to $350,000. This ranged estimate represents a:

    A. Cost estimate.

    B. Budgeted estimate.

    C. Rough order of magnitude estimate.

    D. Variable estimate.

8. Which of the following process sequences is correct?

    A. Create WBS, then Determine Budget, then Estimate Costs.

    B. Create WBS, then Estimate Costs, then Determine Budget.

    C. Determine Budget, then Estimate Costs, then Create WBS.

    D. Estimate Costs, then Budget Costs, then Create WBS.

9. One of your team members makes a change to the budget with your approval. In what process is he engaged?

    A. Plan Costs.

    B. Estimate Costs.

    C. Cost Management.

    D. Control Costs.

Chapter Notes:

_____

_____

_____

_____

_____

_____

_____

_____

_____

_____

_____

_____

_____

_____

_____

_____

Cost Management: Questions

Chapter Seven

Chapter Notes:

_____

_____

_____

_____

_____

_____

_____

_____

_____

_____

_____

_____

_____

_____

_____

10. After measuring expected project benefits, management has four projects from which to choose. Project 1 has a net present value of $100,000 and will cost $50,000. Project 2 has a net present value of $200,000 and will cost $75,000. Project 3 has a net present value of $500,000 and will cost $400,000. Project 4 has a net present value of $125,000 and will cost $25,000. Which project would be BEST?

   A. Project 1.

   B. Project 2.

   C. Project 3.

   D. Project 4.

11. Your project office has purchased a site license for a computerized tool that assists in the task of cost estimating on a very large construction project for a downtown skyscraper. This tool asks you for specific characteristics about the project and then provides estimating guidance based on materials, construction techniques, historical information, and industry practices. This tool is an example of:

   A. Bottom-up estimating.

   B. Parametric modeling.

   C. Analogous estimating.

   D. Activity duration estimating.

12. If the Earned Value of a project on January 15 was $127,253, the Budgeted at Completion was $275,000, and the Schedule Performance Index was 0.77, how much work was expected to have been completed at that point?

   A. $97,985

   B. $127,253

   C. $165,264

   D. $211,750

13. You are managing a project that is part of a large construction program. During the execution of your project you are alerted that the construction of a foundation is expected to experience a serious cost overrun. What would be your FIRST course of action?

   A. Evaluate the cause and size of the overrun.

   B. Halt execution until the problem is solved.

   C. Contact the program manager to see if additional funds may be released.

   D. Determine if you have sufficient budget reserves to cover the cost overrun.

14. If earned value = $10,000, planned value = $8,000, and actual cost = $3,000, what is the schedule variance?

   A. −$2,000

   B. $2,000

   C. $5,000

   D. $-5,000

15. Estimate to complete indicates:

   A. The total projected amount that will be spent, based on past performance.

   B. The projected remaining amount that will be spent, based on past performance.

   C. The difference between what was budgeted and what is expected to be spent.

   D. The original planned completion cost minus the costs incurred to date.

Chapter Notes:

_____

_____

_____

_____

_____

_____

_____

_____

_____

_____

_____

_____

_____

_____

Chapter Seven

Chapter Notes:

_____

_____

_____

_____

_____

_____

_____

_____

_____

_____

_____

_____

_____

16. The project team has been working significant overtime on a project for the past three months. The sponsor wants to know what the CPI will need to be from this point forward in order to meet original cost expectations. You know that at this point the Earned Value is $1,124,767, the total budget is $3,111,845, the Planned Value is $950,000, and the project has spent $1,000,975. What should you tell the sponsor?

A.   0.84

B.   0.94

C.   1.0

D.   1.21

17. If a project has a CPI of .95 and an SPI of 1.01, this indicates:

A.   The project is progressing slower and costing more than planned.

B.   The project is progressing slower and costing less than planned.

C.   The project is progressing faster and costing more than planned.

D.   The project is progressing faster and costing less than planned.

18. The best definition of Earned Value is:

A.   The measure of work performed expressed in terms of the budget authorized to perform that work.

B.   Actual % Complete X the BAC.

C.   The value of the project at a point in time expressed in terms of the work performed.

D.   Managing project performance in order to achieve expected results.

19. Project A would yield $100,000 in benefit. Project B would yield $250,000 in benefit. Because of limited resources, your company can perform only one of these. They elect to perform Project B because of the higher benefit. What is the opportunity cost of performing Project B?

A. −$150,000.

B. $150,000.

C. −$100,000.

D. $100,000.

20. As a project manager, your BEST use of the project cost baseline would be to:

A. Measure and monitor cost performance on the project.

B. Track approved changes.

C. Calculate team performance bonuses.

D. Measure and report on variable project costs.

21. The value of all work that has been completed so far is:

A. Earned value.

B. Estimate at complete.

C. Actual cost.

D. Planned value.

22. If the EAC for a project is $201,500, the ETC is $25,010, the SPI is 1.0, and the CPIc is 1.06, what is the BAC?

A. 23,594.

B. 190,094.

C. 201,500.

D. 213,590.

Chapter Notes:

Chapter Notes:

_____

_____

_____

_____

_____

_____

_____

_____

_____

_____

_____

_____

_____

_____

_____

23. **If you have a schedule variance of $500, this would indicate:**

   A. Planned value is less than earned value.

   B. Earned value is less than the estimate at completion.

   C. Actual cost is less than earned value.

   D. The ratio of earned value to planned value is 5:1.

24. **If budgeted at complete = $500, estimate to complete = $400, earned value = $100, and actual cost = $100, what is the estimate at complete?**

   A. $0.

   B. $150.

   C. $350.

   D. $500.

25. **You have spent $322,168 on your project to date. The program manager wants to know why costs have been running so high. You explain that the resource cost has been greater than expected and should level out over the next six months. What does the $322,168 represent to the program manager?**

   A. Earned value.

   B. Actual cost.

   C. Planned value.

   D. Cost performance index.

COST MANAGEMENT

ANSWERS

1. C. Planned Value is calculated by multiplying the Budgeted At Completion by planned % complete. Our cost per mile is planned at $1,250,000 ($5,000,000 ÷ 4 miles), and our Budgeted At Completion is 32 miles x 1,250,000/mile = $40,000,000. We planned to be 50% complete. Therefore, $40,000,000 x .50 = $20,000,000.

2. A. Understanding the concepts behind the earned value calculations is important for the exam and will help you with questions like this one. In this question, the terrible cost performance index indicates that we are getting ten cents of value for every dollar we spent; thus the project is doing very poorly on cost performance.

3. B. Determine Budget takes the activity cost estimates (one of the project documents) and uses them to create a budget. 'A' is incorrect because Estimate Costs is the process that creates the activity cost estimates, so it stands to reason that they would be an output and not an input. 'C' sounds like a decent guess, but it is not a real process. 'D' is incorrect because the process of Control Costs is not concerned with just the individual activity cost estimates. Instead, it uses inputs of the cost baseline.

4. D. With Benefit Cost Ratios, the bigger the better! BCR is calculated as benefit ÷ cost, so the more benefit, and the less cost, the higher the number.

5. C. There is a difference between present value and net present value. Present value tells the expected value of the project in today's dollars. Net present value is the same thing, but it subtracts the costs after calculating the present value.

Chapter Notes:

_____

_____

_____

_____

_____

_____

_____

_____

_____

_____

_____

_____

_____

_____

6. D. Kayla is performing reserve analysis, which is one of the forms of data analysis. If you were trying to decide between choice 'B' and 'D, you would look at what she is doing and why she is doing it. She is making sure that she has enough money, which is not an estimating activity, and that eliminates 'B'. It is a monitoring and controlling activity. Choice 'C' is not a real process, and 'A' would have been performed much earlier and is not descriptive of what Kayla is doing. 'D' emerges as the best choice since she is comparing the plan (budget) with actual performance (spending). This is classic for a monitoring and controlling process, and Control Costs is the only monitoring and controlling process in the list of choices.

7. C. Rough order of magnitude estimates are −25% to +75%. In this example, $150,000 and $350,000 are −25% to +75% of $200,000.

8. B. This question may not look like it is about inputs and outputs, but it actually is. Create WBS is performed first out of the three processes, and the output is the Work Breakdown Structure (WBS). The WBS is used as an input for the next process of the three, Estimate Costs, where the costs of the activities are estimated and aggregated back to the WBS. Finally, the output of that process, the Cost Estimates, is used as an input into Determine Budget, which occurs last out of the three processes listed. By understanding how the outputs of one process become the inputs into another, it becomes simpler to understand the logical order of many of these processes.

9. D. The main clue here is "change." If they are making approved changes, they are in a control process. 'A' is not a real process. 'B' is incorrect since Estimate Costs is the process where the original estimates are developed and not where they are updated. 'C' is the knowledge area (careful not to get these confused with processes).

10. C. This one was very tricky! Net present value already has costs factored in, so they can be ignored here. The net present value is the only value you need to consider, and bigger is better!

11. B. This is an example of parametric modeling. Parametric modeling is common in some industries, where you can describe the project in detail, and the modeling tool will help provide estimates based on historical information, industry standards, etc.

12. C. The first step in answering any question is to determine what is being asked. In this case, the question asked "how much work was expected to have been completed" at a point in time. That is the definition of Planned Value (PV). In most scenarios, PV is given to you in order to calculate something else, but in this case you have to calculate it.

    One way to do this using the information we have is to use the formula for SPI.

    SPI = EV ÷ PV. Using simple algebra, we can change it around to also say that PV= EV ÷ SPI, or PV = $127,253 ÷ 0.77 = $165,264.

    We can see that the project is behind schedule at this point and has not earned as much value as was expected.

    The Budgeted at Completion (BAC) is not of any use here since we don't know when the project was supposed to be completed or other helpful variables.

13. A. This question illustrates one of the biggest exam biases. Your job as a project manager is almost always to evaluate and understand first. Know what you are dealing with before you take action, and don't just accept anyone's word for it. Verify the information yourself!

14. B. Schedule Variance is calculated as EV−PV. In this example, $10,000 − $8,000 = $2,000.

15. B. The Estimate To Complete is what we expect to spend from this point forward, based on our performance thus far.

Chapter Notes:

_____

_____

_____

_____

_____

_____

_____

_____

_____

_____

_____

_____

_____

_____

16. B. 0.94. The sponsor is asking for the To-Complete Performance Index for cost (TCPIc). This scenario was a little bit tricky. Just because the team has been working overtime does not necessarily mean that they are behind schedule or over budget. In this situation they have recently been working overtime and are still under budget.

To calculate the TCPIc, we'll use the standard formula:

TCPIc = (BAC – EV) ÷ Remaining funds.

The BAC is given as the total budget in this question and is $3,111,845. The EV is also given at $1,124,767. Now we have to calculate remaining funds, which is the original budget minus actual costs. We know that the original budget was $3,111,845 and the project has incurred actual costs so far of $1,000,975, which leaves $2,110,870 remaining funds. Now it becomes a matter of plugging numbers into the formula.

TCPIc = (BAC – EV) ÷ Remaining Funds

TCPIc = ($3,111,845 - $1,124,767) ÷ $2,110,870

TCPIc = $1,987,078 ÷ $2,110,870

TCPIc = 0.94

This value of 0.94 means that the project could run somewhat over budget for the remainder of the time and still finish on target.

17. C. Did the wording trip you up on this one? Make sure you read the questions and answers carefully since things were switched around on this one. A schedule performance index greater than 1 means that the project is progressing faster than planned. A cost performance index that is less than 1 means that the project is costing more than planned. Therefore choice 'C' is the only one that fits.

18. A. This is the definition of Earned Value. 'B' is a formula for Earned Value, but it is not the definition. 'C' does not work since Earned Value is about the value earned and not just the costs expended. For example, it is possible to expend a lot of cost, materials, and manpower and earn very little value. 'D' is close to a definition of earned value management (EVM), but it is too generic and does not match the definition of Earned Value.

19. D. Opportunity cost is simply how much benefit you are passing up. In this case, by choosing project B. You are foregoing $100,000 in expected benefit from project A, and that $100,000 represents the opportunity cost.

20. A. The cost baseline is used to track cost performance based on the original plan plus approved changes.

21. A. Earned value is defined as the value of all work completed to this point.

22. D. The formula for EAC is EAC = BAC ÷ CPIc. There is quite a bit of information here, but the only numbers that are relevant are the EAC and the CPIc. In this case we can use simple algebra to restate the formula as BAC = EAC × CPI, or BAC = $213,590, which is answer 'D'.

23. A. This is another tricky question because of the way it is worded. Schedule variance is calculated as earned value – planned value. In this case, schedule variance could only be positive if earned value is greater than planned value (or stated otherwise, if planned value is less than earned value). 'A' is the only choice that has to be true.

Chapter Notes:

_____

_____

_____

_____

_____

_____

_____

_____

_____

_____

_____

_____

_____

24. D. The estimate at complete is what we expect to have spent at the end of the project. It is calculated by taking our budgeted at complete and dividing it by our cost performance index. Step 1 is to calculate our cost performance index. It is earned value ÷ actual cost, and in this case, it equals 1. Budgeted at complete is $500, and $500 ÷ 1 = $500. Therefore, 'D' is the correct answer, indicating that we are progressing exactly as planned. Note that there are many ways to calculate the EAC, and not all of them agree perfectly. One other common way is EAC = AC + ETC, which yields the same answer of $500 for this example.

25. B. Look at the first sentence "You have spent $322,168…" Actual Cost is what you have spent to date on the project.

Quality Management

PHILOSOPHY:

Quality touches virtually every piece of the project, so it is very important. It is easy to think about the quality of the product, but project managers also care about the quality of the process. In fact, how something gets carried out is as important as the end result. The philosophy of quality covered in this chapter is derived from several leading theories, including TQM, ISO-9000, Six Sigma, and others. We will look at each of these theories in terms of the tools and techniques they provide.

The philosophy of quality is also a very proactive approach. Whereas early approaches to quality relied heavily on inspection, current thinking is focused on prevention since it costs more to fix an error than it does to prevent one. Keep in mind that you can never inspect quality into a product, but you can deliberately plan for it from the start.

The responsibility for quality rests heavily on the project manager. Everyone on the team can contribute to project quality; however, it is management's responsibility to provide the resources to make quality happen, and the project manager is ultimately responsible and accountable for the quality of the project.

Watch The Video
http://**prep.pm**/8-1

Difficulty:
HIGH

Memorization:
HIGH

Exam Importance:
MEDIUM

Chapter Notes:

The processes of Quality Management with their primary outputs

Chapter Notes:

_____

_____

_____

_____

_____

_____

_____

_____

_____

_____

_____

_____

_____

_____

When it comes to quality, the way in which things are done is perhaps more important here than most other places. Plan Quality Management, Manage Quality, and Control Quality map closely to the Plan-Do-Check-Act cycle as described by Deming, and you should expect that several questions on the exam will rely heavily on your understanding of how quality activities flow and connect.

It is also important to understand that some of the investment in quality is usually borne by the organization since it would be far too expensive for each project to have its own quality program. An example would be a company investing in a site license for a software testing product that can be used across numerous projects.

IMPORTANCE:

Project quality management has fewer processes than many chapters, but it is important on the exam, and you should expect to see several exam questions that will relate directly to this chapter. It will be necessary to become acquainted with the terms and theories as described below. Then reread this chapter to ensure that you have mastered the topic.

In real world practice, quality formulas abound; however, you do not need to memorize or apply them here. This chapter focuses on the processes, concepts and terms. Some parts of this topic will be revisited in later chapters to show how quality fits into the overall project management context.

PREPARATION:

You will need to learn and understand the content in this chapter. Special attention will be paid to the key quality theories that are exam favorites, as well as terminology that you need to know.

Pay careful attention to the differences between Plan Quality Management, Manage Quality, and Control Quality. These distinctions can be trickier than most planning, executing, monitoring and controlling combinations for many people on the exam.

Definition of Quality

The definition of quality you should know for the exam is "the degree to which a set of inherent characteristics fulfills requirements." It is also important to know that the requirements or needs of the project may be stated or merely implied. A product may be low-grade and high-quality at the same time if the requirements call for a low-grade product. If you find this concept confusing, this chapter should help clear things up and get you ready for the exam.

Quality Management Processes

There are only three processes within project quality management, as listed in the table below. In the framework, these processes touch three process groups: planning (Plan Quality Management), executing (Manage Quality), and monitoring & controlling (Control Quality).

Process Group	Quality Management Process
Initiating	(none)
Planning	Plan Quality Management
Executing	Manage Quality
Monitoring & Controlling	Control Quality
Closing	(none)

The primary outputs associated with the three quality management processes are shown in the table below.

Process	Primary Outputs
Plan Quality Management	Quality Management Plan Quality Metrics
Manage Quality	Change Requests, Test and Evaluation Documents
Control Quality	Quality Control Measurements Verified Deliverables

Chapter Eight

QUALITY TERMS AND PHILOSOPHIES:

Each of these quality management terms are important for the exam.

Total Quality Management (TQM) - A quality theory popularized after World War II that states that everyone in the company is responsible for quality and is able to make a difference in the ultimate quality of the product. TQM applies to improvements in processes and in results. TQM also includes statistical process control.

TQM was invented by Walter Shewhart at Western Electric; however, it was W. Edwards Deming who made it popular by implementing it successfully in Japan after World War II. Today, Japan gives the Deming Prize as their national award for quality.

TQM shifts the primary quality focus away from the product that is produced and looks instead at the underlying process of how it was produced. It involves all employees in the quality process.

In other words, how something is produced becomes more important than what is actually produced, because a good process will ultimately yield good results.

Continuous Improvement - Also known as "Kaizen," from the Japanese management term. A philosophy that stresses constant process improvement, in the form of small changes in products or services. It comes from the Plan-Do-Check-Act cycle described by Shewhart and Deming. Continuous improvement seeks to make an ongoing series of small changes to improve the product and the process.

Kaizen - (See *Continuous Improvement*)

Just-In-Time (JIT) - A manufacturing method that brings inventory down to zero (or near zero) levels. It forces a focus on quality, since there is no excess inventory on hand to waste.

Chapter Notes:

_____

_____

_____

_____

_____

_____

_____

_____

_____

_____

_____

_____

_____

ISO 9000 - Part of the International Organization for Standardization to ensure that companies document what they do and do what they document.

ISO 9000 is not directly attributable to higher quality, but may be an important component of Manage Quality, since it ensures that an organization follows their processes.

Statistical Independence - When the outcomes of two processes are not linked together or dependent upon each other, they are statistically independent. Rolling a six on a die the first time neither increases nor decreases the chance that you will roll a six the second time. Therefore, the two rolls would be statistically independent.

Mutually Exclusive - A statistical term that states that one choice excludes the others. For example, painting a house yellow and painting it blue or white are mutually exclusive events. Likewise, flipping a coin results in an outcome of heads or tails. One result excludes the other.

Standard Deviation - The concept of standard deviation is an important one to understand for the exam. Standard deviation is a statistical calculation used to measure and describe how a set of data is organized. The following graphic of a standard bell curve illustrates standard deviation.

The standard deviation, represented by the Greek symbol σ (sigma), is calculated first by averaging all data points to get the mean, then calculating the difference between each data point and the mean, squaring each of the differences, and dividing the sum of the squared differences by the number of data points minus one. Finally, take the square root of that number, and you have the standard deviation of the data set. If the data set is "normally distributed," as it is in the following chart, the following statistics will be true:

- 68.25% of the data points (or values) will fall within 1 σ from the mean.

- 95.46% of the values will fall within 2 σ from the mean.

- 99.73% of the values will fall within 3 σ from the mean.

- 99.99966% of the values will fall within 6 σ from the mean.

Chapter Eight

Chapter Notes:

_____

_____

_____

_____

_____

_____

_____

_____

_____

_____

_____

_____

_____

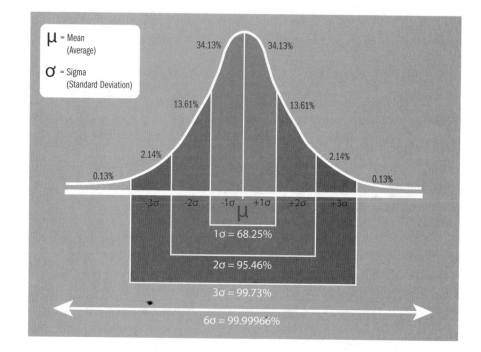

The standard deviation may be used in a few different ways in quality. For instance, the higher your standard deviation, the more diverse your data points are. It is also used to set quality levels (see the Six Sigma topic later in this chapter), and to set control limits to determine if a process is in control (see the Control Charts topic later in this chapter).

Even though you should not expect to have to perform standard deviation calculations for the exam, you will likely see questions related to the application of the standard deviation. The more you understand about this concept, the more prepared you will be for the exam.

Six Sigma - Six Sigma is a popular philosophy of quality management that focuses on achieving very high levels of quality by controlling the process and reducing defects (a defect is defined as anything that does not meet the customer's quality standards).

A σ (sigma) is defined as 1 standard deviation from the mean. At the level of 1 sigma quality, 68.25% of all outputs will meet quality standards.

At the 3 sigma quality level, that number jumps to 99.73% of all outputs that meet quality standards. At the 6 sigma level, the number is 99.99966% of all outputs that meet quality standards. This means that when quality reaches six sigma standards, the results will be such that only 3.4 out of every 1,000,000 outputs do not meet quality standards.

Six sigma quality strives to make the overwhelming majority of the bell curve fall consistently within customer quality limits.

Six sigma puts a primary focus on quantifying, measuring, and controlling the quality of products, services, and results. It is based on the underlying theory that anything will vary if measured to a fine enough level. The goal is to refine the process so that human error and outside influence no longer influence results, and any remaining variations are completely random.

If done properly, the statistical outcome should follow the bell curve illustrated previously under the topic of standard deviation. The goal is to make six standard deviations (sigmas) of the outputs fall within the customer's quality limits.

If this seems like a lot of information, the most important things to know for the exam are that six sigma is a quality management philosophy that sets very high standards for quality, 1 sigma quality is the lowest quality level, allowing 317,500 defects per 1,000,000 opportunities, 3 sigma quality is higher, allowing 2,700 defects per 1,000,000 opportunities, and 6 sigma quality is the highest of these, allowing only 3.4 defects per 1,000,000 opportunities.

Also know that six sigma quality levels may not be high enough for all projects or all industries. For instance, the pharmaceutical industry, the airline industry, and power utilities typically strive for higher levels of quality than six sigma would specify in some areas of their production and operations.

Prevention vs. Inspection - Prevention is simply keeping defects from occurring, while inspection is about identifying and catching the errors that have occurred before they impact others outside the project.

Project management strongly favors prevention over inspection.

Chapter Notes:

Quality Management Terms

Chapter Eight

Chapter Notes:

_____

_____

_____

_____

_____

_____

_____

_____

_____

_____

_____

_____

_____

_____

Attribute Sampling vs. Variable Sampling - Attribute sampling is binary; either a work result conforms to quality or it does not. Variable sampling, on the other hand, measures how well something conforms to quality. Consider, for example, a production facility making prescription drugs. Using attribute sampling, they would define tolerances, a batch of product would be tested, and it would either pass or fail that inspection. Using variable sampling, however, the batch of product would be rated on a continuous scale (perhaps on parts per billion) that showed how well the batch conformed to ideal quality.

Special Causes vs. Common Causes - Within the topic of statistical process control (see Control Charts later in this chapter), there is a concept of special causes and common causes.

Special causes are typically considered unusual and preventable, whereas common causes are normal. For instance, if your manufacturing process produced 250 defects per 1,000,000 due to assembly errors, that might be considered a special cause, whereas if your manufacturing process produced one defect in a million due to fluctuations in the quality of the raw materials, that might be considered a common cause. Special causes are considered preventable by process improvement, while common causes are generally accepted.

Tolerances vs. Control Limits - Tolerances deal with the limits your project has set for product acceptance. For instance, you may specify that any product will be accepted if it weighs between 13.7 grams and 15 grams. Those weights would represent your tolerances. Control limits, on the other hand, are a more complex concept. Typically, control limits are set at three standard deviations above and below the mean. As long as your results fall within the control limits, your process is considered to be in control.

Control limits are explained further under the topic of Control Charts, covered later in this chapter.

To sum up this topic, consider that tolerances focus on whether the product is acceptable, while control limits focus on whether the process itself is acceptable.

Customer Satisfaction - The concept of customer satisfaction runs throughout quality management. There are two main components to this: fitness for use and conformance to requirements. The easiest way to think about this is to look at whether the deliverable solves the underlying need and whether it works properly. In other words, does it do the right thing, and does it do the thing right.

Management Responsibility - Everyone from the top to the bottom is responsible for quality, but it is management's job to make sure that the focus stays on quality management and that initiatives have adequate resources and funding.

Mutually Beneficial Partnership with Suppliers - In a quality-driven organization, relationships with vendors and the supply chain are particularly critical. These suppliers are an extended part of the organization, and strong, positive relationships that benefit both parties are key. Because of this, decisions are made for the long term and not for a quick advantage.

Agile Projects - Adaptive and agile methodologies' approach to quality is to get the product in the customer's hands as quickly as possible and to prioritize and adapt constantly. Quality is an integral part of the project from the start and the focus continues throughout. To make this work, agile takes on small tasks, gets feedback from users, and improves the product. If a problem occurs, it should be detected early and thus cost less and require fewer resources to fix than if it were detected later.

Chapter Notes:

Quality Management Terms

Chapter Eight

···· PLANNING

PLAN QUALITY MANAGEMENT

6th Edition PMBOK® Guide
Cross Ref. pg 277

WHAT IT IS:

Plan Quality Management is named very appropriately. It is the process where the project team identifies what the quality specifications are for this project and how these specifications will be met on the project.

WHY IT IS IMPORTANT:

A very important concept for the exam is that quality is "planned in" from the start, and not "inspected in" after the product has been designed and constructed. Plan Quality Management is the process where this planning is performed to make sure that the resulting product is of acceptable quality. It also explains how quality will be defined and measured.

Watch The Video
▶ http://prep.pm/8-2

WHEN IT IS PERFORMED:

Plan Quality Management begins early in the project. In fact, it typically is performed concurrently with other planning processes and the development of the project management plan.

The reason Plan Quality Management is performed early in project planning is that decisions made about quality can have a significant impact on other decisions such as scope, time, cost, and risk.

Chapter Notes:

_____

_____

_____

_____

_____

_____

_____

_____

HOW IT WORKS / INPUTS:

Project Charter - The charter often provides acceptance criteria that could include quality standards for acceptance.

Project Management Plan - The project management plan is brought into Plan Quality Management, with particular attention paid to the four components covered here.

Requirements Management Plan - The level of quality and how it will be measured is often part of the requirements for the project. In this case, it will be contained in the requirements management plan.

Risk Management Plan - Quality can be a significant area of project risk. For example, it may be identified that there may be issues related to customer acceptance or satisfaction if quality is not satisfied. The risk management plan will define how these particular risks will be identified and managed.

Stakeholder Engagement Plan - There may be stakeholders with expertise in quality, or who work in a quality-related department, who should be involved in the Plan Quality Management process, or who have a particular interest in the outcome.

Scope Baseline - Most project management practitioners view scope and quality as inseparable, which is why the scope baseline is so important to Plan Quality Management. The scope baseline defines the full project requirements, and it also specifies the acceptance criteria for these requirements.

Chapter Notes:

_____

_____

_____

_____

_____

_____

_____

_____

_____

_____

_____

_____

_____

Plan Quality Management

Chapter Eight

Chapter Notes:

_____

_____

_____

_____

_____

_____

_____

_____

_____

_____

_____

_____

_____

Project Documents — See Ch. 2, Common Inputs

Enterprise Environmental Factors — See Ch. 2, Common Inputs

Organizational Process Assets - Assets such as quality management plans from previous projects should be considered and used as part of your project plan. Also, the performing organization's quality policy should be brought into this process. The quality policy is usually brief and defines the performing organization's attitudes and standards related to quality across all projects. It must be considered if it exists. If it does not exist, the project team should write one for this project.

HOW IT WORKS / TOOLS:

Expert Judgment — See Ch. 2, Common Tools

 Data Gathering - Looking at other projects (benchmarking) to determine the right approach to quality, brainstorming, and interviews with others are some ways to gather data for this process.

 Data Analysis - Quality can be expensive to achieve; however, there is a golden rule in quality that all benefits of quality activities must outweigh the costs.

No activities should be performed that cost more (or even the same) as the expected benefits. These anticipated benefits potentially include acceptance, less rework, and overall lower costs.

A technique of evaluating the cost of quality (often abbreviated as COQ) looks at all of the costs that will be realized in order to achieve quality. The costs of items that do not conform to quality are known as "cost of poor quality," often abbreviated as CoPQ.

 Decision Making - This technique is a common one, but it is marked as key here due to the importance of multicriteria decision analysis. This is a matrix that allows several factors to be ranked and prioritized so that the most important or critical ones become evident.

⊕ **Data Representation** - Process flow diagrams, or flowcharts, are a way to show all quality activities and decisions. Also logical data models, matrix diagrams, and mind mapping are popular ways of visualizing data.

Flowchart	Logical Data Model
Matrix Diagram	Mindmap

One flowcharting tool that is popular in quality management is the SIPOC value chain. It helps visualize the flow of (S)uppliers and (I)nputs through the (P)rocess to create (O)utputs to the (C)ustomers.

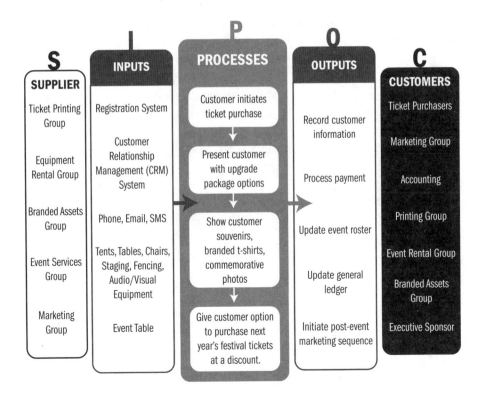

S

INPUTS

SUPPLIER

Ticket Printing Group

Equipment Rental Group

Branded Assets Group

Event Services Group

Marketing Group

Registration System

Customer Relationship Management (CRM) System

Phone, Email, SMS

Tents, Tables, Chairs, Staging, Fencing, Audio/Visual Equipment

Event Table

P

PROCESSES

Customer initiates ticket purchase

Present customer with upgrade package options

Show customer souvenirs, branded t-shirts, commemorative photos

Give customer option to purchase next year's festival tickets at a discount.

O

OUTPUTS

Record customer information

Process payment

Update event roster

Update general ledger

Initiate post-event marketing sequence

C

CUSTOMERS

Ticket Purchasers

Marketing Group

Accounting

Printing Group

Event Rental Group

Branded Assets Group

Executive Sponsor

Chapter Notes:

Plan Quality Management

Test and Inspection Planning - Inspection is still an important part of quality even though it is true that quality cannot be inspected in. These inspections and tests should be scheduled and planned from the start.

Meetings — See Ch. 2, Common Tools

HOW IT WORKS / OUTPUTS:

Quality Management Plan - The quality management plan defines the standards, tools, responsibilities, and activities needed to achieve the quality goals. It also specifies the quality activities and roles needed to carry them out.

Eventually the quality management plan will become integrated into the project plan.

Quality Metrics - By itself, "quality" can be a fuzzy concept, but it can become very meaningful when metrics are applied. Quality metrics are objective, and they allow quality to be measured, quantified, and defined. They are an output here, but they will be an important input into the Control Quality process.

Metrics such as the number of defects, weights and measures, amount of overtime logged, the hours spend on rework, downtime, customer survey results, or response time would all be beneficial.

Project Management Plan Updates —
See Ch. 2, Common Outputs

Project Documents Updates — See Ch. 2, Common Outputs

Plan Quality Management

···· EXECUTING

MANAGE QUALITY

WHAT IT IS:

For many people, Manage Quality can be one of the trickiest of the 49 processes to understand. One of the most common mistakes exam takers make is to confuse Manage Quality with Control Quality (covered next), and the difference between the two can appear subtle at times since the two processes go hand in hand.

Manage Quality is sometimes referred to as Quality Assurance, and it relates to both product design and to process improvement.

Manage Quality is an executing process, and it has two primary purposes:

1. To put the quality management plan into practice and to see that the product, service, or result achieves quality.

2. To improve and streamline the overall process of producing the product, service, or result.

WHY IT IS IMPORTANT:

Manage Quality is important because if the quality of the process and activities is improved, then quality of the product should also improve, and an overall reduction of cost should follow.

On waterfall projects, the project manager is ultimately responsible for quality, while on agile projects, the entire team is jointly responsible for quality.

6th Edition PMBOK® Guide
Cross Ref. pg 288

Watch The Video

▶ http://**prep.pm/8-3**

Chapter Notes:

_____
_____
_____
_____
_____
_____
_____
_____

Chapter Eight

Chapter Notes:

_____

_____

_____

_____

_____

_____

_____

_____

_____

_____

_____

_____

_____

WHEN IT IS PERFORMED:

The process of Manage Quality is performed as an ongoing activity in the project life cycle. It typically begins early and continues throughout the life of the project. Because Manage Quality uses many of the outputs of Plan Quality Management, it is not undertaken until after Plan Quality Management has been performed.

HOW IT WORKS / INPUTS:

Project Management Plan — See Ch. 2, Common Inputs

Project Documents — See Ch. 2, Common Inputs

Organizational Process Assets — See Ch. 2, Common Inputs

HOW IT WORKS / TOOLS:

Data Gathering - One common data gathering technique is to use checklists. These are used to ensure that all steps were performed and were carried out in the proper sequence and to make sure the needed requirements were met. These may be developed internally or standard ones may be available for some tasks from outside sources.

 Data Analysis - This tool is covered in Ch 2 but you should know that the most important techniques it uses are alternatives analysis, process analysis, and root cause analysis.

Decision Making — See Ch. 2, Common Tools

 Data Representation - Visualizing data can be a tremendous help in understanding problems and identifying trends.

> **Affinity Diagrams** - Affinity diagrams help visually relate bits of information to other bits of information. They are used to help discover or create meaningful systems of organization. Most mind mapping techniques make use of affinity diagrams to help represent information the way the human brain processes and stores information.

Another hypothetical use of an affinity diagram would be to initially write production problems onto individual sticky note cards and place them randomly on the wall, then use the affinity system to create four categories and move each note card under one of the categories.

Cause-and-Effect Diagrams - Also called Ishikawa diagrams, fishbone diagrams, and why-why diagrams, these charts are used to help identify root causes. Quality problems are traced back to their root causes so that prevention may be used instead of inspection.

Flowcharts - Flowcharts show how various components relate in a system. Flowcharting can be used to predict where quality problems may happen since quality issues are often the result of a combination of risk occurrences. In addition to traditional flow charts, cause-and-effect diagrams, described above, are a type of flowcharting.

Histograms - Histograms are primarily used in manage quality to show the number of times an issue occurs. A Pareto chart is a histogram where issues are ranked by frequency of occurrence from greatest to least.

Chapter Notes:

_____

_____

_____

_____

_____

_____

_____

_____

_____

_____

_____

_____

Manage Quality

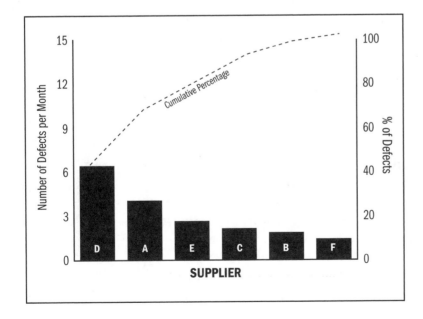

Example of a Pareto Chart, a type of histogram.

Chapter Eight

Chapter Notes:

_____

_____

_____

_____

_____

_____

_____

_____

_____

_____

_____

_____

_____

_____

Matrix Diagrams - A matrix diagram shows the relationship between the different elements by describing the type of relationship for each cell where a row and column intersect. This description could be the characteristic of the relationship or the quality or strength of it. Different shapes and dimensions are useful, depending on how many items there are to evaluate.

Scatter Diagrams - Scatter diagrams are a particularly powerful tool for spotting trends in data. Consider the following three scatter diagrams:

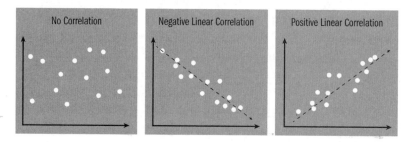

These diagrams show how data may be correlated along an X and Y axis. For example if the Y (vertical) axis were your score on an exam, and the X (horizontal) axis represented the number of hours you spent preparing, you might expect a positive, linear correlation; however, if you were using bad information to prepare, you might see no correlation or even a negative linear correlation.

Scatter diagrams can help you identify a pattern from multiple data points that may not be evident otherwise.

Audits - Quality audits are a key tool in Manage Quality. The reason for this is that audits review the project to evaluate which activities taking place on the project should be improved and which meet quality standards. The goal of the audits is to improve both the acceptance of the product and the overall cost of quality.

Keep in mind that you are auditing the quality of the process and the activities.

Quality audits are usually carried out by an objective person or team, and it is best if they are not part of the project team.

Design for X - One important consideration in quality management is that everything cannot be the top priority. Organizations, engineers, and project planners need to decide which things are the most important. That is where Design for Excellence (DfX) comes in.

DfX is a methodology where design is applied to the top priorities. For example, a popular smart phone had major issues with assembly of the components where there simply was not enough space inside the case for the technicians to put it together. A luxury car manufacturer had an issue where the back seat had to be removed and the carpet in the floor had to be cut in order to access the car's battery. These are examples of design decisions that had a significant impact on the project.

There are several notable prioritizations for DfX including:

- DfC (Design for Cost). Designing with cost efficiency being the key priority.

- DfA (Design for Assembly). Designing to prioritize for ease, accuracy, and efficiency of assembly of the components.

- DfM (Design for Manufacturing). Designing to prioritize around the best way to manufacture the product and its components.

- DfL (Design for Logistics). Designing to prioritize sourcing components from the most efficient locations.

- DfS (Design for Serviceability). Designing to prioritize optimal ease of repair and service.

Chapter Notes:

Manage Quality

Chapter Eight

Chapter Notes:

_____

_____

_____

_____

_____

_____

_____

_____

_____

_____

_____

_____

_____

_____

Problem Solving - It is common for problems to be uncovered in this process. Particularly in the world of quality management, problem solving takes on a structured approach. The following diagram illustrates the overall way that problems are approached in Manage Quality.

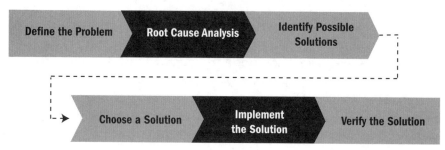

 Quality Improvement Methods - As the previous tool of problem solving is implemented, it is common to find opportunities for quality improvement. The process of Plan-Do-Check-Act and Six Sigma are the two that are most frequently used.

HOW IT WORKS / OUTPUTS:

Quality Reports - The important thing to keep in mind with quality reports is that these reports can be quantitative (numerical) or qualitative (based on the qualities of something rather than numerical measures).

Test and Evaluation Documents - When it comes to the process of Manage Quality, more things are structured and measured than in most other processes. Test and evaluation documents include things like quality checklists and requirements traceability matrices.

Change Requests — See Ch. 2, Common Outputs

Project Management Plan Updates —
See Ch. 2, Common Outputs

Project Document Updates — See Ch. 2, Common Outputs

···· MONITORING & CONTROLLING

CONTROL QUALITY

WHAT IT IS:

If you are inspecting the product or looking at some kind of result, you are probably performing the process of Control Quality. This process looks at specific results to determine if they conform to the quality standards. It involves both product and project deliverables, and it is done throughout the project, not just at the end.

In many cases, Control Quality uses statistical sampling rather than looking at each and every output. Many volumes have been written about sampling techniques, and the practice is often very complex and is highly tailored to industry.

This process uses the tool of inspection to make sure the results of the work are what they are supposed to be. Any time you find a part being inspected for quality, you can be sure that you are in Control Quality.

WHY IT IS IMPORTANT:

Control Quality is the process where each deliverable is inspected, measured, and tested. This process makes sure that everything produced meets quality standards.

WHEN IT IS PERFORMED:

This process typically takes place throughout much of the project. It is performed beginning with the production of the first product deliverable and continues until all of the deliverables have been accepted.

6th Edition PMBOK® Guide
Cross Ref. pg 298

Watch The Video
http://**prep.pm/8-4**

Chapter Notes:

_____

_____

_____

_____

_____

_____

_____

_____

Chapter Eight

Chapter Notes:

_____

_____

_____

_____

_____

_____

_____

_____

_____

_____

_____

_____

_____

HOW IT WORKS / INPUTS:

Project Management Plan - The quality management plan is the main component of the project management plan that is of interest here. It provides the plan for how Control Quality will be carried out.

Project Documents - Usually project documents are generic and are not broken out as a key input; however, in this case they are. The documents here include the lessons learned register, the quality metrics, and the test and evaluation documents. These provide the documentation to show how effective the quality management activities are.

Approved Change Requests - These flow into this process from Perform Integrated Change Control.

Deliverables - In controlling processes, you want the plan and the results of executing that plan so that the two may be compared. In this case, the deliverables represent the results of the execution, and they are compared against the quality management plan to see how the two line up.

Work Performance Data - Keep in mind that how the work is being carried out can be every bit as important as the deliverables themselves. Even if the product is of acceptable quality, if it took significant rework or overtime to achieve, that would be an issue. The work performance data can shed light on the current state of the how the deliverable is being provided.

Enterprise Environmental Factors — See Ch. 2, Common Inputs

Organizational Process Assets — See Ch. 2, Common Inputs

HOW IT WORKS / TOOLS:

Data Gathering - Checklists, check sheets, statistical sampling, and questionnaires and surveys are the key methods of data gathering used here. They are used to gather information about how the quality management plan is lining up with reality.

Data Analysis — See Ch. 2, Common Tools

Inspection - The tool of inspection is the most important tool in this process. It looks at the product, service, or result to ensure that its quality is within the specification. As important as inspection is, you should remember that quality cannot be inspected into the product; it has to be planned in from the start.

Testing / Product Evaluations - This is similar to the previous tool, inspection, although inspection typically deals with a physical product, and testing may also include things like software. Testing and product evaluation may include things like:

Stress testing – applying unusual loads or circumstances

Unit testing – reviewing small components individually

Usability testing – monitoring how users will interact with the system

Regression testing – ensuring that the product being evaluated is compatible with previous versions

Integration testing – making sure new components integrate with existing components and that the system as a whole works

Burn-in testing – performing a long-term test to ensure overall stability

Data Representation - The goal of data representation is summed up in the adage "a picture is worth a thousand words." The goal is to show data in order to make it more easily understood. Common data representation techniques in quality management include cause-and-effect diagrams, control charts, histograms, and scatter diagrams.

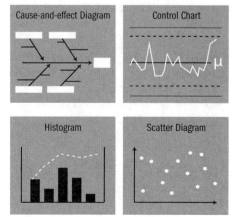

Chapter Eight

Chapter Notes:

_____

_____

_____

_____

_____

_____

_____

_____

_____

_____

_____

_____

_____

_____

Control Charts - Control charts are part of a set of quality practices known as Statistical Process Control. If a process is statistically "in control," it does not need to be corrected. If it is "out of control," then there are sufficient variations in results to the point where production is generally stopped until it can be brought back statistically in line. A control chart is one way of depicting variations and determining whether or not the process is in control.

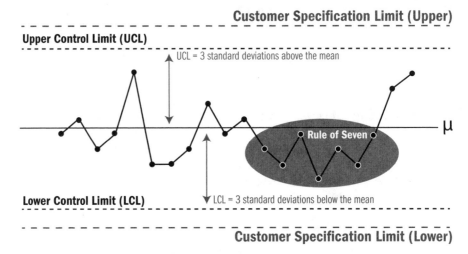

A sample control chart

Control charts graph the results of a process to show whether or not they are in control. The mean of all of the data points is represented by a line drawn through the average of all data points on the chart. The upper and lower control limits are set at three standard deviations above and below mean.

If measurements fall outside of the control limits, then the process is said to be out of control. The assignable cause should then be investigated and determined.

An interesting rule that is used with control charts is known as the rule of seven. It states that if seven or more consecutive data points fall on one side of the mean, they should be investigated. This is true even if the seven data points are within the control limits.

Some control charts, especially those used in a manufacturing environment, represent the upper and lower limits of a customer's specification for quality as lines on the control chart. Everything between those lines would be considered within the customer's quality specification.

Meetings — See Ch. 2, Common Tools

HOW IT WORKS / OUTPUTS:

Quality Control Measurements - The results of control quality should be documented and measured. The quality management plan specifies how this will take place.

Verified Deliverables - The project's verified deliverables are one of the most important outputs in any project. The deliverables have been inspected and measured to ensure that they conform to quality standards.

These verified deliverables become inputs to the Validate Scope process where the team seeks final approval of the product, service, or result.

Work Performance Information —
See Ch. 2, Common Outputs

Change Requests — See Ch. 2, Common Outputs

Project Management Plan Updates —
See Ch. 2, Common Outputs

Project Documents Updates — See Ch. 2, Common Outputs

Chapter Notes:

_____

_____

_____

_____

_____

_____

_____

_____

_____

_____

_____

_____

_____

Control Quality

Chapter Eight

Chapter Notes:

_____

_____

_____

_____

_____

_____

_____

_____

_____

_____

_____

_____

_____

_____

 **The Agile Perspective on Quality Management**

The Agile perspective on quality management is to place the product in the hands of the customer very early to get a sense of its fitness for use. Quality activities begin early on the project and they break work into short iterations with small batches of features. The advantage is that customer feedback may be gathered quickly, and problems or issues may be detected earlier, helping the project to stay on track.

Agile retrospective takes place at the end of each iteration, with small adjustments being made to the process in order to improve quality.

QUALITY MANAGEMENT
QUESTIONS

1. You are a project manager, and your manager wants to meet with you to evaluate your project's performance in order to see how it is meeting the quality standards supplied by the company. In what process is your boss engaged?

    A. Total Quality Management.

    B. Control Quality.

    C. Plan Quality Management.

    D. Manage Quality.

2. If you were using a fishbone diagram to determine root causes of problems, you would be involved in:

    A. Perform Quality Inspection.

    B. Perform Quality Prevention.

    C. Control Quality.

    D. Perform Quality Audits.

3. Plan Quality Management includes all of the following outputs EXCEPT:

    A. Quality management plan.

    B. Accepted deliverables.

    C. Quality metrics.

    D. Project management plan updates.

Chapter Notes:

_____

_____

_____

_____

_____

_____

_____

_____

_____

_____

_____

_____

_____

_____

_____

Chapter Notes:

_____

_____

_____

_____

_____

_____

_____

_____

_____

_____

_____

_____

_____

_____

4. **In a control chart, the mean is represented as a horizontal line. This represents:**

   A. The average of the control limits.

   B. The average of all data points.

   C. The average of all data points that are within control limits.

   D. A means of identifying assignable cause.

5. **The quality team is meeting to discuss quality as it pertains to a new building product. The group is having some difference of opinion as to the Cost of Quality (COQ). Which of the four statements made by the team is true regarding the cost of quality?**

   A. COQ does not include testing, destructive tests, and inspections in the calculations.

   B. COQ should categorize all product failures as preventable or non-preventable.

   C. COQ should include all costs to prevent nonconformance over the life of the product.

   D. All other things being equal, a lower overall COQ is indicative of a higher-quality product.

6. **Quality audits are an important part of quality management because:**

   A. They allow for quantification of the risk.

   B. They randomly audit product results to see if they are meeting quality standards.

   C. They check to see if the quality process is being followed.

   D. They are conducted without prior notice and do not allow team members time to cover up defects.

7. If the results of Activity A have no bearing on the results of Activity B, the two activities would be considered:

   A. Statistically unique.

   B. Statistically independent.

   C. Correlated, but not causal.

   D. Mutually exclusive.

8. The BEST tool to use to look for results that are out of control is:

   A. Pareto chart.

   B. Control chart.

   C. Ishikawa diagram.

   D. Statistical sampling.

9. You are a project manager with limited resources on the project. Several quality defects have been discovered, causing the stakeholders to be concerned. You wish to begin by attacking the causes that have the highest number of defects associated with them. Which tool shows defects by volume from greatest to least?

   A. Pareto chart.

   B. Control chart.

   C. Ishikawa diagram.

   D. Cause-and-effect diagram.

10. A SIPOC diagram is mostly closely associated with which quality management tool/technique?

    A. Cost of Quality.

    B. Test and inspection planning.

    C. Data representation.

    D. Design for X.

Chapter Notes:

_____

_____

_____

_____

_____

_____

_____

_____

_____

_____

_____

_____

_____

_____

Quality Management: Questions

Chapter Notes:

_____

_____

_____

_____

_____

_____

_____

_____

_____

_____

_____

_____

_____

_____

11. In the process of managing a construction project, you discover a very serious defect in the way one particular section has been built. Your engineers analyze the section of the building and decide that the problem is actually relatively minor. In which process are you involved?

   A. Plan Quality Management.

   B. Manage Quality.

   C. Control Quality.

   D. Project Quality Management.

12. You are performing a project that has a lot in common with a project completed by your company two years ago. You want to use the previous project to help you determine quality standards for your project. Which of the following tools would be the BEST one to help you with this?

   A. Benchmarking.

   B. Control chart.

   C. ISO 9000.

   D. Total Quality Management.

13. Which of the following is most representative of the Total Quality Management philosophy?

   A. Decreasing inventory to zero or near zero levels.

   B. Everyone can contribute to quality.

   C. Zero defects.

   D. Continuous improvement is preferred over disruptive change.

14. **Which of these quality standards is the highest?**

    A. It is impossible to determine without further information.

    B. 99% quality.

    C. Three sigma quality.

    D. Six sigma quality.

15. **Which quality process is performed first?**

    A. Plan Quality Management.

    B. Manage Quality.

    C. Control Quality.

    D. Quality Definition.

16. **If a project team is drawing a tree diagram on the board, which of the following would mostly likely be used?**

    A. An organizational breakdown structure.

    B. A cause-and-effect diagram.

    C. A finite branch diagram.

    D. A network diagram.

Chapter Notes:

_____

_____

_____

_____

_____

_____

_____

_____

_____

_____

_____

_____

_____

_____

Quality Management: Questions

Chapter Notes:

_____

_____

_____

_____

_____

_____

_____

_____

_____

_____

_____

_____

_____

_____

17. **A project team is having their first quality meeting and plans to review the organization's quality policy when it is discovered that the company has never developed an organizational quality policy. The project manager is very concerned about this discovery. What would be the BEST course of action?**

   A. Document the absence of a quality policy in the quality management plan and take corrective action.

   B. Write a quality policy just for this project.

   C. Substitute benchmark data for the quality policy.

   D. Delay execution until the organization provides clarity.

18. **On a control chart, the customer's acceptable quality limits are represented as:**

   A. Control limits.

   B. Mean.

   C. Specification.

   D. Normal distribution.

19. **A customer is concerned that the quality process is not being followed as laid out in the quality management plan. The best way to see if this claim is accurate is:**

   A. Random sampling.

   B. Kaizen.

   C. Personally participate in the quality inspections.

   D. Audits.

20. Which of the following would NOT be associated with data representation techniques used in quality-related activities:

    A. Affinity diagram.

    B. Kanban board.

    C. Histogram.

    D. Scatter diagram.

21. Your organization practices just-in-time management. Which of the following would be the highest concern for a project manager operating in this company?

    A. Absenteeism.

    B. Lower quality of parts.

    C. Conflicting quality processes.

    D. Inventory arriving late.

22. Reduced quality on a project would MOST likely lead to which of the following?

    A. Rework and increased cost risk.

    B. Absenteeism and decreased cost.

    C. Increased inspections and decreased cost.

    D. Reduced quality limits.

Chapter Notes:

_____

_____

_____

_____

_____

_____

_____

_____

_____

_____

_____

_____

_____

_____

_____

Quality Management: Questions

Chapter Notes:

_____

_____

_____

_____

_____

_____

_____

_____

_____

_____

_____

_____

_____

23. An organization had a defective unit of product returned. They have asked the team that designed the product to investigate the cause of the failure. After a careful review, the team determines that the product failure is unusual and is related to poor raw materials. They have sampled products from the same batch and have determined that it was not affected by the same problem. The project manager has to report to the Vice President of Quality. How should she describe this problem?

A. A process problem.

B. A quality assurance issue.

C. A special cause.

D. A common cause.

24. Which of the following is NOT a part of the Plan Quality Management process?

A. Benchmarking.

B. Audits.

C. Cost-benefit analysis.

D. Flowcharts

25. A project manager wants to perform a code review, but over two million lines of code have already been written for this project, and more are being produced every day. Rather than reviewing each line of code, the manager should consider:

A. Automated testing tools.

B. Trend analysis.

C. Statistical sampling.

D. Regression analysis.

QUALITY MANAGEMENT
ANSWERS

1. D. In this example your boss is auditing you to see if you are following the process. Remember that audits are a tool of Manage Quality.

2. C. Control Quality is the correct answer here.

3. B. This one should have been one of the easier questions. Accepted deliverables is not an output of Plan Quality Management. It is an output of Verify Scope.

4. B. The mean represents the average of all of the data points shown on the chart, calculated simply by adding the values together and dividing by the number of values. 'C' is not correct because the mean includes everything. If only the values that were within the control limits were used, it could make the mean look better than it should.

5. C. The Cost of Quality (COQ) looks at all costs incurred to prevent nonconformance throughout the life of the product. 'A' is incorrect because it includes all costs related to producing a product that conforms to quality. The ones listed are prime examples of costs that should be included. 'B' is incorrect because product failures are categorized as "Internal" (found through inspection or testing, and "External" (found by the customer) and not as preventable or non-preventable. 'D' is incorrect because spending less overall on quality is not indicative of a higher-quality product. If anything, the opposite would likely be true.

6. C. Audits are a tool of Manage Quality that checks to see if the process is being followed. Choices 'A' and 'D' are incorrect, and choice 'B' is referring to inspection, which is a tool of Control Quality.

7. B. If two events have no bearing on each other, they are statistically independent. Choice 'D' is when two events cannot both happen at the same time.

Chapter Notes:

_____

_____

_____

_____

_____

_____

_____

_____

_____

_____

_____

_____

_____

_____

8. B. That is how a control chart is used. It visually depicts whether a process is in or out of control. Choice 'A' is used in Control Quality to rank problems by frequency. 'C' is used in Control Quality to anticipate problems in advance. Choice 'D' is used in Control Quality to pick random samples to inspect.

9. A. Pareto charts rank defects from greatest to least, showing you what should get the most attention.

10. C. A SIPOC diagram is a way of representing data on a high-level process map that shows the flow from suppliers, inputs, processes, outputs, to customers.

11. C. Control Quality is the best choice here. Your clue here was the fact that your engineers had inspected something specific. This wasn't related to planning or process – it was a physical inspection of a work result, and that is what happens during the Control Quality process.

12. A. Benchmarking takes results from previous projects and uses them to help measure quality on your project. Benchmarks give you something against which you can measure.

13. B. Total Quality Management stresses, among other things, that everyone contributes to the quality of the product and process.

14. D. Six sigma represents that 99.99966% of all work results will be of acceptable quality in the manufacturing process. This is higher than 99% or 3 sigma, which represents a 99.73% quality rate.

15. A. Plan Quality Management should always happen first. Manage Quality and Control Quality would come after the quality management plan is in place. 'D' is not a project management process. Keep in mind that the quality processes do run in a cycle, but planning should always happen first.

16. A. The WBS, RBS, and OBS are examples of tree diagrams. 'B' was a close guess, but it is not a type of tree where one parent node may have multiple child nodes. 'C' was a made up term. 'D' does not work well. Network diagram is its own category and does not fit the concept of a tree diagram.

17. B. If no organizational quality policy exists, you should develop one for this project. 'A' and 'C' are incorrect since you should not proceed without a quality policy. 'D' would be a good way to lose your job! You should try to fix this problem yourself rather than force your organization to write a quality policy.

18. C. The quality specification is the customer's quality requirements. 'A' represents the limits for what is in and out of statistical control, typically set at three standard deviations from the mean. 'B' is the average of all of the data points. 'D' is a statistical term relating to the way the data points are scattered.

19. D. Audits, part of the Manage Quality process, review the process and make sure that the process is being followed.

20. B. Kanban boards are used to represent items flowing through various stages in the workflow. 'A', 'C', and 'D' are data representation techniques.

21. D. The PMP Exam has several questions structured like this one. You could have any of the problems listed here, but the one you would be most concerned with is parts arriving late. An organization that practices just-in-time (JIT) does not keep spare inventory on hand. Instead, the inventory is ordered so that the parts arrive only slightly before they are needed.

22. A. Rework and increased cost and risk are likely outcomes of low quality. 'B' and 'C' are incorrect since decreased cost is not related to low quality. 'D' is incorrect, because you would not lower the quality limits or specifications just because the quality is bad.

Chapter Notes:

_____

_____

_____

_____

_____

_____

_____

_____

_____

_____

_____

_____

_____

_____

Quality Management: Answers

Chapter Eight

Chapter Notes:

_____

_____

_____

_____

_____

_____

_____

_____

_____

_____

_____

_____

_____

_____

23. D. This was a tougher question. A common cause is one that is generally considered not to be preventable, and this falls into that category. 'A' and 'B' are not good answers since we are given no information that points to the fact that there is a process failure that contributed in any way. This problem is related to product failure, and that should have narrowed it down to 'C' or 'D'. 'C' would have been correct if the product had been assembled incorrectly or if there were something that was purely preventable by the project team, but that is not the case. 'D' emerges as the best answer.

24. B. Audits are part of Manage Quality. Choices 'A', 'C', and 'D' are all part of Plan Quality Management.

25. C. Statistical sampling (may appear as random sampling) is the best choice. If the overall population is too large, accurate sampling can give you the same statistical results as measuring the entire population. 'A' might be a good choice in the real world, but you should focus on the inputs, tools, and outputs contained in the *PMBOK® Guide* for the exam, and automated testing tools are not a part of quality management.

Resource Management

PHILOSOPHY:

Resource management has expanded and changed quite a lot with the sixth edition of the *PMBOK® Guide*. Previously, it focused exclusively on human resources, but now it also includes physical resources such as facilities and equipment.

It includes six processes, which makes it one of the more content-rich knowledge areas.

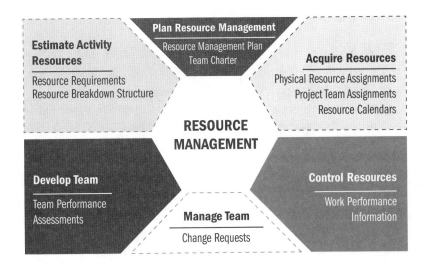

There should be few surprises in this chapter. It follows the standard flow of plan, execute, and monitor and control. You should expect to see several questions on the exam that cover a variety of theories, including leadership, motivation, conflict resolution, and roles within a project.

Watch The Video
http://**prep.pm/9-1**

Difficulty:
MEDIUM
●●●●●○○○○○

Memorization:
MEDIUM
●●●●●●○○○○

Exam Importance:
MEDIUM
●●●●●●○○○○

Chapter Notes:

_____

_____

_____

_____

_____

_____

_____

Chapter Nine

Chapter Notes:

_____

_____

_____

_____

_____

_____

_____

_____

_____

_____

_____

_____

_____

Much of the content in this section is drawn from basic management theory, organizational behavior, psychology, and of course, the field of human resource management. If you have ever studied these subjects, you have probably seen many of the theories in this chapter.

Project managers must also lead people. Some project managers may excel at organizing tasks and planning activities and be dismal at motivating other people; however, in order to be successful, a manager should be able to do both.

This chapter covers the six processes, along with the inputs, tools, and outputs and management theories you will need to know in order to pass the exam.

The approach to the area of resource management is twofold:

1. Define and carefully manage the physical resources on the project.

2. Define a role for everyone on the project and define the responsibilities for each of these roles. Many people make the mistake of only understanding the role of the project manager and never understanding the proper role of senior management, the sponsor, or the team. Project managers must help define roles and influence everyone on the project.

The philosophies of leadership and power are based on the realization that project managers are rarely given complete and unquestioned authority. Instead, they must be able to motivate and persuade people to act in the best interest of the project and must be able to build a team and lead members to give their best efforts.

Also, it is important to understand that although project managers are ultimately responsible for the project, they should delegate assignments to the team. This delegation takes the form of responsibility and authority. The project manager gives responsibility and authority to the team and expects positive results and accountability in return.

An important theme that supports this chapter is that of emotional intelligence (EI). Project managers should be able to identify, assess, and manage their personal emotions as well as the emotions of a group of stakeholders. Managing people requires a different skill set than managing physical resources.

Virtual teams are another area where changes in process and technology have impacted projects. A virtual team is one that works on the same project but not in the same location. There are advantages to the project for using a virtual team. Resources may be available at a lower price or with higher expertise than would otherwise be practical. Other cost savings such as office space and travel may come into play. As good as this sounds, virtual teams present particular challenges to projects and project managers. Communication and collaboration can be more difficult, and team building can be harder since people often never meet or physically interact with their team members.

IMPORTANCE:

Project resource management questions are considered by many people to be among the easiest questions on the exam. This is because this is one of the few sections where many of the questions can often be answered by using common sense. Unless you find these questions particularly difficult, it is a good idea to get comfortable with the information in this chapter and focus your attention on more challenging areas. A careful review of the theories and content prior to taking the exam should be enough to help you through this section.

PREPARATION:

The focus of this chapter will be on resource management along with roles and responsibilities, motivational theories, forms of power, and leadership styles. While this knowledge area is not the most difficult one on the exam, take the time to learn it. Questions from this section will appear on the exam.

You should expect to see questions relating to Tuckman's Ladder, Maslow's Hierarchy, Herzberg's Hygiene Factors, and other theories covered in this chapter on your exam.

Chapter Notes:

Chapter Notes:

_____

_____

_____

_____

_____

_____

_____

_____

_____

_____

_____

_____

_____

This chapter, in particular, contains a significant amount of content that is not found in the *PMBOK® Guide*.

Project Resource Management Processes

There are six processes within project resource management. In the framework, these processes touch three process groups: planning (Plan Resource Management and Estimate Activity Resources), executing (Acquire Resources, Develop Team, and Manage Team), and monitoring and controlling (Control Resources).

Process Group	Resource Management Process
Initiating	(none)
Planning	Plan Resource Management, Estimate Activity Resources
Executing	Acquire Resources, Develop Team, Manage Team
Monitoring & Controlling	Control Resources
Closing	(none)

The primary outputs associated with the six resource management processes are shown in the table below.

Process	Primary Outputs
Plan Resource Management	Resource Management Plan , Team Charter
Estimate Activity Resources	Resource Requirements Resource Breakdown Structure
Acquire Resources	Physical Resource Assignments Project Team Assignments Resource Calendars
Develop Team	Team Performance Assessment
Manage Team	Change Requests
Control Resources	Work Performance Information

···· PLANNING

PLAN RESOURCE MANAGEMENT

WHAT IT IS:

It is a common pattern throughout this book to have a knowledge area that starts off with a planning process to set the tone for the remaining processes in that area. This is the case with resource management, which begins with Plan Resource Management. This process gives guidance to the rest of the resource management processes, defining the roles and responsibilities and creating the resource management plan.

6th Edition *PMBOK® Guide*
Cross Ref. pg 312

WHY IT IS IMPORTANT:

This process lays out how you will staff, manage, team-build, assess, and improve the project team.

Watch The Video

▶ http://**prep.pm/9-2**

WHEN IT IS PERFORMED:

Plan Resource Management typically takes place very early on the project, and it may be performed iteratively. In other words, you may do some work on the scope, some work on the schedule, and then plan resources, and then do more work on the scope, returning again to resources, and so on. It should not be thought of as a process that is tackled only one time.

Chapter Notes:

_____

_____

_____

_____

_____

HOW IT WORKS / INPUTS:

Project Charter — See Ch. 2, Common Inputs

Project Management Plan — See Ch. 2, Common Inputs

_____

_____

_____

Project Documents — See Ch. 2, Common Inputs

Enterprise Environmental Factors — See Ch. 2, Common Inputs

Organizational Process Assets — See Ch. 2, Common Inputs

HOW IT WORKS / TOOLS:

Expert Judgment — See Ch. 2, Common Tools

Data Representation - There are many ways to represent who will be working on the project and what they will be responsible for doing. You need to know about three primary formats:

Hierarchical Charts - A hierarchical chart illustrates responsibilities and relationships. This could be any kind of breakdown structure that shows how responsibilities for deliverables, team members, or resources are allocated and organized. These charts may also be for physical resources, organized logically by type.

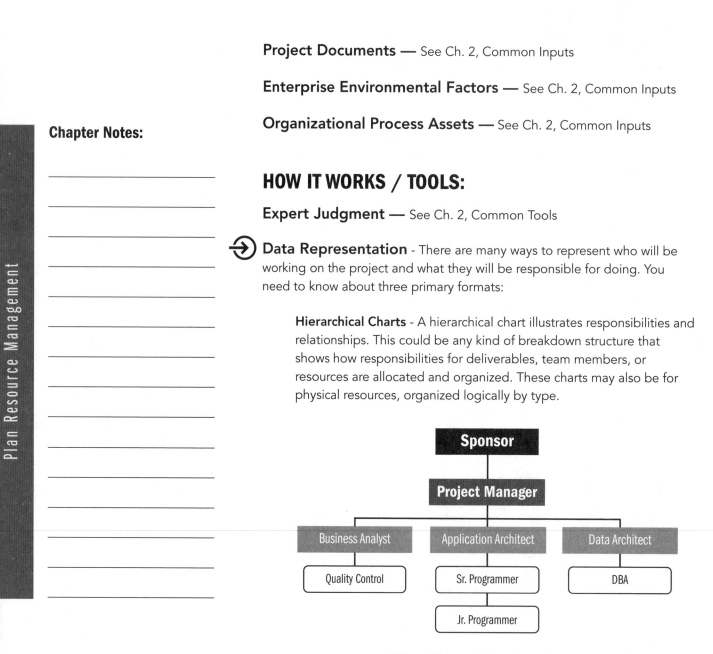

A hierarchical organization chart with positions

Responsibility Assignment Matrix - Matrix charts are another way to depict which roles on the project will be responsible for specific work packages and what their responsibilities will be. One of the most popular categories is the Responsibility Assignment Matrix (RAM),

Chapter Notes:

Plan Resource Management

which displays work packages in the rows and roles in the columns. Each cell shows how a specific role will work on a particular work package.

One common type of the RAM is known as the RACI chart (pronounced "ray-cee"). RACI charts, such as the one that follows, list each work package in the rows and list the roles in the columns. RACI charts derive their name from the way each cell is assigned either an 'R' for Responsible, 'A' for Accountable, 'C' for Consult, or 'I' for Inform. Generally, only one person is assigned accountability for a work package, but more than one person may be responsible for performing the work on a work package.

WORK PACKAGE / ROLE	Project Manager	Business Analyst	Data Architect	Application Architect	Jr. Programmer	Sr. Programmer	Quality Control
Document Scope	C	A					R
Review Scope	A	I	C	C	C	C	C
Approve Scope	A	R	R	R	R	R	R
Create Database	C	C	A	I			
Design Application	I	I	I	A	I	R	C
Code Application	I	I	I	I	R	A	C
Application Testing	I	I	I	I	I	I	A

R = Responsible, A = Accountable, C = Consult, I = Inform

An example of a RAM chart in RACI format

Text-Oriented Formats - Text formats basically follow the format of a position description, detailing out what responsibilities each position on the project will involve and what qualifications will be needed to fill these positions. This tool can be particularly useful in recruiting.

Plan Resource Management

➜ **Organizational Theory** - Groups behave differently than individuals, and it is important to understand how organizations and teams behave. Familiarizing yourself with the vast amount of work that has been done to understand organizational theory can pay dividends throughout the project.

Meetings — See Ch. 2, Common Tools

Chapter Notes:

_____

_____

_____

_____

_____

_____

_____

_____

_____

_____

_____

_____

_____

HOW IT WORKS / OUTPUTS:

➜ **Resource Management Plan** - As you might expect, the resource management plan is the main output of the Plan Resource Management process. It has three main components: identification of resources, plan for acquiring resources, and staffing roles and responsibilities.

The identification of resources includes both people and physical resources needed to complete the project. The plan for acquiring resources details how and when the project will be staffed, how and when the staff will be released, and other key human resources components such as how they will be trained in addition to how and when physical resources will be procured.

One common component of the resource management plan is a resource histogram. A resource histogram (see example following) simply shows the resource usage for a given period of time. On most projects, resource usage increases from the conceptual phase through planning, hits its peak in construction and testing, and falls off through implementation and closure.

The timeline for the staffing needs is also a component of the resource management plan. It helps the project and the organization anticipate and plan for the staffing needs.

Another element of the resource management plan is a release plan. How the project team will be released from the project is important: especially to individual members and their functional managers.

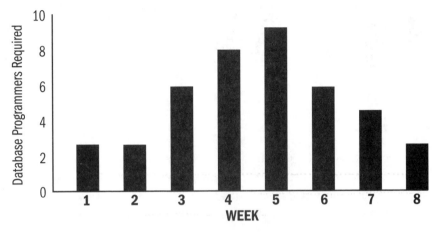

An example of a resource histogram, showing usage by weeks

Other elements of this plan are the staff training needs, rewards systems, safety procedures, compliance needs, and a plan for how the staff will be released at the appropriate time. The resource management plan tells how those specific needs will be addressed on the project.

Team Charter - The team charter communicates the ground rules. It specifies how the team will interact, communicate, reach decisions, hold meetings, and any other elements that are important to this team.

Ground rules may vary project to project, but everyone on the team should know what they are. They define team expectations, whether these are written or implied.

Project Document Updates — See Ch. 2, Common Outputs

Chapter Notes:

6th Edition *PMBOK® Guide*
Cross Ref. pg 320

PLANNING

ESTIMATE ACTIVITY RESOURCES

WHAT IT IS:

How long an activity takes is usually a function of determining the effort needed to perform the activity, the quantity of resources that will be applied to it, and the resource availability. This process is all about analyzing the project's schedule activities to determine the resource requirements.

WHY IT IS IMPORTANT:

Understanding the number of resources required to complete an activity and determining how long they will be used for that activity is an important step in project planning and an essential ingredient to the schedule, which will be developed later.

WHEN IT IS PERFORMED:

Because the process of Estimate Activity Resources uses the activity list and activity attributes (brought in as part of the project documents), it must be performed after the Define Activities process since that is where these documents are produced. Additionally, since the output of this process is used to build the project schedule, this process must be performed before Develop Schedule. This process often goes hand in hand with Estimate Costs, since cost and schedule are closely linked, so they may be performed at the same time, or in an iterative cycle.

Watch The Video

http://**prep.pm**/9-3

Chapter Notes:

_____

_____

_____

_____

_____

_____

_____

_____

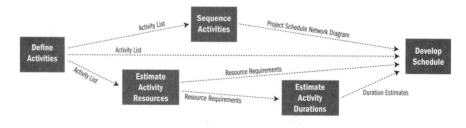

HOW IT WORKS / INPUTS:

Project Management Plan — See Ch. 2, Common Inputs

Project Documents - The key documents brought into this process are the activity list, the activity attributes, and the resource calendars. These provide insight into what activities need to be accomplished and when resources are available. The risk register may also provide information about which activities have higher risks and may require more resources or attention.

Enterprise Environmental Factors — See Ch. 2, Common Inputs

Organizational Process Assets — See Ch. 2, Common Inputs

HOW IT WORKS / TOOLS:

Expert Judgment — See Ch. 2, Common Tools

Bottom-Up Estimating - This is essentially the same technique as the one used in the Estimate Activity Durations process (covered in schedule management), except that this time we are aggregating individual resource estimates. These estimates will be added up on parent nodes, with some of these summary nodes, known as control accounts, being tracked more carefully than others. Using this technique, the topmost node on the WBS should contain all of the estimated resources for the project.

Bottom-up estimating is generally a favored technique on the exam.

Analogous Estimating - Like the previous tool, analogous estimating is used the same way here was it was in Estimate Activity Durations.

Parametric Estimating - Parametric estimating in this process also mirrors the way it was used in Estimate Activity Durations. It uses historical performance to extrapolate and estimate future resource usage.

Data Analysis - The main kind of data analysis used here is alternatives analysis. It is used to evaluate each activity to see if there are other ways of completing it. This may include using different resources or different quantities of resources.

Chapter Notes:

Project Management Information System (PMIS) - The PMIS is a software system that helps the project manager with routine tasks or tedious calculations. It can help the project manager store and organize information, experiment with alternatives, and rapidly optimize resource usage, and calculate schedules.

Meetings — See Ch. 2, Common Tools

HOW IT WORKS / OUTPUTS:

Resource Requirements - The resources required for each schedule activity are the primary output of Estimate Activity Resources. These resources include the kind of resource and the number of these resources. The activity resource requirements need to specify, for instance, if two senior programmers are required for six months or if three junior programmers are required for five months.

Each activity resource requirement should be documented with sufficient detail to explain the decision-making process used to arrive at these estimates.

Basis of Estimates - All three of the estimating processes that are tied to activities (Estimate Activity Resources, Estimate Costs, and Estimate Activity Durations) include the basis for estimates along with the estimates themselves. Including this supporting detail is always a good idea.

→ **Resource Breakdown Structure** - The resource breakdown structure, or RBS, is similar in many ways to the WBS. It is graphical and hierarchical, logically arranged from top to bottom, and it organizes the resources by category and type.

Chapter Notes:

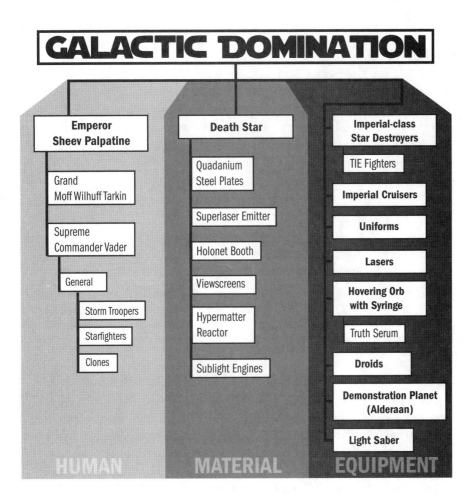

Estimate Activity Resources

Project Document Updates — See Ch. 2, Common Outputs

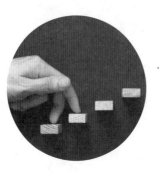

6th Edition *PMBOK® Guide*
Cross Ref. pg 328

.... EXECUTING

ACQUIRE RESOURCES

WHAT IT IS:

Acquire Resources is another process that sounds exactly like what it is. This process focuses on staffing the project and procuring the materials and facilities needed to perform the work. Because it is an executing process, you can think of it as a key process that carries out the resource management plan.

WHY IT IS IMPORTANT:

This process gets the right people working with the right materials on the project. Careful attention to this process should pay off in the form of the quality of staff and materials you bring on.

WHEN IT IS PERFORMED:

Make sure that you understand that the process of Acquire Resources is typically performed throughout the project, as you may need different skill sets and materials throughout the life of the project. For instance, you may need business analysts early on in the life of the project, while you may need more quality engineers later in the project. Acquire Resources would be performed as long as the project was adding team members or replacing existing staff. On a construction project, the raw material needs may be low at the beginning but will likely ramp up quickly during construction. Likewise, on an application development project, the need for servers and bandwidth may increase as the product is prepared for public rollout.

Watch The Video
http://**prep.pm/9-4**

Chapter Notes:

_____

_____

_____

_____

_____

_____

_____

HOW IT WORKS / INPUTS:

Project Management Plan — See Ch. 2, Common Inputs

Project Documents — See Ch. 2, Common Inputs

Enterprise Environmental Factors — See Ch. 2, Common Inputs

Organizational Process Assets — See Ch. 2, Common Inputs

HOW IT WORKS / TOOLS:

Decision Making - Since there are often many variables that influence which resources to select, a multi-criteria decision analysis tool may be used. This is a weighted matrix to objectively score potential candidates or resources on the various factors that matter the most to the project. The criteria and weightings are determined in advance, and candidates are scored against them, with the highest-scoring candidate being selected for the position.

	Availability	Cost	Experience	Knowledge	Skill	Attitude	Location	Total
	1-10	0-25	0-5	0-5	0-10	0-5	0-3	
Jarred	6	12	4	4		5	3	34
Michele	3	9	4	5		4	1	26
Adriana	8	20	5	5		5	3	46
Edward	7	10	4	5		3	1	30
Colin	4	6	3	2		2	3	20
Karl	2	5	5	5		1	3	21
Lisa	7	15	3	4		3	3	35

Interpersonal and Team Skills — See Ch. 2, Common Tools

Pre-Assignment - It is normal for some roles to be defined first. Later, resources are assigned to perform those roles and fulfill the responsibilities; however, occasionally specific resources will be pre-assigned to fill a role. This may occur before the resource management plan has been created and even before the project formally begins.

Chapter Notes:

_____
_____
_____
_____
_____
_____
_____
_____
_____
_____
_____
_____
_____
_____

 Virtual Teams - As the internet has transformed the way many people do their jobs, virtual teams have become much more popular. A virtual team is a group of individuals who may or may not see each other in person. Instead, they typically use electronic tools to communicate, meet online, share information, collaborate on documents and deliverables, work different shifts, and reduce time and travel expense.

HOW IT WORKS / OUTPUTS:

Physical Resource Assignments - This output documents the assignment of the non-human resources needed to complete the project.

Project Team Assignments - The assigned staff is the primary output of this process. Each role that was defined should have a resource assigned to it. Understand that these assignments may happen several times throughout the process as resources are needed. For instance, it might be difficult to assign a particular person to a role if that resource will not be needed for a year.

Resource Calendars - The resource calendars flow into this process through the project documents, and the updated resource calendars, reflecting the resource utilization, dates, and durations, flows out.

Change Requests — See Ch. 2, Common Outputs

Project Management Plan Updates —
See Ch. 2, Common Outputs

Project Documents Updates — See Ch. 2, Common Outputs

Enterprise Environmental Factors Updates - As you use or commit physical resources or commit people to project roles, it needs to be documented for the organization and for other project teams.

Organizational Process Assets Updates —
See Ch. 2, Common Outputs

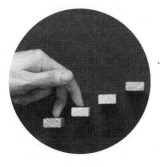

···· EXECUTING

DEVELOP TEAM

WHAT IT IS:

Where the exam is concerned, Develop Team is the most important process in Resource Management. It is an executing process that focuses on building a sense of team and improving its performance.

6th Edition *PMBOK® Guide*
Cross Ref. pg 336

WHY IT IS IMPORTANT:

A good team performs better than a group of disconnected individuals, and the performance difference can be dramatic.

WHEN IT IS PERFORMED:

The process of Develop Team is performed throughout the project. In other words, as long as there is a team on the project, you should perform this process. It is considered to be most effective when it is begun early in the project's life cycle, and it becomes even more important over time.

Watch The Video
http://**prep.pm/9-5**

Chapter Notes:

HOW IT WORKS / INPUTS:

Project Management Plan — See Ch. 2, Common Inputs

Project Documents — See Ch. 2, Common Inputs

Enterprise Environmental Factors —
    See Ch. 2, Common Inputs

Organizational Process Assets — See Ch. 2, Common Inputs

_____

_____

_____

_____

_____

_____

_____

_____

Chapter Notes:

_____

_____

_____

_____

_____

_____

_____

_____

_____

_____

_____

_____

_____

_____

HOW IT WORKS / TOOLS:

Colocation - Colocation is the act of physically locating team members in the same general space. The most common example of this is to create a war room where all the team members work or to colocate the project team at the customer's site. Team building and communication are also easier.

Virtual Teams - Virtual teams can present a challenge to developing a team. They may offer advantages for cost or having access to resources that would not otherwise be practical, but it almost always presents difficulty for creating a sense of team. Successful virtual teams typically use software and tools to improve communication and collaboration.

Communication Technology - Communication is very important regardless of whether the team is collocated or virtual. This can include portals such as SharePoint or cloud-based tools, sites for video and audio conferencing, email and chat. Regardless of the technology used, the point is to reduce barriers to communication.

Interpersonal and Team Skills - The tool of interpersonal skills is often called soft skills. This represents the ability to get along with others, to ensure their cooperation, and to motivate people to give extra effort and do their best for the project.

The Alpha Study of project managers found that many of the project managers who ranked themselves highly in the areas of soft skills were often ranked among the lowest in soft skill competency by their stakeholders.

Strong interpersonal skills are very important where the team is concerned. Soft skills can be a thorny area for project managers. Many project managers are not fully aware of how they are relating to their teams.

Recognition and Rewards - Recognition and reward systems are most commonly associated with the resource management plan. In general, desirable behaviors should be rewarded and recognized. For the exam, you should focus on win-win rewards as the best choices for team building. Win-lose rewards, such as a contest where one team member wins and the others do not, can be detrimental to the sense of team.

There is a substantial body of knowledge on recognition and reward theories. These theories, also known as Theories of Motivation, are traditional exam favorites. A thorough understanding of several theories is needed to be fully prepared to pass the exam, including Tuckman's Ladder, Maslow's Hierarchy of Needs, Expectancy Theory, McGregor's Theory X and Y, Contingency Theory, Herzberg's Motivation-Hygiene Theory, and McClelland's Theory of Needs.

Tuckman's Ladder

An important theory that speaks to the development of the team is Tuckman's Ladder of Team Development. It defines five levels of performance: Forming, Storming, Norming, Performing, and Adjourning.

1. Forming is the first stage where the team understands the project and their roles.

2. Storming is the stage where the team begins to do the work, but there is typically a good bit of conflict and difficulty. This stage may be chaotic.

3. Norming is the stage where the behavior normalizes and members begin to work as a team. In this stage, the project manager shares more leadership with the team.

4. Performing is the stage where the team is working at an efficient level that exceeds what individuals could accomplish alone. The project manager's role changes to be one of overseeing and delegating.

5. Adjourning is the stage where the project is closed and the team is released. Since individuals tend to fear change, this stage can be difficult on everyone.

Chapter Notes:

Develop Team

Chapter Nine

Develop Team

Chapter Notes:

_____

_____

_____

_____

_____

_____

_____

_____

_____

_____

_____

_____

_____

Maslow's Hierarchy of Needs

Maslow's Hierarchy of Needs is a basic theory of human motivation that project managers should understand. Abraham Maslow grouped human needs into five basic categories as illustrated in the following diagram.

Maslow's theory states that these needs form a hierarchy since the needs at the bottom must be satisfied before the upper needs will surface. As an example, people cannot reach their full potential if they do not have sufficient food or safety.

Every project manager should understand the needs of the team members and how they interrelate so that he can help them to perform at their full potential.

Expectancy Theory

Expectancy Theory is a motivational theory developed by Victor Vroom. It says that team members make choices based on the expected outcomes. For project work, it most directly applies by saying that team members will only work hard toward a goal if they believe that goal is achievable.

McGregor's Theory X and Theory Y

McGregor's organizational theory states that there are two ways to categorize and understand people in the workplace.

Managers who ascribe to Theory X presume that team members are only interested in their own selfish goals. They are unmotivated, they dislike work, and they must be forced to do productive work. Theory X managers believe that constant supervision is necessary to achieve desired results on a project.

Those who practice Theory Y assume that people are naturally motivated to do good work. "Y managers" believe that their team members need very little external motivation and can be trusted to work toward the organization's or project's goals.

An assembly-line organization may treat everyone as an "X Person," monitoring and measuring every move, whereas an organization that encourages telecommuting might be more prone to treat employees as "Y People." However, it should be understood that it is the manager, not the organization, that ascribes to Theory X or Theory Y, and the style of management is not necessarily determined by the type of work being performed.

Contingency Theory

The Contingency Theory, developed by Fred E. Fiedler in the 1960s and 1970s, states that a leader's effectiveness is contingent upon two sets of factors. The first set of factors measures whether the leader is task-oriented or relationship-oriented. The second set evaluates situational factors in the workplace, such as how stressful the environment is.

The practical application of this theory suggests that in stressful times, a task-oriented leader will be more effective, while in relatively calm times, a relationship-oriented leader will function more effectively. The inverse is also true. What makes a leader effective in one setting may actually work against them in another.

Chapter Notes:

_____

_____

_____

_____

_____

_____

_____

_____

_____

_____

_____

_____

Develop Team

Chapter Nine

Chapter Notes:

_____
_____
_____
_____
_____
_____
_____
_____
_____
_____
_____
_____
_____

Herzberg's Motivation-Hygiene Theory

This theory has nothing to do with personal hygiene as the name might incorrectly lead you to conclude. Instead, Herzberg conducted studies to quantify what factors influence satisfaction at work.

Similar to Maslow's theory, Herzberg's Motivational-Hygiene theory states that the presence of certain factors does not make someone satisfied, but their absence can make someone unsatisfied. In this case, hygiene factors must be present, but they do not motivate by themselves. Motivation factors will motivate, but they will not work without the hygiene factors in place.

These **motivate** if hygiene factors are present.	**Motivation Factors**	
	Achievement	Responsibility
	Recognition	Advancement
	Work	Growth

Hygiene Factors		These factors **don't motivate** but are needed for motivation factors to work.
Paycheck	Company Policy	
Personal life	Supervision	
Status	Good relationship with boss	
Security	Working conditions	
Relationship with co-workers		

McClelland's Three Need Theory

Also called Achievement Theory, or McClelland's Theory of Needs, this states that employees are motivated out of three primary needs:

Achievement: Team members with a high need for achievement (nAch) have a need to stand out. They gravitate toward other team members with a high nAch. They may also prefer to work alone. High risk projects are often not appealing to nAch team members since their individual effort may be thwarted by the risk of the project. Also, very low-risk projects may not appeal since individual effort may not be recognized.

Power: Team members with the need for power (nPow) generally desire either institutional (social) power or personal power. Individuals with a desire for social power are usually more effective team members than those with a desire for personal power.

Affiliation: Individuals with the need for affiliation (nAff) want to belong to a team. They seek to maintain good relationships and do well in customer-facing team positions.

By understanding the needs of individual team members (nAch, nPow, or nAff), the project manager can work to manage roles and motivate the overall project team to reach peak performance.

Forms of Power

There are various forms of power that a project manager may have. Understanding the forms of power can help the project manager maximize his or her ability to influence and manage the team.

Reward Power: Reward power is the ability to give rewards and recognition. Examples include a pay raise, time off, or any other type of reward that would motivate a team member.

Expert Power: Expert power exists when the manager is an expert on the subject. For example, the person who architected a part of a software system would probably have significant expert power on a project that used that system. People would listen to the architect because they had credibility. A subject matter expert usually has significant power to influence and control behavior.

Legitimate: Also known as formal power, legitimate power is the power that the manager has because of their position. This type of power comes from being formally in charge of the project and the people and has the backing of the organization.

Strong, broad-based, formal authority for a project manager is unusual and would typically indicate a projectized organizational structure.

Chapter Notes:

_____

_____

_____

_____

_____

_____

_____

_____

_____

_____

_____

_____

Develop Team

Chapter Notes:

_____

_____

_____

_____

_____

_____

_____

_____

_____

_____

_____

_____

_____

_____

_____

Referent: Referent power is a form of power that is based on respect or the charismatic personality of the manager. It is ultimately rooted in a persuasive ability with people. Another usage of referent power is when a less powerful person allies with a more powerful person and leverages some of the superior's power. For instance, if the project manager is very close to the CEO of the company, their power will probably be higher because of that alliance.

Punishment: Also known as coercive power, this type of influence is the ability to punish an employee if a goal is not met. "If this module does not pass quality control by the end of next week, you are all fired," would be an example of a manager using punishment power.

Best Forms of Power

In addition to being able to identify the different types of power a project manager can use, you should also know that the exam favors reward and expert as the most effective forms of power and punishment as the least effective.

Training - Training can include a wide range of activities, but it may be thought of as any instruction or acquisition of skills that increases the ability of the team or individuals to perform their jobs.

If a team member does not have the skills needed to carry out his responsibilities, then training may be a good option. In general, training is highly favored for the exam. In most cases you encounter on the exam, it should be paid for by the performing organization or the functional manager and not by the customer or the project.

Individual and Team Assessments - Assessments are powerful ways for team members and managers to gain insights into relational styles, strengths, and weaknesses. In addition, 360-degree feedback assessments can help individuals understand how they are perceived by others both inside and outside of the organization. Assessments are not the end goal. They are a means to create awareness so that an improvement plan may be undertaken.

Meetings — See Ch. 2, Common Tools

HOW IT WORKS / OUTPUTS:

Team Performance Assessments - Team evaluations are performed by the project manager to focus on areas that should be improved. It is the project manager's job to increase team performance. It is also important for the project manager to identify the right tools and resources needed to help develop the team.

Change Requests — See Ch. 2, Common Outputs

Project Management Plan Updates —
    See Ch. 2, Common Outputs

Project Documents Updates — See Ch. 2, Common Outputs

Enterprise Environmental Factors Updates - As employees develop new skills, these need to be documented for the organization.

Organizational Process Assets Updates —
    See Ch. 2, Common Outputs

Chapter Notes:

_____

_____

_____

_____

_____

_____

_____

_____

_____

_____

_____

_____

Develop Team

···· EXECUTING

MANAGE TEAM

6th Edition *PMBOK® Guide*
Cross Ref. pg 345

WHAT IT IS:

This executing process has most of the attributes of a monitoring and controlling process. In fact, it used to be a monitoring and controlling process in an earlier edition of the *PMBOK® Guide*. This is important to know. In this process, you are actively managing the project team to ensure that they perform according to the plan.

WHY IT IS IMPORTANT:

Out of all the areas on a project, the human resource side often has the most trouble with execution. People can be unpredictable. Some leave the project, teams experience unexpected conflict, individuals suffer from low morale, and all of these events directly affect objective measures such as the budget, the schedule, and quality.

Watch The Video
http://**prep.pm/9-6**

This uncertainty becomes even more challenging when you consider that team members often report to different functional managers and only have "dotted line" responsibilities to the project manager.

Chapter Notes:

In the Manage Team process, the project manager considers all of these factors and works to keep the team at optimal performance.

WHEN IT IS PERFORMED:

Manage Team is performed as soon as and as long as there is a team on the project. On larger projects, it is unusual for the entire team to stay exactly the same throughout the project, since different skill sets will roll on and off as needed. The goal is to create and maintain peak team performance, and this lasts as long as there is a team.

HOW IT WORKS / INPUTS:

Project Management Plan — See Ch. 2, Common Inputs

Project Documents — See Ch. 2, Common Inputs

➔ **Work Performance Reports** - The work performance reports come from the process Monitor and Control Project Work. Keep in mind that reports should be actionable, so this should provide a helpful picture as to how the work is being carried out, and that will influence how the team is managed. For example, if the team is producing an excellent product but is working significant overtime, that would show up in the work performance reports and would be considered a problem.

➔ **Team Performance Assessments** - This input, produced in the previous process, Develop Team, is similar to the previous input of work performance reports. The team performance assessments give insight into the overall health of the team.

Enterprise Environmental Factors — See Ch. 2, Common Inputs

Organizational Process Assets — See Ch. 2, Common Inputs

HOW IT WORKS / TOOLS:

➔ **Interpersonal and Team Skills** - Project managers and project coaches often need to help resolve team conflict.

Consider the problem of a door that is stuck shut. There are several ways to approach this:

- You may want to throw your weight against the door, pounding it with your shoulder.

- You might elect to try to go in the room from another point of entry.

- You could try to take the hinges off the door to make it come apart.

Chapter Notes:

_____
_____
_____
_____
_____
_____
_____
_____
_____
_____
_____
_____
_____
_____
_____
_____

Manage Team

Chapter Nine

Manage Team

Chapter Notes:

———————————————
———————————————
———————————————
———————————————
———————————————
———————————————
———————————————
———————————————
———————————————
———————————————
———————————————
———————————————
———————————————
———————————————

- You might choose to ignore the problem of the stuck door, avoiding it altogether, or hope that someone else will take care of it.

- You could attempt to find out why the door was stuck in the first place and deal with that problem.

In the same way, there are several ways to approach conflict resolution. Because conflict is inevitable with any team, you should be aware of the common ways of handling it:

Problem-Solving - Problem-solving involves confrontation, but it is confrontation of the problem and not the person. It means dealing with the problem head on. Using this technique, the project manager gets to the bottom of the problem and resolves the root causes of the conflict.

One common term in problem-solving is "confrontation." Although the word confrontation may have negative connotations, this type of conflict resolution is highly favored as it is proactive, direct, and deals with the root of the problem. Consequently, it is most often the correct answer on the exam when questions of conflict resolution arise.

Collaboration - Collaboration is a favored technique for resolving conflict. When collaborating, individuals (or teams) work together with other individuals (or teams) to come to a solution. This is a favored technique for the exam, second only to problem-solving.

Compromise - Compromise, also referred to as "reconcile", takes place when both parties sacrifice something for the sake of reaching an agreement. On the test, compromise may be presented as "lose – lose" since both parties give up something.

Forcing - Forcing is exactly what the name implies. It is bringing to bear whatever force or power is necessary to get the door open. Although forcing may work well in the case of a stuck door, this is considered to be the worst way to resolve project conflict. Forcing doesn't help resolve the underlying problems, it reduces team morale, and it is almost never a good long-term solution.

Smoothing (also called "Accommodating") - Using smoothing or accommodating, the project manager plays down the problem and turns attention to what is going well. The statement "We shouldn't be arguing with each other. Look at how well we've done so far, and we're ahead of schedule," would be an example of smoothing.

Smoothing downplays conflict instead of dealing with it head on and does not produce a solution to the conflict. Instead, smoothing merely tries to diminish the problem.

Withdrawal - Withdrawal is technically not a conflict resolution technique but a means of avoidance. A project manager practicing withdrawal is merely hoping the problem will go away by itself. Needless to say, this is not a favored method of conflict resolution because the conflict is never resolved. It will never be a correct answer on the exam unless the question describes a bad behavior or asks you about something not to do.

Constructive and Destructive Team Roles

Related to the area of conflict management is the project manager's ability to recognize and deal with constructive and destructive roles on his or her team.

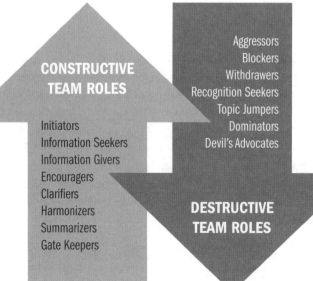

CONSTRUCTIVE TEAM ROLES

Initiators
Information Seekers
Information Givers
Encouragers
Clarifiers
Harmonizers
Summarizers
Gate Keepers

Aggressors
Blockers
Withdrawers
Recognition Seekers
Topic Jumpers
Dominators
Devil's Advocates

DESTRUCTIVE TEAM ROLES

Chapter Notes:

Manage Team

Chapter Notes:

_____

_____

_____

_____

_____

_____

_____

_____

_____

_____

_____

_____

_____

Decision Making

Good decision making involves several components, including following a process, keeping focused on the goals, soliciting input and listening to it, and taking all information into consideration.

Emotional Intelligence

Awareness of the importance of emotional intelligence has been growing in recent years. It is a concept that came out of research by John Mayer and Peter Salovey and was brought into public awareness through Daniel Goleman's book Emotional Intelligence: Why It Can Matter More Than IQ. You may see Emotional Intelligence abbreviated as "EQ" or as "EI."

The concept is that traditional IQ tests measure how good someone is at solving problems and at relating, grouping, and associating information; however, some of the world's most successful leaders did not have particularly high IQs. Instead, they leveraged a strong ability to read people, to relate to them, to assess situations, or to work with a team. Conversely, many people have experienced working for a highly intelligent person who could not manage or relate to people effectively.

High emotional intelligence comes through a combination of elevated self-awareness and social awareness and by being able to gauge the mood and emotions of a group or team.

A high self-awareness means that the individual knows his or her personal strengths and weaknesses. A high social awareness means that the individual is very aware of how he or she is being perceived by others and has the ability to tailor behavior as needed.

The benefits to a high EI are many. Because so much of a project is accomplished through team effort and consensus, the project manager needs to have a strong ability to relate and to negotiate. Abrasive and divisive people, even when technically knowledgable and capable, usually do not make good project managers.

Possessing and employing a high EI to deal with issues or problems should be highly favored on the exam.

Influencing

Most project managers have limited authority on a project, and this is particularly true when it comes to the team. In this case, the skill of influencing becomes more important. Project managers have to be able to influence stakeholders through persuasion, listening, and building trusting relationships.

Leadership

There is a difference between leading and managing on a project. Managing has been defined as producing key results, while leading involves establishing direction, aligning people to that direction, and motivating and inspiring.

There are several different styles of leading that are recognized throughout the field of project management. The following graphic may prove very helpful for the exam. In the early phases of the project, the project manager should take a very active role in the leadership of the project, usually directing the activities and providing significant leadership. As the project progresses, however, other styles of leading may be more appropriate. These styles of leading are less heavy-handed. Of course, the particular style of leading needed will vary from one project to the next.

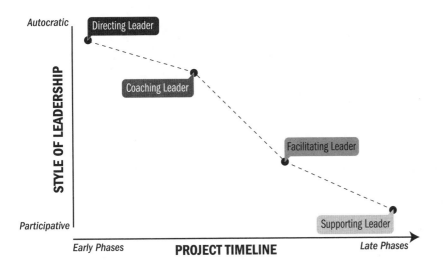

Project Management Information System (PMIS) —
See Ch. 2, Common Tools

Chapter Notes:

_____

_____

_____

_____

_____

_____

_____

_____

_____

_____

_____

_____

HOW IT WORKS / OUTPUTS:

Change Requests — See Ch. 2, Common Outputs

Project Management Plan Updates —
See Ch. 2, Common Outputs

Project Documents Updates — See Ch. 2, Common Outputs

Enterprise Environmental Factors Updates - Some of the enterprise environmental factors that may be updated are skill at managing resources and the organizational performance appraisals.

.... MONITORING & CONTROLLING
CONTROL RESOURCES

WHAT IT IS:

6th Edition *PMBOK® Guide*
Cross Ref. pg 352

This monitoring and controlling process has nothing to do with the human resources. It is about the physical resources on the project and making sure that their availability and uninterrupted flow and usage line up with the resource management plan.

WHY IT IS IMPORTANT:

This is an easy process. In fact, the inputs, tools, and outputs are all commonly used ones, so nothing really stands out. But it is a new process with this edition of the *PMBOK® Guide*, and is ripe for exploitation on the exam.

Watch The Video
http://**prep.pm/9-7**

What you need to know for the exam is that this process is the one that monitors and makes adjustments to the physical resource usage or to the resource management plan.

Chapter Notes:

WHEN IT IS PERFORMED:

All monitoring and controlling processes are performed as needed. If you are acquiring resources or using resources on the project, then you will need to perform this process.

HOW IT WORKS / INPUTS:

Project Management Plan — See Ch. 2, Common Inputs

Project Documents — See Ch. 2, Common Inputs

Chapter Notes:

_____

_____

_____

_____

_____

_____

_____

_____

_____

_____

_____

_____

⊕ Work Performance Data - This is key because it provides the raw data of the quantity and types of resources used. These will be analyzed, processed, and transformed into the key output of work performance information.

Agreements — See Ch. 2, Common Inputs

Organizational Process Assets — See Ch. 2, Common Inputs

HOW IT WORKS / TOOLS:

⊕ Data Analysis - This tool is generic enough in many ways, but you should recognize alternatives analysis, cost-benefit analysis, performance reviews, and trend analysis as ways in which it is carried out. Each of these looks at hard data to see how effective resource management is.

⊕ Problem Solving - Problem solving is a favorite answer for the exam. In fact, if you ever see it as a choice, you should give it very careful consideration. The general approach for problem solving is shown here:

	IDENTIFY	*Isolate the problem*
	DEFINE	*Understand the problem*
	INVESTIGATE	*Get more information*
PROBLEM	**ANALYZE**	*Determine the root cause*
SOLVING	**SOLVE**	*Find the best solution*
	CHECK	*Verify the results*

Interpersonal and Team Skills — See Ch. 2, Common Tools

Project Management Information System (PMIS) — See Ch. 2, Common Tools

HOW IT WORKS / OUTPUTS:

→ **Work Performance Information** - the WPI differs from the input of the work performance data because it is in a more refined form that can be compared with the resource management plan.

Change Requests — See Ch. 2, Common Outputs

Project Management Plan Updates —
　　　See Ch. 2, Common Outputs

Project Documents Updates — See Ch. 2, Common Outputs

Chapter Notes:

_____

_____

_____

_____

_____

_____

_____

_____

_____

_____

_____

_____

_____

Control Resources

Chapter Nine

Chapter Notes:

_____

_____

_____

_____

_____

_____

_____

_____

_____

_____

_____

_____

→ The Agile Perspective on Resource Management

The more agile the project, the less you rely on a pre-set plan. You rely, instead, on the team's ability to adapt. Agile methodologies have changed the way project teams form and operate. One prominent feature of self-organizing teams is that they do not include the role of a traditional project manager. On agile projects, the team is collectively responsible for the quality and deliverables. There is generally a coach (sometimes referred to by other titles) rather than a project manager, who works to remove obstacles and to facilitate open communication on the project. Self-organizing teams are staffed with interchangeable team members known as generalizing specialists rather than individual experts.

Physical resources on an agile project are often procured in smaller quantities in order to satisfy the needs of a single iteration.

RESOURCE MANAGEMENT

QUESTIONS

1. If you hear a project manager saying to a customer "We all agree that this project is important. Let's not fight over a few thousand dollars," what conflict resolution technique is the project manager trying to use?

    A. Smoothing.

    B. Problem Solving.

    C. Forcing.

    D. Compromising.

2. Who manages the resources in a matrix organization?

    A. Senior management.

    B. Functional managers.

    C. Project manager.

    D. Human resources.

3. Trey, a functional manager of his organization's information technology domain, has supplied a database developer to a project managed by Vickie; however, it has become apparent that the developer lacks the knowledge to work on the operating environment the team is using. Trey and Vickie meet and determine that the resource can attend a training class and close the gap in skills, but there is a question as to who should pay for it. How should they resolve this?

    A. They should escalate the conflict to senior management.

    B. Trey's department should pay for the training.

    C. Vickie's project should pay for the training.

    D. They should seek a compromise.

Chapter Nine

Chapter Notes:

_____

_____

_____

_____

_____

_____

_____

_____

_____

_____

_____

_____

_____

4. What is considered the LEAST desirable form of power for a project manager to exercise?

   A. Formal.

   B. Referent.

   C. Punishment.

   D. Forcing.

5. Which statement below BEST matches a Theory X manager's beliefs?

   A. People want to be rewarded for their work.

   B. People have higher needs that will not emerge until the lower needs have been satisfied.

   C. People will contribute to work if left alone.

   D. People cannot be trusted.

6. The resource management plan:

   A. Should be provided by the human resources department.

   B. Is a part of the resource overview plan.

   C. Is used as a tool in Develop Project Team.

   D. Is an output of the Plan Resource Management process.

7. A project manager is tracking his team through a process of development that includes Storming and Adjourning. Which expert developed the theory this is based upon?

   A. Maslow.

   B. Herzberg.

   C. McClelland.

   D. Tuckman.

8. Which technique produces the most lasting results?

   A. Problem-solving.

   B. Smoothing.

   C. Compromising.

   D. Withdrawing.

9. The most important role of the project sponsor is to:

   A. Manage and resolve conflicts between the team and upper management.

   B. Provide and protect the project's financial resources.

   C. Provide and protect the project's human resources.

   D. Balance the project's constraints regarding time, scope, and cost.

10. Resource management encompasses:

    A. Organizational Planning, Acquire Project Team, Report Performance, and Manage Project Team, Monitor and Control Resources.

    B. Plan Resource Management, Acquire Project Team, Report Performance, and Develop Project Team, Monitor and Control Resources.

    C. Plan Resource Management, Estimate Activity Resources, Staff Acquisition, Develop Project Team, and Monitor and Control Resources, Release Project Team.

    D. Plan Resource Management, Estimate Activity Resources, Acquire Resources, Develop Team, Manage Team, Control Resources.

Chapter Notes:

Chapter Nine

Chapter Notes:

_____

_____

_____

_____

_____

_____

_____

_____

_____

_____

_____

_____

_____

_____

11. **Which of the following is NOT an input into Plan Resource Management?**

   A. Enterprise environmental factors.

   B. The team charter.

   C. Organizational process assets.

   D. The stakeholder register.

12. **Which of the following is a constructive team role?**

   A. Information seeker.

   B. Recognition seeker.

   C. Blocker.

   D. Devil's advocate.

13. **A project manager is trying to rank and quantify three variables for his team which he has labeled on a dry-erase board as follows: nAch, nPow, and nAff. Which expert developed the theory this is this based upon?**

   A. Maslow.

   B. Herzberg.

   C. McClelland.

   D. Tuckman.

14. Maslow's Hierarchy of Needs theory states that:

A. The strongest motivation for work is to provide for physiological needs.

B. Hygiene factors are those that provide physical safety and emotional security.

C. Psychological needs for growth and fulfillment can be met only when lower-level physical or security needs have been fulfilled.

D. The greater the financial reward, the more motivated the workers will be.

15. Which of the following is NOT true of team building?

A. Team agreement should be obtained on all major actions.

B. Team building requires role modeling on the part of the project manager.

C. Team building becomes less important as the project progresses.

D. Teamwork cannot be forced.

16. Team building is primarily the responsibility of:

A. The project team.

B. The project manager.

C. Senior management.

D. The project sponsor.

17. A war room is an example of:

A. Contract negotiation tactics.

B. Resource planning tools.

C. A functional organization.

D. Colocation.

Chapter Notes:

Chapter Nine

Chapter Notes:

_____

_____

_____

_____

_____

_____

_____

_____

_____

_____

_____

_____

_____

18. Which processes make use of the project manager's interpersonal skills?

    A. Acquire Resources and Control Resources.

    B. Develop Team and Manage Team.

    C. Plan Resource Management and Develop Team.

    D. Develop Team and Transition Team.

19. Which of the following is NOT a resource management process?

    A. Plan Resource Management.

    B. Acquire Resources.

    C. Report Team Performance.

    D. Develop Team.

20. A project coordinator is distinguished from a project manager in that:

    A. A project coordinator has no decision-making power.

    B. A project coordinator has less decision-making power.

    C. A project coordinator has no authority to assign work.

    D. A project coordinator has more decision-making power.

21. Which of the following is NOT a tool used in Develop Team?

    A. Interpersonal skills.

    B. Recognition and rewards.

    C. Meetings.

    D. Encouragement.

22. An organization is undertaking a strategic project to develop a new technology that would provide them with a market advantage. The project manager has been brought in early to help with pre-planning, when a senior manager informs him that there is a specific resource that he wants to be on the project as a quality engineer. Is this situation acceptable?

    A. No. The project manager is ultimately responsible for the project and should have the opportunity to approve or reject the acquisition of all resources.

    B. No. If a resource is pre-assigned, the functional manager should be the one to make that assignment to ensure that the individual has the proper skills.

    C. Yes. Pre-assignment may occur as a part of Acquire Resources.

    D. Yes, as long as it does not adversely affect the project.

23. **One potential disadvantage of a matrix organization is:**

    A. Highly visible project objectives.

    B. Rapid responses to contingencies.

    C. Team members must report to more than one boss.

    D. The matrix organization creates morale problems.

Chapter Notes:

_____

_____

_____

_____

_____

_____

_____

_____

_____

_____

_____

_____

_____

_____

Chapter Notes:

_____

_____

_____

_____

_____

_____

_____

_____

_____

_____

_____

_____

_____

24. A project manager in Detroit is having difficulty getting the engineers in his company's Cleveland office to complete design documents for his project. He has sent numerous requests to the VP of Engineering (also in Cleveland) for assistance in getting the design documents, but so far his efforts have been unsuccessful. What kind of organization does this project manager work in?

A. Functional.

B. Hierarchical.

C. Strong matrix.

D. Projectized.

25. Which of the following is not true about a project's ground rules?

A. Ground rules should be communicated to all team members.

B. Ground rules should be consistent across projects in an organization.

C. Ground rules should be clearly defined.

D. Ground rules define behavioral boundaries on a project.

RESOURCE MANAGEMENT
ANSWERS

1. A. Smoothing occurs when the person trying to resolve the conflict asks everyone to focus on what they agree upon and diminishes the items on which there is disagreement.

2. B. The functional manager has resource responsibilities in a matrix organization. In this type of organizational structure, the project manager must work with the functional managers to secure resources for a project. If you were tempted to choose 'C', keep in mind that the project manager primarily manages the project. The benefit of a matrix organization is that the project manager does not need to divert as much attention to managing the resources as he or she would in a projectized organization.

3. B. Remember this: unless it is a very unusual circumstance, the project does not pay for training. Trey supplied the developer to work on the project, and it is the functional organization's responsibility to provide competent and trained resources. If you were in a hurry, you might have chosen 'A'. After all, senior management does resolve conflict between project managers and functional managers; however, not every disagreement or conflict should be escalated in such a hair-trigger manner. 'D' is incorrect since compromise is not overly favored for the exam to begin with, and compromise would not be in the project's best interest here.

4. C. Punishment. 'D' is a problem solving technique – not a form of power.

5. D. Theory X managers believe that people cannot be trusted and must be watched and managed constantly.

6. D. The resource management plan is created during the Plan Resource Management process.

7. D. Tuckman's theory of team development, also known as Tuckman's Ladder, includes the phases of Forming, Storming, Norming, Performing, and Adjourning.

Chapter Notes:

_____

_____

_____

_____

_____

_____

_____

_____

_____

_____

_____

Resource Management: Answers

Chapter Nine

Resource Management: Answers

Chapter Notes:

_____

_____

_____

_____

_____

_____

_____

_____

_____

_____

_____

_____

8. A. Problem-solving (sometimes referred to as confrontation) is getting to the root of the problem and is the best way to produce a lasting result and a real solution.

9. B. This question comes from Chapter 2 – Foundational Terms and Concepts. The project sponsor provides the funds for the project. He may or may not take on other roles, but this is his defining role on the project.

10. D. The six processes are: Plan Resource Management, Estimate Activity Resources, Acquire Resources, Develop Team, Manage Team, Control Resources, and yes, you do need to know all of them before taking the exam.

11. B. The easiest way to answer questions like this one is to start by narrowing the choices down. Three of the answers will be valid inputs, and enterprise environmental factors and organizational process assets are inputs into almost every planning process. That will eliminate answers 'A' and 'C'. In order to narrow it down between 'B' and 'D', think about the process and consider what it does. The process creates a resource management plan, and choice 'D' sounds like something that would be produced as part of that plan and not an input. The stakeholder register, brought in as a project document, would be useful to produce the resource management plan. 'B' emerges as the best choice.

12. A. Information seeker. Recognition seekers are more concerned with getting in the spotlight than with facilitating communication. Blockers reject others' viewpoints and shut down discussion. Devil's advocate – bringing up alternative viewpoints - can be either positive or negative, but it is listed in most project management literature as a destructive team role because when it is negative it is very negative! Information seekers are constructive because they ask questions to gain information.

13. C. McClelland developed the Three Need Theory that states that people have the basic needs for Achievement (generally abbreviated as nAch), Power (nPow), and Affiliation (nAff). This is what the project manager is analyzing on the dry-erase board.

14. C. This question might have been difficult for you. 'A' is not necessarily true, because Maslow stated that any level of his "pyramid" provides the greatest level of motivation when the needs of the levels below have already been met. Thus physiological needs such as food and shelter will be the greatest motivator for workers to do a good job when those needs are unmet. But once the lower level needs are met, the needs of the next level become the greatest motivators.

15. C. Successful team building begins early in project development, but it is a continuous process throughout the life of the project.

16. B. Team building must be carried out under the direction of a strong leader. The project manager has the only project role that allows for regular, direct interaction with the team.

17. D. Colocation is the practice of locating all team members in a central location. Another variation of a war room is a conference room devoted exclusively for a particular project team. It is a tool of Develop Team used in resource management.

18. B. Develop Team and Manage Team both have interpersonal skills as a tool. Even if you did not have that memorized, the answer might have been intuitive since team development and management are enhanced by strong interpersonal skills. 'D' had the name of a made-up process in it and should have been eliminated immediately.

19. C. Report Team Performance is not a real process.

20. B. A project coordinator has some authority and some decision-making power, but less than a project manager.

Chapter Notes:

_____

_____

_____

_____

_____

_____

_____

_____

_____

_____

_____

_____

_____

Resource Management: Answers

Chapter Notes:

—————————————————

—————————————————

—————————————————

—————————————————

—————————————————

—————————————————

—————————————————

—————————————————

—————————————————

—————————————————

—————————————————

—————————————————

—————————————————

21. D. Encouragement may be a great idea, but it is not specified as a tool of Develop Team. 'A', 'B', and 'C' all are. If you missed this question keep in mind that you should favor the terms, vocabulary, and phrases you see here on the exam. Few people can commit all of the inputs, tools and techniques, and outputs to memory, but you should learn to recognize them and pick out the ones that do not belong.

22. C. Pre-assignment of individuals to a defined role is a tool of Acquire Resources. There are many reasons this might be necessary, including contractual agreements. Many times the project manager is not the first person recruited onto the project, making pre-assignment a reality for many projects and project managers. 'A', 'B' and 'D' all have some merit to them, but they are not the best answer in this case since pre-assignment is a formally-defined tool.

23. C. In a matrix organization, team members report to both the project manager and the functional manager. This can sometimes cause confusion and can lead to conflict on a project and within the organization.

24. A. The clue in the question that indicates a functional organization is the project manager's low authority; he must appeal to the head of the engineering department rather than making his request directly to the team members.

25. B. Ground rules may be unique to the project, and they certainly don't have to be the same across all projects in an organization. For instance, a project that has high security might have more stringent ground rules than a less secure one. 'A' and 'C' are incorrect because clearly defining ground rules and communicating them to everyone helps to make sure they are understood and will be followed. 'D' is incorrect because that is exactly what ground rules do – they define the boundaries of behavior that team members should respect.

Communications Management

Readers who study this chapter are sometimes surprised that it is not related to the skill of communication through oral and written media in areas such as project writing styles, persuasion, and presentation methods. Rather, communications management covers all tasks related to producing, compiling, sending, storing, distributing, and managing project records. This knowledge area is now made up of only three processes to determine what to communicate, to whom, how often, and when to reevaluate the plan. It involves understanding who your stakeholders are and what they need to know.

Communications management also requires that you accurately report on the project status, performance, change, and earned value, and that you pay close attention to controlling the information to ensure that the communication management plan is working as intended.

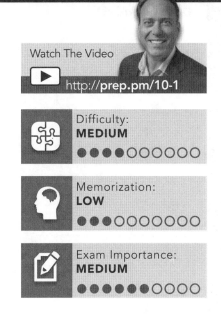

Watch The Video
http://**prep.pm/10-1**

Difficulty:
MEDIUM
●●●●○○○○○○

Memorization:
LOW
●●●○○○○○○○

Exam Importance:
MEDIUM
●●●●●●○○○○

PHILOSOPHY:

There is an old joke in project management circles about "mushroom project management" in which you manage projects the same way you grow mushrooms – by keeping everyone buried in manure, leaving them in the dark, and checking back periodically to see what has popped up.

Chapter Notes:

_____

_____

_____

_____

_____

_____

_____

_____

Chapter Ten

Chapter Notes:

_____

_____

_____

_____

_____

_____

_____

_____

_____

_____

_____

_____

_____

The philosophy presented here is quite different. It focuses on keeping the stakeholders properly informed throughout the project. Communication under this philosophy may be a mixture of formal and informal, written and oral, but it is always proactive and thorough. It is essential that the project manager distribute accurate project information in a timely manner and to the right audience.

IMPORTANCE:

Communications management is of medium importance on the exam, bordering on high. You may see several questions that relate directly to this chapter, so it will be necessary to become acquainted with the processes, terms, and theories presented here.

PREPARATION:

Although the volume of material in communications management is smaller than most of the other areas, there are key concepts that must be learned. Be prepared for several questions on the test specifically related to the inputs, tools and techniques, and outputs for each process. The reason the focus is on these areas is that they are critical to the smooth operation of the processes, and most test-takers do not find them intuitive.

Two other areas of key importance are the communications model and understanding channels of communication. You can expect to see questions about these on the exam.

Communications Management Processes

There are three processes within project communications management, following the familiar pattern of plan, execute, and control. These processes touch three process groups: planning (Plan Communications Management), executing (Manage Communications), and monitoring and controlling (Monitor Communications).

Process Group	Communications Management Process
Initiating	(none)
Planning	Plan Communications Management
Executing	Manage Communications
Monitoring & Controlling	Monitor Communications
Closing	(none)

The primary outputs associated with the three communications management processes are shown in the table below.

Process	Primary Outputs
Plan Communications Management	Communications Management Plan
Manage Communications	Project Communications
Monitor Communications	(No Key Outputs)

Project Manager's Role in Communications

The project manager's most important skill set is the ability to communicate effectively. It is integral to everything he or she does. You may see questions on your exam asking you what the project manager's most important job or most important skills are, or how most of the project manager's time is spent. The answer is almost always related to communications. It is estimated that an effective project manager spends about 90% of his time communicating, and fully 50% of that time is spent communicating with the project team.

Also note that while communications take up a majority of the project manager's working day, one individual cannot control everything that is communicated on a project, nor should they try. Project managers who ask that every single e-mail or conversation be filtered through them first are demonstrating that they are not in control on the project. Instead, the project manager should be *in control* of the communications process. This is done by creating a strong communications management plan, adhering to it, and regularly monitoring and controlling the results.

.... PLANNING

PLAN COMMUNICATIONS MANAGEMENT

6th Edition *PMBOK® Guide*
Cross Ref. pg 366

WHAT IT IS:

For the exam you should consider that Plan Communications Management is all about the communications management plan, its only significant output. The communications management plan is, as you might guess, the plan that drives communication on the project. It defines:

- How often communications will be distributed and updated

- In what format the communications will be distributed (e.g., e-mail, meetings, printed copy, web site, etc.)

- What information will be included in the communications

- Which project stakeholders will receive these communications

Watch The Video
http://**prep.pm/10-2**

WHY IT IS IMPORTANT:

The communications management plan sets stakeholders' expectations on the project, letting them know what information they will receive and when and how they will receive it. If the project manager invests time in defining these lines of communication up front, conflict should be less than if it were undefined. Keep in mind that projects will vary greatly in how formally they define the communications management plan. On a small project, it may not make sense for the project manager to go to great lengths to define an overly formal communications management plan.

Chapter Notes:

_____

_____

_____

_____

_____

_____

_____

WHEN IT IS PERFORMED:

Like many planning processes, Plan Communications Management is typically performed early on the project, before regular project communications commence; however, it may be revisited as often as needed. It does depend on the process of Identify Stakeholders, so it would be performed after that process has been completed.

HOW IT WORKS / INPUTS:

Project Charter — See Ch. 2, Common Inputs

Project Management Plan - The key component of the project management plan here is the stakeholder engagement plan. Communications is almost always the primary way in which stakeholders are kept engaged.

Project Documents - The most important document to bring into this process is the stakeholder register which shows which stakeholders will receive project communications.

Enterprise Environmental Factors — See Ch. 2, Common Inputs

Organizational Process Assets — See Ch. 2, Common Inputs

HOW IT WORKS / TOOLS:

Expert Judgment — See Ch. 2, Common Tools

Communication Requirements Analysis - This one can cover quite a bit of ground. It is relatively simple to define, but sometimes quite tricky to perform on an actual project. The goal of this technique is to identify which stakeholders should receive project communications, what communications they should receive, how they should receive these communications, and how often they should receive them.

Chapter Notes:

_____
_____
_____
_____
_____
_____
_____
_____
_____
_____
_____
_____
_____
_____

Plan Communications Management

Chapter Ten

Chapter Notes:

_____

_____

_____

_____

_____

_____

_____

_____

_____

_____

_____

_____

_____

_____

Communication Channels

A significant part of analyzing the project's communication requirements is determining the communication channels, or paths of communication, that exist within it. Expect at least a couple of questions on the exam to relate directly to this topic. Because the project manager needs to manage and be in control of project communications, it is important to understand that adding a single person on a project can have a significant impact on the number of paths or channels of communication that exist between people.

The formula is: Channels = $n \times (n-1) \div 2$
(Where n = the number of people on the project)

The formula above for calculating communication channels should not scare you. It is a very simple geometric expansion. Before memorizing the formula, refer to the two illustrations below. You can see from the drawing that four people produce six communication channels, as is confirmed by the formula:

$4 \times (4-1) \div 2 = 6$.

If there were five people, the formula would be applied as:

$5 \times (5-1) \div 2 = 10$

By understanding the illustrations that follow and the way people interrelate to form communication channels, the concept should be easy to comprehend.

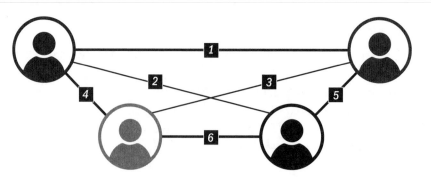

Four people create six communication channels, as illustrated above.

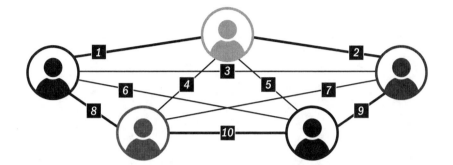

Five people create ten communication channels, or paths, as depicted in the illustration above.

Official Channels of Communication

The number of communication channels is of specific concern when analyzing the project's communication requirements. If there are a large number of channels of communication on the project, the project manager should work to define which communication channels are official. For example, it may be necessary to determine who can officially communicate with the customer or with key subcontractors.

Communication Technology - Technology is a tool, and the right tool should be selected for a given communications need. Whereas face-to-face meetings may be needed for some projects, a project web site, portal, or e-mail may be more appropriate for others. The technology should be tailored to the need. Sensitivity and security of information should also come into consideration when choosing the right technology.

Chapter Notes:

_____

_____

_____

_____

_____

_____

_____

_____

_____

_____

_____

_____

_____

_____

Plan Communications Management

Chapter Ten

Chapter Notes:

_____

_____

_____

_____

_____

_____

_____

_____

_____

_____

_____

_____

_____

_____

Communication Models - The communication model is a formal way of understanding how messages are sent and received. This model defines the responsibilities between the sender and the receiver.

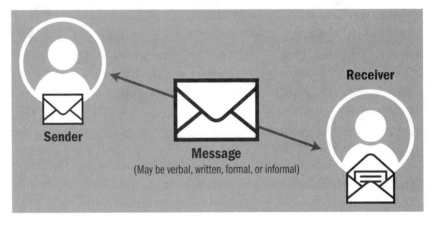

The sender's responsibilities are to:

- Encode the message clearly

- Select a communication method

- Send the message

- Confirm that the message was received and understood by the receiver

The receiver's responsibilities are to:

- Decode the message

- Acknowledge (Confirm that the message was received)

- Respond and give feedback

Often, it is not so easy to simply transmit a message and assume it will be received, decoded, and understood properly. "Noise" can interfere with a message's transmission. Noise can be anything that affects the receiver's ability to understand a message. For instance, language and cultural issues, method of transmission, distance, and bias can all inject noise into the message. Both the sender and receiver must be consciously aware of noise and work to prevent it from compromising the message.

Messages can be conveyed in verbal and nonverbal ways. Below are some terms related to different ways of communicating:

Active listening - Active listening requires the receiver to take steps to ensure that the sender's message was understood. It is similar to effective listening (below).

Effective listening - Effective listening requires the listener's full thought and attention. To be effective as a listener means to monitor nonverbal and physical communications and to provide feedback indicating whether the message has been clearly understood.

Feedback - Feedback refers to the verbal and nonverbal cues a speaker must monitor to see whether the listener fully comprehends the message. Nodding and smiling might be considered positive feedback and indicate that the message is understood and received, whereas nodding and a blank stare might indicate that the message needs to be re-coded for better communication. Asking questions or repeating the speaker's words are also ways to give feedback.

Nonverbal - Nonverbal communication takes place through body language such as facial expressions, posture, hand motions, etc. In fact, most communication between the sender and receiver is nonverbal. Therefore, in order to understand the message, a good listener must carefully attend to nonverbal communication.

Paralingual - Paralingual communication is vocal but not verbal – for example, tone of voice, volume, or pitch. A high-pitched squeal does not employ words, but it certainly communicates.

Communication Blockers - A communication blocker is anything that interferes with the sender encoding the message or with the receiver decoding it. It can include anything that disrupts the communication channels.

Chapter Notes:

_____
_____
_____
_____
_____
_____
_____
_____
_____
_____
_____
_____
_____

Plan Communications Management

Ten

Chapter Notes:

_____

_____

_____

_____

_____

_____

_____

_____

_____

_____

_____

_____

_____

➔ **Communication Methods** - There are methods of communication you will need to know, and it is very important to understand what they are and how and when they are used. Many people find the difference between formal and informal to be non-intuitive the first time they encounter it. The methods of communication are covered in the following table.

Method	Examples	When used
Informal Written	E-mail messages, memorandum	Used frequently on the project to convey information and communicate.
Formal Written	Contracts, legal notices, project documents (e.g, the Charter), important project communications	Used infrequently, but essential for prominent documents that go into the project record. The project plan is a formal written document.
Informal Oral	Discussions, phone calls, conversations	Used to communicate information quickly and efficiently.
Formal Oral	Meetings, speeches, mass communications, presentations	Used for public relations, special events, company-wide annoucements, sales.
Internal	Emails to the team, Memos or presentations to senior management	Used to communicate within the performing organization.
External	Messages or presentations to customers, regulators, the public, or investors	Used to communicate with stakeholders outside of the performing organization.
Official	Communication to government or regulatory bodies.	Used to communicate with any party that operates in an oversight role for the project.
Unofficial	Anything that is not official, including the majority of project communication to internal or external stakeholders.	Used for most project commuications to ensure successful delivery.

Be aware that not just the message but also the medium determines whether a form of communication is formal or informal.

Another way of framing communications is to think of them in one of the following three categories:

Category	Examples
Interactive	A meeting where people can ask questions
Push	A bulk e-mail blast
Pull	A website where a video presentation or white paper can be downloaded

Interpersonal and Team Skills - This tool shows up frequently in this book, but it is particularly important when it comes to communication. Understanding your communication style, and being politically and culturally aware are important aspects of interpersonal and team skills.

 Data Representation - The stakeholder engagement assessment matrix is a powerful tool to show how stakeholders relate to the project.

Meetings — See Ch. 2, Common Tools

HOW IT WORKS / OUTPUTS:

 Communications Management Plan - The communications management plan is part of the project management plan, and it defines the following:

- Who should receive project communications

- What communications they require and what should be included

- Who should send the communication

- Who should approve sensitive communications

- How the communication will be sent

- How often it will be updated

- Definitions so that everyone has a common understanding of terms

Project Management Plan Updates —
See Ch. 2, Common Outputs

Project Documents Updates — See Ch. 2, Common Outputs

Chapter Notes:

_____

_____

_____

_____

_____

_____

_____

_____

_____

_____

_____

_____

_____

_____

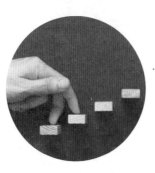

···· EXECUTING

MANAGE COMMUNICATIONS

6th Edition *PMBOK® Guide*
Cross Ref. pg 379

WHAT IT IS:

It is easiest to consider the process of Manage Communications as the execution of the communications management plan. In other words, the communications management plan lays out how communications will be handled, and the process of Manage Communications carries that out.

Keep in mind that while Manage Communications is performed according to the communications management plan, it must also be flexible so that unplanned information requests may be handled.

Watch The Video
▶ http://**prep.pm**/10-3

WHY IT IS IMPORTANT:

Manage Communications is the process where the bulk of project communications takes place.

The approach to this process may be summed up in the following four statements:

Chapter Notes:

1. Always deal with the problem

2. Always communicate directly

3. Always tell the truth

4. Always distribute accurate information

_____

_____

_____

_____

_____

_____

_____

WHEN IT IS PERFORMED:

Manage Communications generally updates stakeholders on the progress of the project according to the communications management plan. It may start quite early on the project, but it typically elevates in importance and activity during the construction phases of the project.

HOW IT WORKS / INPUTS:

Project Management Plan — See Ch. 2, Common Inputs

Project Documents — See Ch. 2, Common Inputs

Work Performance Reports - Much of project communication will be related to the project's performance, and the performance reports are the source of that.

Enterprise Environmental Factors — See Ch. 2, Common Inputs

Organizational Process Assets — See Ch. 2, Common Inputs

HOW IT WORKS / TOOLS:

Communication Technology: See description under the tools of previous process, Plan Communications Management.

Communication Methods: See description under the tools of previous process, Plan Communications Management.

Communication Skills - This tool includes your ability to formulate a message, your ability to stay on topic, and well as how well you receive feedback. It also includes how you conduct presentations and how you set and manage communications expectations with your stakeholders. For the exam, the same things that apply for a high Emotional Intelligence will apply here.

Chapter Notes:

_____
_____
_____
_____
_____
_____
_____
_____
_____
_____
_____
_____
_____
_____

Manage Communications

Chapter Notes:

_____

_____

_____

_____

_____

_____

_____

_____

_____

_____

_____

_____

_____

_____

_____

Project Management Information System —
    See Ch. 2, Common Tools

Project Reporting - This is very similar to the work performance reports. Project Reporting includes any communications about the deliverables, whereas the other work performance reports look more at how the work is progressing.

 **Interpersonal and Team Skills** - The skills of active listening, conflict management, effective meeting management, and political awareness are the key skills to recognize here.

Meetings — See Ch. 2, Common Tools

HOW IT WORKS / OUTPUTS:

Project Communications - Any time information is being exchanged with stakeholders, this output comes into play. Recall from earlier in this chapter that communications may be formal or informal, oral or written. These communications will include information about how the project is progressing, how the team is performing, and how the deliverables are shaping up.

Project Management Plan Updates —
    See Ch. 2, Common Outputs

Project Documents Updates — See Ch. 2, Common Outputs

Organizational Process Assets Updates —
    See Ch. 2, Common Outputs

···· MONITORING & CONTROLLING

MONITOR COMMUNICATIONS

WHAT IT IS:

Monitoring and controlling processes look at what was planned and compare that with the work that was executed. Monitor Communications does exactly that. It compares the results of the previous process (Manage Communications) with the communications management plan. If there are differences, adjustments are made to the plan or to the way the work is being carried out.

WHY IT IS IMPORTANT:

Communication issues are responsible for more than their share of project problems and failures. Getting the plan right and then executing it well is extremely important.

The important things to know about this process are the nature of what it does, how it is carried out, and how the tool of Data Representation is used.

WHEN IT IS PERFORMED:

Monitor Communications is started early in the project and is performed periodically throughout. As long as there are project communications taking place, it would be an appropriate time to perform this process.

6th Edition *PMBOK® Guide*
Cross Ref. pg 388

Watch The Video

▶ http://**prep.pm**/10-4

Chapter Notes:

_____

_____

_____

_____

_____

_____

_____

_____

Chapter Ten

Chapter Notes:

_____

_____

_____

_____

_____

_____

_____

_____

_____

_____

_____

_____

_____

_____

HOW IT WORKS / INPUTS:

Project Management Plan — See Ch. 2, Common Inputs

Project Documents — See Ch. 2, Common Inputs

Work Performance Data — See Ch. 2, Common Inputs

Enterprise Environmental Factors — See Ch. 2, Common Inputs

Organizational Process Assets — See Ch. 2, Common Inputs

HOW IT WORKS / TOOLS:

Expert Judgment — See Ch. 2, Common Tools

Project Management Information System — See Ch. 2, Common Inputs

Data Representation - The idea here can be expressed in the axiom "a picture is worth a thousand words." Graphics, images, charts, and tables can be used to help people visualize and understand data. One area that is used in communications management is the stakeholder engagement assessment matrix (covered in chapter 13 in the Plan Stakeholder Engagement process). It provides a way to group and display how stakeholders are participating on the project.

For the exam, think of this tool as showing data in a meaningful format.

Interpersonal and Team Skills - Once again, this tool appears as key. Observation and conversation, sometimes referred to as MBWA (Manage By Walking Around), is key here. In other words, stay engaged with your team.

Meetings - Meetings are an important part of communications, and they are always classified as formal communication even if the meeting is ad-hoc. One type of meeting you should be aware of is a lessons learned meeting, sometimes referred to as a post mortem meeting or an after action review. These meetings ask one simple question: "if we had this activity to do over again, what would we do differently knowing what we know now?" The results of these become lessons learned, which may be useful for this project and for future projects.

HOW IT WORKS / OUTPUTS:

Work Performance Information — See Ch. 2, Common Outputs

Change Requests — See Ch. 2, Common Outputs

Project Management Plan Updates —
See Ch. 2, Common Outputs

Project Documents Updates — See Ch. 2, Common Outputs

Chapter Ten

Chapter Notes:

_____

_____

_____

_____

_____

_____

_____

_____

_____

_____

_____

_____

_____

→ The Agile Perspective on Communications Management

Communication stands out as being markedly more open and dynamic on agile projects. Because the team is often colocated, agile projects benefit from "osmotic communication" where the team benefits from and absorbs information gleaned from other conversations.

In this environment, communication should be rapid, and barriers to direct, transparent communication should be actively removed. Agile projects also employ stand-up meetings and frequent reviews which facilitate communication. Conversation and engagement are highly encouraged over adhering to a plan.

Healthy agile teams avoid communication silos and instead foster the collective understanding of the team.

EXERCISES

1. Calculate the number of communication channels that would exist between eight people.

2. Draw a line connecting the specific form of communication on the left to the corresponding type of communication on the right.

Email

Testimony before Congress

Speech at a trade show

Contracts addendum

Hallway conversation with a coworker

Informal Written

Formal Written

Informal Verbal

Formal Verbal

Chapter Notes:

_____

_____

_____

_____

_____

_____

_____

_____

_____

_____

_____

_____

_____

_____

Chapter Ten

Chapter Notes:

_____

_____

_____

_____

_____

_____

_____

_____

_____

_____

_____

_____

ANSWERS TO EXERCISES

1. **Calculate the number of communication channels for 8 people.**

With 8 individuals, there are 28 communication channels as proven by the formula $8 \times (8-1) \div 2 = 28$

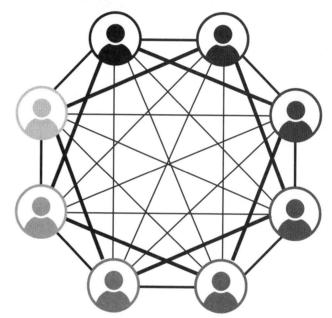

A graphical depiction of the 28 communication channels between the 8 people

2. **The forms of communication are illustrated below**

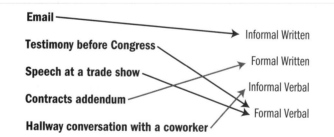

Email ——→ Informal Written

Testimony before Congress —→ Formal Written

Speech at a trade show —→ Informal Verbal

Contracts addendum —→ Formal Verbal

Hallway conversation with a coworker —→

COMMUNICATIONS MANAGEMENT

QUESTIONS

1. If there were 4 people on the project team and 9 more are added, how many additional channels of communication does this create?

   A. 6.

   B. 30.

   C. 36.

   D. 72.

2. The process to create a plan showing how all project communication will be conducted is known as:

   A. Communications Modeling.

   B. Plan Communications Management.

   C. Information Method.

   D. Communication Distribution Planning.

3. The responsibility of decoding the message rests with:

   A. The sender.

   B. The receiver.

   C. The communications management plan.

   D. The communications model.

Chapter Notes:

_____

_____

_____

_____

_____

_____

_____

_____

_____

_____

_____

_____

4. **Which of the following is FALSE regarding Manage Communications?**

    A. Manage Communications is an executing process.

    B. Manage Communications ends when the product has been accepted.

    C. Manage Communications may involve unexpected requests from stakeholders.

    D. Manage Communications carries out the communications management plan.

5. **Acknowledgement in the context of the communication model indicates:**

    A. Confirmation of receipt.

    B. Comprehension of the sender's message.

    C. Agreement with the sender's message.

    D. Agreement upon the protocol and frequency of communication.

6. **Your latest review of the project status shows it to be more than three weeks behind schedule. You are required to communicate this to the customer. This message should be:**

    A. Formal and written.

    B. Informal and written.

    C. Formal and oral.

    D. Informal and oral.

7. **Which of the following statements is TRUE regarding issues?**

   A. All issues must be resolved in order for the project to be closed.

   B. The issue log is a tool for stakeholders to manage project issues.

   C. Each issue should be assigned to a single owner.

   D. Issue management may be treated as a sub-project on larger, more complex projects.

8. **The majority of a person's communication is:**

   A. Verbal.

   B. Nonverbal.

   C. Documented.

   D. Unnecessary.

9. **Which of the following communication techniques is the most effective for resolving conflict?**

   A. Instant messaging.

   B. Conference calls.

   C. Paralingual communication.

   D. Face-to-face communication.

10. **Communication skills would be used most during which of the following processes?**

    A. Manage Communications.

    B. Status Meetings.

    C. Direct and Manage Project Work.

    D. Communications Change Control.

Chapter Notes:

_____

_____

_____

_____

_____

_____

_____

_____

_____

_____

_____

_____

_____

_____

_____

Communications Management: Questions

Chapter Ten

Chapter Notes:

_____

_____

_____

_____

_____

_____

_____

_____

_____

_____

_____

_____

_____

11. The communications management plan typically contains all of the following EXCEPT:

A. The expected stakeholder response to the communication.

B. The stakeholder communication requirements.

C. What technology will be used to communicate information.

D. A glossary of terms.

12. You are about to attend a biweekly status meeting with your program manager when she calls and asks you to be certain to include earned value analysis in this and future meetings. Why is earned value analysis important to the communications process?

A. It communicates the likelihood of the project's success.

B. It communicates how the project is doing against the plan.

C. It communicates the date the project deviated from the plan.

D. It communicates the value-to-cost ratio.

13. You receive a last-minute status report from a senior member of the project team that you believe is incorrect. It shows tasks as being complete that you are almost certain are no more than 60% complete, and it documents deliverables as having been turned over to the customer that you do not believe are finished yet. You are walking into a communication meeting with key stakeholders. What is the BEST way to handle this problem?

A. Ask the team member who wrote the report to sign it.

B. Ask the stakeholders to wait a few minutes while you try to verify the information.

C. Summon the project team to the meeting and get to the bottom of the discrepancy.

D. Do nothing with this status and provide an amended report at the next meeting with the stakeholders.

14. The MOST important skill for a project manager to have is:

A. Good administrative skills.

B. Good planning skills.

C. Good client-facing skills.

D. Good communication skills.

15. Project reporting is a tool that is most closely associated with which process?

A. Plan Communications Management.

B. Manage Communications.

C. Report Performance.

D. Monitor Communications.

16. The best definition of noise is:

A. Any unsupportable information that finds its way onto written or oral project communications.

B. Anything that interferes with transmission and understanding of a message.

C. Any communication that takes place through unofficial project channels.

D. A communications acronym for Normal Operational Informing of Select project Entities.

Chapter Notes:

_____

_____

_____

_____

_____

_____

_____

_____

_____

_____

_____

_____

_____

_____

Chapter Notes:

_____

_____

_____

_____

_____

_____

_____

_____

_____

_____

_____

_____

_____

_____

17. A project manager is holding a meeting with stakeholders related to the status of a large project for constructing a new runway at a major airport. The runway project has a CPI of 1.2 and an SPI of 1.25, and the manager is going to have to deliver the message to the stakeholders that a crucial quality test has failed. What kind of communication does this meeting represent?

    A. Informal oral.

    B. Formal oral.

    C. Paralingual.

    D. Nonverbal.

18. You have just assumed the role of project manager for the construction of a new runway for a major airport. The project is already in progress, and there are over 200 identified stakeholders on the project. You want to know how to communicate with these stakeholders. Where should you be able to find this information?

    A. It depends on the type of project.

    B. The stakeholder register.

    C. The communications management plan.

    D. Communication requirements.

19. Mary is using forecasting to determine her project's estimate at complete. What would be the most likely place to include this information?

    A. The communications management plan.

    B. The project activity report.

    C. Project communications.

    D. The stakeholder engagement report.

20. Marie is a project manager who is involved in a meeting with the customer. After the customer makes a statement, Marie carefully reformulates and restates the message back to them. What is Marie practicing in this case?

    A. Listening skills.

    B. Project communications management.

    C. Professional courtesy.

    D. Passive listening.

21. Lessons learned should contain:

    A. The collective wisdom of the team.

    B. Feedback from the customer as to what you could have done better.

    C. Information to be used as an input into project closure.

    D. Analysis of the variances that occurred from the project's baseline.

22. In which process would work performance information be produced?

    A. Plan Communications Management.

    B. Monitor Communications.

    C. Report Performance.

    D. Manage Communications.

23. Information sent to specific recipients who need to receive it but that is not confirmed to be received or understood by the receiver is known as:

    A. The communication model.

    B. Push communication.

    C. Pull communication.

    D. Noise.

Chapter Notes:

_____

_____

_____

_____

_____

_____

_____

_____

_____

_____

_____

_____

_____

_____

24. Information sensitivity and security would be of greatest concern when:

A. Working on government projects.

B. Evaluating the communications model.

C. Choosing the appropriate communications technology.

D. Rumors or inaccurate information are being circulated.

25. The issue log is used in which communications management process?

A. Plan Communications Management.

B. Push Communication.

C. Distribute Communications.

D. Monitor Communications.

COMMUNICATIONS MANAGEMENT

ANSWERS

1. D. If you tried to take a shortcut here, chances are you missed this one and guessed 'C'. If there were 4 people, there would have been 6 communication channels. 9 more would create 13, which translates to 78 communications channels. The question is asking how many additional channels were created, so the answer is 78 - 6 = 72.

2. B. Plan Communications Management is the process for determining how the overall communication process will be carried out. It is the general plan for communications. None of the other three answers were terms used in this book, but the real giveaway was that only one answer 'B' was even the name of a process.

3. B. In the communication model, it is the sender that encodes, and the receiver decodes the message.

4. B. Did you get tricked by this one? Manage Communications doesn't always end when acceptance has occurred, so this is the answer that doesn't fit. Some stakeholders will need information distributed on the closure of the contracts and projects. 'A' is true, because Manage Communications is an executing process. 'C' is true because Manage Communications carries out predetermined communication, but also will be used to respond to unplanned requests from stakeholders. 'D' is true because Manage Communications is the process that executes the communications management plan.

5. A. Within the communication model, acknowledgement only indicates confirmation of receipt. It does not mean that the receiver understood the message or agreed with the message.

6. A. Communication on schedule slippage, cost overruns, and other major project statuses should be formal and in writing. That doesn't mean you can't pick up the phone to soften the blow, but the formal and written aspects of the communication are what count here.

Chapter Notes:

_____

_____

_____

_____

_____

_____

_____

_____

_____

_____

_____

_____

_____

7. C. Each issue should be assigned to an owner and be assigned a target completion date. 'A' is incorrect since a project could be closed (successfully) and still have outstanding issues. Sometimes the issues are out of the project manager's control. 'B' is incorrect since the issue log is not for the stakeholders – it is for the project manager to use to manage issues. 'D' is incorrect because issues are managed within the context of a project. If you were even considering creating a separate project to manage issues, your project is probably beyond hope.

8. B. Most of a person's communication takes place non verbally. It is body language that carries much of the message. 'A' is the opposite of the correct answer. 'C' is incorrect since most of the communication is nonverbal, but not written (documented). 'D' may well be true for some people, but it is not the correct answer here.

9. D. Face-to-face communication is the most effective means of resolving conflict. This fits an overall theme that direct, clear, and personal communication is favored for project managers. If you guessed 'A', go find a place to hide in shame, or at least go sit in time out for a few minutes. 'B' and 'C' might seem like appropriate choices in some situations, but face-to-face is still more effective.

10. A. Your communications skills are used as a tool in Manage Communications. 'B' and 'D' should have been easy to eliminate since they are not real processes. 'C' is a real process but it is not the correct answer.

11. A. The expected response you will receive is not part of the communications management plan. The communications management plan focuses on how you will communicate to stakeholders and not how they will communicate to you. 'B', 'C', and 'D' are all typically part of the communications management plan.

12. B. Earned value analysis is a communication tool, and it's all about how the project is doing against the plan. 'A' is incorrect, because "success" involves more than good earned value.

13. B. This is a hard scenario, but be prepared for questions like this on the exam. The reasoning behind answer 'B' is this: a project manager should always communicate accurate information and should always report the truth. 'A' is wrong because it isn't about getting your team member to sign off. Accurate information is more important than accountability. 'C' is incorrect because it is not the team's job to go to these meetings. They should be executing the work on the project. 'D' is incorrect because waiting only postpones the situation and delays getting accurate information to the stakeholders. Choice 'B' is best in this case because it is the only one that gets accurate information to the stakeholders as quickly as possible.

14. D. Good communication skills are the most important skills a project manager can have! Project managers spend more time communicating than anything else.

15. B. Project reporting is a tool of the Manage Communications process. 'C' would have been a good choice years ago when such a process existed, but it is not a process for this edition of the exam.

16. B. Noise is anything that interferes with the transmission and understanding of a message. If you guessed 'D', then you were, indeed, guessing.

17. B. Meetings are classified as formal, whether they are regular or ad-hoc.

18. C. This information would be contained in the communications management plan.

19. C. Project communications is the main output of the Manage Communications process. This is the place for updated earned value information such as the estimate at complete. 'A' was the only other answer that contained a term that is used in this book, and it is not an appropriate match for this question.

20. A. Marie is practicing good listening skills to make sure she communicates well with her customer.

Chapter Notes:

_____

_____

_____

_____

_____

_____

_____

_____

_____

_____

_____

_____

_____

_____

Communications Management: Answers

Chapter Notes:

_____

_____

_____

_____

_____

_____

_____

_____

_____

_____

_____

_____

_____

_____

21. D. This is important. Lessons learned focus on variances from the plan and what would be done differently in the future in order to avoid those variances.

22. B. The WPI is the main output of Monitor Communications. It provides information on how the communication is performing compared to the plan.

23. B. Push communication is communication that is pushed out (think bulk email), but the drawback is that there is no reliable confirmation by the receiver that it was received or understood.

24. C. One of the key, deciding factors when selecting the right communication technology is how sensitive or confidential the information is. 'A' might look like a good answer at first, but not all government projects are particularly confidential or sensitive.

25. D. Even if you didn't memorize all of the inputs, tools, and outputs, it may have been intuitive to you that the issue log was tied to the monitoring and controlling process here. It is one of the documents used as an input into Monitor Communications.

Risk
Management

If the previous chapter seemed light and easy, we are about to make up for that. Risk management is a rich field, full of information and tools for statistical analysis. In the real world, actuaries anticipate risk and calculate the probability of risk events and their associated costs, and entire volumes are written on risk analysis and mitigation. In this section, you do not need to know every tool and technique associated with risk. Instead, focus your study on the high-level interactions within the different risk processes.

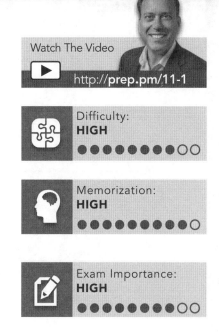

Watch The Video
http://**prep.pm**/11-1

Difficulty:
HIGH
●●●●●●●●○○

Memorization:
HIGH
●●●●●●●●●○

Exam Importance:
HIGH
●●●●●●●●○○

PHILOSOPHY:

By this time, you should have picked up on the fact that very few of these processes are reactive. The overriding philosophy is that the project manager is in control and proactively managing events, avoiding as many problems as possible. The project manager must understand how to anticipate and identify areas of risk, how to quantify and qualify them, and how to plan for them.

Chapter Notes:

IMPORTANCE:

Risk is one of the areas some people find challenging on the exam. The material may be new or unfamiliar, and the techniques may take some work in order to master.

Chapter Eleven

Chapter Notes:

_____

_____

_____

_____

_____

_____

_____

_____

_____

_____

_____

_____

_____

_____

_____

PREPARATION:

In order to pass this section of the exam, you need to understand the risk management plan and the terms related to risk. The seven risk management processes contain 82 inputs, tools, and outputs! All of these components to the processes are important, but the secret is that most of them are either common sense or they are not frequent exploits on the exam. This chapter puts more emphasis on the essential elements that you need to know. Material is organized around these seven processes, building upon the different components that go with each one.

There are seven processes within project risk management, and these processes touch three process groups: planning (Plan Risk Management, Identify Risks, Perform Qualitative Risk Analysis, Perform Quantitative Risk Analysis, Plan Risk Responses), executing (Implement Risk Responses), and monitoring and controlling (Monitor Risks)

Process Group	Risk Management Process
Initiating	none
Planning	Plan Risk Management, Indentify Risks, Perform Qualitative Risk Analysis, Perform Quantitative Risk Analysis, Plan Risk Responses
Executing	Implement Risk Responses
Monitoring & Controlling	Monitor Risks
Closing	none

The primary outputs associated with the seven risk management processes are shown in the table below.

Process	Primary Outputs
Plan Risk Management	Risk Management Plan
Identify Risks	Risk Register, Risk Report
Perform Qualitative Risk Analysis	(No Key Outputs)
Perform Quantitative Risk Analysis	(No Key Outputs)
Plan Risk Responses	(No Key Outputs)
Implement Risk Responses	Change Requests
Monitor Risks	(No Key Outputs)

Risk

The usage of the word "risk" here has a different meaning than many project managers and organizations may have encountered before. Risk has three characteristics that must be understood for the exam:

1. Risk is related to an uncertain event.

2. A risk may affect the project for good or for bad. Although risk usually has negative connotations, it may well have an upside. This is a favorite exploit on the exam.

3. There is a difference between Individual Project Risk and Overall Project Risk. An Individual Project Risk threatens an objective. For example, if a decision is made to move something from a local server into the cloud in order to save money and improve uptime, there might be an individual risk associated with that. If the move could not be carried out, it might threaten the objectives of saving money and increasing uptime, but it could still be moved back to the local server and continue the project. Overall Project Risks are things that threaten the success of the project. Both of these examples were things that threatened elements of the project, but in reality, these risks can be positive or negative.

Risks may occur for different reasons. Some of those may be because the situations are naturally variable such as the weather. Others may occur because things are purely uncertain or ambiguous such as whether or not a piece of technology will be readily available.

The risk approach you choose needs to be tailored to fit with the factors that influence your project.

Chapter Notes:

_____

_____

_____

_____

_____

_____

_____

_____

_____

_____

_____

_____

_____

Size of Project — Project Complexity — Inherent Project Risk — Project Methodology — Importance

Tailored Risk Approach

Chapter Eleven

···· PLANNING

PLAN RISK MANAGEMENT

6th Edition *PMBOK® Guide*
Cross Ref. pg 401

WHAT IT IS:

Plan Risk Management is the process that is concerned with one thing: creating the risk management plan. Your understanding of that plan is the key to unlocking this process and will form the foundation for the other risk management processes.

In Plan Risk Management, the remaining six risk management processes are planned. How they will be conducted is documented in the risk management plan, which is typically general and high-level in nature. This means that when performing Plan Risk Management, you usually are not concerned with specific project risks. Instead, you will focus on how risk will be approached on the project.

Watch The Video
▶ http://**prep.pm**/11-2

WHY IT IS IMPORTANT:

Think of this process as creating your roadmap for the six processes of Identify Risks, Perform Qualitative Risk Analysis, Perform Quantitative Risk Analysis, Plan Risk Responses, Implement Risk Responses, and Monitor Risks. By creating a plan (the risk management plan) for these five processes, you are being deliberate and proactive with risk on the project.

The more risk that is inherent on the project, and the more important the project is to the organization, the more resources you would typically apply to performing this process.

By far the most important component of this process is the sole output, the Risk Management Plan. The rest of it is predictable and unlikely to be exploited on the exam.

Chapter Notes:

_____

_____

_____

_____

_____

_____

_____

_____

WHEN IT IS PERFORMED:

This process is general and high-level in nature and therefore takes place early on the project, usually before many of the other planning processes are performed. The reason it usually takes place very early is that the results of this (and other risk processes) can significantly influence decisions made about scope, time, cost, quality, and procurement.

HOW IT WORKS / INPUTS:

Project Charter - The charter may contain information about risk tolerance or constraints and assumptions that need to be factored into the risk management plan.

Project Management Plan - This process brings in as much information as is known about the project in order to create a risk management plan with compatible approach.

Project Documents - The stakeholder register is the important document in this process because it lists stakeholders who may be able to give input about risk approaches and who may be affected by risk management decisions.

Enterprise Environmental Factors — See Ch. 2, Common Inputs

Organizational Process Assets — See Ch. 2, Common Inputs

Chapter Eleven

Chapter Notes:

_____

_____

_____

_____

_____

_____

_____

_____

_____

_____

_____

_____

HOW IT WORKS / TOOLS:

Expert Judgment — See Ch. 2, Common Tools

Data Analysis — See Ch. 2, Common Tools

Meetings — See Ch. 2, Common Tools

HOW IT WORKS / OUTPUTS:

Risk Management Plan - As stated in the introduction to Plan Risk Management, creating the risk management plan is the real purpose of this process. In fact, it is the process's sole output.

The risk management plan is a road map to the other six risk management processes. It defines what level of risk will be considered tolerable for the project, how risk will be managed, who will be responsible for risk activities, the amounts of time and resource that will be allotted to risk activities, and how risk findings will be communicated.

Another important part of the risk management plan is a description of how risks will be categorized. This will be a significant help in the subsequent risk processes. One tool for creating consistent risk categories is the risk breakdown structure (RBS).

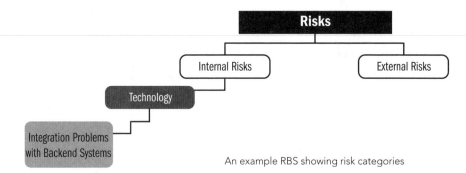

An example RBS showing risk categories

The RBS, like its cousin the WBS, is a graphical, hierarchical decomposition used to facilitate understanding and organization.

In this case, however, we are breaking down the categories of risks and not the work. One important thing to note with the RBS is that we are not breaking down the actual risks (they won't all be known until we perform the Identify Risks process). Instead, we are breaking down the categories of risks that we will evaluate.

The risk management plan may contain more information such as standard vocabulary about probability and impact that apply to the project.

Chapter Notes:

_____

_____

_____

_____

_____

_____

_____

_____

_____

_____

_____

_____

_____

Plan Risk Management

Chapter Eleven

···· PLANNING

IDENTIFY RISKS

6th Edition *PMBOK® Guide*
Cross Ref. pg 409

Watch The Video
▶ http://**prep.pm/11-3**

WHAT IT IS:

Identify Risks is a planning process that evaluates the project to create a list of the risks that could potentially impact the project and to understand the nature of those risks.

The output of the risk register will help you understand this process. It is a list of all risks, their causes, and any possible responses to those risks that can be identified at this point in the project.

Be aware that Identify Risks, like many processes discussed in this book, is often performed multiple times on the project. This may be especially true in this case since your understanding of risk, and the nature of the risks themselves, will change and evolve as the project progresses.

WHY IT IS IMPORTANT:

Chapter Notes:

_____

_____

_____

_____

_____

_____

_____

_____

Identify Risks builds the risk register, which is needed before the remaining five risk processes (Perform Qualitative Risk Analysis, Perform Quantitative Risk Analysis, Plan Risk Responses, Implement Risk Responses, and Monitor Risks) may be performed. This list of risks will drive the other risk processes.

WHEN IT IS PERFORMED:

Although Identify Risks is typically performed early on in the project, risks change over time, and new risks arise. It may be necessary to perform this process multiple times throughout the project.

HOW IT WORKS / INPUTS:

Project Management Plan — See Ch. 2, Common Inputs

Project Documents — See Ch. 2, Common Inputs

Agreements – You should treat the word "agreement" as if it were a contract when you are preparing for the exam. Contracts almost always have enforcements and penalties if the terms are not met, and oftentimes they have rewards if the terms are met or exceeded. These potential penalties and rewards represent a type of risk.

Procurement Documentation – Portions of the project that are procured from outside organizations (covered in the next chapter) carry their own inherent risks. The procurement documentation brought into this process will help the team spot (identify) these risks.

Enterprise Environmental Factors — See Ch. 2, Common Inputs

Organizational Process Assets — See Ch. 2, Common Inputs

HOW IT WORKS / TOOLS:

Expert Judgment — See Ch. 2, Common Tools

Data Gathering – Brainstorming and checklists are the two techniques to remember here for the exam. They are important to help make sure the right risks are identified.

Chapter Notes:

_____

_____

_____

_____

_____

_____

_____

_____

_____

_____

_____

_____

➜ **Data Analysis** - The primary tools used to analyze data in this process are:

Root Cause Analysis - This is using Ishikawa (fishbone) diagrams, or the 5 why technique to trace risk events back to identify the underlying factors that led to them. For example, if many of the risks are traced back to a root cause of outdated or poorly maintained equipment, then this might lead to a decision to update that equipment or it might lead to the identification of more risks.

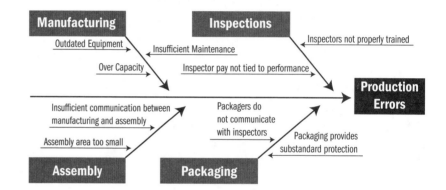

In addition to Ishikawa diagrams, there is the practice of asking why five times to uncover root causes. This technique, pioneered at Toyota, looks at a problem and asks "why?", then takes that response and asks "why?" again, five times in all. Generally, by the fifth iteration of this technique you will have reached the root cause.

Consider the following example of the five whys technique:

Effect: The vehicle failed its annual emissions test.

Why? The check engine light was on.

Why? The oxygen sensor had failed.

Why? The fuel injectors had not been properly cleaned, resulting in an improper burn.

Why? The mechanic did not follow manufacturer's guidelines.

Why? The staff was not factory trained for maintenance.

Asking the five whys can help the team get below the surface and understand the real underlying issues at work. In the preceding example, the root cause that was uncovered may well lead to other maintenance problems.

Assumptions and Constraint Analysis - The project management plan is largely built around assumptions and constraints, and these need to be analyzed and challenged from time to time. If the project finds that they can relax a constraint (e.g., this project needs to use all open source software), this may open the door for more options in planning and execution. Likewise, if an assumption (positive or negative) is found to be incorrect (e.g., the external software APIs the project needs will be available before development begins), it can greatly impact the project.

SWOT Analysis - SWOT analysis is particularly useful since it is a tool used to measure the project's strengths (S), weaknesses (W), opportunities (O), and threats (T). Each one of these is plotted, and the quadrant where the weaknesses (usually internal) and threats (usually external) represent the highest negative risks, and the quadrant where strengths (again, usually internal), and opportunities (usually external) are highest will represent the highest positive risks on the project.

SWOT analysis can give you another perspective on risk that will often help you identify your most significant project risk factors.

Chapter Notes:

_____

_____

_____

_____

_____

_____

_____

_____

_____

_____

_____

_____

_____

Identify Risks

	Helpful	Harmful
Internal	Strength J F	Weakness L O N E D
External	Opportunity C A M G H	Threat P K I B

Illustration of one type of SWOT analysis where each letter corresponds to a specified risk from the risk register

Chapter Eleven

Chapter Notes:

_____

_____

_____

_____

_____

_____

_____

_____

_____

_____

_____

_____

_____

Document Analysis - Reading the project documentation may not be the most entertaining activity described in this book, but it can be a very good way to identify the risks. Remember that risk is defined as uncertainty, and areas where project documentation is not clear might be an indicator of underlying risks.

Interpersonal and Team Skills — See Ch. 2, Common Tools

Prompt Lists - A prompt list is used by the project team to help facilitate a risk review. They are often used periodically or between each phase to serve as a kind of framework for identifying new risks that might have arisen. The _PMBOK® Guide_ lists three different frameworks PESTLE (political, economic, social, technological, legal, environmental), TECOP (technical, environmental, commercial, operational, political), and VUCA (volatility, uncertainty, complexity, ambiguity).

An example of how this might be used is at the end of a phase, a project team might ask the questions "since our last review, what political, economic, social, technological, legal, environmental changes or developments have there been that could impact our project?"

This underscores the fact that risk management is not something a project team does once and then forgets. It is an ongoing set of processes, and prompt lists give you a framework to make this easier.

Meetings — See Ch. 2, Common Tools

HOW IT WORKS / OUTPUTS:

Risk Register - The risk register provides a list of all identified risks on the project, what the possible reactions to this risk are, what the root causes are, and what categories the risks fall into. It is also common to update the RBS with the more specific information as the following example illustrates.

The risk register contains the identified risks, the potential risk owners, and a list of potential responses to those risks. The potential risk owners will be validated in Perform Qualitative Risk Analysis, and the potential responses will be validated in Plan Risk Responses, both covered later in this chapter.

The risk register is an essential input into the remaining risk management processes and may be updated throughout the life of the project.

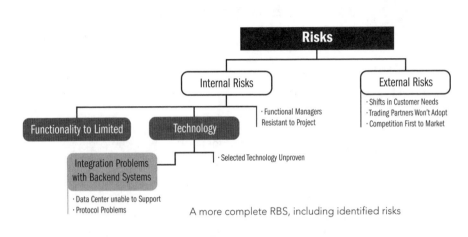

A more complete RBS, including identified risks

Risk ID	Risk	Responses	Root Cause	Categories
R001	Threat of being hacked	Firewall; intrusion detection software	Poorly designed security; Outdated techonolgy	Security

Fragment of Risk Register

Risk Report - The risk report looks at the factors contributing to risk and high-level information on the identified risks. It has some similarities to the risk register; however, the risk report is more of a summary document and will likely be more verbose about what things are contributing to project risk.

Project Documents Updates — See Ch. 2, Common Outputs

Chapter Notes:

Identify Risks

···· PLANNING

PERFORM QUALITATIVE RISK ANALYSIS

6th Edition *PMBOK® Guide*
Cross Ref. pg 419

WHAT IT IS:

The process of Perform Qualitative Risk Analysis is usually done rapidly in order to determine which risks are the highest priority on the project.

This process takes each risk from the risk register and works to analyze the probability it will occur and its impact if it does. By using the probability and impact matrix (PIM), a prioritization and ranking can be created, which is updated on the risk register.

Watch The Video
http://prep.pm/11-4

WHY IT IS IMPORTANT:

This process helps you rank and prioritize the risks so that you can put the right emphasis on the right risks. It helps to ensure that time and resources are spent in the right risk areas.

Chapter Notes:

_____

_____

_____

_____

_____

_____

_____

WHEN IT IS PERFORMED:

Perform Qualitative Risk Analysis, like many other risk processes, is usually performed more than once on a project. The reason for this is twofold:

1. Perform Qualitative Risk Analysis can usually be performed fairly quickly relative to other planning processes.

2. It is normal for risks and their underlying characteristics to change over the life of the project, making this process important to revisit often.

HOW IT WORKS / INPUTS:

Project Management Plan — See Ch. 2, Common Inputs

Project Documents — See Ch. 2, Common Inputs

Enterprise Environmental Factors — See Ch. 2, Common Inputs

Organizational Process Assets — See Ch. 2, Common Inputs

HOW IT WORKS / TOOLS:

Expert Judgment — See Ch. 2, Common Tools

Data Gathering — See Ch. 2, Common Tools

Data Analysis - Data Analysis is a significant part of this process.

> **Risk Data Quality Assessment** - There is a saying "garbage in equals garbage out." If the data about risks is not high quality, then the decisions you make will naturally have more uncertainty. The data should be objectively evaluated to determine whether or not it is accurate and of acceptable quality. For instance, if you were evaluating weather risk for a construction project, you would need to evaluate the quality of the weather data you were using.

Chapter Notes:

Chapter Eleven

Chapter Notes:

_____

_____

_____

_____

_____

_____

_____

_____

_____

_____

_____

_____

_____

➔ Risk Probability and Impact Assessment / Probability and Impact Matrix

When evaluating risks to determine what the highest priorities should be, the probability impact matrix (PIM) can assist you. The way it is used is that each risk in the risk register is evaluated for its likelihood of occurring and its potential impact on the project. Each of these two values is given a ranking (such as low, medium, high, or 1 through 10) and are multiplied together to get a risk score. This resulting score is used to set the priorities.

Assessment of Other Risk Parameters - Take time to familiarize yourself with the following terms before taking the exam. Not all of them may be intuitive.

Urgency - How much time you have to respond to a risk event. A short amount of time does not necessarily make the risk important, but it does make it urgent. Lower urgency is more desirable.

Proximity - How much time you have before the risk impacts project goals. Lower proximity is more desirable.

Dormancy - How much time will likely pass after the risk has occurred but before it is detected. A home water leak in a rarely-used room might have more dormancy than a water leak in the kitchen. Likewise, computer malware can sometimes go undetected for long periods of time before the results are detected. Lower dormancy (that is, a shorter period of time before it is detected) is more desirable.

Manageability - How easily a risk's impact can be managed. Higher manageability is more desirable.

Controllability - How easily a risk event can be changed. Software backups might be a way to help control the outcome of the earlier example of malware. Higher controllability is more desirable.

Detectability - How easily a risk event can be noticed or recognized. Higher detectability is more desirable.

Connectivity - Many negative project events that occur are actually a combination of numerous risk events. Often the way that risks occur is similar to the way dominoes fall, with one impacting the next and setting off a chain reaction. Understanding how risks are connected is important, and lower risk connectivity is more desirable.

Strategic Impact - How likely the risk event is to impact the organization's strategic goals. Lower strategic impact is more desirable.

Propinquity - Propinquity is the measure of how important the project's stakeholders perceive this risk to be. Lower propinquity is more desirable.

Interpersonal and Team Skills — See Ch. 2, Common Tools

Risk Categorization - Categorizing the detailed risks can help you build a better big-picture of the risks. This may help you understand which parts of the project have the highest degree of uncertainty. The RBS is a common way to help organize the identified risks into categories.

Chapter Notes:

_____

_____

_____

_____

_____

_____

_____

_____

_____

_____

_____

_____

Perform Qualitative Risk Analysis

Chapter Eleven

Chapter Notes:

_____

_____

_____

_____

_____

_____

_____

_____

_____

_____

_____

 **Data Representation**

Hierarchical Charts - One example of a hierarchical chart is a bubble chart, which shows rankings plotted on a X and Y axis and a third dimension of data is shown by the size of the data point.

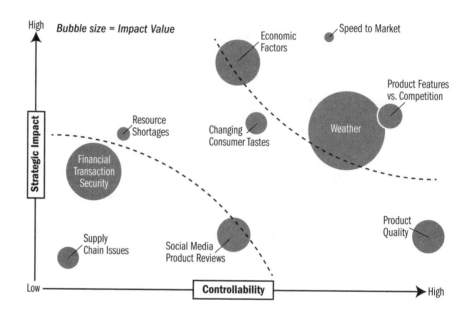

Meetings — See Ch. 2, Common Tools

HOW IT WORKS / OUTPUTS:

Project Documents Updates — See Ch. 2, Common Outputs

···· PLANNING

PERFORM QUANTITATIVE
RISK ANALYSIS

WHAT IT IS:

This process is very easy to confuse with the previously covered Perform Qualitative Risk Analysis, and in reality the processes have quite a lot in common; however, Perform Quantitative Risk Analysis seeks to assign a projected value to quantify the risks that have been ranked by Perform Qualitative Risk Analysis. This likely value is most often specified in terms of cost or time. Make sure to be able to differentiate between this process and the previous one before taking the exam.

6th Edition *PMBOK® Guide*
Cross Ref. pg 428

WHY IT IS IMPORTANT:

One important point to note is that not all projects need to perform this process. For many projects, the previous process of Perform Qualitative Risk Analysis will be sufficient; however, if your project is large, complex, strategic, required by contract, or required by a key stakeholder, you may decide to carry it out.

Perform Quantitative Risk Analysis updates the risk register, and this information will be used by the next three processes (Plan Risk Responses, Implement Risk Responses, and Monitor Risks). Without performing this process, the information about the identified risk may be less complete and less useful.

Watch The Video
http://**prep.pm**/11-5

Chapter Notes:

_____

_____

_____

_____

_____

_____

_____

_____

Chapter Eleven

Chapter Notes:

_____

_____

_____

_____

_____

_____

_____

_____

_____

_____

_____

_____

_____

WHEN IT IS PERFORMED:

Perform Quantitative Risk Analysis is usually performed right after Perform Qualitative Risk Analysis; however, in some cases they may be performed at the same time.

HOW IT WORKS / INPUTS:

Project Management Plan — See Ch. 2, Common Inputs

Project Documents — See Ch. 2, Common Inputs

Enterprise Environmental Factors — See Ch. 2, Common Inputs

Organizational Process Assets — See Ch. 2, Common Inputs

HOW IT WORKS / TOOLS:

Expert Judgment — See Ch. 2, Common Tools

Data Gathering — See Ch. 2, Common Tools

Interpersonal and Team Skills — See Ch. 2, Common Tools

➔ **Representations of Uncertainty** - The project team needs to have some way of showing the likelihood of a risk occurrence. For the exam, you should be prepared to recognize the common types of probability distributions, Triangular and Beta. There are other ways to represent probability, but these are the ones most commonly used.

Chapter Notes:

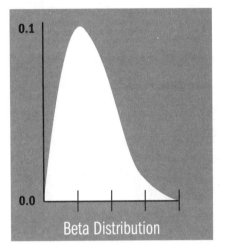

Beta Distribution

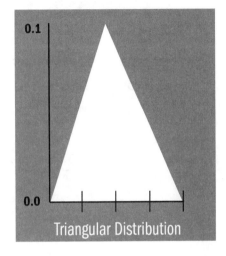

Triangular Distribution

➔ **Data Analysis**

> **Simulation** - The most common type of risk simulation is Monte Carlo Analysis, and it is a perennial favorite topic for the exam. Monte Carlo analysis, also discussed in Chapter 6 – Schedule Management, is a tool that takes details and assembles a big picture. Performed by computer, Monte Carlo analysis throws large numbers of "what if" scenarios at the schedule activities or at individual costs to see the impact of certain risk events. This technique will show you what is not always evident by simply looking at the schedule or the budget. It will often identify tasks that may not appear inherently high risk, but in the event they are delayed or that they exceed budget, the whole project may be adversely affected.

Perform Quantitative Risk Analysis

Chapter Eleven

Chapter Notes:

_____

_____

_____

_____

_____

_____

_____

_____

_____

_____

_____

_____

_____

_____

_____

Sensitivity Analysis - A commonly used data analysis tool to depict sensitivity to risk is a tornado diagram, named for the funnel shape of its bars. A tornado diagram provides a way to depict the project's sensitivity to cost or other risk factors. This is a type of sensitivity analysis which shows the impact of one change while holding other factors constant.

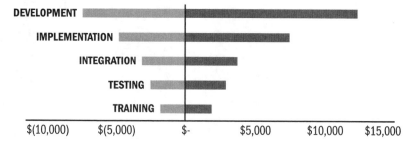

Change in project cost due to a 10% change in labor costs with all other project costs held constant.

Change in Project Costs: A tornado diagram, used to depict risks

The tornado diagram above depicts the effects of a 10% change in labor costs on the project. If labor costs increase by 10% and all other costs hold steady, development would be affected the most.

Specifically, if the costs rise by 10%, then the development costs will rise by approximately $13,000. If the labor costs fall by 10%, development costs will fall by approximately $7,000. This shows how sensitive each analyzed area of the project is to risk (in this case, the risk of a cost increase).

By running this analysis against various risks, it will help the team understand which risks pose the greatest threats (or potential rewards – remember that risks may be positive or negative) to the project.

A tornado diagram ranks the bars from greatest to least on the project so that the chart takes on a funnel or tornado-like shape.

Decision Tree Analysis - Decision trees are used to show probability and arrive at a dollar amount associated with each risk.

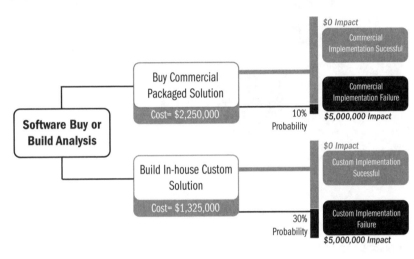

For each branch of the decision tree, compute the expected monetary value (EMV) for the event. The EMV should take into consideration each probability included in the branch. The numbers for this decision tree work out as follows:

	Initial Cost	Risk Cost	Probability	Total
Commercial Package	$2,250,000	$5,000,000	10 %	$2,750,000
Custom Package	$1,325,000	$5,000,000	30 %	$2,825,000

The totals above were calculated by multiplying the risk cost by the probability and adding that value to the initial cost.

Influence Diagrams - An influence diagram is another useful data analysis tool. It depicts the actors (or entities), influences, and possible outcomes.

Chapter Notes:

_____

_____

_____

_____

_____

_____

_____

_____

_____

_____

_____

_____

_____

_____

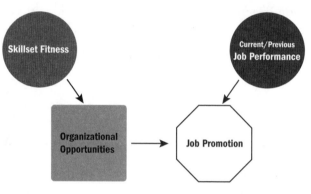

HOW IT WORKS / OUTPUTS:

Project Documents Updates

Risk Report - The risk report, created earlier in the Identify Risks process, is updated here to include the results of your quantitative analysis. This can include anything from a ranking of the risks to the diagrams used in the data analysis section.

The main point of this is to update recommended risk responses which will feed the next process.

.... PLANNING

PLAN RISK RESPONSES

WHAT IT IS:

6th Edition *PMBOK® Guide*
Cross Ref. pg 437

Earlier, in the process of Plan Risk Management, we created a general approach to risk (the risk management plan). Then, in Identify Risks, we created a list of risks and started our risk register. Next we qualitatively and quantitatively analyzed the risks, and now we are ready to create a detailed plan for managing them. That is precisely what Plan Risk Responses does; it creates a plan for how each risk will be handled.

Remember that risk can be a positive or negative event (e.g., there is a risk that the project will finish late, but there is also a risk that it will finish early). Therefore, careful consideration must be given to each risk, whether the impact of that risk is positive or negative.

This is the last planning process within risk (there are five in all, which gives you an idea of the importance of this topic), and this is the one that is most oriented toward taking action.

Watch The Video
http://**prep.pm**/11-6

Chapter Notes:

WHY IT IS IMPORTANT:

Up to this point, all we have done is identify and analyze the risks, but now that the analysis is complete, we need to create a specific plan. The resulting plan is actionable, meaning that it assigns specific tasks and responsibilities to specific team members.

Chapter Eleven

Chapter Notes:

_____

_____

_____

_____

_____

_____

_____

_____

_____

_____

_____

_____

_____

_____

WHEN IT IS PERFORMED:

Plan Risk Responses is performed after all of the other risk planning processes have been completed. The risk register flows in as an input, and the updated risk register emerges as its primary output.

HOW IT WORKS / INPUTS:

Project Management Plan — See Ch. 2, Common Inputs

Project Documents — See Ch. 2, Common Inputs

Risk Register - The risk register, created earlier in Identify Risks, contains a list of risks, positive and negative, on the project. The main purpose of this process is to update that register.

Enterprise Environmental Factors — See Ch. 2, Common Inputs

Organizational Process Assets — See Ch. 2, Common Inputs

HOW IT WORKS / TOOLS:

Expert Judgment — See Ch. 2, Common Tools

Data Gathering — See Ch. 2, Common Tools

Interpersonal and Team Skills — See Ch. 2, Common Tools

Strategies for Threats - Threats are anything that could potentially jeopardize the goals of the project. Five key ways of dealing with threats are presented here:

Escalate - In general, escalation is not a favored choice when dealing with risk. It should only be used when a risk response is outside of the project manager's authority (and remember, the project manager is large and in charge). If a threat is escalated, there needs to be a very clear handoff of responsibility. After a threat has been escalated, it becomes someone else's responsibility.

Avoid - Avoidance is a very appropriate tool for working with undesirable risk in some circumstances. For instance, a software project may choose to avoid the risk associated with using a particular piece of cutting-edge technology in favor of using a slower but more reliable technology.

Transfer - To transfer a risk to another party outside of the project is to make it their responsibility. Contractual agreements and insurance are common ways to transfer risks. The key here is that the risk is moved outside of the performing organization.

Mitigate - To mitigate a risk simply means to make it less. For instance, if you were concerned about the risk of weather damage to a construction project, you might choose to construct the building outside of the rainy season. It does not eliminate the risk, but mitigating should diminish it.

Accept - Acceptance is often a perfectly reasonable strategy for dealing with risk, whether positive or negative. When accepting a risk, you are simply acknowledging that the best strategy may not be to escalate, avoid, transfer, or mitigate it. Instead, the best strategy may be simply to accept it and continue with the project. Many people miss questions on the exam related to this because they don't have the mindset that acceptance may be the best strategy if the cost or impact of the other strategies is too great or the likelihood is low. If you are struggling with this concept, consider that even the act of getting out of bed each day carries risks, but these are risks that most people readily accept.

Chapter Notes:

_____

_____

_____

_____

_____

_____

_____

_____

_____

_____

_____

_____

Plan Risk Responses

Chapter Notes:

_____

_____

_____

_____

_____

_____

_____

_____

_____

_____

_____

_____

_____

_____

Acceptance may be active or passive. Passive acceptance requires no proactive steps. Active acceptance may involve setting aside a contingency reserve in case the risk event occurs.

Strategies for Opportunities - As is stressed throughout this chapter, risks can be positive or negative, and where positive risks are concerned, the project manager wants to take steps to make them more likely. The following are specific strategies taken to capitalize on the positive risks.

Escalate - Escalated opportunities are managed at a level above the project manager. For example, if the risk of a technological breakthrough on the project is much bigger than the project, it may be appropriate to escalate this higher within the organization.

Exploit - The definition for risk is uncertainty. Where the strategy of exploitation is concerned, you are trying to remove any uncertainty. For instance, if a positive risk of finishing the project early is identified, then adding additional people to increase the possibility that the project is completed early would be an example of exploiting the risk.

Share - In order to share a positive risk, the project seeks to improve the chances of the risk occurring by working with another party. For example, if a defense contractor identifies a positive risk of getting a large order, they may determine that sharing that risk by partnering with another defense firm, or even a competitor, would be an acceptable strategy.

Enhance - Enhancing a positive risk first requires that you understand the underlying causes of the risk. By working to influence the underlying risk triggers, you can increase the likelihood of the risk occurring. For example, an airline might add flights to a popular route during holidays in order to enhance traffic and profitability during heavy travel times.

Accept - See explanation under Strategies for Threats.

Contingent Response Strategies - A contingent response strategy, also known as a contingency plan or a fallback plan, is one where the project team may make one decision related to risk, but make that decision contingent upon certain conditions. For example, a project team may decide to mitigate a technology risk by hiring an outside firm with expertise in that technology, but that decision might be contingent upon the outside firm meeting intermediate milestones related to that risk.

Strategies for Overall Project Risk - The same strategies listed earlier in this section for dealing with individual project risk may be used for dealing with overall project risk. The point is to establish your project's overall posture toward risk, to understand and analyze the risks, and to plan appropriate action.

Data Analysis - Two analytical techniques are frequently used here.

The first is alternatives analysis, used to look at alternative ways to deal with risk events in general. For example, if there are too many unknowns related to a particular building material, an alternative material may be the rational choice.

The second analytical technique is cost-benefit analysis. Many risks come down to an impact in terms of money. Using this technique, you would make sure that the response does not cost more than the risk.

Decision Making — See Ch. 2, Common Tools

HOW IT WORKS / OUTPUTS:

Change Requests — See Ch. 2, Common Outputs

Project Management Plan Updates —
See Ch. 2, Common Outputs

Project Documents Updates - The updated risk register is the primary output of this process. It now contains the planned responses for each risk.

Chapter Notes:

Plan Risk Responses

Chapter Eleven

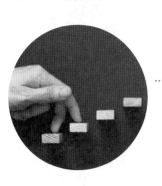

···· EXECUTING

IMPLEMENT RISK RESPONSES

6th Edition *PMBOK® Guide*
Cross Ref. pg 449

WHAT IT IS:

This process is new with the sixth edition *PMBOK® Guide*. It is an executing process that puts the risk response plan into action.

WHY IT IS IMPORTANT:

Plans are written to be implemented, and when it comes to risk, you have done a lot of planning in the previous five processes. Most processes, when they make their debut in the *PMBOK® Guide*, start off a bit light and then grow denser over time. New processes are ripe for exploitation on the exam, so even though there is nothing special about this process, you should still become familiar with what it is, when it is performed, and the fact that it belongs to the executing process group.

Watch The Video
http://**prep.pm/11-7**

WHEN IT IS PERFORMED:

When Implement Risk Responses is performed depends upon the risks you have identified. It may be begun as soon as you have completed the preceding process of Plan Risk Responses.

Chapter Notes:

HOW IT WORKS / INPUTS:

There is nothing special about the way this process works. In fact, it should be fairly intuitive for you at this point. Instead, focus your study primarily on the preceding paragraphs that describe the process.

Project Management Plan — See Ch. 2, Common Inputs

Project Documents — See Ch. 2, Common Inputs

Organizational Process Assets — See Ch. 2, Common Inputs

HOW IT WORKS / TOOLS:

Expert Judgment — See Ch. 2, Common Tools

Interpersonal and Team Skills — See Ch. 2, Common Tools

Project Management Information System — See Ch. 2, Common Tools

HOW IT WORKS / OUTPUTS:

Change Requests - It is a bit unusual to have change requests as a key output since they are so common; however, it is the main point of this process. After risks have been identified, analyzed, and the responses planned, the change requests are the primary way those responses are implemented.

Project Documents Updates — See Ch. 2, Common Outputs

Chapter Notes:

_____
_____
_____
_____
_____
_____
_____
_____
_____
_____
_____
_____
_____
_____
_____

Implement Risk Responses

···· MONITORING & CONTROLLING

MONITOR RISKS

6th Edition *PMBOK® Guide*
Cross Ref. pg 453

WHAT IT IS:

At this point, you have seen a pattern with the knowledge areas repeated many times. They have a monitoring and controlling process toward the end that looks back over the plans and any execution that has taken place and compares them with each other. In these monitoring and controlling processes, you are asking questions such as: "Did we plan properly?" "Did the results come out the way we anticipated?" "If the results did not match the plan, should we take corrective action by modifying the plan or by changing the way we are executing?" "Are there lessons learned that we need to feed into future activities or projects?"

Watch The Video
http://**prep.pm**/11-8

Chapter Notes:

WHY IT IS IMPORTANT:

Plans have to be reassessed and reevaluated. Where risk is concerned, we've done quite a bit of planning, identifying, analyzing, and predicting, but the process of Monitor Risks takes a look back to evaluate how all of that planning is lining up with reality.

WHEN IT IS PERFORMED:

Monitor Risks is a process that is performed almost continually throughout the project. That is not to say that you do these activities without stopping or that someone is necessarily assigned full time to carry them out, but rather that monitoring and controlling the risk is an ongoing concern.

HOW IT WORKS / INPUTS:

Project Management Plan — See Ch. 2, Common Inputs

Project Documents — See Ch. 2, Common Inputs

Work Performance Data - Work performance data is used as an input here since monitoring and controlling processes compare the plan to the results. The plan is brought in as an input above, and the work performance data provides information on the results. For instance, the status of a deliverable provides helpful information related to schedule risk, cost risk, or other areas of concern.

Work Performance Reports - The work performance reports do not focus so much on what has been done as they do on how it was done. For instance, whereas the work performance information provides information on the status of deliverables, the work performance reports focus on cost, time, and quality performance. Where the performance reports are concerned, the actual results are compared against the baselines to show how the project is performing against the plan.

Chapter Notes:

_____

_____

_____

_____

_____

_____

_____

_____

_____

_____

_____

_____

_____

Monitor Risks

Chapter Eleven

Chapter Notes:

_____

_____

_____

_____

_____

_____

_____

_____

_____

_____

_____

_____

_____

HOW IT WORKS / TOOLS:

Data Analysis - There are two important ways of analyzing data that are associated with Monitor Risks.

Technical Performance Analysis
The first is to analyze the technical performance of the project. This compares the results with the plan. For example, a project to construct a roadway might measure specific lengths of road with what they had planned to have completed at a point in time.

Reserve Analysis
The second way is through reserve analysis for cost and schedule. This review would alert the project manager if reserves fall below a threshold.

Audits - The important thing to know about risk audits is that they are focused on overall risk management. In other words, they are more about the top-down process than they are about individual risks. Periodic risk audits evaluate how the risk management plan and the risk response plan are working as the project progresses and also whether or not the risks that were identified and prioritized are actually occurring.

Meetings - This particular technique is not necessarily suggesting that you have specially-called status meetings related to risk. Instead, it is suggesting that you create a project culture where bringing up items related to risk is always acceptable and risk is discussed regularly.

HOW IT WORKS / OUTPUTS:

Work Performance Information — See Ch. 2, Common Outputs

Change Requests - When risk events occur, change requests to the project are a normal outcome. In addition, even when the events do not occur, the project may be changed as a result of new risk-related information gathered during this process.

Project Management Plan Updates —
    See Ch. 2, Common Outputs

Project Documents Updates - New risk information, whether it is changes to your risk estimates or actual numbers (such as costs related to weather damage), should be regularly updated in the risk register.

Org. Process Assets Updates — See Ch. 2, Common Outputs

Chapter Notes:

Monitor Risks

Chapter Eleven

Chapter Notes:

_____

_____

_____

_____

_____

_____

_____

_____

_____

_____

_____

_____

_____

→ The Agile Perspective on Risk Management

Because agile projects typically perform less planning on the front end of a project, there is often less risk planning. Agile projects seek to identify risks early and to respond to them rapidly. They take smaller steps to minimize risk. As uncertainty on a project evolves and changes, it may change the prioritization of backlogged work.

RISK MANAGEMENT

QUESTIONS

1. You are managing the construction of a data center, but the location is in an area highly prone to earthquakes. In order to deal with this risk, you have chosen a type of building and foundation that is particularly earthquake-resistant. This is an example of:

   A. Risk transfer.

   B. Risk avoidance.

   C. Risk mitigation.

   D. Risk acceptance.

2. You are evaluating the risk by trying to produce a risk score for each risk. This is an example of which tool?

   A. Monte Carlo analysis.

   B. Probability impact matrix.

   C. RACI Chart.

   D. Cause-and-effect diagrams.

3. As part of your project, you have identified a significant risk of cost overrun on a software component that is integral to the product. Which represents the BEST strategy in dealing with this risk?

   A. Outsource the software development.

   B. Insure the cost.

   C. Double the estimate.

   D. Eliminate the need for this component.

Chapter Notes:

_____

_____

_____

_____

_____

_____

_____

_____

_____

_____

_____

_____

_____

_____

_____

4. Meetings and data analysis are used in which process?

   A. Manage Stakeholder Expectations.

   B. Perform Quantitative Risk Analysis.

   C. Plan Risk Responses.

   D. Plan Risk Management.

5. Refer to the diagram below. What is the expected value of Result A?

   A. $200,000.

   B. $100,000.

   C. $50,000.

   D. $25,000.

Risk 1 — 50% Probability — Risk 2 — 25% Probability — Result A — $200,000 Value; 75% Probability — Result B — $400,000 Value

6. Refer to the diagram from the previous question. What type of risk management analysis is employed in this diagram?

   A. Earned value management.

   B. Sensitivity analysis.

   C. Decision tree analysis.

   D. Flowcharting.

7. Marie is meeting with her project team to evaluate each identified risk and try to assign an estimated dollar amount or time impact estimate to it. Which process is her team performing?

   A. Perform Quantitative Risk Analysis.

   B. Perform Qualitative Risk Analysis.

   C. Plan Risk Responses.

   D. Control Risks.

8. The project team has missed an important milestone, and their SPI is 0.77. The sponsor has notified the project manager that she intends on getting more involved in project decisions until they are back on track. She has asked the team to activate their contingency response strategy for this scenario. Which choice below best describes what the team would likely do?

   A. Implement a contingent response to deal with the missed milestone and poor performance.

   B. Spend reserve money to get the SPI back to 1.0 or greater.

   C. Perform a root cause analysis on the late milestone and performance.

   D. Identify the risks associated with the missed milestone.

9. If a project manager is recommending that immediate corrective action be taken, which process is she performing?

   A. Perform Qualitative Risk Analysis.

   B. Plan Risk Management.

   C. Identify Risks.

   D. Implement Risk Responses.

Chapter Eleven

Chapter Notes:

_____

_____

_____

_____

_____

_____

_____

_____

_____

_____

_____

_____

_____

_____

_____

_____

10. What is the BEST source of information about potential risk on your project?

    A. Computer risk analysis.

    B. Interviews with team members from other projects.

    C. Historical records from similar projects.

    D. Your own experience in this industry.

11. You have just finished a thorough Monte Carlo analysis for your project. Which of the following would the analysis MOST likely identify?

    A. Divergent paths causing risk.

    B. Points of schedule risk.

    C. Points of schedule conflict that lead to risk.

    D. Gaps in the project path that could create risk.

12. Senior management in an organization is concerned about risk on a project. The concern has escalated to the sponsor who has asked the project manager to evaluate a particular risk. The project manager responded by saying this risk had numerous interdependencies and was related to many other potential risks, but the sponsor asked that its potential impact be evaluated while holding all of the other risks at their current state. What would be the best tool for the project manager to use in this case?

    A. Root cause analysis.

    B. Tornado diagram.

    C. Decision tree analysis.

    D. Risk categorization.

13. **Your company is beginning a new building project and has assigned you the role of project manager. During the first few meetings with stakeholders you become aware of several risks that are of concern to the project sponsor. The topic of risk management, however, has yet to be addressed. What is the first thing you should do to address the project risks?**

    A. Develop a risk management plan.

    B. Identify project risks.

    C. Plan responses to project risks.

    D. Determine how risks will be controlled.

14. **Plan Risk Management is:**

    A. A process of identifying potential risks for a project.

    B. Deciding how risk management activities will be structured and performed.

    C. Assessing the impact and likelihood of project risks.

    D. Numerical analysis of the probability of project risks.

15. **Which of the following is an output of Identify Risks?**

    A. Risk register.

    B. Probabilistic analysis.

    C. Risk-related contractual agreements.

    D. Recommended cash reserves.

16. **Which of the following would NOT be a strategy for dealing with negative risk?**

    A. Avoid.

    B. Transfer.

    C. Share.

    D. Mitigate.

Chapter Eleven

Chapter Notes:

_____

_____

_____

_____

_____

_____

_____

_____

_____

_____

_____

_____

_____

_____

17. A risk probability and impact assessment is used in:

A. Identify Risks.

B. Perform Qualitative Risk Analysis.

C. Perform Quantitative Risk Analysis.

D. Plan Risk Responses.

18. A project team is meeting to review a document provided to them by the project management office. The document contains categories of risks to periodically review. What is the team using in this scenario?

A. An enterprise environmental factor.

B. A risk register.

C. Risk categorization.

D. A prompt list.

19. The BEST definition of risk management is:

A. The process of identifying, analyzing, and responding to risk.

B. The process of reducing risk to the minimum level possible for the project.

C. The process of proactively ensuring that all project risk is documented and controlled.

D. Creation of the risk response plan.

20. A tool that depicts a set of entities with directional arrows showing how they relate to the project would best describe which of the following?

A. Sensitivity analysis.

B. SWOT analysis.

C. Influence diagram.

D. Tornado diagram.

21. Which of the following is NOT a tool or technique for gaining expert opinion as it relates to risk?

    A. Brainstorming.

    B. Delphi technique.

    C. Monte Carlo analysis.

    D. Expert interviews.

22. Which of the following would NOT be contained in the risk management plan?

    A. A risk breakdown structure.

    B. A description of the overall approach to risk on the project.

    C. Risk roles and responsibilities.

    D. A list of identified risks.

23. Which of the following statements is TRUE regarding risk?

    A. All risk events must have a planned workaround.

    B. All risk events are uncertain.

    C. All risk events are negative.

    D. All risk events should be covered by a contingency budget or schedule amount.

Chapter Notes:

_____

_____

_____

_____

_____

_____

_____

_____

_____

_____

_____

_____

_____

_____

Risk Management: Questions

Chapter Eleven

Chapter Notes:

_____

_____

_____

_____

_____

_____

_____

_____

_____

_____

_____

_____

_____

24. Which of the following is NOT a valid way to reduce risk?

    A. Select a contract type that reduces risk.

    B. Insure against the risk.

    C. Create a workaround for the risk.

    D. Plan to mitigate the risk.

25. You are the project manager for a global change management project. The Vice President of Operations is a key project stakeholder, and she has expressed concern about the way risk is being managed on the project. She is particularly concerned that the project may fail if even one of several risk events occur. She has called a meeting to discuss this with you. What would be the best document to bring to this meeting.

    A. The results of your project's sensitivity analysis.

    B. The results of your project's risk modeling.

    C. The results of your project's EMV analysis.

    D. The results of your probability distributions.

RISK MANAGEMENT

ANSWERS

1. C. The best answer here is risk mitigation since you are taking steps to lessen the risk. 'A' is incorrect because you are not transferring the risk to anyone else. 'B' is incorrect because you would need to relocate in order to completely avoid the risk of earthquake. 'D' is incorrect because you are not merely accepting the risk – you are taking steps to make it less severe.

2. B. The probability impact matrix (PIM) derives a risk score by multiplying the probability of the risk by its impact (both of these numbers are estimated). This resulting risk score may be used to help prioritize the risk register.

3. A. Outsourcing the software development could allow you to cap the cost. 'B' is not a good choice because costs for development such as this cannot be insured in a cost-effective manner. 'C' is not correct because doubling the estimate does not deal with the root of the problem. It only arbitrarily changes the estimate. 'D' is incorrect because you cannot simply eliminate every high risk component in the real world.

4. D. Meetings and data analysis are tools of the process of Plan Risk Management.

5. D. The way this problem is solved is by multiplying out the probabilities times the value. In this case, it is the 50% probability of Risk 1 × the 25% probability of Risk 2 × the $200,000 value of Result A. .5 × .25 × 200,000 = $25,000.

6. C. This is an example of decision tree analysis.

7. A. You should have seen the fact that Marie's team was quantifying the risks by seeking to assign a dollar or time estimate to them, and Perform Quantitative Risk Analysis is the process that does this.

Chapter Notes:

_____

_____

_____

_____

_____

_____

_____

_____

_____

_____

_____

_____

_____

_____

Risk Management: Answers

Chapter Eleven

8. A. Contingent response strategies are generally only activated once a milestone is missed or some key measurement is triggered. At that point a contingency plan kicks in. 'B' is not a bad answer, but it assumes too much. For instance, we don't even know if there are reserve monies. 'C' and 'D' might be very reasonable steps, but it wasn't what the sponsor specifically requested.

9. D. Corrective action is defined as anything done to bring future results in line with the plan. This would be accomplished through change requests in the Implement Risk Responses process.

10. C. Historical records from similar projects would provide you with the best source of information on potential risks. 'A', 'B', and 'D' are all good sources, but they would not be as pertinent or helpful as the records from other similar projects. Historical information gets brought into your planning processes as an organizational process asset.

11. B. One of the things Monte Carlo analysis would show you is where schedule risk exists on the project. 'A' is incorrect, because it is typically convergent and not divergent tasks that create schedule risk. 'C' is incorrect because it is not looking for schedule conflicts – those would be corrected in Develop Schedule. 'D' is incorrect because gaps in the project path do not, by themselves, cause risk.

12. B. The sponsor is asking to evaluate the impact of one risk while holding the others at a baseline, and a tornado diagram is the tool to accomplish that. 'A', 'C', and 'D' are all tools used in risk assessment, but the tornado diagramming technique is custom-made for this assignment.

13. A. You should develop the risk management plan. A risk management plan will outline how all risk planning activities and decisions will be approached. Methods of identification, qualification, quantification, response planning, and control will all follow the development of the risk management plan.

14. B. Plan Risk Management is not planning for actual risks (which include choices 'A', 'C', and 'D'); it is the PROCESS of deciding how all risk planning activities and decisions will be approached. It is the plan for how to plan.

15. A. The risk register is the only output of Identify Risks, and it is updated in Perform Qualitative Risk Analysis, Perform Quantitative Risk Analysis, Plan Risk Responses, and Control Risks.

16. C. There are five identified strategies for dealing with negative risks. They are: mitigate, transfer, avoid, escalate and accept. The reason that 'C' was incorrect is that share is a strategy for managing a positive risk or opportunity.

17. B. The hardest part about risk is keeping the various processes straight. Since the outputs are similar (for the most part), focus more of your study on the processes themselves and their tools. In this question, the Data Analysis tool of risk probability and impact assessment is a tool of Perform Qualitative Risk Analysis.

18. D. Prompt lists are used to help guide the team in reviewing risk categories. For example, one category may be "political" to prompt the team to review whether any new political risks have been introduced since the last risk identification. 'A' is incorrect because this might be an organizational process asset, but it is not a good example of an enterprise environmental factor. 'B' is incorrect because a risk register is a list of actual risks that have been identified. 'C' is incorrect because risk categorization is the practice of organizing risks into categories. That is not what is described here.

19. A. The process of identifying, analyzing, and responding to risk is the definition of risk management. It would be a better definition if it also mentioned monitoring risks, but out of the four choices, 'A' is the best.

20. C. An influence diagram, used in Perform Quantitative Risk Analysis, shows entities and their direction of influence. The description in the question was not complete, but it only fit this choice.

21. C. Monte Carlo analysis, which is a computer-based analysis, might be useful for revealing schedule risk, but it would not be useful for gaining expert opinion. Choices 'A', 'B', and 'D' are all tools used as part of project risk management.

22. D. The risk management plan does not contain the identified risks. It is more general and high-level than that. The identified risks will be listed in the risk register, produced after the risk management plan.

Chapter Notes:

_____

_____

_____

_____

_____

_____

_____

_____

_____

_____

_____

_____

Risk Management: Answers

Chapter Notes:

_____

_____

_____

_____

_____

_____

_____

_____

_____

_____

_____

_____

_____

23. B. Risk events are, by definition, uncertainties. These could either be positive or negative. 'A' is incorrect because some risks are simply accepted and have no workaround. 'C' is incorrect because a risk may be positive or negative. 'D' is incorrect because not all risks are budgeted. Some are transferred to other parties or are too small or unlikely to consider.

24. C. Read these questions carefully! The workaround is what you do if the risk occurs, but it does not reduce the risk as the question specified. 'A', 'B', and 'D' all focus on reducing risk by transferring or mitigating it.

25. A. Your VP of Operations is concerned about your project's sensitivity to risk. Other answers might be applicable to one degree or another, but 'A' stands out as the best match to the problem you are trying to address. The results of sensitivity analysis directly addresses your stakeholder's concern.

Procurement Management

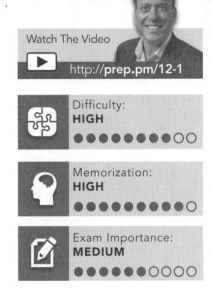

Procurement management is the set of processes that are used to obtain goods, services, or scope from outside the organization.

Even though it is relatively small, procurement management can be a challenging knowledge area on the exam. One reason it can be so difficult is that few project managers have formal procurement training in their backgrounds, and even if they do, it may differ in key ways from what is presented here.

Watch The Video
http://**prep.pm**/12-1

Difficulty:
HIGH
●●●●●●●●○○

Memorization:
HIGH
●●●●●●●●●○

Exam Importance:
MEDIUM
●●●●●●○○○○

PHILOSOPHY:

This procurement management approach is steeped in formal government procurement practices.

The over arching philosophy of procurement management is that it should be formal. Many people's practical experience may differ from this rigid approach, but it is necessary to understand it and to be able to apply this philosophy on the exam.

Chapter Notes:

IMPORTANCE:

Several questions on the exam will be drawn from the material in this chapter. If formal procurement is new to you, this will be especially important. You will also need to master the concept and formula for Point of Total Assumption (PTA).

Conduct Procurements
Selected Sellers
Agreements

Control Procurements
Closed Procurements
Work Performance Info

PROCUREMENT MANAGEMENT

Plan Procurement Management
Bid Documents
Source Selection Criteria
Procurement Strategy
Make or Buy Decisions

Procurement Management Plan
Independent Cost Estimates
Procurement Statement of Work

453

Chapter Twelve

Chapter Notes:

_____

_____

_____

_____

_____

_____

_____

_____

_____

_____

_____

_____

_____

PREPARATION:

As mentioned earlier, it would be wise to take special care in this section if you do not have a background in formal procurement activities.

Keep in mind as you approach this material that it was not written to be memorized. It was written to be practiced and applied. For this chapter in particular, understanding is more important than memorizing.

This also applies to key terms, concepts, the processes, and their components.

If formal procurement is a new concept, you would do well to read this chapter carefully and then skim Chapter 12, Project Procurement Management, in the 6th Edition *PMBOK® Guide*.

Procurement Management Processes

There are three processes in procurement management. These processes are displayed in the figure at the beginning of the chapter and summarized in the following tables.

Process Group	Procurement Management Process
Initiating	(none)
Planning	Plan Procurement Management
Executing	Conduct Procurements
Monitoring & Controlling	Control Procurements
Closing	(none)

Process	Primary Outputs
Plan Procurements Management	Procure. Mgt. Plan, Independent Cost Estimates, Make or Buy Decisions, Procure. Strateg, Bid Documents, Procure. S.O.W., Source Selection Criteria
Conduct Procurements	Selected Sellers, Agreements
Control Procurements	Closed Procurements, Work Performance Info, Change Req.

Procurement Roles

In procurement management, there are two primary roles defined, and the project manager could play either of these roles. In fact, it is not uncommon for project managers to play both roles on the same project. The roles are:

Buyer - The organization or party purchasing (procuring) the goods or services from the seller.

Seller - The organization or party providing or delivering the goods or services to the buyer.

Contract Types

When procuring goods or services, the type of contract that governs the deal can make a significant difference in who bears the risk. There are four categories of contracts you must know for the exam. They are listed below with information on each one:

Type of Contract	Who Bears the Risk	Explanation
Fixed Price	Seller	Since the price is fixed, cost overruns may not be passed on to the buyer and must be borne by the seller.
Cost Plus Fixed Fee	Buyer	Since all costs must be reimbursed to the seller, the buyer bears the risk of cost overruns.
Cost Plus Incentive Fee	Buyer and Seller	The buyer bears most of the risk here, but the incentive fee for the seller motivates that seller to keep costs down.
Time and Materials	Buyer	The buyer pays the seller for all time and materials the seller applies to the project. The buyer bears the most risk of cost overruns.

Fixed Price Contracts (AKA Lump Sum Contracts) - Fixed price contracts are the easiest ones to understand. There is generally a single fee, although payment terms may be specified so that the cost is not necessarily a lump sum, payable at the end.

This type of contract is very popular when the scope of work is thoroughly defined and completely known. Three types of fixed price contracts are:

Chapter Twelve

Chapter Notes:

——————————————
——————————————
——————————————
——————————————
——————————————
——————————————
——————————————
——————————————
——————————————
——————————————
——————————————
——————————————

Firm Fixed Price (FFP) - The price is fixed, with no provision for cost or performance overruns. The risk is entirely shifted to the seller.

Fixed Price Incentive Fee (FPIF) - The price is fixed, with an incentive fee for meeting a target specified in the contract (such as finishing the work ahead of schedule). With FPIF contracts, both parties agree to a price ceiling, and all costs above the price ceiling must be covered by the seller.

Fixed Price Economic Price Adjustment (FP-EPA) - This type of contract is popular in cases where fluctuations in the exchange rate or interest rate may impact the project. In this case, an economic stipulation may be included to protect the seller or the buyer. The economic stipulation may be based on the interest rate, the consumer price index, cost of living adjustments, currency exchange rates, or other indices.

Cost Reimbursable Contracts

Another type of contract is cost reimbursable where the buyer agrees to pay the seller for actual costs plus a fee that is actually the seller's profit. There are three common varieties of this type of agreement:

Cost Plus Fixed Fee (CPFF) - The seller passes the cost back to the buyer and receives an additional fixed fee upon completion of the project. The fee is calculated as a percentage of the planned costs.

Cost Plus Incentive Fee (CPIF) - The seller passes the cost back to the buyer and gets an incentive fee for meeting a target (usually tied back to keeping costs low) specified in the contract.

Cost Plus Award Fee (CPAF) - The seller passes the costs back to the buyer, but the seller's profit (award fee) comes from a decision on whether or not to grant it, made subjectively by the buyer based on the seller's performance. The decision may not be appealed by the seller.

Time and Materials Contracts

In a time and materials contract, the seller charges for time plus the cost of any materials needed to complete the work.

Point of Total Assumption

Because there are numerous types of contracts where the risk is shared to one degree or another, it is important to be able to calculate how risk is allocated between the buyer and seller. One consideration, particularly when using Fixed Price Incentive Fee contracts, is the Point of Total Assumption.

The Point of Total Assumption (PTA) is the cost point in the contract where a subcontractor assumes responsibility for all additional costs. This concept can be challenging to understand at first, so to help with this, consider the following situation. Company ABC is subcontracting out the installation of industrial shelving to company XYZ for an estimated $75,000. The selected contract is Fixed Price Incentive Fee, so ABC pushes for a cap (called a price ceiling) to protect them from serious cost overruns. The terms of the contract are that XYZ's target cost is $71,000, the target price to ABC is $75,000 and XYZ's ceiling price to ABC is $84,000; however, for every dollar over the target cost, the share ratio is 3:1. This means that ABC (the buyer) will pay $0.75, while XYZ (the seller) will have to pay $0.25 of every dollar overrun. Knowing this information, it is fairly simple to calculate the PTA.

The formula is: Target cost + (ceiling price – target price) ÷ ABC's % share of cost overrun.

In this case, it would be $71,000 + ($84,000 - $75,000) ÷ .75, which simplifies to $71,000 + $12,000 = $83,000.

In other words, at the point the cost reaches $83,000, the subcontractor (XYZ) would assume the total burden of cost overrun. The ceiling price is still $84,000, but XYZ is bearing 100% of the cost overrun burden above $83,000 in cost (the PTA). The PTA is important, because it helps identify the cost point in the contract where the seller has the most motivation to bring things to completion.

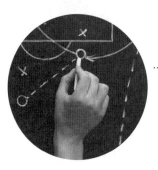

···· PLANNING

PLAN PROCUREMENT MANAGEMENT

6th Edition PMBOK® Guide
Cross Ref. pg 466

WHAT IT IS:

This process involves looking at the project and determining which components or services of the project will be made or performed internally and which will be "procured" from an external source. After that decision is made, the project manager must determine a strategy for conducting procurements and the appropriate type of contracts to be used on the project.

Watch The Video

▶ http://**prep.pm**/12-2

WHY IT IS IMPORTANT:

This process has a lot of important outputs, and your understanding of them will help you on the exam. Currently, best practices in the field of project management favor buying externally vs. building internally, all other things being equal; however, there are numerous factors that should go into your decision on whether to "make or buy."

Carefully planning what to procure and how to go about the processes of procurement will ensure that the right things are procured in the right way.

Chapter Notes:

_____

_____

_____

_____

_____

_____

_____

_____

_____

WHEN IT IS PERFORMED:

Because a project may have multiple subcontractors, potentially in every phase of the project, any of the procurement processes could be performed repeatedly and at any time throughout the project.

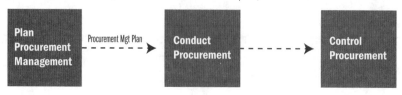

A diagram showing the order of the three Procurement Management processes

HOW IT WORKS / INPUTS:

Project Charter — See Ch. 2, Common Inputs

Business Documents - The business case and the benefits management plan are key documents that will help the project team plan procurements. Each may influence why project components are being created and how and when the project expects to deliver benefits.

Project Management Plan - The project management plan describes what will be done and how it will be accomplished. This information will be useful to review when considering what components of the scope should be procured (i.e., performed by groups outside of the organization).

Project Documents

> **Requirements Documentation** - Requirements are a key part of the project plan and may carry legal or contractual obligations that need to be considered in procurement.

Enterprise Environmental Factors - There may be factors at work in an organization that have a strong influence on procurement. For instance, an organization may have a strong culture of building internally rather than buying, or they could have a strong culture of buying from a few trusted sellers. All of this should be factored in when making procurement decisions.

Organizational Process Assets — See Ch. 2, Common Inputs

HOW IT WORKS / TOOLS:

Expert Judgment — See Ch. 2, Common Tools

Data Gathering — See Ch. 2, Common Tools

Chapter Notes:

_____
_____
_____
_____
_____
_____
_____
_____
_____
_____
_____
_____
_____
_____
_____

Plan Procurement Management

Chapter Twelve

Chapter Notes:

_____

_____

_____

_____

_____

_____

_____

_____

_____

_____

_____

_____

_____

Data Analysis - The tool of data analysis used here is make-or-buy analysis, and it is difficult to sum up succinctly. The analysis looks at all of the factors that could sway the decision toward making internally or buying externally, including risk factors, cost, releasing proprietary information, and a host of other decision points.

When using this tool, the decision-makers must often look outside of the project itself. For instance, writing a software component may not make as much sense as procuring it externally where only the project is concerned; however, if the performing organization has an interest in developing the capability to build that kind of software, it may make sense for the project to make vs. buy.

Source Selection Analysis - This tool is essentially deciding how you are going to select a seller. Consider the following possible ways:

Least Cost - This may work well when the quality is not in question. For example, if your project is purchasing a component that complies with an ISO standard, then you can probably assume that anything that complies with this standard would suffice for your project.

Qualifications Only - When a product or service is small enough that it does not warrant an elaborate procurement process, the buyer may use "qualifications only" as the sole criterion. In this case, the buyer makes a short list of sellers and makes a selection based on qualifications such as experience, references, etc.

Quality-Based (technical score) - Most procurements come down to value (quality and cost). The seller with the highest quality ranking is selected if a suitable financial arrangement can be negotiated.

Quality and Cost-Based - This is very similar to the previous one except that quality and cost are both ranked and are both considered in the decision.

Sole Source - This is an unusual type of proposal that is requested from only one vendor. In that case, the buyer negotiates with that one seller. There is no competition in this scenario, which can eliminate much of the benefit of conducting a procurement.

Fixed Budget - In this procurement scenario, the buyer discloses the budget to the seller, and the two parties negotiate on scope, quality, and schedule. This type of procurement would not work well when scope changes are anticipated.

Meetings — See Ch. 2, Common Tools

HOW IT WORKS / OUTPUTS:

➔ **Procurement Management Plan** - The procurement management plan is an important output of the Plan Procurement Management process. It defines how all of the other procurement management processes will be carried out. This includes defining what will be procured on the project, how a seller will be selected, what types of contracts will be used, how risk will be managed, and how sellers will be managed, including how their performance will be measured.

➔ **Procurement Strategy** - The procurement strategy defines how the procurements will be organized, how the contracts will be structured, and which procurement phases will be carried out.

➔ **Bid Documents** - There are quite a few types of procurement documents that vary from organization to organization. Don't worry about the differences between an Invitation For Bid (IFB) and a Request For Proposal (RFP). For the exam, know that the bid documents of work are written by the buyer and provided to the prospective seller(s). They provide a narrative description of the work to be performed.

Chapter Notes:

_____

_____

_____

_____

_____

_____

_____

_____

_____

_____

_____

_____

_____

Plan Procurement Management

Chapter Notes:

_____

_____

_____

_____

_____

_____

_____

_____

_____

_____

_____

_____

_____

_____

➜ **Procurement Statement of Work** - Many people find this document confusing at first, but it is important for the exam. If you recall the project scope statement, produced as part of the Define Scope process, then you will know that the project's scope has been defined at this point. A procurement statement of work is not merely a replication of what was done in Define Scope. Instead, a procurement statement of work helps explain a section of the scope to potential sellers in enough detail so that they can decide whether or not they want to (or are qualified to) pursue the work in question. Expect statements pertaining to the previous sentence to be on the exam. One other point about the procurement statement of work is that it should usually focus on the outcome more than the steps to get there to allow sellers to be creative in their approach.

➜ **Source Selection Criteria** - The key to remember for this output is that the source selection criteria are determined before the seller is selected. This helps keep the procurement process objective and unbiased. For instance, it may be that you will choose the lowest-priced qualified bidder (in which case the qualifications need to be spelled out), or you may want the bidder that represents the highest technical competency or the lowest risk. Whatever the criteria, ensure that they are specified before the other procurement activities are conducted. Also keep in mind that these source selection criteria may or may not be shared with the prospective sellers.

➜ **Make-or-Buy Decisions** - During this process, the project team performed make-or-buy analysis as part of data analysis, and now it is time to act upon the data gathered. The decisions should be made and documented, and enough information to justify these decisions should be included.

➜ **Independent Cost Estimates** - Think of this as a procurement sanity check to ensure that costs are in line with what they should be. These cost estimates may be created by outside companies or internally.

Change Requests — See Ch. 2, Common Outputs

Project Documents Updates — See Ch. 2, Common Outputs

Organizational Process Assets Updates —
See Ch. 2, Common Outputs

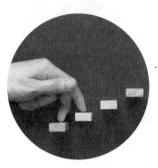

.... EXECUTING

CONDUCT PROCUREMENTS

WHAT IT IS:

6th Edition PMBOK® Guide
Cross Ref. pg 482

Most of the processes in this book do exactly what they sound like. In this case, Conduct Procurements does just that. It carries out the procurement management plan, selects one or more sellers, and awards the procurement, usually in the form of a contract.

WHY IT IS IMPORTANT:

This executing process gets the ball rolling with procurement. So far you have decided what you want to procure and written the procurement management plan. Now it's time to issue the bid package to potential sellers, hold bidder conferences, evaluate proposals you receive from potential sellers, and select one of them. You know, however, that real life isn't that simple, and this can be a very tricky area on the exam as well.

Watch The Video
http://**prep.pm**/12-3

Chapter Notes:

WHEN IT IS PERFORMED:

To state the obvious, this process is performed when you are ready to conduct your procurement activities. This means that it will occur after Plan Procurement Management.

Like the other procurement processes, Conduct Procurements is performed as needed. It may be performed multiple times if there are multiple contracts, or it is not performed at all if the project is not procuring anything.

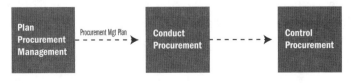

Chapter Twelve

Chapter Notes:

_____

_____

_____

_____

_____

_____

_____

_____

_____

_____

_____

_____

_____

_____

HOW IT WORKS / INPUTS:

Project Management Plan — See Ch. 2, Common Inputs

Project Documents — See Ch. 2, Common Inputs

Procurement Documentation — See Ch. 2, Common Inputs

Seller Proposals - Prospective sellers provide proposals for doing the work, and these should include how they intend to satisfy the bid request, the technical aspects of their proposal, the price, and the terms. Ideally, the price should be separated from the other components so the proposals can be evaluated on their technical merit and then on price.

Enterprise Environmental Factors — See Ch. 2, Common Inputs

Organizational Process Assets — See Ch. 2, Common Inputs

HOW IT WORKS / TOOLS:

Expert Judgment — See Ch. 2, Common Tools

 Advertising - If you need to expand the seller responses you are getting, advertising the bid may be the best way. Trade publications, online sources, and even newspapers can help get your bid request in front of a large and more carefully targeted audience to improve the volume and quality of responses. Sometimes advertising is required for compliance with law or regulations.

Bidder Conferences - Bidder conferences are conducted to provide information to potential sellers, while keeping all of them on a level playing field. It is important that the project manager conduct everything out in the open, with no secret meetings or communications with some vendors or excluding others.

Conduct Procurements

➜ **Data Analysis** - Seller proposal evaluations are a common way of analyzing data here. It is helpful to imagine them being compared against the seller evaluation matrix and the proposal statement of work.

➜ **Interpersonal and Team Skills** - The main focus of interpersonal and team skills in this process is negotiation. This is where the project manager works with all parties (buyers, sellers, teams, organizations) to reach a mutual agreement. Negotiations may happen with groups or individuals inside and outside the organization. The goal of negotiating is to create a win-win outcome that is sustainable for all parties.

HOW IT WORKS / OUTPUTS:

➜ **Selected Sellers** - The RFP has been generated, the sellers have submitted their proposals in response, the negotiations have taken place, and now a seller is selected to provide goods or services on the project.

➜ **Agreements** - The agreements that come out of this process, often in the form of a contract, are formal documents governing the relationship between the buyer and seller. In general, when you see the word "agreement" on the exam, you should think "contract."

Contracts are legal documents with highly specialized and technical language and should be written and changed only by people specializing in that field (e.g., the contracting officer, procurement office, legal counsel). The project manager should not attempt to write, negotiate, or change the contract on his own.

The contract describes the work to be performed and perhaps the way in which that work will be performed (e.g., location, work conditions). It may specify who will do the work, when and how the seller will be paid, and delivery terms.

In reality, there is very little that the contract cannot specify in one way or another, so long as the terms and conditions are legal and they are mutually agreed upon by buyer and seller. Several other legal factors may come into play, depending on the country that governs the contract, legal consideration, and other technical legal matters that are outside the scope of this discussion.

Chapter Notes:

_____

_____

_____

_____

_____

_____

_____

_____

_____

_____

_____

_____

_____

Conduct Procurements

Chapter Twelve

Chapter Notes:

_____

_____

_____

_____

_____

_____

_____

_____

_____

_____

_____

_____

_____

_____

An important component to include with the contract is how disputes (also called claims) will be resolved. This includes the process of dispute resolution, the parties who will be involved, and where the dispute resolution will take place.

Change Requests — See Ch. 2, Common Outputs

Project Management Plan Updates —
See Ch. 2, Common Outputs

Project Documents Updates — See Ch. 2, Common Outputs

Organizational Process Assets Updates —
See Ch. 2, Common Outputs

···· MONITORING & CONTROLLING

CONTROL PROCUREMENTS

WHAT IT IS:

6th Edition PMBOK® Guide
Cross Ref. pg 492

In a nutshell, Control Procurements is the monitoring and controlling process where the buyer and seller review the contract and the work results to ensure that the results match the contract. This typically includes a review of:

- Are the goods or services being delivered?

- Are the goods or services being delivered on time?

- Are the right amounts being invoiced or paid?

- Are additional conditions of the contract being met?

- Is the buyer/seller relationship being properly managed and maintained?

Watch The Video
http://prep.pm/12-4

The process of Control Procurements is a process performed by both the buyer and the seller, and because of the ramifications of any issues here, the project managers from both the buyer and seller should use whatever resources are necessary to explore the potential effects of any decisions.

Chapter Notes:

_____

_____

_____

_____

WHY IT IS IMPORTANT:

_____

When looking at this from a project management perspective, the contract may be viewed as a plan (albeit a very specialized and binding type of plan). The process of Control Procurements ensures that the results of the project match this plan and that all conditions of the contract are met.

_____

_____

_____

Chapter Twelve

Chapter Notes:

_____

_____

_____

_____

_____

_____

_____

_____

_____

_____

_____

_____

_____

_____

WHEN IT IS PERFORMED:

Control Procurements, like the other procurement management processes, may be performed throughout the project whenever goods or services are being procured. It typically occurs for a given contract at predefined intervals, but may also be performed as requested or needed.

HOW IT WORKS / INPUTS:

Project Management Plan — See Ch. 2, Common Inputs

Project Documents — See Ch. 2, Common Inputs

Agreements - The agreements (remember to think "contracts" when you see this word) that were produced in the previous process are brought in here. The agreements are the intent and will be compared with the results.

Procurement Documentation - This input includes everything you will need related to procurements. It is not important to memorize the list, but anything that could be useful here would be included.

Approved Change Requests - Approved change requests flow out of the Perform Integrated Change Control process. They need to be brought into this process since a change to scope, price, schedule or other aspects of the project may well impact procurements.

Work Performance Data — See Ch. 2, Common Inputs

Enterprise Environmental Factors — See Ch. 2, Common Inputs

Organizational Process Assets — See Ch. 2, Common Inputs

HOW IT WORKS / TOOLS:

Expert Judgment — See Ch. 2, Common Tools

➜ **Claims Administration** - Claims are basically disagreements. They may be about scope, the impact of a change, or the interpretation of some piece of the contract. The essential (legally binding) elements of the process for claims administration are defined in the contract itself, but there may be additional components in the procurement management plan.

The most important thing about claims administration is to understand that disputes must be managed and ultimately resolved and that the process for doing so should be defined in advance of the claim.

Contracts are completed when all terms, conditions, and claims against the contract are satisfied. Ideally, this is objective, and everyone agrees; however, that is not always the case. Sometimes mediation or arbitration may be necessary. Both of these are forms of Alternative Dispute Resolution (ADR). Litigation is another option, but it is the least desirable course of action to achieve closure and should only be used as a last resort when all forms of ADR have been exhausted.

➜ **Data Analysis** - This is used by the buyer to make sure the seller is performing according to the agreement. Use the tools of performance reviews, earned value analysis (EVA), and trend analysis to review how things are progressing.

➜ **Inspection** - This tool focuses on the product itself and its conformance to specifications. Inspections do not seek to measure the seller's performance (i.e., how quickly or cost-effectively they are delivering the results). Instead, the buyer may use them to help the seller find problems in the way they are delivering the work results.

➜ **Audits** - Whereas the previous tool of inspection focuses on the product, audits focus on the procurement process.

Chapter Notes:

_____
_____
_____
_____
_____
_____
_____
_____
_____
_____
_____
_____
_____
_____
_____

Control Procurements

Chapter Twelve

Chapter Notes:

_____

_____

_____

_____

_____

_____

_____

_____

_____

_____

_____

_____

_____

_____

_____

HOW IT WORKS / OUTPUTS:

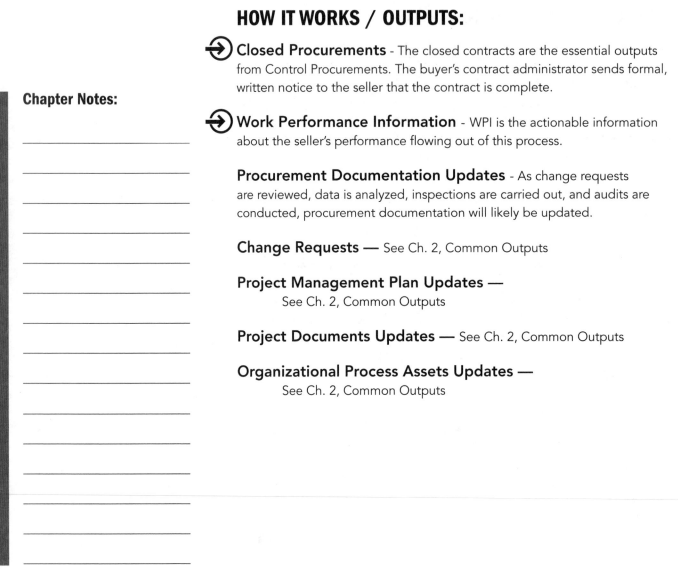

Closed Procurements - The closed contracts are the essential outputs from Control Procurements. The buyer's contract administrator sends formal, written notice to the seller that the contract is complete.

Work Performance Information - WPI is the actionable information about the seller's performance flowing out of this process.

Procurement Documentation Updates - As change requests are reviewed, data is analyzed, inspections are carried out, and audits are conducted, procurement documentation will likely be updated.

Change Requests — See Ch. 2, Common Outputs

Project Management Plan Updates —
See Ch. 2, Common Outputs

Project Documents Updates — See Ch. 2, Common Outputs

Organizational Process Assets Updates —
See Ch. 2, Common Outputs

→ The Agile Perspective on Procurement Management

Agile projects approach vendor relationships as opportunities for collaboration. In fact, some sellers may actually become part of the team.

Because procurement may be very formal, agile or adaptive methodologies may perform the procurement activities in a highly adaptive way without changing the procurement process.

Chapter Notes:

_____

_____

_____

_____

_____

_____

_____

_____

_____

_____

_____

_____

Agile Perspective on Procurement Management

Chapter Twelve

Chapter Notes:

_____

_____

_____

_____

_____

_____

_____

_____

_____

_____

_____

_____

_____

_____

_____

PROCUREMENT MANAGEMENT

QUESTIONS

1. The contract type that represents the highest risk to the seller is:

   A. Fixed price plus incentive.

   B. Cost reimbursable.

   C. Fixed price.

   D. Cost reimbursable plus incentive.

2. You have been tasked with managing the seller responses to a request for proposal issued by your company. The seller responses were numerous, and now you have been asked to rank the proposals from highest to lowest in terms of their response. What are you going to use as a means to rank the sellers?

   A. Expert judgment.

   B. Request for quotation.

   C. Seller response guidelines.

   D. Seller selection matrix.

3. Make-or-buy analysis is a tool used in which process?

   A. Plan Procurement Management.

   B. Conduct Procurements.

   C. Control Procurements.

   D. Analyze Procurements.

4. **Which of the following represents the right sequence of processes?**

    A. Analyze Procurements, Plan Procurement Management, Conduct Procurements, Close Procurements.

    B. Determine Make or Buy, Control Procurements, Conduct Procurements, Close Procurements.

    C. Plan Purchases and Acquisitions, Conduct Procurements, Control Procurements, Close Procurements.

    D. Plan Procurement Management, Conduct Procurements, Control Procurements, Close Project or Phase.

5. **An organization is trying to close out a procurement sub-project, but the vendor has not delivered on a key piece of contracted technology. The project manager has been negotiating with the vendor for several weeks to no avail. Recently the vendor representative stated that he believed the performing organization had no real legal recourse; however, the project manager disagrees. How should the project manager approach the next steps?**

    A. With the attitude that litigation is a perfectly acceptable option if negotiations fail.

    B. With the attitude that alternative dispute resolution would be preferable to litigation.

    C. With the attitude that a final, equitable settlement is to be prioritized below stakeholder satisfaction.

    D. With the attitude that alternative dispute resolution is binding, while mediation is not.

Chapter Notes:

_____
_____
_____
_____
_____
_____
_____
_____
_____
_____
_____
_____
_____
_____
_____
_____

Procurement Management: Questions

Chapter Twelve

Chapter Notes:

_____

_____

_____

_____

_____

_____

_____

_____

_____

_____

_____

_____

_____

_____

6. You are managing a large software project when the need for a new series of database tables is discovered. The need was previously unplanned, and your organization's staff is 100% utilized, so you decide to procure this piece of work from outside the company. When you meet with prospective sellers, you realize that the scope of work is not completely defined, but everyone agrees that the project is relatively small, and your need is urgent. Which type of contract makes the MOST sense?

A. Fixed price.

B. Time and materials.

C. Open ended.

D. Cost plus incentive fee.

7. Your project plan calls for you to go through procurement in order to buy a specialty motor for an industrial robot. Because of patent issues, this motor is only available from one supplier that is across the country. After investigation, you believe that you could procure the motor from this company for a price that is within your budget. What is your BEST course of action?

A. Revisit the design and alter the specification to allow for a comparable motor.

B. Procure the motor from this source even though they are the sole source.

C. See if the component may be produced in another country, avoiding your country's patent issues.

D. Take the product out of the procurement management process.

8. You have a supplier that is supplying parts to you under contract. The terms and conditions give you the right to change some aspects of the contract at any time, and you need to significantly lower the quantities due to a change in project scope. How should you notify the supplier?

   A. Take them to lunch and explain the situation gently to preserve the relationship.

   B. Have your attorney call the supplier's attorney.

   C. Communicate with the supplier via e-mail.

   D. Send them a formal, written notice that the contract has been changed.

9. Source selection analysis is used in which procurement process?

   A. Plan Procurement Management.

   B. Select Sellers.

   C. Conduct Procurements.

   D. Evaluate Proposals.

10. A team has adopted an agile approach to their software development project. They have elected to procure one section from an outside seller. Which of the following would be true?

   A. The selected seller would also need to adopt an agile approach as part of development.

   B. They may extend the team by adding the selected seller.

   C. Control procurements will take on more importance within this agile project.

   D. Agile projects often perform procurement management iteratively, which may change the flow of the procurement management processes.

Chapter Notes:

_____

_____

_____

_____

_____

_____

_____

_____

_____

_____

_____

_____

_____

_____

_____

Chapter Notes:

_____

_____

_____

_____

_____

_____

_____

_____

_____

_____

_____

_____

_____

_____

_____

11. You are evaluating proposals from prospective sellers. What process are you involved in?

   A. Analyze Procurements.

   B. Plan Procurement Management.

   C. Conduct Procurements.

   D. Control Procurements.

12. Your project scope calls for a piece of software that will control a valve in a pressurized pipeline. Your company has some experience with this type of software, but resources are tight, and it is not part of your company's core competency. You are considering involving other sellers but want to decide whether it is a better decision to produce this within your company or source it externally. What activity are you performing?

   A. Source selection.

   B. Make-or-buy analysis.

   C. Rational project procurement.

   D. Source evaluation.

13. Martina is managing a global project that will attempt to get significant portions through sourcing. When the first bids are received, they seem surprisingly high and there is very little variance among them. Which of the following would prove most useful in this case?

   A. Negotiation.

   B. Proposal Evaluation Techniques.

   C. Bidder Conferences.

   D. Independent Cost Estimates.

14. Your organization is holding a bidder conference to discuss the project with prospective sellers, and a trusted seller you have worked with many times in the past has asked if they can meet with the project manager the day before the conference to cover some sensitive questions they do not wish to ask in front of other sellers. Should your organization meet with the seller?

    A. Yes, the more that prospective sellers know about the project, the better.

    B. Yes, they are your primary seller, and past history should be factored in.

    C. No, prospective suppliers should be kept on equal footing.

    D. No, that would represent an illegal activity.

15. The most important thing to focus on in contract negotiations is:

    A. To negotiate the best price possible for your project.

    B. To maintain the integrity of the scope.

    C. To negotiate a deal that both parties are comfortable with.

    D. To make sure legal counsel or the contract administrator has approved your negotiating points.

16. If a project manager was performing Control Procurements, which of the following duties might he or she be performing?

    A. Evaluating proposals.

    B. Negotiating the contract.

    C. Closing out the procurement.

    D. Weighing seller responses.

Chapter Notes:

_____

_____

_____

_____

_____

_____

_____

_____

_____

_____

_____

_____

_____

_____

17. A buyer is engaging with a seller to move equipment from one location to another and to properly install the equipment in the new location. The buyer has received an estimate for this work of $28,000, and they have structured their agreement to have a ceiling price of $30,000 and that for every dollar in excess of $25,000 (the seller's anticipated cost), the buyer and seller would share costs evenly. At what point would the seller assume responsibility for all additional costs?

A. $28,000

B. $29,000.

C. $29,500.

D. $30,000.

18. Who generally bears the risk in a time and materials contract?

A. The buyer.

B. The seller.

C. The buyer early in the project and the seller later on.

D. It depends on the materials used.

19. Your company is outsourcing a project in an area where it has little experience. The procurement documents should be:

A. Completely rigid to ensure no deviation from sellers.

B. Flexible enough to encourage creativity in seller responses.

C. Informal.

D. Reviewed by senior management.

20. The procurement statement of work should provide:

    A. Enough detail for the prospective seller to complete the project.

    B. Enough detail to describe the product, but not so much as to divulge trade secrets or sensitive information.

    C. Enough detail to perform make-or-buy analysis.

    D. Enough detail for the prospective seller to know if they are qualified to perform the work.

21. You are ready to close out a procurement. Where is the best place to look for guidance in how to perform this activity?

    A. Contract.

    B. Correspondence.

    C. Records management system.

    D. Seller performance evaluations.

22. You are the project manager for a seller who has been selected to construct an industrial kitchen for a large food services company. Before the contract negotiations, the buyer confides in you that design is not finalized, and they want you to begin work with incomplete specifications. What type of contract should you ask for in negotiations?

    A. Fixed price.

    B. Cost plus incentive fee.

    C. Time and materials.

    D. Cost plus fixed fee.

Chapter Notes:

_____

_____

_____

_____

_____

_____

_____

_____

_____

_____

_____

_____

_____

_____

_____

Procurement Management: Questions

Chapter Twelve

Chapter Notes:

_____

_____

_____

_____

_____

_____

_____

_____

_____

_____

_____

_____

_____

_____

23. The product or result of the project is created during which process group?

    A. Project life cycle.

    B. Control Procurements.

    C. Project executing.

    D. Work package processing.

24. Your customer has asked to meet with you and inspect the work you have completed to date on the project to ensure that it meets the contractual agreements. What is your customer manager engaged in?

    A. Close Procurements.

    B. Seller Efficiency Audit.

    C. Seller Administration.

    D. Control Procurements.

25. You have completed a project and delivered the full scope of the contract. The buyer agrees that you have technically satisfied the terms of the contract but is not completely satisfied with the end results. In this case, the contract is:

    A. Contested.

    B. Complete.

    C. Poorly written.

    D. Lacking terms and conditions.

PROCUREMENT MANAGEMENT
ANSWERS

1. C. This question was easier than it may have first appeared to be. Fixed price is the highest risk to the seller since the seller must bear the risk of any cost overruns. Choice 'B' would provide the highest risk to the buyer.

2. A. By this time you should be thinking that if you see "expert judgment," it is likely the right answer. Expert judgment is a favored technique in project management, and it is correct in this case because you are conducting the Conduct Procurements process. It is the only tool/technique among the potential answers that is a part of that process.

3. A. Make-or-buy analysis is a tool used during the Plan Procurement Management process where you are deciding which deliverables should be procured and which should be created internally. 'D' is not a real process, and 'B' and 'C' are incorrect because by the time you conduct or Control Procurements, you need to already know what you are going to make and what you are going to buy.

4. D. Plan Procurement Management, Conduct Procurements, Control Procurements, Close Project or Phase. The easiest explanation for this one is that 'A', 'B', and 'C' all contain at least one made-up process.

5. B. Alternative dispute resolution (ADR), which includes mediation and arbitration, is preferable to litigation. 'A' is not a good choice because litigation should only be entered into as a last resort. 'C' is incorrect because a final, equitable resolution is very important and would not be prioritized below satisfaction. 'D' is not correct. ADR includes mediation, so the statement does not even make sense. It may be binding or non-binding.

6. B. Time and Materials. Choice 'A' is incorrect because the scope is not defined enough to establish a fair fixed price. Choice 'C' is a made-up type of contract. Choice 'D' would not make sense in this case since the seller's costs are not abundantly clear, and this type of contract would create too much risk.

Chapter Notes:

———————————————
———————————————
———————————————
———————————————
———————————————
———————————————
———————————————
———————————————
———————————————
———————————————
———————————————
———————————————
———————————————
———————————————

7. B. This one may trick some who think that it is wrong to use a sole source. In many cases it is the only choice. 'A' would not be good since the design has nothing to do with this. 'C' is not necessary in this case, since the issue is not a legal issue. Choice 'D' would be completely invalid since the item is still being procured outside of your organization.

8. D. Choices 'A' and 'B' are verbal. Contract changes should always be made in writing! 'C' is written, but e-mail is not the proper forum for making important contractual changes.

9. A. Plan Procurement Management. This is the tool where you plan how you are going to select a seller. For example, you choose how important competing factors such as cost, quality, seller qualifications, and others are, and you do this before you conduct procurements.

10. B. Agile projects may extend their team to incorporate selected sellers. This makes sense if you understand the way agile projects work. 'A' is not necessarily true. They may be purchasing something that has already been developed, so the seller would not necessarily need to adopt agile. 'C' is not a good choice since that process is no more or less important just because it is agile. 'D' is not a good choice because procurement is not a particularly iterative activity. Put another way, how would you purchase something iteratively? You will find that procurement management changes less between waterfall and agile than other knowledge areas.

11. C. If you are evaluating seller responses, you are performing the process of Conduct Procurements. The seller proposals are brought into this process, and they are screened, weighted, rated, and evaluated against the criteria.

12. B. Make-or-buy analysis is the process where an organization decides whether it should produce the product internally or outsource it. This is one of the data analysis techniques performed as part of the Plan Procurement Management process.

13. D. Independent cost estimates would be most appropriate. Martina needs to check and see if the bids are valid or if there may be some sort of collusion going on. 'A' might be a good step after getting some independent estimates. 'B' is a way of scoring and ranking vendors, but that might be premature at this point. 'C' is a way to inform bidders, but that should have taken place before the bids were received and would not be the best choice at this point.

14. C. If you are involved in formal procurement, you should make every effort to keep sellers on equal footing. If one seller is provided with an advantage, it negates much of the value of the procurement process.

15. C. The most important point is to create a deal that everyone feels good about. 'A' sounds like a good choice, but it is incorrect; the best possible price might not be fair to your seller, and that could create a bad scenario for the project in the future. 'B' is important, but that is not the primary focus of negotiations. 'D' may or may not be necessary, depending on the situation.

16. C. One of the outputs of Control Procurements is closed procurements. Make sure to learn the primary inputs, tools, techniques, and outputs for the processes.

17. B. This question is asking for the Point of Total Assumption (PTA). The formula is: Target cost + (ceiling price – target price) ÷ buyer's % share of cost overrun.

    Since buyer and seller are sharing costs 50/50 for any overrun up to the ceiling, the math works out as follows: $25,000 + (30,000 – 28,000) ÷ .5 = $29,000

    If you knew the formula but still got the wrong answer, remember that math is performed in the order of parentheses, exponents, multiplication, division, addition, then subtraction.

18. A. In a time and materials contract, the buyer has to pay the seller for all time and materials, and often it involves an incomplete scope definition. Therefore, the buyer is the one most at risk.

Chapter Notes:

_____

_____

_____

_____

_____

_____

_____

_____

_____

_____

_____

_____

_____

_____

Procurement Management: Answers

Chapter Twelve

19. B. In this scenario, you want sellers to respond with their own ideas. Procurement documents should be rigid enough to get responses to the same scope of work, and flexible enough to allow sellers to interject their own good ideas and creativity. Many people incorrectly choose 'A' because they assume that a rigid approach is almost always correct, but in this example, you do not have sufficient experience to rigidly manage the process, and you want your sellers to give you some guidance in their proposals. 'C' was clearly incorrect as procurement is something that should be done formally. 'D' is incorrect because senior management has many functions in an organization, but they would not be expected to review procurement documents.

20. D. Procurement statements of work should be as complete and concise as possible. At a minimum, they should contain enough information for the seller to determine if they are qualified to do the work.

21. A. The contract, often referred to as an agreement, specifies how the procurement will be closed. Any of the other choices might provide supporting information, but the best place to look for guidance would be the contract.

22. C. The major clue here is that the scope of work is not completely defined and they want you to begin work anyway. In that case, the project is at a higher risk, and a time and materials contract shifts much of that risk back to the buyer.

23. C. This question ties back to Chapter 3– Process Framework. The actual work packages are completed (or executed) during the Executing process group.

24. D. Procurement performance reviews are a tool of Control Procurements, where the buyer arranges a meeting with the seller to review the seller's performance against the plan. This question presents a near-textbook case of this.

25. B. If the scope of the contract is complete, no other terms were breached, and no claims against the contract have been filed, then the contract is complete. 'A' is not a good choice since no claim was filed. 'C' is not a good guess here since you don't have enough information to state that the problem was that the contract was poorly written.

Stakeholder Management

This knowledge area is still relatively young, but meaningful content has been added over the last few years. On a project, stakeholder management can have a powerful impact on its success or failure.

PHILOSOPHY:

Stakeholder management focuses on identifying the relevant stakeholders, creating a plan, executing that plan, and monitoring and controlling. The idea that drives this is to work to manage the expectations that drive stakeholder satisfaction.

Stakeholder management is defined as "the creation and maintenance of relationships with the aim to satisfy needs." This is an expansive definition that covers activities throughout the project life cycle.

The approach is driven by the fact that stakeholders need to be identified and have their needs understood before they are managed. They should be communicated with and involved at the proper level through the life of the project.

IMPORTANCE:

Stakeholder management has a few key tools and outputs that are important for the exam. It is far more important on an actual project than it is on the exam.

Watch The Video
http://prep.pm/13-1

Difficulty:
MEDIUM
●●●●●○○○○○

Memorization:
MEDIUM
●●●●●○○○○○

Exam Importance:
MEDIUM
●●●●●○○○○○

Chapter Notes:

_____

_____

_____

_____

_____

_____

_____

_____

Identify Stakeholders
Stakeholder Register

Monitor Stakeholder Engagement
(No Primary Outputs)

STAKEHOLDER MANAGEMENT

Plan Stakeholder Engagement
Stakeholder Engagement Plan

Manage Stakeholder Engagement
Issue Log

485

Chapter Thirteen

PREPARATION:

This knowledge area presents no real surprises other than the fact that there is an initiating process. Since a significant number of questions come from the initiating process group, and there are only two initiating processes, it is a safe assumption that this particular process is important.

Stakeholder Management Processes

There are four processes in stakeholder management. These processes are displayed in the figure at the beginning of the chapter and summarized in the tables below.

Process Group	Stakeholder Management Process
Initiating	Identify Stakeholders
Planning	Plan Stakeholder Engagement
Executing	Manage Stakeholder Engagement
Monitoring & Controlling	Monitor Stakeholder Engagement
Closing	(none)

Process	Primary Outputs
Identify Stakeholders	Stakeholder Register
Plan Stakeholder Engagement	Stakeholder Engagement Plan
Manage Stakeholder Engagement	Issue Log
Monitor Stakeholder Engagement	(No Primary Outputs)

···· INITIATING

IDENTIFY STAKEHOLDERS

WHAT IT IS:

6th Edition PMBOK® Guide
Cross Ref. pg 507

Identify Stakeholders is the process that focuses on creating the stakeholder register to list all of the stakeholders and describe their involvement on the project.

Identify Stakeholders is one of only two initiating processes.

Keep in mind that a stakeholder may be anyone with an interest in the project, and that interest may be positive or negative.

WHY IT IS IMPORTANT:

If the stakeholders are not properly identified on the project and their needs are not understood, then there is little chance of meeting expectations. Many projects are derailed because they did not understand the needs of the stakeholders and address them on the project.

On the exam, quite a few questions will come from the initiating process group, so you should expect several questions to be directly related to this process.

Watch The Video
► http://prep.pm/13-2

Chapter Notes:

_____

_____

_____

_____

_____

_____

_____

WHEN IT IS PERFORMED:

Identify Stakeholders will typically be one of the first processes you perform on a project or project phase; however, it may be performed multiple times throughout the project's life cycle. If your project had six phases, you may well perform it six times (or even more). You will need to perform it after the process of Develop Project Charter has been completed.

Chapter Thirteen

Chapter Notes:

_____

_____

_____

_____

_____

_____

_____

_____

_____

_____

_____

HOW IT WORKS / INPUTS:

Project Charter - The charter describes the project in broad brush strokes, and it may also describe some of the stakeholders and their interests in the project or its product.

Business Documents - The business case and benefits management plan outline who is expected to benefit from the project's product, service, or result. These groups, in particular, are considered key stakeholders.

Project Management Plan — See Ch. 2, Common Inputs

Project Documents — See Ch. 2, Common Inputs

Agreements — See Ch. 2, Common Inputs

Enterprise Environmental Factors — See Ch. 2, Common Inputs

Organizational Process Assets — See Ch. 2, Common Inputs

HOW IT WORKS / TOOLS:

Expert Judgment — See Ch. 2, Common Tools

Data Gathering - The primary tools used here are questionnaires and surveys and brainstorming. The point of these is to cast a wide net for identifying potential stakeholders.

Data Analysis - This one tool can cover quite a bit of ground. In this case, the data you are analyzing is data about stakeholders. It is relatively simple to define, but it is often quite tricky to perform on an actual project. The goal of this is to identify which stakeholders should receive project communications, what communications they should receive, how they should receive these communications, and how often they should receive them.

Not all stakeholders should be treated equally on the project. Some are more important than others, and it is the job of the project manager (with

488

help from the sponsor) to understand stakeholders and their abilities to influence the organization and their interests in the project.

There are many ways to accomplish this, but one technique is to plot stakeholders on a grid to visualize their impact and influence.

For the purposes of stakeholder analysis, a stakeholder would be anyone who creates or causes a need, is affected by the need, or would be affected by the solution.

When performing stakeholder analysis, the underlying needs that the stakeholders have related to this project should be ranked from greatest to least. There are a number of ways to rank them, including interest, influence rights, ownership, knowledge, and contribution.

➡️ **Data Representation** - This tool is essentially a graphical way of representing the information in the previous tool. Some possible ways are:

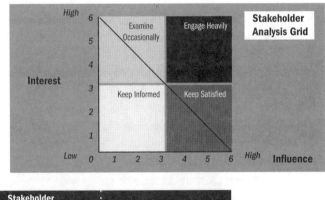

Chapter Notes:

_____

_____

_____

_____

_____

_____

_____

_____

_____

_____

_____

_____

Meetings — See Ch. 2, Common Tools

HOW IT WORKS / OUTPUTS:

➔ **Stakeholder Register** - The stakeholder register is a document that lists all of the project stakeholders, describes them, and classifies them. The classification will become particularly important when you are planning the communication and want to group stakeholders together.

The stakeholder register contains three main sections:

1. Stakeholder identification – the names, titles, and project roles of the people involved with the project.

2. Stakeholder assessment – what their needs are and when those needs are expected to arise in the life of the project.

3. Stakeholder classification – a logical grouping of stakeholders in any way that makes communication easier

This document may be published with other project documentation or kept in reserve for the project manager's use only.

Change Requests — See Ch. 2, Common Outputs

Project Management Plan Updates — See Ch. 2, Common Outputs

Project Documents Updates — See Ch. 2, Common Outputs

Chapter Notes:

_____

_____

_____

_____

_____

_____

_____

_____

_____

_____

_____

_____

_____

_____

Identify Stakeholders

···· PLANNING

PLAN STAKEHOLDER ENGAGEMENT

WHAT IT IS:

The process of Plan Stakeholder Engagement looks at how the team will relate to the stakeholders and what stakeholder involvement will be in all aspects of the project.

WHY IT IS IMPORTANT:

For the exam, the sole output of this process is all that matters. On a real project it is important because it is necessary to be proactive and deliberate when considering how to involve stakeholders on the project.

WHEN IT IS PERFORMED:

This process would generally be performed very early on the project and may be revisited often as project work progresses. If it is not performed early in the project's life cycle, the project runs the risk of marginalizing and alienating stakeholders.

HOW IT WORKS / INPUTS:

Project Charter — See Ch. 2, Common Inputs

Project Management Plan — See Ch. 2, Common Inputs

Project Documents — See Ch. 2, Common Inputs

Agreements — See Ch. 2, Common Inputs

6th Edition PMBOK® Guide
Cross Ref. pg 516

Watch The Video
http://**prep.pm**/13-3

Chapter Notes:

_____

_____

_____

_____

_____

_____

_____

_____

Chapter Thirteen

Chapter Notes:

_____

_____

_____

_____

_____

_____

_____

_____

_____

_____

_____

_____

_____

Enterprise Environmental Factors — See Ch. 2, Common Inputs

Organizational Process Assets — See Ch. 2, Common Inputs

HOW IT WORKS / TOOLS:

Expert Judgment — See Ch. 2, Common Tools

Data Gathering — See Ch. 2, Common Tools

Data Analysis — See Ch. 2, Common Tools

Decision Making — See Ch. 2, Common Tools

➔ **Data Representation** - Stakeholders, and particularly their level of engagement, must be understood and analyzed, with particular attention paid to the current and desired levels of engagement.

Stakeholder engagement is often plotted on a Stakeholder Engagement Assessment Matrix such as the one that follows.

Stakeholder	Unaware	Resistant	Neutral	Supportive	Leading
Carla T.		Current ——————————————————➝			Desired
Siva S.			Current ——➝ Desired		
Ken P.	Current ——————————————➝			Desired	

The purpose of this is to chart the current and desired states of project stakeholders, which will inform the stakeholder engagement plan.

Meetings — See Ch. 2, Common Tools

HOW IT WORKS / OUTPUTS:

➔ **Stakeholder Engagement Plan** - The stakeholder engagement plan will become a component of the project management plan. It describes how the team will engage the stakeholders and how it will manage expectations and deal with issues. It also describes how communication will be conducted.

The stakeholder engagement plan may or may not be shared with most stakeholders.

Chapter Notes:

_____

_____

_____

_____

_____

_____

_____

_____

_____

_____

_____

_____

_____

_____

_____

Plan Stakeholder Engagement

.... EXECUTING

MANAGE STAKEHOLDER ENGAGEMENT

6th Edition PMBOK® Guide
Cross Ref. pg 523

WHAT IT IS:

Manage Stakeholder Engagement was first introduced in the previous edition *PMBOK® Guide*. It is an executing process that revolves around using change and the issue logs to help ensure that the right stakeholders are involved at the right level and in the right way.

For this executing process, know that stakeholders should be managed according to their needs and how the project scope addresses those needs.

Think of your stakeholders as strategic partners working with you toward the success of the project. You should go into the exam with an attitude of strong stakeholder cooperation. If you and your stakeholders are not aligned toward a mutually successful solution, that should serve as a red flag.

Watch The Video

http://prep.pm/13-4

Chapter Notes:

_____

_____

_____

_____

_____

_____

_____

_____

WHY IT IS IMPORTANT:

Stakeholder satisfaction may be the single most significant ingredient in project success. While much of that may have to do with benefits realization and product quality, quite a bit of it has to do with whether or not the stakeholders were happy with the way the project was conducted, whether or not they were properly involved, and whether or not they had a voice on the project. This process helps to ensure that they are properly engaged throughout the life of the project.

It is vital that the project manager keep the stakeholders engaged at the appropriate level throughout the project. The concept is straightforward, but the execution can be very tricky. The project manager should constantly be thinking about how the stakeholders wish to be engaged and to participate in the project, what their goals and concerns are, what information they need and how they want to receive that information.

WHEN IT IS PERFORMED:

Stakeholders typically influence the project from very early (often before it is even a project) until it is closed. This process happens as long as there are stakeholders with whom you need to work.

HOW IT WORKS / INPUTS:

Project Management Plan — See Ch. 2, Common Inputs

Project Documents — See Ch. 2, Common Inputs

Enterprise Environmental Factors — See Ch. 2, Common Inputs

Organizational Process Assets — See Ch. 2, Common Inputs

HOW IT WORKS / TOOLS:

Expert Judgment — See Ch. 2, Common Tools

Communication Skills - Feedback is the important communication skill here. It is used to make sure that communications are being received in the intended way by the stakeholders.

Interpersonal and Team Skills - This tool is frequently used in this book, but it is particularly important here. Conflict management, cultural awareness, negotiation, observation and conversation, and political awareness all play a part. Good project managers use soft skills to help manage stakeholder expectations and engagement.

Ground Rules - The ground rules are often defined in the charter but they may also be unwritten. These are the rules to which everyone is expected to adhere. The ground rules can apply to stakeholders and to the project team.

Meetings — See Ch. 2, Common Tools

Chapter Notes:

_____

_____

_____

_____

_____

_____

_____

_____

_____

_____

_____

_____

_____

Manage Stakeholder Engagement

Chapter Thirteen

Chapter Notes:

_____

_____

_____

_____

_____

_____

_____

_____

_____

_____

_____

HOW IT WORKS / OUTPUTS:

Change Requests — See Ch. 2, Common Outputs

Project Management Plan Updates —
See Ch. 2, Common Outputs

 Project Documents Updates - The issue log is the key document you should focus on as being updated for this process. It is an important tool for managing stakeholder expectations and engagement.

.... MONITORING & CONTROLLING

MONITOR STAKEHOLDER ENGAGEMENT

WHAT IT IS:

This process evaluates how the plan of engaging and involving stakeholders lines up with the results. While there are no surprises with this process with the inputs, tools, and outputs, you should understand what the process is and when and why it is conducted.

6th Edition PMBOK® Guide
Cross Ref. pg 530

WHY IT IS IMPORTANT:

As any professional project manager can attest, stakeholder engagement and management does not always go according to plan, and when things go awry with stakeholder engagement, the entire project can quickly become derailed.

This process does the important work of monitoring and controlling the overall activities related to engaging the stakeholders and makes sure they stay on track or that the plan is updated if necessary.

Watch The Video

http://**prep.pm/13-5**

Chapter Notes:

WHEN IT IS PERFORMED:

Like all monitoring and controlling processes, Monitor Stakeholder Engagement will be performed after there is a plan in place (the stakeholder engagement plan created in Plan Stakeholder Engagement) and as execution of that plan begins (Manage Stakeholder Engagement).

This process will typically be performed from time to time throughout the project's life cycle, but it may take on heightened importance on sensitive projects.

_____

_____

_____

_____

_____

_____

_____

_____

Chapter Thirteen

Chapter Notes:

_____

_____

_____

_____

_____

_____

_____

_____

_____

_____

_____

_____

_____

_____

_____

HOW IT WORKS / INPUTS:

Project Management Plan — See Ch. 2, Common Inputs

Project Documents — See Ch. 2, Common Inputs

Work Performance Data — See Ch. 2, Common Inputs

Enterprise Environmental Factors — See Ch. 2, Common Inputs

Organizational Process Assets — See Ch. 2, Common Inputs

HOW IT WORKS / TOOLS:

Data Analysis — See Ch. 2, Common Tools

Decision Making — See Ch. 2, Common Tools

 Data Representation - The stakeholder engagement assessment matrix is the key tool to help depict how stakeholder are relating to the project.

Communication Skills - Feedback and presentations are the two key communications skills used to monitor stakeholder engagement.

Interpersonal and Team Skills - The skills of active listening, cultural awareness, leadership, networking, and political awareness come into play as you monitor stakeholder engagement. Interpersonal and team skills are important in many parts of the project, but they are particularly important in stakeholder management.

Meetings — See Ch. 2, Common Tools

HOW IT WORKS / OUTPUTS:

Work Performance Information — See Ch. 2, Common Outputs

Change Requests — See Ch. 2, Common Outputs

Project Management Plan Updates —
See Ch. 2, Common Outputs

Project Documents Updates - The key document that would be updated here is the issue log. This is particularly important for stakeholders to see that their issues are being acknowledged and recorded.

Chapter Notes:

_____

_____

_____

_____

_____

_____

_____

_____

_____

_____

_____

_____

_____

_____

Monitor Stakeholder Engagement

Chapter Thirteen

Chapter Notes:

_____

_____

_____

_____

_____

_____

_____

_____

_____

_____

_____

_____

_____

_____

➡ The Agile Perspective on Stakeholder Management

Agile projects are arguably much less formal than more traditional, predictive projects.

The agile approach to stakeholder management is markedly different than the waterfall approach. Stakeholders are actively engaged and may even become part of the team. Information about progress and team performance is posted in public places in what is often referred to as "big, visible charts" with the goal of keeping stakeholders up to date and well informed.

With agile, stakeholders are not viewed as people who must be kept informed. Instead, they are engaged and treated as integral parts of the overall solution.

STAKEHOLDER MANAGEMENT

QUESTIONS

Note that this stakeholder management quiz is intentionally shorter than other chapter quizzes due to the nature of the material. This knowledge area is relatively new and is still maturing.

1. **What are the dimensions measured on a stakeholder grid?**

   A. Access and Availability.

   B. Expertise and Influence.

   C. Interest and Power.

   D. Motive and Opportunity.

2. **Which of the following is not a tool used to manage the stakeholder engagement?**

   A. Communication methods.

   B. Interpersonal Skills.

   C. Management Skills.

   D. Issue Log.

3. **The primary purpose of the stakeholder register is:**

   A. To keep a list of all project stakeholders.

   B. To record stakeholder issues on the project.

   C. To map functional requirements back to the originating stakeholder.

   D. To serve as a project directory.

Chapter Thirteen

Chapter Notes:

_____

_____

_____

_____

_____

_____

_____

_____

_____

_____

_____

_____

_____

4. **The most important element in project success is:**

   A. Stakeholder satisfaction.

   B. How the product meets the requirements.

   C. Overall product quality.

   D. Overall project quality.

5. **Which of the following does not identify someone as a stakeholder during stakeholder analysis?**

   A. Someone who proposes a solution.

   B. Someone who is aware of a need.

   C. Someone who is affected by the need.

   D. Someone who would be affected by the solution.

6. **Stakeholders should be:**

   A. Communicated with frequently.

   B. Qualified.

   C. Analyzed.

   D. Documented before the project begins.

7. Which of the following is not a classification of stakeholder engagement?

    A. Unaware.

    B. Resistant.

    C. Leading.

    D. Participating.

8. Ana is working on a matrix where she is measuring the stakeholder engagement on the project. What dimension would she likely be assessing and plotting?

    A. Power and interest to influence the project.

    B. Ability and urgency to influence the project.

    C. Current and desired levels of interest.

    D. Expertise and availability to engage with the project.

9. Which of the following statements is false regarding stakeholders?

    A. Stakeholders may have a positive or negative interest in the success of the project.

    B. All stakeholders should be identified before the project execution begins.

    C. Stakeholders may not be affected by the outcome but may perceive that they could be affected by the outcome.

    D. Stakeholders may be people, or organizations.

Chapter Notes:

_____

_____

_____

_____

_____

_____

_____

_____

_____

_____

_____

_____

_____

_____

_____

10. **Which of the following is true concerning work performance data and work performance information?**

A. Work performance data is used at the organizational level, while work performance information is used at the project level.

B. Work performance information is more useful than work performance data.

C. Work performance data is collected from monitoring and controlling processes.

D. Work performance information represents raw observations and measurements.

STAKEHOLDER MANAGEMENT

ANSWERS

1. C. When plotting stakeholder interest on a matrix, interest and influence (and sometime involvement) are measured.

2. D. This may have looked hard, but it was not so difficult to reason out. The issue log is the primary output of Manage Stakeholder Engagement, so it could not also be a tool. 'A', 'B', and 'C' are all tools used in that process.

3. A. The stakeholder register is a list of the stakeholders with their assessment and classification as it relates to the project.

4. A. This one should have been easy given the topic of the quiz, but you may well see questions like this on the PMP Exam. While all of the elements are important, stakeholder satisfaction is the most important.

5. B. The term "Stakeholder" is very broad and generally includes quite a few groups; however, someone who is aware of a need is ambiguous enough to not fit well within this list.

6. C. The process of Identify Stakeholders has a prominent tool of Stakeholder Analysis. 'A' may sound good, but not all stakeholders may need or desire frequent communication. 'B' is close, but it is not the best answer since there is no process or tool to see if someone qualifies as a stakeholder. 'D' is not a good choice since stakeholders may enter the project at any point.

7. D. The five states of stakeholder engagement are Unaware, Resistant, Neutral, Supportive, and Leading. "Participating" might seem to make sense, but it is not a classification since the project manager does not typically need to measure the engagement of team members participating on the project.

Chapter Notes:

_____

_____

_____

_____

_____

_____

_____

_____

_____

_____

_____

_____

_____

_____

_____

_____

_____

_____

Chapter Thirteen

8. C. The stakeholder engagement matrix plots the current and desired levels of engagement by stakeholders.

9. B. If you missed this one, don't feel bad. It is best to identify stakeholders early, but the key to getting it right is the word "all." Many of them may not emerge until late in the project.

10. B. WPI and WPD show up in Control Stakeholder Engagement. Remember that work performance data is raw, while work performance information has been analyzed and made more useful. 'A' has no grounding in reality at all, and 'C' and 'D' are opposite of the truth.

How To Pass
The PMP Exam

Passing the PMP on your first try has nothing to do with good luck. It is all about preparation and strategy. While the other chapters in this book are all about the preparation, this chapter focuses on test strategy. It includes techniques on how you can be sure to avoid careless mistakes during your exam.

THE PMP EXAM:

This chapter covers strategies and material related to standardized tests in general and to the PMP exam specifically.

Before we get into the specifics of the PMP exam, it would be a good idea to cover standardized exams. Even if you have taken quite a few standardized exams before, now would be a good time to review some important points.

A standardized exam is a test designed to achieve some statistical consistency. Since the PMP exam is a standardized exam, this essentially means two things:

1. An individual test-taker should perform at approximately the same level on two different versions of the PMP exam.

2. The results of all people taking the exam should be normally distributed. That means they should form a bell curve.

It is important to know that the PMP exam does not cover material only from the *PMBOK® Guide*. People who use the *PMBOK® Guide* as a sole study reference are often surprised to find this out. This is because the *PMBOK® Guide* is not meant to be a sole reference for practitioners or test-takers. It neither instructs you how to manage a

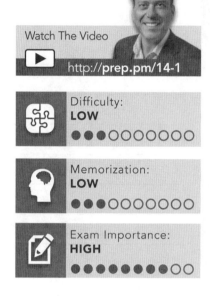

Watch The Video
http://**prep.pm/14-1**

Difficulty:
LOW
●●●○○○○○○○

Memorization:
LOW
●●●○○○○○○○

Exam Importance:
HIGH
●●●●●●●●○○

Chapter Notes:

_____

_____

_____

_____

_____

_____

_____

Chapter Notes:

_____

_____

_____

_____

_____

_____

_____

_____

_____

_____

_____

_____

_____

project, nor how to study for an exam. It is, as its name suggests, a guide to the greater body of knowledge.

As we begin to talk about strategies, it would be helpful to look at how the PMP exam is actually created. The exam is made up of 200 questions, but as was pointed out in Chapter 1, only 175 of those questions count toward your pass/fail score on the exam. The trouble is that you will not be aware of which questions count and which do not. Volunteers are recruited to write questions, and these questions are then vetted, refined, and tested out before they are added to the exam.

If a question is selected, it may be introduced as one of the 25 experimental questions on the exam. Experimental questions should look like every other question on the exam. The key is that when the results for these experimental questions are evaluated, they should perform like every other question on the exam. Questions that are too difficult or too easy may be discarded.

The topic for each question may cover anything as long as it can be cited in a "contemporary project management resource." The problem for the test-taker is that PMI no longer publicly discloses what those contemporary project management resources are (although the author speculates that they are likely books currently for sale in PMI's bookstore).

There is a common way in which standardized exams are created. Questions will generally fall into three categories:

- Easier questions

- Medium questions

- Harder questions

It is important to note, however, that these questions will be scattered randomly throughout the exam.

EASIER QUESTIONS:

Easier questions should be answerable by most test-takers. They generally focus on topics such as ethical questions, questions that require you to support PMI, questions where you are encouraged to follow the process, and questions about obvious inputs, tools, or outputs. Most people find these to be among the easiest questions on the exam. Expect to see as many as 60 of the easier questions on the exam, although they may not seem easy at first glance.

The best way to recognize one of these questions is that after reading it through carefully a couple of times, you should find that one answer clearly stands out as the most likely candidate.

MEDIUM QUESTIONS:

Medium questions are the most common questions on the exam. You should expect to see approximately 80 questions that will fall into this category. These questions will cover topics such as the order in which processes must be performed, earned value calculations, and the application of specific risk and quality tools. They will also delve into more detail to test your understanding of the processes. In order to answer these questions, you will need to fall back to your study. If you are well prepared, you will find that you can generally trust your instincts.

Medium questions may be recognized by the fact that they should generally be more fact-based. You should be able to narrow these questions down to one or two candidate answers with a bit of careful reading.

Chapter Notes:

Question Categories

Chapter Fourteen

HARDER QUESTIONS:

The harder questions will generally make the difference between those who pass and those who do not. One of the telltale signs of these questions is that you may be left scratching your head as to what is even being asked. This is an important clue! When you reach a question where you are not sure what is being asked, and remember that there may be as many as 60 of them, pause for a moment and shift mental gears. The harder questions on the exam are designed so that only the most prepared exam-takers will get them right.

When dealing with the harder questions, it is important to note that most test-takers will not naturally gravitate toward the right answer.

Consider the following example:

> Q: Mike is midway through execution and has a CPI of .98 and an SPI of .96 on his project. His project sponsor has requested a meeting with him to discuss the project's CPI and SPI as well as certain decisions he has made and how they might have led to recent issues that have arisen. Mike does not agree with the sponsor. What is the best way for Mike to handle this?

> A. Generate current performance reports before the meeting.

> B. Meet with the sponsor to show how the project is within tolerance.

> C. Explain to the sponsor why he made the decisions he did.

> D. Evaluate why the sponsor wants to meet.

There are many confusing things about this question. First of all, the question is asking "what is the best way to handle this," but the reader is no more certain what 'this' even is. Beyond that, none of the answers really seems to fit.

'A' is a fine thing to do, but it doesn't really address any of the issues in the question. 'B' seems problematic since even though the project is very close to being on track, we do not know what tolerances are. 'C' sounds like a defensive response, and while 'D' looks great at first glance (trigger word: "evaluate"), it doesn't really seem to solve anything.

Now, let's look more closely. What is the question actually asking? While we cannot be certain from the way it is worded, the question basically states that the sponsor has asked for a meeting about a couple of points and that there is a disagreement on those points. Reformulating the question now adds a bit of clarity. Whenever you have to restate the question in order to understand it, you can feel confident that it is one of the harder questions on the exam.

Next, look for the trap. Remember that most exam-takers will initially pick the wrong answer on the harder questions. In this case, the most likely answer would be 'D'. It is comfortable, it does no harm, and it uses one of the trigger words we like to see. Remember, however, that a trigger word does not guarantee that it is the right answer. Instead, it should be given extra consideration. Looking at it this way, 'D' now looks like a trap. It is the answer that most test-takers would pick, and it is incorrect.

This brings us to an important strategy for strong test-takers. When you recognize a harder question, you should look for the trap and eliminate it first; however, be sure that you are, indeed, on one of the harder questions. Also keep in mind that this strategy may backfire on the easy and medium questions.

In this case, we are reasonably confident that this is one of the harder questions, so we will eliminate 'D'. Reviewing the remaining answers, 'A' does not appear to be very helpful either. Updated performance reports do not really pertain to the question in any way. That leaves answers 'B' and 'C'. Take a closer look at choice 'C'. Although the wording is such that it sounds defensive, project managers have an aspirational goal of transparency in the decision-making process. Transparency is a good thing, and 'C' fits that model.

This strategy works best with a lot of practice, so be sure to use the key in the inside back cover of your book and practice using InSite before you try it on the PMP Exam!

Chapter Notes:

_____

_____

_____

_____

_____

_____

_____

_____

_____

_____

_____

_____

Question Categories

Chapter Fourteen

Chapter Notes:

_____

_____

_____

_____

_____

_____

_____

_____

_____

_____

_____

_____

_____

_____

READING THE QUESTIONS:

A critical step to passing the PMP is to read and understand each question. Questions on the exam may be long and have many twists and turns. They are often full of irrelevant information thrown in intentionally to distract you from the relevant facts. Those who pass the PMP know to read the questions carefully. Many times the only relevant information is contained at the very the end. Consider the following example:

Q: Mark has a project where task A is dependent on the start and has a duration of 3. Task B is dependent on start and has a duration of 5. Task C is dependent on A and has a duration of 4. Task D is dependent on B and has a duration of 6, and the finish is dependent on tasks C and D. Mark is using his project network diagram to help create a schedule. The schedule for the project is usually created during which process?

   A. Estimate Costs.

   B. Determine Budget.

   C. Control Schedule.

   D. Develop Schedule.

Questions like the one above are not uncommon on the PMP Exam. If you take the time to draw out a complex project network diagram, you will have wasted valuable time, when the question was only asking you to pick the process (the answer is 'D').

On lengthy questions, the best practice is to quickly skip down to the last sentence for a clue as to what the question is asking. Then read the entire question thoroughly. Most of them have a very short final sentence that will summarize the actual question. Make sure, however, to read the entire question at least once! Don't simply rely on the last sentence.

Just as important as carefully reading the questions is reading each of the four answers. You should never stop reading the answers as soon as you find one you like. Instead, always read all four answers before making your selection.

A GUESSING STRATEGY:

By simply reading the material in this book, you will immediately know how to answer many of the questions on the exam. For many others, you will have an instinctive guess. If you have studied the other chapters, you should trust that instinct. It is not there by chance. Your instinct was created by exposing yourself to this material in different ways. Your mind will begin to gravitate toward the right answer even if you are not explicitly aware of it.

Guessing on the PMP does not have to be left purely to chance. If you do not know the answer immediately, begin by eliminating wrong answers, or ones you suspect are wrong. Let's take a fairly difficult question as an example:

Q: Organizational Process Assets are used as an input to all of the following processes EXCEPT:

    A. Define Activities.

    B. Develop Project Charter.

    C. Validate Scope.

    D. Perform Quantitative Risk Analysis.

Unless you have memorized all of the inputs to all of the processes (the *PMBOK® Guide* lists 1444 inputs, tools, and outputs including their sub-points), you are going to have to guess at this one. However, if you throw up your hands and pick one, you only have a 25% chance of getting it right. Instead, you should think about what is being asked. Organizational process assets are used as an input to processes all over the *PMBOK® Guide*, so that doesn't offer help, but when you stop to consider that it is used primarily in initiating and planning processes, suddenly the picture becomes a little clearer. Now you can see that 'A', 'B', and 'D' are probably not the right answer. Any of these would be a good fit for historical information, which is an organizational process asset. Even if you could only narrow the choices down to 'C' and 'D', you would have a 50% chance. Look at them more carefully and ask yourself where would historical information most likely be used an input? Perform Quantitative Risk Analysis is a good guess, since

Chapter Notes:

Chapter Notes:

_____

_____

_____

_____

_____

_____

_____

_____

_____

_____

_____

_____

_____

you might use past results (an organizational process asset) to help you analyze and quantify risk. So now, you are left with choice 'C', Verify Scope, as the one that looks least likely to have an organizational process asset as an input. It is also the one process that takes place after execution, when historical information might not be as valuable. It may be a guess, but it is a very educated one.

The method here is simply to think about each answer and eliminate ones that are obviously wrong. Even if you only knock off one wrong answer, you have significantly increased your odds of choosing the right one. You will find that most times you can knock off at least two, evening your chances of answering the question correctly.

SPOTTING TRICKS AND TRAPS:

The exam does have trick questions. They are designed specifically to catch people who are coming in with little formal process experience, those who have thumbed through the *PMBOK® Guide* a few times and are now going to take the exam. These people try to rely on their work experience, which often does not line up with PMI's prescribed method for doing things. As a result, they typically don't even come close to passing the exam.

At times, however, these trick questions can also fool a seasoned pro! Listed below are some techniques you can use so that you will not fall into these traps.

FOLLOW THE PROCESS:

This is always the right answer. There will be questions on your exam that give you "common sense" scenarios that will give you a seemingly innocent way to skip the formal process and save time, or perhaps avoid some conflict by not following procedure. This is almost certainly a trap. The right answer is to follow PMI's process! Do not give in to pressure from irate customers, stakeholders, or even your boss to do otherwise.

DON'T TAKE THE EASY WAY OUT:

There will often be choices that allow you to postpone a difficult decision, dodge a thorny issue, or ignore a problem. This is almost never the right thing to do for questions on the exam.

ACT DIRECTLY AND SAY WHAT YOU MEAN:

In PMI's world, project managers communicate directly. They do not dance around the issue, gossip, or imply things, and they do not communicate through a third party. If they have bad news to tell the customer, they go to the customer and tell them the facts – and the sooner, the better. If they have a problem with a team member, they confront the person, usually directly, although at times it may be appropriate to get the team member's functional manager involved.

STUDY THE ROLES:

By the time you take the exam, you should be confident about the roles of stakeholders, sponsors, customers, team members, functional managers, the project office, and most importantly, the project manager (plus the other roles that are discussed in Chapter 2 – Foundational Terms and Concepts). Expect several "who should perform this activity" type questions. If you have absolutely no clue, guessing the "project manager" is a good idea.

Additionally, understand the difference between the different types of organizations (projectized, matrix, and functional). Most of your questions will pertain to matrix organizations, so focus your study on that one.

Chapter Notes:

General Advice

Chapter Notes:

_____

_____

_____

_____

_____

_____

_____

_____

_____

_____

_____

_____

PROJECT MANAGER'S ROLE:

Expanding on the previous point, project managers are the ones who make decisions and carry them out. They have the final decision on most points, can spend budget, can change schedules, and can approve or refuse scope. For the test, assume that the project manager is "large and in charge!"

Another attribute of project managers is that they are proactive in their approach to managing tasks and information. They do not wait for changes to occur. Instead, they are actively influencing the factors that contribute to change. Instead of waiting for information to come to them, they are actively communicating and making certain they have accurate and up-to-date information.

DON'T GET STUCK:

You should expect to find a few questions on the exam that you do not know how to answer. You will look at these and see 4 correct answers, making it impossible to pick just 1. In such cases, do not agonize. Even using every good technique, you will still have to make an educated guess at some questions. Some test-takers can get quite upset at this, and it can undermine their confidence. If a question stumps you, simply mark it for review and move on. Never spend 15 minutes staring at a single question unless you have already answered all the others. One question is only worth a fraction of a percent on the exam, so if you do not know the answer, do not obsess over it.

You may even discover that a block of questions seems especially difficult to you. This experience can be discouraging and may cause your confidence to waver. Don't be alarmed if you happen upon several difficult questions in a row. Keep marking them for review and keep moving until you come to more familiar ground. You may find that questions later in the test will offer you hints or jog your memory, helping you with those you initially found difficult.

EXAM TIME MANAGEMENT:

You will have a few minutes at the beginning to go through a tutorial. You may not find much value in the actual tutorial; however, you absolutely should take it. After going through it, you will be given a chance to wait before taking the test. Use that time to write down essential formulas and processes on your scratch paper.

SCRATCH PAPER:

You will be given five to six sheets of scratch paper when you walk into the exam. You may not carry your own paper into the test. When you sit down to begin the exam, you should write down a few key things. Regardless of how well you know this material, at a minimum, write the following on your first sheet of scratch paper.

1. Earned Value formulas (EV, PV, AC, CPI, CPIc, SPI, CV, SV, BAC, EAC, ETC, TCPIc) from Chapter 7. You will probably need to refer to these several times during the exam, and it will save time and improve your accuracy if you have written them out.

2. The schedule management formulas for the three-point estimates and standard deviation.

3. The communication channels formula described in Chapter 10.

Even if you are tempted to skip this step, don't! When you come to a lengthy and confusing question that requires you to calculate several different values, you will be glad that you already have your formulas written down for review. This will free your mind to concentrate on the specific question rather than on recalling a formula.

Chapter Notes:

_____

_____

_____

_____

_____

_____

_____

_____

_____

_____

_____

_____

_____

Scratch Paper

Chapter Fourteen

Chapter Notes:

_____
_____
_____
_____
_____
_____
_____
_____
_____
_____
_____
_____
_____
_____

BUDGETING YOUR TIME:

Going into the exam, you may be fast or you may be a slower test-taker. Everyone should walk into the exam with a strategy for managing their time, based on their own pace. Do not underestimate how hard it is to sit for a 200 question, 4 hour exam. The test-taking process is strenuous and mentally and physically taxing.

If you have a test time management strategy that has served you well in the past, you should use that. If not, here is a generic strategy that many people have used "as is" to take and pass the PMP.

1. Sit for the tutorial to gain familiarity with the testing software.

2. When the exam begins, quickly download your memorized information to your scratch paper.

3. Take the first 75 questions, pacing yourself to take approximately 45 minutes.

4. Take your first break. Spend 5 minutes stretching and get a bite of food from your locker.

5. Take the next 75 questions, again pacing yourself to take 45 to 50 minutes.

6. Take your 2nd break. Spend approximately 10 minutes, go to the bathroom, and get a snack.

7. Answer the final 50 questions and then return to answer any ones you did not answer the first time. Budget approximately 45 minutes for this as well. You may not take that long, but it is normal for your pace to slow down as the test wears on.

8. Take a bigger 15 minute break (relishing the fact that you have now answered all the questions on the PMP).

9. At this point, you should have used approximately three hours of your allotted time.

10. Perform a review of the first 100 questions. Pace yourself to finish this in about 25 minutes.

11. Take a short 5 minute stretch break if needed.

12. Review last 100 questions and any other ones in your remaining time.

MANAGING YOUR REVIEW:

When you make a review pass through the exam, you will come across questions that you missed the first time but that are apparent when you look at them again. This is normal, and you should not hesitate to change any answers that you can see you missed. Many people change as many as 10% of the answers on their review. If you catch yourself changing more than that, be careful! You may be second guessing yourself and actually do more harm than good.

When you go through your review pass on the exam, do not take the whole test over again. Instead, employ three rapid fire steps:

1. Did you read the question correctly the first time?

2. Did your selected answer match what was being asked?

3. Perform a complete check of your math where applicable.

Managing Your Review

Chapter Fourteen

Chapter Notes:

_____

_____

_____

_____

_____

_____

_____

_____

_____

_____

_____

DIFFICULTY:

Everyone wants to know what the hardest topic on the exam is. That is a difficult question to answer for two reasons:

1. The *PMBOK® Guide* and the test are divided differently. There are ten knowledge areas in the *PMBOK® Guide*, each given its own chapter. But all of this material also fits into one of five process groups. To make it more confusing, the *PMBOK® Guide* is arranged by knowledge area, but the test is graded by process group. You will not be aware of this while you are taking the exam, but it can heighten the confusion when evaluating your test results!

2. The other reason that difficulty is hard to predict is that everyone's experience will differ. No two tests are alike just as no two people have identical backgrounds. If you have heavy finance and accounting experience, time and cost may be easy subjects for you. If you have a strong legal background or have worked for the government, then questions about procurement may be easy for you. If you have human resource or psychology training, human resource management may be easiest.

Based on a typical profile of someone who had earned an undergraduate degree in management and had non-industry specific experience managing projects, the material would roughly rank as shown below:

Topic	Rank	Difficulty
Process Framework	1	**HARDER**
Foundational Concepts	2	
Integration	3	
Cost	4	
Schedule	5	
Risk	6	**MEDIUM DIFFICULTY**
Procurement	7	
Quality	8	
Scope	9	
Resource	10	**EASIER**
Communications	11	
Stakeholder	12	

The preceding scale is relative since very little of the material on the exam is considered "easy" to everyone. Ultimately, your professional experience and study can significantly change the order of this list for you.

GENERAL ADVICE:

Professional Responsibility is no longer a category on the exam, but there are questions that will be related to the "right thing to do," and some of these may surprise the test-taker who has not thoroughly prepared. Many of the questions may create very difficult situations that would be easier to ignore or dodge in real life; however, PMI requires that the project manager deal with these situations in a direct and open manner.

If there were one simple phrase that sums up this category of questions section of the test, it would be "Do the right thing," even (especially) if it is painful or would be tempting to avoid. If a test question offers you an easy way out, beware! You have likely spotted a trap. If the exam presents you with an option that represents a shortcut, do not take it.

There are a number of specific points you should understand in this area. International law can be a fairly tricky and sometimes ambiguous area, but you should expect questions on the exam to be generally straightforward in this regard. The rule for the exam is this: if you are asked to do something in another country that is not customarily done in your culture, you should first evaluate and investigate it, determine if it is unethical or illegal, and then act accordingly. This may be difficult for those who are not accustomed to international dealings. For instance, if you are asked to make a payment to a city council in another country in order to get a work permit, evaluate whether or not the payment is a bribe. If it is a bribe, do not make the payment. If it is not a bribe and it is customary, or even the law, then make the payment.

A short way of looking at it is that if it is illegal or unethical in any way then it is wrong. Otherwise, the custom in the country where the work is being performed should prevail.

There are infinite possibilities as to what may be asked here. Questions of bribery, discrimination, and illegal activity are among the favorites, but by following the thought process previously described, these questions should present no problem. Only make sure that you are not thinking so concretely that you think anything is wrong if it is different from the customary practices in your home country.

Chapter Notes:

_____

_____

_____

_____

_____

_____

_____

_____

_____

_____

_____

_____

_____

General Advice

Chapter Fourteen

Chapter Notes:

_____

_____

_____

_____

_____

_____

_____

_____

_____

_____

_____

_____

_____

A rule to keep in mind is that your organization's policies must be followed at all times. If you have an interest that conflicts with a policy, the policy is to be considered first. If your organization has a policy that all travel must be booked through the company's travel agency but you find that you can get a cheaper rate through your mother's travel agency, you should adhere to the company policy and use the corporate travel agency.

Integrity may be defined as sticking to high moral principles. For the test, the important concept is that you should do what you said you would do, deal with problems openly and honestly, and do not put personal gain ahead of the project.

Company and professional politics may play a prominent role in your life or company, and many project managers learn to be quite adept at managing them, but they are relegated to a low position on the exam.

Keep in mind that carrying out the right choice may involve standing up to the company's president, refusing an order from your boss, telling the customer the whole truth, and many other things that might have unpleasant consequences.

If a choice appears sneaky, underhanded, or dishonest in any way, it is probably not the correct answer. If the behavior is not direct, open, and straightforward, it is probably not the right behavior – even if it would ultimately appear to help the project! This will help you eliminate wrong choices on many questions.

Questions about professionalism on the exam are testing your knowledge of how a project manager acts as a professional in the workplace. According to the code of professional conduct, a project manager is to follow the process and act with respect toward others.

One key to these questions is to take the 49 processes outlined in this book seriously. The process framework is not just a formality or a theoretical best-case scenario. It is a serious set of processes, inputs, tools and techniques, and outputs that will reduce risk and improve time, cost, and quality. That said, the process is not painless. For the exam, however, the process must be followed. If your customer asks you to cut corners on the process in order to save money, you should not agree.

PMI expects Project Management Professionals to stay engaged and further the profession. The PMP certification was not designed for people to earn and never use. This is reflected on the exam with questions about activities that don't necessarily relate directly to a project.

Any time a project manager has an opportunity to further the project management training or learning of someone else, such as sharing lessons learned, mentoring, teaching, or leading in best practices, there is a very good chance that is the correct choice.

PMPs are encouraged to publish, teach, write, and disseminate the methodology and process as much as they can. Answers that offer a variant of these activities as the choice are often correct.

Project management certification is quite a milestone in one's career, but it is by no means the end. Project managers are expected to continue to study, learn, and grow professionally. As you have no doubt seen, any one of the knowledge areas could consume an entire career, so do not assume that you have learned all there is to know. Even one topic, such as quality, or risk, could provide more than a lifetime's worth of material to study and master.

Another favorite key here is that you know your own areas of weakness and continue to develop them. Do you know what your professional weaknesses are? Are you strong at planning but weak in communication? Are you good at planning tasks but poor at leading people? Everyone has strong suits as well as areas that need to be developed. It is important that the project manager knows what his or her professional growth needs are and pays attention to them.

Additionally, project managers can contribute more to the body of knowledge if they are familiar with their industries. They should study their industries, learn them well, and thus enhance their ability to apply the project management processes to their work.

You should also expect to see questions that put you in a situation of taking a hard look at your abilities, or learning where it is that you are weak. In these scenarios, the project manager should strive for continued improvement, growth, and increased proficiency.

Chapter Notes:

_____

_____

_____

_____

_____

_____

_____

_____

_____

_____

_____

_____

General Advice

Chapter Fourteen

General Advice

Chapter Notes:

_____

_____

_____

_____

_____

_____

_____

_____

_____

_____

_____

_____

_____

The project manager must accurately identify the stakeholders, then understand them, and then seek to balance their interests. This can be nearly impossible at times! For the exam, keep these principles in mind:

- Be fair to everyone and respect the differences of the group.

- Resolve stakeholder conflict in favor of the customer.

- Be open and honest about the resolution. Don't hide things from one stakeholder in order to please another.

- Do the ethical thing in all decisions.

It is tempting for some people to approach questions with a sense of "fairness" about how hard someone should work, but work ethics vary from country to country, and project managers should take that into account. That does not mean that laziness or negligence should be tolerated, but it does mean that different cultures place different values upon work, and it is not the project manager's job to force them to the level of his or her home country.

As stated previously, cultural differences on the team should be respected (notice how many times the concept of "respect" is mentioned in this chapter), and multiculturalism is something PMI promotes heavily. Your dealings with your team and the many stakeholders on a project should be professional and mindful of their customs.

As in other areas, communication should be open and regular so that people are aware of what is going on with the project.

Organizations are accountable for social, environmental, and economic impacts to their projects. Project managers should factor in the interests of the community, the environment, and society when making decisions.

On the exam, you may encounter a question that poses a situation where the project would benefit but society would suffer. The project manager should avoid all such situations and scenarios. If the situation becomes untenable or unresolvable, the project manager should disclose the situation and, as a last resort, resign the project.

Sustainability is another favored answer on the exam. Answers that encourage sustainable usage of resources and sustainable team work practices are good candidates for the right answer.

MANAGING ANXIETY:

Finally, if test-taking has always been a fear-inducing activity for you, there is one simple strategy that may help you manage the physical symptoms of anxiety so that your thinking and memory are not impaired: Take a deep breath. This may sound like obvious advice, but it is based on sound research. Studies in the field of stress management have shown that feelings of anxiety (the "fight or flight" response) are linked with elevated levels of adrenaline and certain brain chemicals. One way to bring your brain chemistry back into balance is to draw a deep breath, hold it for about six seconds, and slowly release it. Repeat this breathing pattern whenever you begin to feel panicky over particular questions. It will help to slow your heart rate and clear your mind for greater concentration on the task at hand.

Another thing to remember is that many people who take the exam do not pass – especially on their first attempts. While no one wants to fail the test, you can turn around immediately and apply to take it again (at a reduced rate). You can take the exam up to three times in a year starting with the time you receive your letter of eligibility from PMI.

If you do have to take the exam again, use it as a learning experience. You will have a much higher chance for success on your next attempt, and you will have your post-exam evaluation sheet that gives you a breakdown of where you need to study. As the inspired Jerome Kern once penned to music, "Take a deep breath; pick yourself up; dust yourself off; start all over again."

Chapter Notes:

Managing Anxiety

···· PROJECT MANAGEMENT INSTITUTE

PROFESSIONAL CONDUCT

PMI CODE OF CONDUCT:

Carefully review the code of conduct printed on the following pages. Applicants sign this statement when applying to take the exam. While there is no longer a formal "professional responsibility" section on the PMP exam, there are still questions that relate directly back to this material. Understanding the code of conduct will give you excellent guidance in answering questions on the exam, especially when you have narrowed the correct answer down to two choices.

Watch The Video

▶ http://**prep.pm**/14-2

Chapter Notes:

_____

_____

_____

_____

_____

_____

_____

CODE OF ETHICS AND PROFESSIONAL CONDUCT:

CHAPTER 1. VISION AND APPLICABILITY

1.1 Vision and Purpose

As practitioners of project management, we are committed to doing what is right and honorable. We set high standards for ourselves and we aspire to meet these standards in all aspects of our lives—at work, at home, and in service to our profession.

This Code of Ethics and Professional Conduct describes the expectations that we have of ourselves and our fellow practitioners in the global project management community. It articulates the ideals to which we aspire as well as the behaviors that are mandatory in our professional and volunteer roles.

The purpose of this Code is to instill confidence in the project management profession and to help an individual become a better practitioner. We do this by establishing a profession-wide understanding of appropriate behavior. We believe that the credibility and reputation of the project management profession is shaped by the collective conduct of individual practitioners.

We believe that we can advance our profession, both individually and collectively, by embracing this Code of Ethics and Professional Conduct. We also believe that this Code will assist us in making wise decisions, particularly when faced with difficult situations where we may be asked to compromise our integrity or our values.

Our hope is that this Code of Ethics and Professional Conduct will serve as a catalyst for others to study, deliberate, and write about ethics and values. Further, we hope that this Code will ultimately be used to build upon and evolve our profession.

1.2 Persons to Whom the Code Applies

The Code of Ethics and Professional Conduct applies to:

1.2.1 All PMI members

1.2.2 Individuals who are not members of PMI but meet one or more of the following criteria:

1. Non-members who hold a PMI certification

2. Non-members who apply to commence a PMI certification process

3. Non-members who serve PMI in a volunteer capacity.

Comment: Those holding a Project Management Institute (PMI®) credential (whether members or not) were previously held accountable to the Project Management Professional (PMP®) or Certified Associate in Project Management (CAPM®) Code of Professional Conduct and continue to be held accountable to the PMI Code of Ethics and Professional Conduct. In the past, PMI also had separate ethics standards for members and for credentialed individuals. Stakeholders who contributed input to develop this Code concluded that having multiple codes was undesirable and that everyone should be held to one high standard. Therefore, this Code is applicable to both PMI members and individuals who have applied for or received a credential from PMI, regardless of their membership in PMI.

Chapter Notes:

_____

_____

_____

_____

_____

_____

_____

_____

_____

_____

_____

_____

_____

Professional Conduct

Chapter Fourteen

Chapter Notes:

_____

_____

_____

_____

_____

_____

_____

_____

_____

_____

_____

_____

_____

_____

1.3 Structure of the Code

The Code of Ethics and Professional Conduct is divided into sections that contain standards of conduct which are aligned with the four values that were identified as most important to the project management community. Some sections of this Code include comments. Comments are not mandatory parts of the Code, but provide examples and other clarification.

1.4 Values that Support this Code

Practitioners from the global project management community were asked to identify the values that formed the basis of their decision-making and guided their actions. The values that the global project management community defined as most important were: responsibility, respect, fairness, and honesty. This Code affirms these four values as its foundation.

1.5 Aspirational and Mandatory Conduct

Each section of the Code of Ethics and Professional Conduct includes both aspirational standards and mandatory standards. The aspirational standards describe the conduct that we strive to uphold as practitioners. Although adherence to the aspirational standards is not easily measured, conducting ourselves in accordance with these is an expectation that we have of ourselves as professionals—it is not optional.

The mandatory standards establish firm requirements, and in some cases, limit or prohibit practitioner behavior. Practitioners who do not conduct themselves in accordance with these standards will be subject to disciplinary procedures before PMI's Ethics Review Committee.

Comment: The conduct covered under the aspirational standards and conduct covered under the mandatory standards are not mutually exclusive; that is, one specific act or omission could violate both aspirational and mandatory standards.

There are a few important points to note in this section. The first is that the code of conduct does not apply to everyone in the world. Instead, it applies to project managers who are affiliated with PMI. While there are many nuances to this, for the exam, use the simple rule that if someone has any real contact with PMI, even if they are not a member, then they should follow the code of conduct. You will always be safer on the exam adhering to the rule that any person in question should follow the code of conduct.

The second thing you should know about the code of conduct is that it is divided into four sub-chapters, each based on a value. The four values are: Responsibility, Respect, Fairness, and Honesty. Each of these are expanded in the following sections.

Finally, there are two more divisions for each of the four sub-chapters. They are mandatory and aspirational standards. As you might guess, mandatory conduct must be followed, while aspirational conduct is a goal.

CHAPTER 2. RESPONSIBILITY

2.1 Description of Responsibility

Responsibility is our duty to take ownership for the decisions we make or fail to make, the actions we take or fail to take, and the consequences that result.

2.2 Responsibility: Aspirational Standards

As practitioners in the global project management community:

2.2.1 We make decisions and take actions based on the best interests of society, public safety, and the environment.

2.2.2 We accept only those assignments that are consistent with our background, experience, skills, and qualifications.

Chapter Notes:

_____

_____

_____

_____

_____

_____

_____

_____

_____

_____

_____

_____

Professional Conduct

Chapter Fourteen

Chapter Notes:

_____

_____

_____

_____

_____

_____

_____

_____

_____

_____

_____

_____

_____

Comment: Where developmental or stretch assignments are being considered, we ensure that key stakeholders receive timely and complete information regarding the gaps in our qualifications so that they may make informed decisions regarding our suitability for a particular assignment.

In the case of a contracting arrangement, we only bid on work that our organization is qualified to perform and we assign only qualified individuals to perform the work.

2.2.3 We fulfill the commitments that we undertake – we do what we say we will do.

2.2.4 When we make errors or omissions, we take ownership and make corrections promptly. When we discover errors or omissions caused by others, we communicate them to the appropriate body as soon they are discovered. We accept accountability for any issues resulting from our errors or omissions and any resulting consequences.

2.2.5 We protect proprietary or confidential information that has been entrusted to us.

2.2.6 We uphold this Code and hold each other accountable to it.

2.3 Responsibility: Mandatory Standards

As practitioners in the global project management community, we require the following of ourselves and our fellow practitioners:

Regulations and Legal Requirements

2.3.1 We inform ourselves and uphold the policies, rules, regulations and laws that govern our work, professional, and volunteer activities.

2.3.2 We report unethical or illegal conduct to appropriate management and, if necessary, to those affected by the conduct.

Comment: These provisions have several implications. Specifically, we do not engage in any illegal behavior, including but not limited to: theft, fraud, corruption, embezzlement, or bribery. Further, we do not take or abuse the property of others, including intellectual property, nor do we engage in slander or libel. In focus groups conducted with practitioners around the globe, these types of illegal behaviors were mentioned as being problematic.

As practitioners and representatives of our profession, we do not condone or assist others in engaging in illegal behavior. We report any illegal or unethical conduct. Reporting is not easy and we recognize that it may have negative consequences. Since recent corporate scandals, many organizations have adopted policies to protect employees who reveal the truth about illegal or unethical activities. Some governments have also adopted legislation to protect employees who come forward with the truth.

Ethics Complaints

2.3.3 We bring violations of this Code to the attention of the appropriate body for resolution.

2.3.4 We only file ethics complaints when they are substantiated by facts.

Comment: These provisions have several implications. We cooperate with PMI concerning ethics violations and the collection of related information whether we are a complainant or a respondent. We also abstain from accusing others of ethical misconduct when we do not have all the facts. Further, we pursue disciplinary action against individuals who knowingly make false allegations against others.

2.3.5 We pursue disciplinary action against an individual who retaliates against a person raising ethics concerns.

The value of Responsibility is an important one for the exam. In fact, most professional responsibility questions will likely touch on this value in some way.

Chapter Notes:

Professional Conduct

Chapter Fourteen

Chapter Notes:

_____

_____

_____

_____

_____

_____

_____

_____

_____

_____

_____

_____

_____

_____

Each of the four values is divided into mandatory and aspirational conduct, and it is important that you know the difference between them.

In this case, mandatory conduct focuses primarily on laws, regulations, policies, and ethics. The easiest way to interpret these questions is to always take the high road. For instance, if a question gives you a scenario where it appears that the right thing to do is to follow the law or a corporate policy, but it would be very difficult to you professionally, you can be confident that the right answer is to follow the law or policy.

Aspirational values generally take the mandatory ones a good step further. In the value of Responsibility, project managers aspire to not getting in over their heads, taking ownership of their actions (including mistakes), and most importantly, doing what they say they will do.

CHAPTER 3. RESPECT

3.1 Description of Respect

Respect is our duty to show a high regard for ourselves, others, and the resources entrusted to us. Resources entrusted to us may include people, money, reputation, the safety of others, and natural or environmental resources.

An environment of respect engenders trust, confidence, and performance excellence by fostering mutual cooperation — an environment where diverse perspectives and views are encouraged and valued.

3.2 Respect: Aspirational Standards

As practitioners in the global project management community:

3.2.1 We inform ourselves about the norms and customs of others and avoid engaging in behaviors they might consider disrespectful.

3.2.2 We listen to others' points of view, seeking to understand them.

3.2.3 We approach directly those persons with whom we have a conflict or disagreement.

3.2.4 We conduct ourselves in a professional manner, even when it is not reciprocated.

Comment: An implication of these provisions is that we avoid engaging in gossip and avoid making negative remarks to undermine another person's reputation. We also have a duty under this Code to confront others who engage in these types of behaviors.

3.3 Respect: Mandatory Standards

As practitioners in the global project management community, we require the following of ourselves and our fellow practitioners:

3.3.1 We negotiate in good faith.

3.3.2 We do not exercise the power of our expertise or position to influence the decisions or actions of others in order to benefit personally at their expense.

3.3.3 We do not act in an abusive manner toward others.

3.3.4 We respect the property rights of others.

This value may be challenging to implement in real life, but it should be a bit easier to navigate on the exam.

The project manager shows respect to others. This extends not only to individuals, but to cultures. PMI is a strong advocate of multiculturalism, and questions on the test will often reflect this bias. Just as PMI does not advocate forcing in other areas, the project manager is not to force or impose his culture or personal beliefs upon others. Multicultural and "politically correct" answers are usually good choices for questions related to professionalism.

Chapter Notes:

_____

_____

_____

_____

_____

_____

_____

_____

_____

_____

_____

_____

_____

Professional Conduct

Chapter Fourteen

Chapter Notes:

_____

_____

_____

_____

_____

_____

_____

_____

_____

_____

_____

_____

_____

_____

Another area of respect that often appears on the test is the respect for confidentiality. This covers confidentiality of client information, trade secrets, project information, and any personal information that may be disclosed during the course of the project.

The mandatory standard is that we negotiate in good faith and do not abuse others. The respect we extend to others includes interpersonal respect and the respect of others' property, including intellectual property.

The aspirational standard here takes the mandatory standard further by valuing other people, cultures, and opinions. Keep in mind that answers that sound "politically correct" are generally considered favorable for the exam.

CHAPTER 4. FAIRNESS

4.1 Description of Fairness

Fairness is our duty to make decisions and act impartially and objectively. Our conduct must be free from competing self interest, prejudice, and favoritism.

4.2 Fairness: Aspirational Standards

As practitioners in the global project management community:

4.2.1 We demonstrate transparency in our decision-making process.

4.2.2 We constantly reexamine our impartiality and objectivity, taking corrective action as appropriate.

Comment: Research with practitioners indicated that the subject of conflicts of interest is one of the most challenging faced by our profession. One of the biggest problems practitioners report is not recognizing when we have conflicted loyalties and recognizing when we are inadvertently placing ourselves or others in a conflict-of-interest situation. We as practitioners must proactively search for potential conflicts and help each other by highlighting each other's potential conflicts of interest and insisting that they be resolved.

4.2.3 We provide equal access to information to those who are authorized to have that information.

4.2.4 We make opportunities equally available to qualified candidates.

Comment: An implication of these provisions is, in the case of a contracting arrangement, we provide equal access to information during the bidding process.

4.3 Fairness: Mandatory Standards

As practitioners in the global project management community, we require the following of ourselves and our fellow practitioners:

Conflict of Interest Situations

4.3.1 We proactively and fully disclose any real or potential conflicts of interest to the appropriate stakeholders.

4.3.2 When we realize that we have a real or potential conflict of interest, we refrain from engaging in the decision-making process or otherwise attempting to influence outcomes, unless or until: we have made full disclosure to the affected stakeholders; we have an approved mitigation plan; and we have obtained the consent of the stakeholders to proceed.

Comment: A conflict of interest occurs when we are in a position to influence decisions or other outcomes on behalf of one party when such decisions or outcomes could affect one or more other parties with which we have competing loyalties. For example, when we are acting as an employee, we have a duty of loyalty to our employer. When we are acting as a PMI volunteer, we have a duty of loyalty to the Project Management Institute. We must recognize these divergent interests and refrain from influencing decisions when we have a conflict of interest.

Further, even if we believe that we can set aside our divided loyalties and make decisions impartially, we treat the appearance of a conflict of interest as a conflict of interest and follow the provisions described in the Code.

Chapter Notes:

_____

_____

_____

_____

_____

_____

_____

_____

_____

_____

_____

_____

_____

Professional Conduct

Chapter Fourteen

Chapter Notes:

_____

_____

_____

_____

_____

_____

_____

_____

_____

_____

_____

_____

_____

_____

Favoritism and Discrimination

4.3.3 We do not hire or fire, reward or punish, or award or deny contracts based on personal considerations, including but not limited to, favoritism, nepotism, or bribery.

4.3.4 We do not discriminate against others based on, but not limited to, gender, race, age, religion, disability, nationality, or sexual orientation.

4.3.5 We apply the rules of the organization (employer, Project Management Institute, or other group) without favoritism or prejudice.

The mandatory standard here is pretty clear. We must be especially careful to avoid conflicts of interest, and we never discriminate against others. The conflict of interest point is an important one. For the exam, you should choose answers that go out of their way to avoid a conflict of interest, even if it seems silly. As for discrimination, be especially attuned to situations where you might be passing over one candidate in favor of another due to age, gender, disability, etc.

The aspirational conduct for fairness can generally be summed up in The Golden Rule: "Do unto others as you would have them do unto you." Treat everyone equally, with no discrimination, nepotism, or favoritism. Further, you should make your decisions in a transparent and open way, and treat everyone equally. Finally, it is an aspirational standard for fairness that we regularly examine our own impartiality.

CHAPTER 5. HONESTY

5.1 Description of Honesty

Honesty is our duty to understand the truth and act in a truthful manner both in our communications and in our conduct.

5.2 Honesty: Aspirational Standards

As practitioners in the global project management community:

5.2.1 We earnestly seek to understand the truth.

5.2.2 We are truthful in our communications and in our conduct.

5.2.3 We provide accurate information in a timely manner.

Comment: An implication of these provisions is that we take appropriate steps to ensure that the information we are basing our decisions upon or providing to others is accurate, reliable, and timely.

This includes having the courage to share bad news even when it may be poorly received. Also, when outcomes are negative, we avoid burying information or shifting blame to others. When outcomes are positive, we avoid taking credit for the achievements of others. These provisions reinforce our commitment to be both honest and responsible.

5.2.4 We make commitments and promises, implied or explicit, in good faith.

5.2.5 We strive to create an environment in which others feel safe to tell the truth.

5.3 Honesty: Mandatory Standards

As practitioners in the global project management community, we require the following of ourselves and our fellow practitioners:

5.3.1 We do not engage in or condone behavior that is designed to deceive others, including but not limited to, making misleading or false statements, stating half-truths, providing information out of context or withholding information that, if known, would render our statements as misleading or incomplete.

Chapter Notes:

_____
_____
_____
_____
_____
_____
_____
_____
_____
_____
_____
_____
_____

Professional Conduct

Chapter Fourteen

Chapter Notes:

_____

_____

_____

_____

_____

_____

_____

_____

_____

_____

_____

_____

_____

5.3.2 We do not engage in dishonest behavior with the intention of personal gain or at the expense of another.

Comment: The aspirational standards exhort us to be truthful. Half-truths and non-disclosures intended to mislead stakeholders are as unprofessional as affirmatively making misrepresentations. We develop credibility by providing complete and accurate information

Honesty is the fourth and final value in the code of conduct. The mandatory standard is short and to the point: we never deceive others. For the exam, think of the court oath to tell the truth, the whole truth, and nothing but the truth. This will serve you well on the exam.

The aspirational standard carries this further by saying that we not only try to be truthful, but we try to create an environment where it is encouraged that people tell the truth and are safe in doing so. Also, it is important that the project manager always seeks the truth in all dealings.

Final Exam

IMPORTANT

In addition to this quiz, use your Key to InSite, found on the inside back cover of this book, to access additional content, including new exam questions, expanded content, and simulated PMP exams. If your book did not come with a Key to InSite on the inside back cover, it may not be authentic. If you do not have a Key to InSite, you may purchase one at insite.velociteach.com.

Watch The Video
▶ http://**prep.pm/15-1**

INSTRUCTIONS:

This simulated PMP Exam may be used in several ways. If you take it as a final, you will get a very good idea how you would do if you walked right in to take the PMP Exam. In that way, it can be a very good readiness indicator.

Perhaps the best way to use this exam is to take it again and again, reviewing the answers that go with each question. The answers and explanations will give you insight into the formation of each question and the thought process you should follow to answer it.

Prior to taking the PMP, the best strategy is to take this exam repeatedly, reviewing the answers, until you can make a score of 90% or better.

Chapter Notes:

_____

_____

_____

_____

_____

_____

_____

_____

Chapter Fifteen

Chapter Notes:

_____

_____

_____

_____

_____

_____

_____

_____

_____

_____

_____

_____

_____

If you are taking this as a final exam, you have 4 hours (240 minutes) to complete the following 200 questions, including any breaks you may take.

Each question has only one best answer. Mark the one best answer on your answer sheet by filling in the circle next to A, B, C, or D.

On the actual PMP Exam, only 175 of the 200 questions will be graded, but you do not know which questions count and which do not. A passing score on the PMP Exam is 106 out of 175, which is 61%. For this practice final, you should correctly answer at least 180 out of the 200 possible questions in order to consider yourself ready for the real exam.

FINAL EXAM:

1. There are two processes that are closely related to product or result acceptance from the Customer. Review these four statements and select the one that is the least accurate regarding these two processes.

   A. Validate Scope is generally performed before Control Quality.

   B. Control Quality and Validate Scope can be performed in parallel in some cases.

   C. Control Quality and Validate Scope both use inspection as a key tool.

   D. Validate Scope and Control Quality both make use of deliverables.

2. Lupita is incredibly busy. She is trying to close out the project that she is leading, and there are many items to be addressed. Consider Lupita's priorities. From this list of four, what is the most important thing that Lupita should do?

   A. Perform a lessons-learned review with as many team members present as possible.

   B. Make sure all project records have been updated with the most current information.

   C. Complete performance appraisals for all team members and report those to the members and their functional managers.

   D. Confirm that all the project work is complete and that the project met the stated objectives.

Chapter Fifteen

Chapter Notes:

_____

_____

_____

_____

_____

_____

_____

_____

_____

_____

_____

_____

_____

_____

_____

_____

3. **Plan Communications Management is a process designed to produce the obvious - a communications management plan. Consider the following four statements about communication planning on your project. Select the one false statement.**

   A. Project communication should be both effective and efficient so that only the necessary information is provided at the right time and in the right format.

   B. Communication planning is performed very early in the project life cycle in most cases.

   C. Planning communications is linked closely to enterprise environmental factors because the structure of the organization will have an impact on the communication requirements for the project.

   D. Because communication planning results in a component of the overall project plan and establishes expectations with key stakeholders, this communication plan should not be changed or revised once published.

4. **Alex is a project manager who is trying desperately to motivate his team. He understands that the environment has to be right and certain basic needs must be met in order for any incentives to have affect. However, in his heart, Alex is convinced that the team needs a lot of direct supervision from him in order to stay focused and reach the goals they have set. Which of the following statements best applies to Alex?**

   A. McGregor would classify Alex as a Theory X manager.

   B. McClelland would refer to Alex as a Theory Y manager.

   C. McClelland would categorize Alex as a manager with a need for control.

   D. Maslow would point to Alex as a manager following the Hierarchy of Needs approach to motivation.

5. Which of the following is NOT a primary goal of Perform Integrated Change Control?

   A. Influencing factors that cause change.

   B. Determining that a change has occurred.

   C. Managing change as it occurs.

   D. Denying change whenever possible.

6. Which process makes use of the issue log as an input, and what is the process group associated with this process?

   A. Manage Stakeholder Engagement, Communications Management.

   B. Manage Team, Executing.

   C. Manage Stakeholder Engagement, Stakeholder Management.

   D. Manage Stakeholder Engagement, Monitoring and Controlling.

7. Cleve is taping the latest version of the risk breakdown structure on the wall for the team to view. During which process would Cleve and the project team make use of the tool called Risk Categorization?

   A. Risk Identification.

   B. Perform Quantitative Risk Analysis.

   C. Perform Qualitative Risk Analysis.

   D. Identify Risks.

8. One of the results of the Conduct Procurements process becomes an important input into building the project schedule. Which output of Conduct Procurements is described?

   A. Selected Sellers.

   B. Resource Calendars.

   C. PND.

   D. Contracts.

Chapter Fifteen

Chapter Notes:

_____

_____

_____

_____

_____

_____

_____

_____

_____

_____

_____

_____

9. **The schedule activity list:**

   A. Serves as an extension of the work breakdown structure.

   B. Is synonymous with the work breakdown structure.

   C. Is used to create the project scope statement.

   D. Is included in the project charter.

10. **The team is scrambling - they just received word that their customer had a major reorganization last Friday. Many of the key stakeholders for the project have been let go or reassigned. The team heard that Kelly has risen into a position of considerable power in the customer organization. Kelly has had little involvement with the project team, and the team is frantically searching for early assessments and conclusions reached about Kelly. What document is being described here? What is the team searching for?**

    A. The project charter - it lists assumptions and constraints and sets expectations from the customer perspective.

    B. The project staffing and resource plan - this plan will point out commitments from the project team and the customer side and should provide the supporting data needed by the team in this state of flux.

    C. The team needs the updated version of the change log because that should include Kelly and her related information pertinent to the discussion.

    D. The stakeholder register, including the strategy for managing stakeholders - that is the document that may include notes on Kelly and how to best increase her support.

11. As soon as Sandy discovered that she would be leading the newly launched GreenLamb project, she immediately scheduled an appointment to meet with the program manager. In that meeting, Sandy presented a strong case for recruiting Harold and Jocelyn onto her team based on her prior experience working with both. Sandy left the meeting feeling confident that her wishes would be honored. Which tool most closely fits the description of the actions Sandy took?

   A. Negotiation.

   B. Pre-assignment.

   C. Acquisition.

   D. Collaboration.

12. A subset of the project team was tasked with writing the RFP and selection criteria for the architectural work needed on the project. They have connected with others in the organization who have created similar RFPs for other projects, so they have a good template for a start. Today, the group is looking at the calendar to determine the best time to hold a bidder conference. Given these activities, which process from Procurement Management best describes where the group is and what they are doing?

   A. Control Procurements.

   B. Plan Procurement Management.

   C. Conduct Procurements.

   D. Execute Procurements.

13. Which of the following best fits "corrective action"?

   A. Anything done to bring future results in line with the plan.

   B. Actions taken to fix mistakes.

   C. Typically a required specification or deliverable from the project sponsor.

   D. An output of project planning.

Chapter Notes:

_____

_____

_____

_____

_____

_____

_____

_____

_____

_____

_____

_____

_____

_____

14. You are the PM for a project that has some of the work out for bid. You just ended a phone call with Ben. Ben leads a small consulting firm that has provided excellent work for your organization in the past. In the call, Ben apologized profusely for missing the vendor conference or pre-bid conference your project team held last week. Ben's firm plans to submit a proposal, but he would like to meet with you later this week to discuss the RFP. Given these four choices, what is your best course of action?

   A. Explain to Ben that meeting with him would show favoritism and suggest that his firm bid on future work with your organization.

   B. Agree to meet with Ben but extend the same offer to all companies who attended the bidder conference last week.

   C. Ask Ben to submit his questions about the RFP in email and your team will post the questions and responses so that all vendors can read them.

   D. Share the questions and answers recorded from last week's vendor conference so that Ben knows as much as all other vendors.

15. The Kaylehmda Project has recently migrated to the Implementation Phase. The development team cleared the final quality gates, documentation was completed, and all results and responsibilities have been passed on to the implementation team. Most of these team members are new to the project. Kiki, the new project manager, is getting up to speed in meetings with Vinit, the PM of the prior phase. Vinit and Kiki are reviewing aspects of the charter in order to validate that the known constraints are still applicable. According to the PMBOK® Guide, what process is being carried out?

   A. Project justification and funding.

   B. Develop Project Charter.

   C. Validate Scope.

   D. Close Project or Phase.

16. Tim is bracing himself for a challenging day at work. Several of the team members have reported to Tim that two members are very angry with each other. Tim is rehearsing a few of his conflict management statements of truth in his head while he drives into the office. Which of the following is not a true statement regarding this tool of managing the project team?

   A. Conflict resolution should focus on the present keeping the past in mind as a point of reference.

   B. Conflict is a team issue.

   C. Openness resolves conflict.

   D. Conflict resolution should focus on the issues and not the personalities of those involved.

17. Which of the following is the best explanation of the process called Create WBS?

   A. Decomposing product requirements into smaller features that are easier to manage.

   B. Decomposing project activities into smaller tasks that are easier to manage.

   C. Subdividing project deliverables into smaller components that are easier to manage.

   D. Subdividing project work packages into smaller components that are easier to manage.

18. A project manager is pondering the enterprise environmental factors that may impact how she goes about acquiring human resources to fill out the project team. Which of the following does not represent a valid enterprise environmental factor in this scenario?

   A. A list of the cost rates for these human resources.

   B. The standard policies, processes, and procedures of the company.

   C. The location of the company and where the project will be performed.

   D. The competency level of the staff members being considered for the project team.

Chapter Notes:

_____

_____

_____

_____

_____

_____

_____

_____

_____

_____

_____

_____

_____

The Final Exam

Chapter Notes:

_____

_____

_____

_____

_____

_____

_____

_____

_____

_____

_____

_____

_____

_____

19. Cam walks by the conference room where the new project team is meeting. He overhears a spirited debate between two of the members. They have very different opinions about the level of influence that Bob has within the customer organization. The team will be working with Bob throughout the project, and they are trying to understand where Bob fits. Given this type of team activity and your understanding of the project management framework, what Process Group is being described here?

    A. Initiating.

    B. Integration management.

    C. Stakeholder analysis.

    D. Planning.

20. **Which of the following techniques is not used in Collect Requirements?**

    A. Surveys and questionnaires.

    B. Fibonacci Technique.

    C. A JAD session.

    D. Building a model.

21. **Tia and Anton are busy gathering data and running reports to determine how much money and how many days of schedule have been consumed by risks that have occurred to date on the project. Next, they will compare those totals with the amount of money and amount of time set aside to deal with risks. What tool is being used by Tia and Anton, and what process are they conducting?**

    A. Contingency Reserve Analysis and Perform Quantitative Risk Analysis.

    B. Risk Audits and Monitor Risks.

    C. Expert Judgment and Perform Quantitative Risk Analysis.

    D. Reserve Analysis and Monitor Risks.

22. **What topic is relevant to ADR, and in what process would you find ADR?**

    A. ADR is a contract type and is discussed in Plan Procurement Management.

    B. ADR is an accounting method and is found in the EVM section of Control Costs.

    C. ADR is a method for handling disputes and would be used in Control Procurements.

    D. ADR is an estimating technique and is referenced in Estimate Activity Durations.

23. **You are assigned to replace a project manager on a large software project for a telecommunications company in the middle of executing the work. Portions of the software are being supplied by subcontractors working at your company's offices. You would like to know what performance metrics are going to be tracked for these contract workers. Where could you find such information?**

    A. The project charter.

    B. The procurement management plan.

    C. The WBS.

    D. The organizational process assets.

24. **The team has been dealing with a recurring issue for weeks. A recommendation was made to the project manager to change how the team handles this situation in the future in order to prevent the issue from occurring. The PM has approved the change, and now the project team is implementing it. In which project management process is the team engaged?**

    A. Control Quality.

    B. Monitor and Control Project Work.

    C. Direct and Manage Project Work.

    D. Perform Integrated Change Control.

Chapter Notes:

_____

_____

_____

_____

_____

_____

_____

_____

_____

_____

_____

_____

_____

_____

The Final Exam

Chapter Fifteen

Chapter Notes:

_____

_____

_____

_____

_____

_____

_____

_____

_____

_____

_____

_____

_____

25. One of the Enterprise Environmental Factors that will influence the role of the project manager is the type of organization the PM belongs to. Which of the following statements about a functional organization is most accurate?

    A. Power primarily lies with the project manager.

    B. The project manager is more likely to run into issues obtaining sufficient resources.

    C. Power is shared between the functional manager and project manager.

    D. Staffing issues are rare because the functional manager supplies them from his or her department.

26. What officially authorizes a project?

    A. The assignment of a project manager to the project in the project charter document.

    B. The kickoff meeting is held and the project charter is handed out to team members.

    C. The project initiator signs the project charter.

    D. The PMO or a steering committee finalize the selection of the project and document that choice in a project charter.

27. Members of the project team are scheduling meetings with selected representatives from the Customer. The goal is to further understand the roles of the staff that the team will be working with over the life of the project. Clark gave team members a great template developed from prior Customer engagements. The interview questions ask some basic items, such as job titles, length of service, responsibilities, and some more sensitive questions, such as what do you hope to gain from this project, and what do you fear from this project. Based on this description of activities, determine what process is being conducted. Now, pick the process group associated with that process:

   A. Collect Requirements.

   B. Planning.

   C. Identify Stakeholders.

   D. Initiating.

28. Which of the following statements best describes the Define Scope process?

   A. Developing a detailed description of the project and product.

   B. Developing a detailed description of the project.

   C. Developing a detailed description of the product.

   D. Bridging or connecting documentation from initiating steps to the schedule baseline.

Chapter Fifteen

Chapter Notes:

_____

_____

_____

_____

_____

_____

_____

_____

_____

_____

_____

_____

_____

29. The sponsor, Samantha, is still concerned after her meeting with the project manager, Sherry, that the quality process is not being followed as originally planned. What is the best means for Sherry to illustrate to Samantha that the team is carrying out the quality plan? Choose the best answer from these four:

    A. Present the sponsor with a whitepaper discussing the effectiveness of statistical sampling.

    B. Show the sponsor the various costs of nonconformance identified by the team.

    C. Hand a quality control chart to the sponsor that compares results from this project with results from the prior project.

    D. Provide a quality checklist that indicates when items were carried out.

30. If your organization is considered the Buyer and you are currently reviewing proposals from potential Sellers, which of the following would be valid outputs from this process?

    A. Procurement Statement of Work and Resource Calendars.

    B. Source Selection Criteria and a Contract Award.

    C. An Agreement and a Selected Seller.

    D. A Make or Buy Decision and a Qualified Seller List.

31. Kirk has carried out the planning necessary to develop a human resource plan for his project. Kirk is not sure what comes next. How many executing processes are in the knowledge area of Resource Management, and which executing process should be carried out first?

    A. Two and Develop Team should occur first in the executing processes of resource management.

    B. One executing process and Acquire Resources is the process that should be carried out first.

    C. Two and Acquire Resources should occur first in the executing processes of resource management.

    D. Three and Acquire Resources should occur first in the executing processes of resource management.

32. Your team has encountered recent unanticipated problems. After extensive earned value analysis, you determine that the project has a schedule performance index of .54 and a cost performance index of 1.3. Additionally, your customer has just requested a significant change. What should you do?

    A. Alert management about the schedule delays.

    B. Alert management about the cost overruns.

    C. Alert management about the scope change.

    D. Reject the requested change.

33. The project management plan is a logical input to the process of Manage Quality. What component of this PM plan is most relevant to this process?

    A. Quality Management Plan.

    B. Cost Baseline.

    C. Quality Reports.

    D. Cost Management Plan.

34. Which of the following statements is not accurate regarding the conflict resolution technique of confronting or problem-solving?

    A. It examines many alternatives and treats conflict as a problem to solve.

    B. It requires open dialogue.

    C. It emphasizes areas of agreement rather than differences.

    D. It requires a give-and-take attitude.

Chapter Notes:

Chapter Fifteen

Chapter Notes:

_____

_____

_____

_____

_____

_____

_____

_____

_____

_____

_____

_____

_____

35. You are the PM for a project that was requested and sponsored by three Vice Presidents in your organization. The key objective is to select and implement a customer management system with enhanced capabilities; the old system is a mess and must be replaced. Initial planning is done. The team you are managing is deep into the execution of the work packages. Today, all three VPs have emailed you with separate change requests. To make matters worse, each VP argues that his or her change request is of utmost priority. In this situation, what would be your best course of action?

   A. Request a meeting of the change control board and turn the three requests over to the board.

   B. Look at the three change requests, do the necessary research, and prioritize them.

   C. Request a meeting with each VP and explain that the initial planning is done, the team is fully engaged in execution, and the change request will have to wait.

   D. Look at the three change requests, meet with your manager, and seek advice on how to prioritize them.

36. What would be the most correct sequence of these project processes?

   A. Collect Requirements, Identify Stakeholders, Define Scope, Control Communications.

   B. Identify Stakeholders, Create WBS, Monitor Risks, Close Project or Phase.

   C. Identify Stakeholders, Collect Requirements, Develop Project Charter, Close Project or Phase.

   D. Develop Project Charter, Identify Stakeholders, Create WBS, Define Scope, Close Project or Phase.

37. What is the name of the tool or technique used to sum up the cost elements in the process that derives the project budget? And, what is the proper sequence of summation, from the lowest level of detail to the highest?

    A. Cost Aggregation and the order is activity to work package to control accounts to total project.

    B. Funding Limit Reconciliation and the order is activity to task to control account to work package to summary WBS node to total project.

    C. Cost Aggravation and the order is task to control account to work package to total project.

    D. Cost Aggregation and the order is total project to WBS summary node to work package to control accounts.

38. The project team appears to have stalled, and the heart of the matter is a conflict that has divided the team into two distinct camps. You are the project manager and need to be a decisive leader. Which of the following types of conflict resolution should be avoided when looking for a solution to the problem? Specifically, which method should be your last choice to implement?

    A. Punishment.

    B. Compromising.

    C. Forcing.

    D. Collaboration.

Chapter Fifteen

Chapter Notes:

———————————————

———————————————

———————————————

———————————————

———————————————

———————————————

———————————————

———————————————

———————————————

———————————————

———————————————

———————————————

———————————————

———————————————

39. **Trish and Sal were discussing project management. Sal asked Trish to describe the goal of a certain project management process and to state the purpose in her own words. Trish came up with the following description: "This process is all about making sure the right message is being delivered to the right audience at the right time." What is the name of the process being described, and what is the associated process group?**

    A. Manage Communications, Executing.

    B. Monitor Communications, Monitoring and Controlling.

    C. Communications Management Plan, Planning.

    D. Control Stakeholder Engagement, Monitoring and Controlling.

40. **In regards to EVM, what is considered the most critical metric and why?**

    A. CPI because it reports the value of the work completed compared to the estimated costs that were anticipated to date.

    B. CPI because it measures the cost efficiency of the work completed.

    C. SPI because it measures progress achieved compared to progress planned on the project.

    D. SPI because it reports to key stakeholders a valid snapshot of the work performance of the team to date.

41. Fran and Mark were supposed to be working together to develop the schedule and assign team resources to the various tasks on the schedule. They are feeling a lot of pressure because another PM within their organization just came in and took 4 of their team members to work on her project. The program manager authorized the move and doesn't have replacement resources for Fran and Mark. So, they are stressed by too much work, and too few resources. The two agree that they need to use a combination of critical path and critical chain methods. The point of confusion is over their disparate definitions of critical chain. Which of these definitions do you think is best?

   A. Critical chain is the resource-constrained critical path.

   B. Critical chain is the same as critical path, it was just developed after CPM.

   C. Critical chain is the critical path plus float buffers for risk reserve.

   D. Critical chain is the critical path plus a project buffer placed just after project kickoff.

42. Hirdesh and Anton lead two separate departments that are collaborating on a long-term corporate initiative. The plan is that the group led by Hirdesh will complete the first portion of the development. Then, they will transfer the work product over to Anton's group for the next portion of the initiative. Anton and Hirdesh are meeting in the conference room to map out that transfer, although it will not take place for several more months. According to PMI, what process best describes the meeting that the two department heads are having?

   A. Define Scope.

   B. Close Project or Phase.

   C. Develop Schedule.

   D. Perform Qualitative Risk Analysis.

Chapter Notes:

_____

_____

_____

_____

_____

_____

_____

_____

_____

_____

_____

_____

_____

43. Roger is confused. This is the first time he has been asked to perform variance analysis as a means of reporting the performance of the project back to the Sponsor. Roger is not sure what is expected of him. His project manager tells Roger to look for variance analysis as a Tool in the PMBOK® Guide and use the tool just as it is described there. Given this instruction to Roger, what statement is the best advice for Roger?

A. Data Analysis is listed as a Tool in 10 of the 12 Monitoring and Controlling processes, so Roger should compare the overall project performance measurements with the project plan and baselines, identify and quantify differences and their causes, and report back to the Sponsor.

B. Variance Analysis is a tool listed for Control Quality, so Roger should pinpoint differences in the quality metrics and the work performance data, determine the cause and degree of these differences, and report to the Sponsor.

C. In Cost Management, the tool of Variance Analysis is listed for Control Costs, so Roger should determine differences in the approved budget and the actual expenditures, determine the degree and cause of the differences, and report to the Sponsor.

D. The tool of Variance Analysis is listed for Control Scope, so Roger should determine differences in the work performance data and the requirements documentation, determine the severity and cause of the differences, and report to the Sponsor.

44. Actual results of performing project activities are used in many monitoring and controlling processes to determine potential variances. What are these actual results called and from which process are they generated?

A. Work performance measurements, Manage project execution.

B. Performance reports, Control Communications.

C. Work performance data, Monitor and Control Project Work.

D. Work performance data, Direct and Manage Project Work.

45. Approved budget increases should be:

A. Added to the schedule management plan.

B. Added to the project's cost baseline.

C. Added to the project's reserve fund and used only if needed.

D. Added to the lessons learned.

46. 1. Refer to the table at the right. If task H were increased from 3 to 7, what impact would this have on the project?

Task	Dependency	Duration
Start	None	0
A	Start	3
B	A	2
C	B	2
D	Start	4
E	D	1
F	Start	5
G	F	7
H	B, E	3
I	C, G, H	4
Finish	I	0

A. The project would finish later.

B. The project would finish earlier.

C. The schedule risk would decrease.

D. The critical path would change, but the finish date would not change.

47. Jansen works in the corporate office and is managing a project to upgrade 50 franchise stores at an estimated cost of $250,000 per store. Jansen's team plans to complete the upgrade project in 8 months. What is the planned value for the end of month 2 of the project?

A. $12,500,000.

B. $3,125,000.

C. $1,625,000.

D. $2,500,000.

Chapter Notes:

Chapter Notes:

_____

_____

_____

_____

_____

_____

_____

_____

_____

_____

_____

_____

_____

_____

_____

48. **What should you argue is the most important output of the Acquire Resources process and why?**

    A. Project team assignments because other project managers in the organization need to know that resources are no longer available for their projects.

    B. Project management plan updates because the Resource Management Plan is a vital component of the document that guides execution.

    C. Project team assignments because the team members need to know that they've been assigned to a project and the role they will play.

    D. Resource calendars because these are essential inputs to building a reliable schedule.

49. **In six separate instances, the Customer has formally requested a change to the scope of the project. Each time, the project manager set up a meeting and invited the Customer, a member of the PMO, and his mentor from within the organization. The project team is small, so the PM thought it would be wise to include all team members in these meetings, as well. What does this action tell you about the project manager? Which statement seems most accurate?**

    A. This PM should be replaced.

    B. This PM believes in collaboration and values the judgment of others.

    C. This PM is using change control meetings to drive decisions regarding important change requests.

    D. This PM is demonstrating the need for a well-defined integrated change control system.

50. **In which of the following organizations is the project manager role more likely to be filled as a full-time position?**

    A. Functional.

    B. Strong matrix.

    C. Strong functional.

    D. Projectized.

51. **Which of the following is not produced as a result of initiating a project?**

    A. Project charter.

    B. Summary milestone schedule.

    C. Assignment of the project manager.

    D. Stakeholder engagement plan.

52. **Look at the following list of answers. These are descriptions of possible inputs to the Define Scope process. Logically, which one is not valid?**

    A. The list of requirements.

    B. The list of activities.

    C. The risk register.

    D. A template from a past project.

53. **Your team has begun to develop the project schedule. Important information about the tasks is delaying the team from completing the development. What planning should occur prior to or simultaneously with the creation of the schedule to enable completion of the Gantt Chart that has been requested by the functional management team?**

    A. Determining the budget to obtain the funding limits of the schedule activities.

    B. Diagramming the flow from one task to the next based on logical relationships.

    C. Team meetings to understand the task uncertainties and associated contingency plans.

    D. Stakeholder meetings to assess the project scope relative to the organization's quality policy.

Chapter Notes:

_____
_____
_____
_____
_____
_____
_____
_____
_____
_____
_____
_____
_____

The Final Exam

Chapter Notes:

_____

_____

_____

_____

_____

_____

_____

_____

_____

_____

_____

_____

_____

_____

54. One of the stated purposes of a particular process is to document how the project will demonstrate compliance. What is the name of the process that has this purpose?

A. Plan Quality Management.

B. Define Scope.

C. Control Quality.

D. Validate Scope.

55. What other quality management tool is related to the tool of a Histogram, and how is it related?

A. Histograms and Control Charts both use statistical analysis of project results to determine how the project is performing from a quality standpoint.

B. Histograms are very similar to Run Charts as Run Charts are a presentation of the "history" of a quality metric on the project.

C. Histograms and Run Charts both track and report the historical performance of the project in such a way that quality analysis can be performed easily.

D. Histograms and Pareto Charts are similar because the Pareto Chart is a type of histogram that is ordered by frequency of occurrence.

56. You are managing a team developing a software product. You have contracted out a portion of the development. Midway through the project you learn that the contracting company is entering Chapter 11 bankruptcy. A manager from the subcontracting company assures you that the state of the company will not affect your project. What should you do FIRST?

A. Review the risk register and the contract and act according to those plans.

B. Stop all pending and future payments to the subcontractor until the threat is fully assessed.

C. Contact your legal department to research your options.

D. Meet with senior management to apprise them of the situation.

57. What component of the project management plan is most useful to a project manager while working to manage the expectations of project stakeholders?

   A.   Change management plan.

   B.   Configuration management plan.

   C.   Communications management plan

   D.   Stakeholder engagement plan.

58. Roger is reaching the end of the project, and he wants to ensure that he has carried out all the steps to close the project successfully. Roger is sitting in his office and notices his copy of the PMBOK® Guide on the bookshelf. He flips to the section describing this process, reviews the outputs, and makes notes. What is the name of one of the outputs and the associated item(s) listed under this output that Roger should update?

   A.   The output is deliverables transition and lists the transition of product, service, or result.

   B.   The output is project management plan updates and lists project documents, closure files, and historical information.

   C.   The output is project documents updates, and the item is the lessons learned register.

   D.   The output is final product transition and lists the items of historical information, lessons learned, and supporting files.

59. Alexia and the team are meeting with key stakeholders to begin identifying and gathering project requirements. Which two processes should have already taken place?

   A.   Collect Requirements and Identify Stakeholders.

   B.   Collect Requirements and Develop Project Charter.

   C.   Develop Project Management Plan and Define Schedule.

   D.   Identify Stakeholders and Develop Project Charter.

Chapter Notes:

_____

_____

_____

_____

_____

_____

_____

_____

_____

_____

_____

_____

_____

The Final Exam

Chapter Fifteen

Chapter Notes:

_____

_____

_____

_____

_____

_____

_____

_____

_____

_____

_____

_____

_____

_____

_____

60. Your organization is submitting a proposal for a contract that is well aligned with the expertise of your company. However, the contract that is out for bid is from a government entity that your organization has not worked with in the past. The government entity places a favorable weighting on those companies who are headquartered in the local region. For this reason, your organization has teamed up with a small company in that region to offer a joint proposal. In terms of risk strategies, this scenario describes the use of which one?

A. Transfer.

B. Exploit.

C. Share.

D. Mitigate.

61. Barbara is the new project manager for a project that has been going on for 5 months now. The project is scheduled to deliver final product to the Customer in 3 more months, but the team has had poor quality performance to date. Barbara is considering the best tool to use to solve the quality issues. Here is the situation: the project team is relying on 4 departments to provide timely advice, resources, and expertise in completing project tasks and hitting acceptable quality metrics. What tool will be most beneficial to Barbara to determine where the problems are hiding?

A. Run Charts.

B. Flowcharting.

C. Inspection.

D. Control Charts.

62. A project charter has many elements that are important. Which of the following is not always included in the project charter?

A. The business need that the project addresses.

B. Name of the sponsor of the project.

C. A summary-level schedule or milestones.

D. A strategy for managing stakeholders.

63. GlobalCorp is carrying out a consulting engagement for a firm based in Canada. Vijay is the PM for GlobalCorp on the project, and he is looking at an invoice for training that he authorized for a team member. Vijay and his team realized they needed more training with this particular system in order to carry out the engagement. Now Vijay is pondering which control account and organization to charge for this system training. How would you advise Vijay?

   A. Charge it to the client unless the contract specifies otherwise - the client should pay because the client benefits.

   B. Charge it to the PMO of GlobalCorp - GlobalCorp should pay.

   C. Charge it to the project budget - GlobalCorp should pay.

   D. Charge it to GlobalCorp regardless of what the contract states - GlobalCorp should pay.

64. Brenda is managing a project at her firm to enhance the features of one of their product lines. Her project is going well - it has a CPI of 1.2 and they are slightly ahead of schedule. Brenda gets a call at home on Saturday that the firm she works for was acquired by another company. Her boss assures Brenda that her job is secure, but the project Brenda is leading will be terminated. The acquiring company has a similar product line that has deeper market penetration, and that drove the decision. When Brenda goes to work on Monday, what is the best course of action for her to take?

   A. Analyze the two product lines and make a recommendation to management to either support the decision or offer justification for keeping the current product line.

   B. Find out more about the acquisition, then meet with the team and share an update.

   C. Carry out the close project or phase process.

   D. Since the project is going well, Brenda should meet with the team ASAP to determine what level of effort would be required to complete the work.

Chapter Notes:

_____

_____

_____

_____

_____

_____

_____

_____

_____

_____

_____

_____

_____

_____

65. When communication links are undefined or broken:

   A. The communications management plan should be rewritten.

   B. Conflict will increase.

   C. The project manager's power will decrease.

   D. Project work will stop.

66. Senior Management is reviewing project options for the next funding cycle. The CFO has tasked them to use BCR to determine how the various projects stack up. The first project named Solo has a BCR of 2.3 - which of the following statements is correct about Project Solo?

   A. With a BCR of 2.3, Project Solo should clearly be authorized.

   B. Project Solo will be considered a better choice than other projects that have a Benefit Contingency Risk score of greater than 2.3 because those projects are considered more risky.

   C. With a BCR of 2.3, Senior Management should recommend that the organization not fund Project Solo.

   D. Senior Management should recommend funding Project Solo if no other projects being considered have a BCR greater than 2.3.

67. Henry is in charge of distributing project information to the various stakeholder groups. Which of the following methods does not represent a valid means for Henry to push data to these stakeholders?

   A. Knowledge repository.

   B. Emails.

   C. Press release.

   D. Letters.

68. Reaching the last 3 months of the project, Rochelle is excited to see the positive results being produced by the team. In the weekly meeting, the team brings 2 new risks to the attention of Rochelle. What action should Rochelle take first?

    A. Add the 2 new risks to the Risk Register.

    B. Consult the risk management plan for guidance regarding the process for managing risks that are identified late in the project.

    C. Send the risks through the change control process in Perform Integrated Change Control.

    D. Investigate the risks further by using the tool of expert judgment.

69. The process of managing stakeholder engagement includes 1 input and 1 output that are related to issues and changes. From the list of 4 answers, select the answer that is the most accurate concerning this input and output.

    A. The change log and issue log are both inputs and outputs of this process.

    B. Change Requests are an output of Perform Integrated Change Control and an input to this process, and Issue Requests are an output of this process.

    C. Change Requests are an output of Monitor and Control Project Work and an input to this process, and Issue Lists are an output of this process.

    D. The Issue Log is an output of this process, while the Change Log is an input to this process and an output of Monitor and Control Project Work.

Chapter Notes:

———————————

———————————

———————————

———————————

———————————

———————————

———————————

———————————

———————————

———————————

———————————

———————————

———————————

Chapter Fifteen

Chapter Notes:

_____

_____

_____

_____

_____

_____

_____

_____

_____

_____

_____

_____

_____

_____

70. George is managing a project where some of the work should be performed by subcontractors or vendors. George received several proposals from potential vendors for his company's project. Working with his company's procurement department, George evaluated the proposals and has made a vendor selection decision. Consider the following four phrases or descriptions. Which of the following would not be a result of George's supplier selection decision process?

    A. Resource calendars.

    B. A contract that represents a mutually binding legal agreement between Buyer and Seller.

    C. Change requests, which include those made to the project plan or its subsidiary plans.

    D. Independent estimates to report to all potential Sellers to justify the selection process that was followed.

71. The sponsor and Ankit, the project manager, walk out of the meeting with several follow-up action items. Ankit needs to alert the team to this significant change the sponsor and he have agreed to take. For this project, several objectives will drop from the scope. Hopefully, a follow-up project will pick up these scope items and receive the proper funding and schedule. However, the Sponsor and Ankit agreed that this scope-cutting measure was essential to save the project from a looming large risk. What strategy have the sponsor and project manager agreed to use?

    A. Avoid.

    B. Transfer.

    C. Share.

    D. Accept.

72. When it comes to managing human resources, a project manager may try different tactics for motivating the team to produce desired results. Who authored the motivational theory that describes three categories of needs that people have, and what are those 3 categories?

    A. McClelland and the three needs are for achievement, affiliation, and power.

    B. Maslow and the three are the Need for Control, Need for Belonging, and Need for Power.

    C. McGregor and the three needs are categorized as Theory X, Theory Y, and Theory Z.

    D. McCleveland and the three categories are the Need for Affiliation, Need for Achievement, and Need for Control.

73. If you had to pick from the following 4 choices, during which group of processes is it best to assign someone as the project manager?

    A. Initiating.

    B. Planning.

    C. Executing.

    D. Monitoring and Controlling.

74. This tool of risk identification takes a look at the suppositions and hypotheses related to the project to check for inconsistencies, inaccuracies, or incompleteness. What is the name of the tool?

    A. Checklist analysis.

    B. Decision reviews.

    C. Assumption and constraint analysis.

    D. Predetermined risks.

Chapter Notes:

_____

_____

_____

_____

_____

_____

_____

_____

_____

_____

_____

_____

_____

_____

_____

The Final Exam

Chapter Fifteen

Chapter Notes:

_____

_____

_____

_____

_____

_____

_____

_____

_____

_____

_____

_____

_____

75. **If you are the project manager leading a new team, which of the stages introduced by Tuckman would you want your team to move out of the most quickly and why?**

    A. Norming because this stage is particularly taxing on the project manager as she or he work with team members to coalesce as a team and give up individual pursuits.

    B. Performing because this stage can bring out the insecurities of team members as they act out their false expectations for the project and their role in it.

    C. Forming because this stage is not as productive as others and can put financial and schedule pressure on the team if they remain in this stage too long.

    D. Storming because this can be a destructive stage if the team cannot move past the normal disagreements or differences of opinion that may arise during this stage.

76. **Ozeas is managing the implementation of a financial software system for a large Customer. Ozeas and the team selected a vendor to deliver a reporting solution for the implementation, and the product has been of high quality to date. Today, Ozeas receives word that the vendor will discontinue support of that reporting product in 6 months. Ozeas is considering his options. How would you advise him? What should Ozeas first course of action be?**

    A. Ask members of the team to perform additional risk response planning to manage the risk this presents.

    B. Pause all payments to the vendor until the threat is further analyzed.

    C. Meet face to face with your legal department immediately to determine next steps.

    D. Research the contract and look for any pertinent warranty or support information.

77. **Schedule constraints would likely include all of the following EXCEPT:**

    A. Imposed dates.

    B. Key events.

    C. Major milestones.

    D. Leads and lags.

78. **Why would you use the Delphi Technique when gathering requirements from stakeholders?**

    A. To find out which requirements are most important - you may need to use this technique so that the loudest voice in the room does not take over the process.

    B. To analyze the requirements adequately - you need to use a statistical approach that is more objective than subjective.

    C. To find out which requirements the project should address - you must consider the quality standards or metrics that will serve as targets for your team and drive performance.

    D. To analyze and document the requirements correctly - your goal should be to use a voting system that is fair and equitable.

79. **From the choices provided, identify the exact output of the closing process from the Integration Management area.**

    A. Final Product, Service, or Result.

    B. Closed Procurements.

    C. Closed Contract Awards.

    D. Final Product, Service, or Result Transition.

Chapter Notes:

_____

_____

_____

_____

_____

_____

_____

_____

_____

_____

_____

_____

_____

_____

The Final Exam

Chapter Fifteen

Chapter Notes:

_____

_____

_____

_____

_____

_____

_____

_____

_____

_____

_____

_____

_____

80. **Which of the following documents are you least likely to place on a shared server where the entire team and the Customer can download and view documents?**

A. Procurement SOW.

B. Stakeholder register.

C. Risk register.

D. Issue list.

81. **Creating the work breakdown structure is a vital step for the project team for a number of reasons. 3 of the following statements describe a purpose or result of creating the WBS. Find the statement that does not.**

A. To make the work more manageable.

B. To create a task-oriented decomposition of the work.

C. To create a more refined description of the deliverables at a lower level than the scope statement.

D. To define work packages that can be assigned, monitored, and controlled.

82. CMMI, TQM, Six Sigma, Deming, and Malcolm Baldridge. What do those terms or names have in common, in terms of how they are referenced in the PMBOK® Guide?

   A. These are specific flowcharting techniques and the authors that developed them along with Ishikawa in conjunction with Toyota Motor Corp.

   B. These represent alternative quality management techniques that are not embraced or endorsed by PMI and may be in conflict with the 3 Quality Processes put forth by PMI.

   C. These are references to quality management initiatives that may be used by certain organizations who strive for continuous improvement.

   D. These are sophisticated quality disciplines (and two of the leaders) that emphasize the use of control charts and interviewing to uncover underlying causes to quality issues and are most closely associated with that specific tool of Control Charts.

83. If a project team is experiencing conflict over a technical decision that is negatively affecting project performance, the BEST source of power the project manager could exert to bring about cooperation would be:

   A. Legitimate.

   B. Penalty.

   C. Referent.

   D. Expert.

Chapter Notes:

The Final Exam

Chapter Notes:

_____

_____

_____

_____

_____

_____

_____

_____

_____

_____

_____

_____

_____

84. Brandon is a green project manager - he doesn't have a lot of experience. He has been advised to listen closely to the voice of the Customer, but Brandon is not sure which voice to listen to first, or if he should hear them all! Choose the best list of stakeholders for Brandon to consider, given these 4 groups:

A. The project management office, the customer rep, and the team.

B. Team members, his manager, his sponsor, and the customer.

C. The project management office, his sponsor, the primary point of contact with the customer, the vendors, and the president of the local PMI chapter.

D. The customer, the team members, the manager of Brandon, the project sponsor, and members of the community impacted by the project results.

85. Consider the second process of Project Procurement Management. To which process group does it belong?

A. Executing.

B. Planning.

C. Closing.

D. Monitoring and controlling.

86. If a project manager is unsure who has the authority to approve changes in project scope, what components of the project management plan should they consult?

A. The scope management plan.

B. The scope baseline.

C. The scope management plan and the change management plan.

D. The scope management plan, the configuration management plan, and the change management plan.

87. Consider the following phases of a project and select the phase where you are most likely to be asked for a ROM estimate of costs:

   A. Controlling phase.

   B. Initiating phase.

   C. Executing phase.

   D. Planning phase.

88. A subset of the team is meeting to determine the number of work periods required to complete each task for a given section of the work breakdown structure. Ron has left the room to survey the technical resources and ask for opinions for how long a certain task will take. Ron comes back and states that the value for M is 12 days. What process is being described, and what does M most likely represent in this context?

   A. Estimate Activity Resources and M represents the Most-Likely resource requirements based on opinions of the technical team.

   B. Estimate Activity Durations and M represents the Most-Likely duration estimate that Ron received from the team members.

   C. Create WBS and M represents the Median or average estimate derived from the team.

   D. Determine Activity Durations and M represents the man-days or FTEs estimated by the team.

89. You have reviewed the historical records from the two projects performed last year that align well with your current project. You are excited to discover a Pareto chart that is formatted in a manner that will help your team identify quality control issues throughout the project. The Pareto chart is a specific type of what tool?

   A. Ishikawa diagram.

   B. Vilfredo Pareto Diagram.

   C. Scatter Diagram.

   D. Histogram.

Chapter Notes:

_____

_____

_____

_____

_____

_____

_____

_____

_____

_____

_____

_____

_____

_____

90. Your team is working hard to manage the quality issues that have been persistent the last two weeks. It seems that every time the team puts out one fire, another quality fire starts burning. Things are getting out of control, and you want to help the team focus on those quality issues that are responsible for the majority of the complaints. What tool would be best?

A. Pareto chart.

B. Control chart.

C. Ishikawa diagram.

D. 5 Why technique.

91. The term "slack" is also known as:

A. Lag.

B. Lead.

C. Float.

D. Free float.

92. The project team is gathered in the war room working hard to fully capture the scope of the project. Their goal is to hammer out the scope baseline by the end of the week. The PM encourages them to keep breaking down the work into smaller and smaller chunks. What is the tool that the PM is referring to, and where else might it be used?

A. The tool is top-down analysis, and it is used to define the work packages as well as the schedule tasks.

B. The tool is decomposition, and it may be used in Define Scope and Create WBS processes by the team members or subject matter experts.

C. The tool is decomposition, and it may be used to define the WBS and also to create the list of activities that will go on the schedule.

D. The tool is decomposition, and it is often used along with Expert Judgment in the Define Scope and Define Activities processes.

93. The project has a CPI of 1.2 and a SPI of 1.1 and has been managed from the start by Daphne. No matter what actions Daphne takes with the Customer, it seems that change requests continue to hit the project team too frequently - too many - too fast. Which of the following statements is the most accurate?

    A. Daphne should continue to work with the Customer to influence factors that bring about the change requests.

    B. Daphne should recognize the excellent performance results and not upset the Customer with further discussions about change requests.

    C. Daphne should communicate face to face with the Customer that the project performance cannot be undercut by the risk of any future change requests.

    D. Daphne should commit to the Customer that only those change requests that result in traceable value to the Customer will be accepted in the future.

94. Davicel has been supporting the sales team throughout the engagement with GROWCOM, the new customer. Jake is the primary point of contact for GROWCOM, and Jake is in a high position of management so that he can approve project funding. Davicel and Jake have been working to complete the project charter. When can Davicel know that the project has been formally authorized?

    A. When Davicel and Jake jointly agree that the charter is finished.

    B. When Davicel has the project charter signed by his manager.

    C. When Jake signs the charter.

    D. When Davicel and Jake agree that the charter is complete and a contract has been written.

Chapter Notes:

_____

_____

_____

_____

_____

_____

_____

_____

_____

_____

_____

_____

_____

The Final Exam

Chapter Fifteen

Chapter Notes:

_____

_____

_____

_____

_____

_____

_____

_____

_____

_____

_____

_____

_____

_____

95. **Bob is managing a project that is in month 14 of a 24-month project. The team has just entered the phase that has the greatest uncertainty and was the most difficult to estimate when building the budget for the sponsor. Bob was given numbers this morning that indicate the overall project TCPI has actually dropped below 1 for the first time in the project. What should Bob do with this piece of information?**

A. TCPI is below 1 indicating that the project is performing better than expected, so Bob should share the news with the sponsor as soon as possible.

B. TCPI is below 1 indicating that the project is performing worse than expected, so Bob should share the news with the sponsor as soon as possible.

C. TCPI is below 1 indicating that the project is performing better than expected, so Bob should watch this trend for another month and then report his findings and conclusions to the sponsor.

D. TCPI is below 1 indicating that the project is performing worse than expected, so Bob should watch this trend for another month and then report his findings and conclusions to the sponsor.

96. **The work authorization system can add more complexity to a project - and some team members may complain about it. What is the purpose of the system?**

A. It makes sure that only authorized work is performed by the team per the scope baseline.

B. It makes sure that work is performed at the right time and in the correct sequence by the correct resources.

C. It ensures that work performed will comply with the authorized acceptance criteria.

D. It ensures that the right people are authorized to perform the approved work.

97. At what point in project planning would you decide to change the project scope in order to avoid certain high-risk activities?

    A. Identify Risks.

    B. Qualify Risks.

    C. Control Risks.

    D. Plan Risk Responses.

98. The team has been told to keep a close eye on expenditures and make sure that invoices from the subcontractors are reviewed carefully. Angelina is leading the team and has the most experience applying earned value management principles to analyze spending trends and performance on a project. Given Angelina's level of experience, what statement would she be most likely to make?

    A. We prefer that the project's TCPI is greater than 1 and the CPI is less than 1.

    B. We prefer that the project's SPI is greater than 1 and the CPI is less than 1.

    C. We prefer that the project's CPI is greater than 1 and the TCPI is less than 1.

    D. We prefer that the project's EVI is greater than 1 and the CPI is equal to 1.

99. Your project team has completed identifying risks that might impact the new project. Some time and effort have gone into performing qualitative risk analysis, and the risk register has been updated with the results. The project team members have all suggested next steps to help quantify each risk. Which team member's suggestion should NOT be carried out?

    A. Make use of a decision-tree diagram and calculate EMV.

    B. Perform sensitivity analysis to determine which risks have the largest potential impact on the project.

    C. Calculate risk probability and impact assessments for each remaining risk.

    D. Create an influence diagram to show risk entities, outcomes, and influences.

Chapter Fifteen

Chapter Notes:

_____

_____

_____

_____

_____

_____

_____

_____

_____

_____

_____

_____

100. **Regarding integration management, which of the following statements would you most likely categorize as false?**

   A. Because integration management is vital to project success, it is best to assign a key team member to manage each of these processes.

   B. A primary focus of integration management is to coordinate various elements of the project.

   C. Because integration touches many areas of the project, the project management information system is used and updated a good deal in this area.

   D. The decisions made by the project manager in integration often involve competing project requirements or goals.

101. **The process of Estimate Activity Resources is closely coordinated with another process from a separate Knowledge Area. What is that process and why?**

   A. Collect Requirements because you need to have the right people on the project team who are familiar with the work to be performed to properly document requirements.

   B. Identify Risks because your team needs to have enough experience to carry out risk identification to mitigate project failure.

   C. Control Quality because your team must have staff skilled in using the specific tools of this process.

   D. Estimate Costs because this process determines the cost to conduct an activity based on the type and quantity of resources required.

102. Verified deliverables are referenced by the project team as they validate the documented project scope against the deliverables being produced. Given that verified deliverables are being used here, which of the following statements is the most accurate and complete?

    A. The tool of inspection must have been used to validate deliverables.

    B. The process to Control Quality must have been completed.

    C. The team has already carried out inspections, sampling, Pareto analysis, or used other similar techniques to vet quality.

    D. Verified deliverables indicate that the Validate Scope process has been completed.

103. Assume that your project budget follows a familiar S-curve over time. This is common to most projects. If the S-curve represents the cost baseline, which of the following statements is most accurate?

    A. Project funding requirements are derived from the cost baseline but they probably will not result in the same S-curve because of the timing of funding.

    B. Project funding requirements in total should be slightly less than the cost baseline.

    C. Project funding requirements should track the same S-curve as the cost baseline and remain parallel over the life of the project.

    D. Program funding requirements may be greater than or less than the cost baseline depending on the time period being measured.

Chapter Notes:

_____

_____

_____

_____

_____

_____

_____

_____

_____

_____

_____

_____

_____

_____

_____

The Final Exam

Chapter Notes:

_____

_____

_____

_____

_____

_____

_____

_____

_____

_____

_____

_____

104. Which of the following choices most properly reflects matching roles to responsibilities?

A. Senior management: Signing the project charter, approving schedule change requests, and naming the project manager.

B. Project manager: Signing the project charter, approving schedule change requests, and assigning team resources to activities.

C. Senior management: Communicating the strategic vision, matching portfolio options to the goals, and signing the project charter.

D. Program manager: Coordinating multiple project dependencies, Communicating the program vision, and assigning project team members to activities.

105. This question offers a familiar scenario: you work for a pharmaceutical company that has grown fast and is aggressive in bringing new products to market. The current project you are leading is not that exciting - it involves an upgrade to the customer management system used by the company. When the project kicked off, many of the top resources had rolled off other tasks. You were able to recruit many of the best resources to your team. The project has 9 months remaining on the revised schedule. Today, the marketing department broadcasted a press release indicating that your company won a huge contract with great bonus potential based on performance. Without discussing this with you, one of your team members, named Francis, goes directly to the person who is expected to lead the new project and asks to be a part of the team. What should you do?

A. Go directly to Francis's functional manager and report the offensive behavior.

B. Call a meeting with Francis and your project sponsor so that the 2 of you can discuss Francis's actions with him.

C. Bring the item up in the next team meeting, document it in the team issue log, and monitor it yourself.

D. Discuss the matter with Francis as soon as possible in a meeting with him.

106. You are focused on managing stakeholder expectations about the communication received and have determined that the reports being distributed to the groups of stakeholders are going out too frequently. As a result of this discovery, what output are you most likely to update?

A. Project management plan.

B. Change request.

C. Issue log.

D. Stakeholder management strategy.

107. One of the tools used for estimating the duration of an activity is the three-point estimate. What is the other name of this estimate, and which accompanying statement is accurate?

A. GERT and M should be less than P but greater than O.

B. Triangular Distribution and M should be less than O but greater than P.

C. Triangular Distribution and M should be greater than O but less than P.

D. GERT and O should be greater than P but less than M.

108. The WBS dictionary documents additional information that supports the WBS. Consider the following 4 lists that describe information stored in the WBS dictionary. Which one of the lists contains inappropriate information?

A. Description of work, responsible organization, code of account identifier.

B. Associated schedule activities, list of schedule milestones, resources required.

C. Cost estimates, acceptance criteria, quality requirements.

D. Technical references, contract information, Delphi charts.

Chapter Notes:

_____

_____

_____

_____

_____

_____

_____

_____

_____

_____

_____

_____

_____

_____

109. Which of the following statements about a project is not true?

A. A project can involve a single person.

B. A project must include all unique elements; otherwise, the work is considered ongoing operations.

C. A project may create a capability to provide a service.

D. A project may create a result, such as a research document.

110. Stanley led the team through the vendor selection process, and the team is very happy with the decision. Next comes contract negotiations. Buyer and Seller hope to agree to contract terms that are fair to both parties. They hope to sign the contract quickly and start the work promptly. Read through these descriptions of contract items - things that may be included in a valid agreement. Identify the answer that is the least accurate.

A. Pricing, roles and responsibilities.

B. Performance reporting, pricing, and the period of performance.

C. Limitation of liability, incentives, and make-or-buy decisions.

D. Schedule baseline, SOW, and warranty.

111. Johnson accepted an offer from another company, and Isabel has inherited the project to manage to completion. Johnson cannot be reached, so Isabel is forced to search project documents to get what she needs. She found the contracts to be very helpful, but Isabel wants to make sure she has a full comprehension of the expectations of the sponsor. What two documents would be most useful?

A. The stakeholder register and the communications management plan.

B. The WBS and the project charter.

C. The communication management plan and the scope statement.

D. The communication plan and the stakeholder management strategy.

112. **Group decision-making techniques are often used by project teams to gather, classify, and prioritize requirements. Which of the following are examples of these techniques?**

    A. Dictatorship, majority, minority-voice.

    B. Unanimity, majority, plurality, dictatorship.

    C. Democratic, autocratic, representative.

    D. Majority, autocratic, plurality, proxy.

113. **A normal part of projects involves repairing broken software code, fixing defective products, or revamping the results so that they meet acceptable quality standards. In which process would the team make these types of repairs, fixes, or take corrective action?**

    A. Direct and Manage Project Work.

    B. Control Quality.

    C. Perform Integrated Change Control.

    D. Monitor and Control Project Work.

114. **If the optimistic estimate for an activity is 15 days and the pessimistic estimate is 25 days, what is the realistic estimate?**

    A. 19 days.

    B. 20 days.

    C. 21 days.

    D. Unknown.

Chapter Notes:

The Final Exam

Chapter Fifteen

115. Rochelle is reviewing risk analysis performed by fellow team members. She views a report that shows decision nodes, costs associated with the nodes, chance nodes, rewards associated with these nodes, and a final net path value for each possible path. What process are Rochelle and the team engaged in, and what tool is being used here? Pick the best combination from these four choices:

    A. Perform Qualitative Risk Analysis and Risk Quality Assessment and Analysis.

    B. Perform Qualitative Risk Analysis and Decision Tree Analysis.

    C. Perform Quantitative Risk Analysis and Expected Monetary Value Analysis.

    D. Perform Quantitative Risk Analysis and Probability Impact Analysis.

116. Jorge, Regina, and Lu were tasked with performing the first round of analysis of risks that followed the team brainstorming session. In that session, a list of 59 potential risks was captured. Now, the three team members have completed their initial analysis that precedes quantitative risk analysis. Which of the following would not be appropriate to present, given this stage of risk management activities?

    A. A tornado diagram of all risks.

    B. A list of risks grouped by common categories.

    C. A prioritized list of risks.

    D. A list of risks that require attention in the near-term.

117. Zebra Gear provides equipment, clothing, and apparel to referees and sports officials in the US. The CEO wants to expand slowly into the UK market. One of her concerns is with shipping and order fulfillment in the new market. Your company was hired to perform a gap assessment and produce a series of reports. The reports should highlight likely problems or gaps and recommend solutions. You have been working with your project team to fully define the scope of the new project with the CEO and her core team. Of all the tools listed for the Define Scope process, which one is least likely to be effective or applicable in this situation?

A. Expert judgment because your team will have a hard time finding people with experience with this type of international business.

B. Facilitated workshops because one key to success with those sessions is to have the decision-makers in the room; the CEO is probably very busy and she may not be available.

C. Product analysis because the deliverable for this project is more of a service or result.

D. Decomposition because the nature of gap analysis makes it difficult to get down to work packages.

118. Ralph is leading a project with many internal and external parties of interest. Jamie has submitted a change request that will impact the scope, and the request is sitting on Ralph's desk. Ralph has gone over the request 3 times to make sure he's not missing anything. He needs to respond to Jamie. Which of the following choices describes the best advice for Ralph?

A. Review the KPI from the most current reports and determine the impact this change may have on the progress in the project.

B. Check the configuration management plan to make sure Jamie filled out the change request forms properly before committing resources.

C. Look at the requirements traceability matrix, see who owns the requirements that may be affected by the change, and discuss the change with them.

D. Request a copy of the staffing management plan to determine if Jamie's request is feasible

Chapter Notes:

_____

_____

_____

_____

_____

_____

_____

_____

_____

_____

_____

_____

_____

_____

_____

_____

The Final Exam

Chapter Fifteen

Chapter Notes:

_____

_____

_____

_____

_____

_____

_____

_____

_____

_____

_____

_____

_____

_____

119. The project you are leading has a SPI of 1.2 and a CPI of .98 at this time. Kim comes to you with an idea for an easy improvement to the product you are building. The change will take very little time and add no additional cost. The enhancement was not included in this project but may be needed during the next build. What should you do?

   A. Build to the project scope and do not add the enhancement.

   B. Since the impact on costs is zero, add the enhancement for the current Customer.

   C. Perform risk analysis before making a decision.

   D. Ask the Customer to sign off on the enhancement.

120. Camille is the program manager, and in her weekly meetings, she reviews results with her project managers. Charles and Jose are in Camille's office providing their weekly update. Both of them are expressing the need for more resources, so Camille has asked to see the details of the schedule. First, Camille wants to see the activity list from both projects. The list of activities should include:

   A. The tasks that have been identified and assigned to team members on the respective teams for Charles and Jose.

   B. The schedule activities on the project that have been identified as being on the critical path.

   C. All the tasks or steps that need to take place to create the work packages.

   D. To be efficient with Camille's time, Charles and Jose should identify that subset of tasks that have constrained resources.

121. How would you categorize or describe the work results of the project?

   A. Projects produce products.

   B. Projects result in services, results, or products.

   C. Outputs of projects must pass acceptance criteria.

   D. Change control boards have the ultimate say over those specifications of the final work product produced by the project.

122. Sabrina is managing the internal project for this important upgrade of infrastructure. Elisha approaches Sabrina and asks for time off to join friends on an impromptu vacation. After consulting the schedule, Sabrina is reluctant to grant the time off - Elisha is working on two activities that are on the critical path and is an important contributor. However, Elisha is the niece of Teresa who owns the company. What should Sabrina do?

   A. This is an example of referent power which should be avoided - Sabrina should escalate this situation to her direct manager.

   B. This is an excellent case for using the compression technique of crashing the schedule - bring in other resources and allow Elisha the time off.

   C. This is a case where Sabrina should treat Elisha like any other resource on the team - look for a reasonable substitute and if there is none, she should not allow the time off.

   D. This is a delicate situation that Sabrina should discuss directly with Teresa and follow her advice.

123. Raj, the project manager, is meeting with Sue, the Customer, at the working assembly line to compare the product modifications to the specification. Raj and Sue are most interested in the results of the modifications. The goal of the project is to increase efficiency on this section of the line by 15%. Which tool would be the best for them to use during this meeting?

   A. Variance Analysis.

   B. Inspection.

   C. A Pareto Chart.

   D. Alternatives Generation.

Chapter Notes:

_____

_____

_____

_____

_____

_____

_____

_____

_____

_____

_____

_____

_____

_____

124. Which of the following statements regarding resource requirements is not true?

A. This output results from Estimate Activity Resources and identifies the types of resources required for each activity, and quantities are determined in the following process of Estimate Activity Durations.

B. It is an input into Estimate Costs and Plan Procurement Management.

C. You can take these requirements, sum them up, and determine the resources needed for a work package.

D. It is a good practice to include the basis for these estimates and any assumptions made in developing them

125. Manage Communications is a process that is all about executing the plans that have been made and responding to requests for information as they arise. Which of the following techniques is not considered as relevant to this process as the others?

A. Communication Style Assessment.

B. Conflict Resolution Techniques.

C. Feedback.

D. Presentations.

126. Which answer best completes the following statement: "The project charter is ..."

A. Developed before the business case and after the project plan.

B. Developed after the business case and before the project plan.

C. Developed before the contract and after the project plan.

D. Developed before the contract and before the project plan.

127. Which process is best described as the process of communicating and working with stakeholders to meet their needs and address issues?

   A. Direct and Manage Project Communication.

   B. Perform Integrated Change Control.

   C. Manage Stakeholder Engagement.

   D. Manage Communications.

128. Members of the team have provided data from their respective areas to Chafik. Now, he can analyze the summarized data, draw conclusions, and share them with key stakeholders. Chafik is puzzled because Lisa is in charge of the project schedule and reports a cumulative SPI of .87 while Ankit reports that the CPI is 1.14 - Alex reports a drop in rework and defects for the period. From these four statements, choose the statement that would best describe an interpretation of the data for Chafik.

   A. Tell Chafik that the cost overruns are not due to quality issues but most likely are due to the inefficient work of the team.

   B. Tell Chafik that his project is behind schedule but ahead of budget and to be happy with the quality improvements.

   C. Tell Chafik that his project is ahead of schedule but behind budget and he should be pleased with the quality improvements.

   D. Tell Chafik that there is not enough data to forecast an estimated final budget or delivery date for the project, but focus on the good quality results.

129. As a result of the execution of the Manage Communications process, what are the stakeholders most likely to see?:

   A. Enterprise Environmental Factors Updates.

   B. Project Communications.

   C. Issue Log Updates.

   D. Risk Register Updates.

Chapter Notes:

_____

_____

_____

_____

_____

_____

_____

_____

_____

_____

_____

_____

_____

_____

_____

The Final Exam

Chapter Fifteen

The Final Exam

Chapter Notes:

_____

_____

_____

_____

_____

_____

_____

_____

_____

_____

_____

_____

_____

_____

130. **In the context of project management, what might be the best way to describe WPI and WIP?**

   A. There is no difference - they represent the same concept.

   B. WPI stands for work performance indication; WIP stands for work indicated priority.

   C. WPI is more about how work is being performed; WIP is more about ranking external factors that may threaten the project.

   D. WPI refers to work performance information; WIP often refers to work in progress.

131. **Margaret is gathering information from the last month of project activity as she prepares to meet with key stakeholders, make sure they are getting the data they need, and respond to any issues. Margaret is looking for all supporting data related to a recent request to modify the shipping specifications for vital parts. She recalls that this topic of shipping requirements was a very big concern for one of the customers, but she cannot remember who that person was. What two items will be key inputs to Margaret in this process?**

   A. Requirements documentation and Work performance information.

   B. Issue log and Stakeholder engagement plan.

   C. Change log and Responsibility assignment matrix.

   D. Change log and the Work breakdown structure.

132. **Sal walks by the office of the sponsor and overhears the project manager making a conciliatory statement to the sponsor. The PM says "Listen, I probably should have made you aware of the quality issue with the contractor a month ago, but you and I agree we need to hit the delivery date, right? Completion is more important than arguing over the small stuff... don't you agree?" What conflict resolution technique did Sal overhear the project manager attempting to use with the sponsor?**

   A. Accommodating.

   B. Smothering.

   C. Collaboration.

   D. Forcing.

133. Consider the following four lists related to the process of monitoring and controlling risks. Which list is most accurate, if you start with the output, then list the tool or technique, and finally the input related to this process?

   A. Work performance measurements, Trend analysis, Work performance information.

   B. Work performance information, Audits, Work performance data.

   C. Risk register, Meetings, Project management plan updates.

   D. Risk register, Risk reassessment, Meetings.

134. A project manager may use all of the following tools or techniques when creating the project budget EXCEPT:

   A. Earned value management.

   B. Expert judgment.

   C. Cost aggregation.

   D. Funding limit reconciliation.

135. Which of the following is the best explanation of the differences between the Validate Scope and Manage Quality processes?

   A. They may be performed in parallel, but Validate Scope should be finished last.

   B. Manage Quality is all about correctness, while Validate Scope is all about completeness.

   C. Validate Scope is primarily concerned with acceptance and Manage Quality is primarily concerned with following the quality standards on the project.

   D. Validate Scope is about correctness, and Manage Quality is about completeness.

Chapter Notes:

_____

_____

_____

_____

_____

_____

_____

_____

_____

_____

_____

_____

_____

_____

The Final Exam

Chapter Fifteen

Chapter Notes:

_____

_____

_____

_____

_____

_____

_____

_____

_____

_____

_____

_____

_____

_____

136. **Based on the table at the right, which path listed below represents the LEAST schedule risk?**

Task	Dependency	Duration
Start	None	0
A	Start	3
B	A	2
C	B	2
D	Start	4
E	D	1
F	Start	5
G	F	7
H	B, E	3
I	C, G, H	4
Finish	I	0

   A. Start-A-B-C-I-Finish.

   B. Start-A-B-H-I-Finish.

   C. Start-D-E-H-I-Finish.

   D. Start-F-G-I-Finish.

137. **Which of these statements about a work breakdown structure is not accurate?**

   A. Once the scope baseline is established, the WBS should represent all the official scope of the project.

   B. The number of levels in a WBS will vary.

   C. The goal with decomposing the WBS is to keep going until you don't know enough information to continue decomposing or you've reached the work package level.

   D. The WBS results in many work packages that all have a single schedule activity associated with them.

138. **The stakeholder register contains a list of project stakeholders. Which of the following statements is not true about a stakeholder register?**

   A. No processes use it as a tool.

   B. Only one process creates or generates this list of stakeholders.

   C. It contains the communication requirements for each stakeholder.

   D. The stakeholder register is most closely associated with the process of Identify Stakeholders.

139. Accepted deliverables are an input to the process of closing the project or phase carried out in Integration Management. What process produces those accepted deliverables?

   A. Perform Integrated Change Control.

   B. Monitor Project Execution.

   C. Validate Scope.

   D. Monitor and Control Project Work.

140. Which of the following statements about the work authorization system is not correct?

   A. The work authorization system ensures that work gets performed at the right time in the right order.

   B. The work authorization system is part of the project management information system.

   C. The work authorization system is considered a formal, documented set of procedures.

   D. The work authorization system does not go to the level of detail needed to ascertain approval levels to authorize work.

141. A project team member may have a strong preference to being led by a project manager who practices either Theory X or Theory Y leadership and motivation styles. Who is attributed with development of the Theory X and Theory Y motivational descriptions?

   A. McDonald.

   B. Maslow.

   C. McGregor.

   D. McClelland.

Chapter Notes:

_____

_____

_____

_____

_____

_____

_____

_____

_____

_____

_____

_____

_____

_____

The Final Exam

Chapter Fifteen

Chapter Notes:

_____

_____

_____

_____

_____

_____

_____

_____

_____

_____

_____

_____

_____

_____

142. **Project managers should work to motivate and develop the team to achieve success on the project. To that end, which of the following choices is not in the best interest of the project manager when developing the team?**

A. Create a competitive environment wherein team members strive to outperform each other leading to increased productivity for the team.

B. Create a cohesive team unit by instilling and nurturing trust.

C. Capitalize on any cultural differences and work to decrease unhealthy conflict in the team.

D. Develop improved skills and knowledge in the team members.

143. **Jonas is performing a number of administrative tasks as the contract work is nearly complete for this project. Assume only one contract and one vendor was used on this project. In what order would Jonas and the team perform these processes?**

A. Conduct Procurements, Create WBS, Validate Scope, Control Procurements, Close Project or Phase.

B. Develop Schedule, Create WBS, Validate Scope, Control Procurements, Close Project or Phase.

C. Create WBS, Develop Schedule, Validate Scope, Close Project or Phase, Close Procurements.

D. Create WBS, Develop Schedule, Validate Scope, Control Procurements, Close Project or Phase.

144. **Regarding the overall purpose of the process of Control Procurements, which statement is the most accurate of these four?**

   A. Buyer must ensure that Seller abides by the terms of the contract and that deliverables are of acceptable quality.

   B. Seller must ensure that Buyer does not add to the contractual scope of the work that has been documented and signed by both parties.

   C. Buyer and Seller must ensure that all actions are taken in the best interest of their respective companies, their owners, and their shareholders by law.

   D. Buyer and Seller must ensure that both parties meet their contractual obligations and that their own legal rights are protected.

145. **Throughout the life of a project, there can be a great deal of pressure on the PM to meet the expectations of stakeholders and communicate with them appropriately. Read the following 4 descriptions and choose the one that best describes what this process entails:**

   A. Clarifying and resolving issues that have been identified and documented.

   B. Resolving issues that have been identified and addressing concerns that have not become documented issues yet.

   C. Actively managing the expectations of stakeholders while passively reporting status to the PMO when required.

   D. Actively listening to the needs of stakeholders.

Chapter Notes:

_____

_____

_____

_____

_____

_____

_____

_____

_____

_____

_____

_____

_____

_____

The Final Exam

Chapter Fifteen

Chapter Notes:

_____

_____

_____

_____

_____

_____

_____

_____

_____

_____

_____

_____

_____

146. What is the best description of the goal or purpose of the first process in the Quality Management knowledge area?

   A. Documenting the quality standards or guidelines the team must adhere to on the project.

   B. Determining how to use the tool of audits to ensure that proper quality steps are being carried out consistently.

   C. Identifying the quality requirements and documenting how the team will demonstrate compliance.

   D. Demonstrating an acceptable quality metric to the key stakeholder and receiving buy-in for continuous process improvement.

147. Which of the following statements is least accurate in describing the process of stakeholder identification that a project manager should carry out in a project?

   A. This process should identify stakeholders who may be impacted negatively by the project result or work.

   B. This process should identify both internal and external stakeholders, including vendors or sellers performing work for the project team.

   C. Identifying stakeholders is vital to project planning because it helps determine who should be involved in defining the project scope baseline.

   D. Identifying stakeholders is an initiating process that should be conducted and closed out very early in the project.

148. A project is scheduled to last 20 months with a budget of $1,800,000. At the end of month 5, the project is 25% complete. What is the schedule performance index?

   A. 0.85

   B. 1.25

   C. 0.75

   D. 1

149. Theresa took over for another PM after about half of the project was completed. She is looking for guidance for how she might reward team members for excellent performance. What document is the best source for finding that specific information?

A. Staffing management plan.

B. Resource management plan.

C. Human resource plan.

D. Reward guidelines.

150. When the senior manager walks by the desk of Kiosho, he berates him for reading a book at work. Kiosho explains that his reading is work-related - the book gives tips and ideas for managing people, building teamwork, and drawing out the best performance of others. Kiosho goes on to reference one of the processes of project management and says the book will help him improve in this area. Which process do you think Kiosho would reference, and what is the purpose of that process?

A. Manage Team because that process is all about the key tool of teamwork and finding ways to draw the team into a group that trusts, respects, and desires to work with each other for project success.

B. Manage Team because that process focuses on removing conflict from the team as it is counterproductive to reaching project goals.

C. Develop Team because that process involves teamwork exercises and follows the 5 stages of team development first introduced by McGregor.

D. Develop Team because that process is focused on improving the competencies of the team and creating an environment of trust and support that leads to improved project performance.

Chapter Notes:

_____
_____
_____
_____
_____
_____
_____
_____
_____
_____
_____
_____
_____
_____
_____

The Final Exam

Chapter Fifteen

Chapter Notes:

_____

_____

_____

_____

_____

_____

_____

_____

_____

_____

_____

_____

_____

151. Which of the following processes is not in the Planning process group?

   A. Create WBS.

   B. Determine Budget.

   C. Develop Project Charter.

   D. Collect Requirements.

152. You are in a meeting with the sponsor to review project status, but someone spilled coffee on the one copy of your report, and your laptop is back in the office. You can barely make out some of the numbers. The report shows that schedule variance for the project is $15,000. Planned value = $105,000, and actual cost = $114,000. Do you have enough data to calculate the cost variance, and if you do, what is it?

   A. No, you do not have enough data.

   B. Yes, CV is $6,000.

   C. Yes, CV is ($24,000).

   D. Yes, CV is ($9,000).

153. Teresa has instructed Alysse to stay on top of the contract firm they've hired to help facilitate the current conversion project. Alysse does not know all of the history, but it is apparent that Teresa has had a bad experience with this contract firm on prior projects. Teresa has insisted that Alysse spend the remainder of the month focused on contract administration. Consider the following four choices. Which of the these activities should Alysse not carry out this week?

   A. Schedule an inspection with the contractor to verify compliance with the contract.

   B. Conduct a proactive review of the contract, find the weakest area, create an amendment to address the weakness, and submit it to the legal department for approval.

   C. Determine if the contract allows Alysse to bring along a member of the procurement department on an audit of the contractor.

   D. Read through the contract change control system, get familiar with the provisions, and know what actions your company can take in the case of a future dispute.

154. In the Plan Communications Management process, the concept of communication channels is introduced along with a formula to compute those channels. With what tool of the process is this formula associated?

    A. Communication Model Analysis.

    B. Communication Requirements Analysis.

    C. Communication Technology Analysis.

    D. Communication Methods Analysis.

155. Your company has limited resources and must choose between two projects for the next period. Project Green has a present value of $11,000,000. Project Orange has a present value of $7,500,000. What is the opportunity cost of choosing Project Green?

    A. $7.5 Million.

    B. $3.5 Million.

    C. $11 Million.

    D. $1 Million.

156. The project team is busy performing quality assurance for the current phase of the project. Why is the team most interested in the quality control measurements?

    A. These measurements are compared against the plan to see if the deliverables are of acceptable quality.

    B. These measurements are the results of quality activities so they indicate if the plan is being followed.

    C. These measurements are compared with the quality metrics and the Customer is asked to sign off on those that pass inspection.

    D. These measurements help the team find quality issues, initiate change requests, and implement correction action.

Chapter Notes:

The Final Exam

Chapter Fifteen

Chapter Notes:

_____

_____

_____

_____

_____

_____

_____

_____

_____

_____

_____

_____

_____

_____

157. Which of the following statements is not true regarding the collection of project requirements?

   A. The requirements documentation produced from this process becomes an input to other processes.

   B. The project team or a subset of the team makes use of the project charter, the stakeholder register, and the scope statement to carry out this process to document requirements.

   C. The project manager should be able to tie each work package back to a requirement that was defined in this process.

   D. This process is all about understanding, documenting, and managing customer expectations.

158. Jamal is the project manager for a nine month project, and the team has completed half the deliverables in the first three months. At the end of month three, Jamal gets called into an emergency meeting with his boss and the project sponsor. The sponsor breaks the news that the prior quarter financials for her organization were not good; as a result, the sponsor is forced to shut down funding for four projects, including the project that Jamal is leading. Jamal is very upset - the project is going well and the team is performing excellent work. As he leaves the meeting, Jamal considers what action he should take first. As the Project Manager, what should Jamal do?

   A. Request a formal, written document from the sponsor that indicates project termination.

   B. Take the steps of Close Project or Phase.

   C. Request a meeting with the sponsor and her management to report on the progress made to date on the project.

   D. Take the steps to close out the contract.

159. The system that supports all aspects of the project management processes from initiating through closing is:

A. Information technology.

B. The information distribution system.

C. The project management information system.

D. The work authorization system.

160. Monitoring and controlling risks is a valuable discipline for several reasons. Consider the following four choices, and pick the one that is not a valid purpose of this process:

A. To analyze the economic impact of all risks so that an absolute ranking can be carried out.

B. To modify schedule contingency reserves to align with the current risk assessment.

C. To ensure that risk management policies and procedures are being followed.

D. To determine if an assessed risk can be retired.

161. The most important factor in project integration is:

A. A clearly defined scope.

B. Timely corrective action.

C. Team buy-in on the project plan.

D. Effective communication.

162. The project generates a product, service, or result during which process group?

A. Close Project or Phase.

B. Direct and Manage Project Work.

C. Executing.

D. Create WBS.

Chapter Notes:

_____

_____

_____

_____

_____

_____

_____

_____

_____

_____

_____

_____

_____

163. In a strong matrix organization:

A. More power is given to the functional manager.

B. More power is given to the project manager.

C. More power is given to the project expeditor.

D. More power is given to the project coordinator.

164. The resource management plan may contain:

A. The escalation flowchart.

B. How to develop the Resource Management Plan.

C. The project organizational chart.

D. The work authorization system.

165. You are the project manager for a project, and the Customer just asked for a cost estimate for a group of tasks the team will perform. What type of estimate would you prefer that the Customer request from you?

A. Control.

B. Definitive.

C. ROM.

D. Parenthetical.

166. What is an output of an executing process in resource management, what process does it come from, and where is it used as an input?

A. Resource Calendars, Acquire Resources, Develop Schedule.

B. Project Staff Assignments, Acquire Resources, Control Schedule.

C. Project Staff Assignments, Acquire Resources, Estimate Activity Durations.

D. Project Staffing Plan, Plan Resource Management, Develop Project Management Plan.

167. The project team, including those members who work remotely, are all meeting together for the week in order to test, document, and finalize delivery of the first major project deliverable. What is this practice called that a project manager may use from time to time to help develop the project team?

A. Collaboration.

B. Colocation.

C. Team-building.

D. Quality circles.

168. The team is getting slightly behind on the project schedule, so Francine has moved team members Joseph and Sally from their prior assignments to new tasks. Rick is thrilled because he had been working nights and weekends in an effort to complete the task - now, he has help! What process is being described, and what tool has Francine used?

A. Develop Schedule and the tool of Resource Leveling.

B. Estimate Activity Durations and the tool of Crashing.

C. Develop Schedule and the schedule compression tool of Crashing.

D. Control Schedule and the tool of Resource Optimization.

169. A Responsibility Assignment Matrix (RAM) does NOT indicate:

A. Who does what on the project.

B. Job roles for team members.

C. Job roles and responsibilities for groups.

D. Project reporting relationships.

Chapter Fifteen

Chapter Notes:

_____

_____

_____

_____

_____

_____

_____

_____

_____

_____

_____

_____

_____

_____

170. **Which of the following is the best description of the project plan?**

    A. A formal, approved document that consolidates all subsidiary management plans and baselines from planning processes.

    B. The formal, approved document that integrates planning processes and tells how the project measurement baseline will be defined.

    C. The formal, approved document that contains the work breakdown structure, schedule management plan, budget, contracts, cost management plan, and quality management plan.

    D. The document that outlines all of the work to be performed on a project and how change requests will be managed.

171. **There are 49 Processes, and most of them result in more than one output. One of the outputs of the Direct and Manage Project Work process is:**

    A. The deliverables.

    B. The work authorization system.

    C. Approved change requests.

    D. The key performance information.

172. **David is managing a wind farm construction project in a remote region during the winter season. Today, David receives the latest results from the team. One report shows that weather for the last month was much colder than anticipated, with record-breaking frigid temperatures recorded. A second report indicates that the SPI has ticked up from 1.2 to 1.35 during the same period. How should David interpret this information?**

    A. David is puzzled because the work efficiency of the team improved in spite of the terrible working conditions.

    B. David is puzzled because the work efficiency of the team declined in spite of the risk mitigation plans the team put in place.

    C. David is not surprised because he can point to the decline in work efficiency and blame it on the terrible working conditions.

    D. David is not surprised because he can explain to his Sponsor that the cold temperatures caused the spike in SPI.

173. In order to have a successful project, the project manager must keep the team and key stakeholders focused on a common understanding of the scope. The scope baseline should capture this definition of the project scope. Efforts to manage to this scope involve some monitoring and controlling. Search the following 4 choices. Find the choice that best names and succinctly describes a relevant process.

A. Monitor and Control Scope - process of documenting product acceptance.

B. Validate Scope - the process of formalizing acceptance of completed deliverables.

C. Control Scope - the process of documenting accepted deliverables.

D. Manage Scope - the process of validating project deliverables and documenting change requests.

174. Quality audits are considered an important tool in the quality management knowledge area. Which of the 4 statements best describes the impact a quality audit is most likely to have on the cost of quality?

A. Quality audits should result in an increased cost of quality as the performing organization makes an investment in either internal or external resources to conduct the audits.

B. Quality audits have nothing to do with the cost of quality, which is directly tied to product failure.

C. Quality audits should result in a reduced cost of quality and an increase in customer acceptance of the product of the project.

D. Quality audits should result in a reduced cost of quality but have no direct correlation with customer acceptance of the product of the project.

Chapter Fifteen

Chapter Notes:

_____

_____

_____

_____

_____

_____

_____

_____

_____

_____

_____

_____

_____

_____

175. A stakeholder is:

A. A person or group that invests in a project expecting a return.

B. A person or group that will either benefit or suffer a loss in return for a project investment.

C. A person or group that can steer or influence the direction of the project.

D. A person or group that has an interest in or impact from a project.

176. The project manager, Keisha, is leading the weekly team meeting. Keisha is reviewing the schedule for the following week and mentions that the team will begin focused efforts on risk identification and the development of a risk register. Keisha uses the word "anonymous" as she describes one of the techniques that will be used to gather information about possible risks. Which technique or tool is Keisha referring to?

A. Nominal Group Technique.

B. Delphi Technique.

C. Fibonacci Voting Technique.

D. Australian Secret Ballot.

177. The Monitor Communications process is a fairly straight-forward yet important process related to this area of Communications Management. In this process, who is responsible for ensuring that the data that is collected, analyzed, and distributed is accurate and timely?

A. All members of the team.

B. Members of the team who have been assigned the role of Facilitator.

C. The project manager.

D. The manager of the performing organization.

178. **Regarding the management of changes on a project, which of the following best represents the responsibility of the project manager?**

   A. PM should influence, define, and establish the change control board, driving the standards by which change control meetings will be carried out.

   B. PM should communicate status of change requests to all stakeholders on a regular basis.

   C. PM must assure that only approved change requests are incorporated into the revised baseline.

   D. PM must act quickly and decisively regarding change requests to set a proactive tone for the team and the customer.

179. **The PM has many responsibilities described for the knowledge area of Integration. Of the following four choices, what would you consider the most important function of the project manager during project integration?**

   A. Taking action to make sure the team is unified and on the same page.

   B. Allocating resources, materials, and people to optimize project performance.

   C. Communicating with key stakeholders to maintain support of the Sponsor and buy-in from the influential people.

   D. Problem-solving and decision-making for internal and external resources to keep the project moving forward.

Chapter Notes:

_____

_____

_____

_____

_____

_____

_____

_____

_____

_____

_____

_____

The Final Exam

Chapter Notes:

_____

_____

_____

_____

_____

_____

_____

_____

_____

_____

_____

_____

_____

_____

180. This input to the first process of procurement management involves a description of a specification or capability. Additionally, this input may bring with it contractual or legal implications in areas such as health, safety, performance, preserving the environment, licenses, permits, intellectual property rights, security, and insurance. What is the name of the process? And, what is the name of the input?

A. Plan Contracting and Risk-Related Contract Decisions.

B. Conduct Procurements and Risk-Related Contract Decisions.

C. Plan Contracting and Vendor Contract Awards.

D. Plan Procurement Management and Requirements Documentation.

181. Robert has a crisis on his hands. It is relatively early in the project schedule; Robert has 3 team members in his office all talking at once. Gene, Maria, and Anshul are very upset about their assignments on the project. They contend that they are responsible for more work than they can manage. Robert has very little patience - he's managing 32 full-time staff, including another 8 contractors on this project. The others are not complaining, so why should these 3 be upset? Maria speaks up for the group and suggests Robert make use of one tool to control the schedule more effectively. What tool do you believe Maria suggests to Robert?

A. Schedule Compression.

B. Resource Leveling.

C. Crashing.

D. Performance Reviews.

182. Close Project or Phase should be performed:

A. At the end of the project.

B. Before formal acceptance of the project's product.

C. As a safeguard against risk.

D. By someone other than the project manager.

183. You have a problem with Ted. The project you are leading has high visibility as this is the first phase of a multi-year engagement with a new customer. The contract was negotiated such that the customer can elect to extend the agreement into the next phase upon completion of the prior phase. You selected Ted to be the spokesperson for the project team at the status meetings at the customer site. These take place every other week. Four of these meetings have taken place, and Ted is not performing up to expectations. He does not read his audience well, spending too long on topics of low interest and not long enough on those items of keen interest to the customer. Ted seems ill-prepared and has expressed that this role seems trivial to him. You have met with Ted three times to coach, prepare, and assist him. Things have not improved. The information must be distributed effectively in these meetings - what should you do?

A. Move Ted out of this role of project spokesperson and find someone better suited for the role.

B. Dismiss Ted from the team and recommend to his functional manager that Ted be fired.

C. Place a formal, written letter in the personnel file of Ted regarding this issue.

D. Find someone outside your organization who can provide professional training to Ted in this area.

Chapter Fifteen

Chapter Notes:

_____

_____

_____

_____

_____

_____

_____

_____

_____

_____

_____

_____

_____

184. You work for a pharmaceutical company that has grown fast and is aggressive in bringing new products to market. The current project you are leading is not that exciting - it involves an upgrade to the customer management system used by the company. When the project kicked off, many of the top resources had rolled off other tasks. You were able to recruit many of the best resources to your team. The project has 9 months remaining on the revised schedule. Today, the marketing department broadcasted a press release indicating that your company won a huge contract with great bonus potential based on performance. Given the size and importance of the new project, what action should you take as soon as possible?

A. Either crash or fast track your project to free up key resources as soon as possible.

B. Schedule a meeting with your manager to determine what effect the new project will have on your project.

C. Schedule a team meeting and ask all members to brainstorm time-saving measures to complete early or release key resources earlier than planned.

D. Update your project risk register with this new item and assign resources to investigate the potential negative impacts on your project.

185. You could make the argument that the process of Develop Project Management Plan is the most important process belonging to the Planning process group. Of the following choices, which choice would not be considered a Planning process?

A. Develop project management plan.

B. Identify risks.

C. Identify stakeholders.

D. Perform quantitative risk analysis.

186. Which of the following statements accurately describes the relationship of Control Scope to the other processes of Validate Scope and Create WBS?

   A. All 3 processes have only 1 or 2 tools.

   B. Only 2 of the processes have the Project Management Plan as a specific input.

   C. Control Scope must follow Validate Scope but can happen before Create WBS.

   D. Control Scope and Validate Scope are Monitoring and Controlling processes while Create WBS is an Executing process.

187. Which of the following best describes when a project has been successfully completed?

   A. All quality metrics have been validated and accepted.

   B. Contracts are closed.

   C. The team has delivered product, service, or results to a customer and avoided legal actions, including arbitration.

   D. The team delivers all work packages on time and on budget.

Chapter Notes:

_____

_____

_____

_____

_____

_____

_____

_____

_____

_____

_____

_____

_____

_____

_____

188. Julie is tired of hearing about what could go wrong and delay delivery of a major milestone on the project she is managing. She asked her team for the most likely delivery date - when the deliverable would be done; a prolonged argument broke out. Finally, Julie asked for everyone's attention. She told the team to use Monte Carlo Analysis and report back to her the next day. Of these 4 statements, which one is the best description of this technique and the likely result?

A. The team will create multiple versions of the project schedule based on weighted worst case, best case, and most likely durations.

B. The team will simulate several outcomes based on a range of possible durations for the tasks in the schedule.

C. The team will be able to identify the critical path and delivery date by applying PIM Scores associated with use of this technique.

D. The team will compute the delivery date because this technique involves regression analysis and statistical optimization that will drive out the answer.

189. The key function of the project manager's job in project integration is:

A. Minimizing conflict to promote team unity.

B. Making key decisions about resource allocation.

C. Communicating with people of various backgrounds.

D. Problem-solving and decision-making between project subsystems.

190. As a project manager is developing, managing, and leading the team, that PM should be aware of Tuckman's model. According to this model, how many stages are there, and what factors would most likely affect the duration of each stage?

A. 4 stages and the duration can be influenced by the team size, leadership, and team dynamics - how they interact.

B. 5 stages and how long those stages last may depend upon the team dynamics, size, and the leadership present.

C. 5 stages and the duration of each stage is affected by the presence of these roles - devil's advocate, negotiator, and information seeker.

D. 4 stages and the duration of each stage depends on team diversity, technical complexity, and cultural norms.

191. Read the following descriptions and choose the one that best describes the purpose for the process called **Plan Risk Management**.

A. Defines how to identify, rank, and react to risk events in an organization.

B. Defines how to identify, qualify, and quantify risk threats in your project.

C. Defines the risk register for a given project.

D. Defines how to conduct risk management activities for a project.

Chapter Notes:

The Final Exam

Chapter Fifteen

Chapter Notes:

_____

_____

_____

_____

_____

_____

_____

_____

_____

_____

_____

_____

_____

_____

_____

192. You are building a case for the use of virtual teams as you develop the staffing plan for your next project. Which of the following 4 justifications is not valid?

    A. The use of virtual teams will allow you to use team members who work from home offices and those may be vital resources with unique skills that help your project team.

    B. You may be able to include team members with unique skills who live in other, remote regions or work during different shift or hours.

    C. Lower travel costs and decreased commuting times will benefit the project.

    D. The quality of work will be better as virtual team members make use of osmotic communications and return higher quality results.

193. The project charter provides useful information regarding a new project. Which of the following statements is false regarding the project charter?

    A. The project charter justifies why the project is being undertaken - the document explains the business case.

    B. The project charter assigns a person to the role of project manager.

    C. The project charter shares the summary-level budget.

    D. The project charter summarizes the process to be carried out to perform risk identification.

194. Two project managers are having a discussion about hiring resources. One favors hiring people who can do each other's job, a term she refers to as "generalizing specialists." What is reasonable to infer from her preference?

    A. She does not have an overly technical project.

    B. She is managing a project using an adaptive methodology.

    C. She will likely have difficulty in project integration.

    D. She does not realize the term "generalizing specialist" is a contradiction in the context of project management.

195. Samantha is the sponsor for the project and has set up a meeting next Friday with Sherry, the project manager. Samantha communicated to Sherry that the purpose of the meeting was to analyze project results to date and determine if the project team is fulfilling the quality requirements that Samantha has established. The actions carried out in the meeting would fall into what process?

   A. Control Quality.

   B. Manage Communications.

   C. Plan Quality Management.

   D. Manage Quality.

196. You are managing a project for a new client, Lazor Corp. Enrique is the chief point of contact for your engagement with Lazor. You don't know Enrique that well due to only limited time together so far on the project. You are in a meeting with your team, Enrique, and a few of his technical staff at the Lazor offices. You are going through an explanation of the critical path with the client to get resource commitment. A portion of the schedule is displayed on the wall so everyone can view it together. Your team member is displaying an AON view or diagram. Enrique looks at you and asks you to explain what the arrows represent. What do you say?

   A. The activity or task - an arrow represents the step that must be carried out by the team.

   B. Precedence - an arrow points to a node that must precede the other node.

   C. Dependency - the arrow indicates the task flow from the predecessor to the successor.

   D. Dependency - an arrow points from a successor activity to a predecessor activity from left to right.

Chapter Notes:

_____

_____

_____

_____

_____

_____

_____

_____

_____

_____

_____

_____

197. **During a weekly status meeting, Leah brings up some interesting news. Leah realized that an important testing stage was somehow left out of the project plan. In light of the entire project, the testing stage will not take too long or require excessive resources. Some team members suggest that the testing is not even critical for the go-live delivery. What should the PM do?**

   A. Set up the testing stage as a new mini-project, assign resources, and manage it separately.

   B. This testing stage did not make the project plan, so it should be omitted until the next iteration or sprint is performed.

   C. Meet with senior management, explain the situation, and ask for their input.

   D. Return to planning processes for this testing stage.

198. **When changes are approved and made to the project, those changes should be:**

   A. Added to the project baselines.

   B. Compared against the project baselines.

   C. Added to the project plan.

   D. Compared against the project plan.

199. Carol and Jasper were in charge of the last round of quality audits. As they kicked off their status meeting with the team, Carol took a moment to remind the team of the objectives of a quality audit. Of these four statements, pick the one that Carol should not state to the team:

    A. Identify all best practices that are being implemented.

    B. Share good practices that were implemented in similar projects in the organization or in the industry.

    C. Help the team become more productive by offering to assist in improving the implementation of these processes.

    D. Identify the gaps and shortcomings as long as they do not make the organization liable to legal action later.

200. ZXY Consulting is performing a project for the Customer, ABC Industries. The offices of ABC Industries are a one-hour drive from the offices of ZXY. Early in the project, ZXY consultants discovered that the Customer does not like email and has a strong preference for in-person status meetings. This project will run for more than a year, and many status meetings will take place. What advice is the best advice for the consultants at ZXY?

    A. Reduce the number of status meetings to save time and money.

    B. Build a case for alternative methods for distributing the information and present the ideas to the Customer.

    C. Challenge the Customer to accept email updates for these status meetings pointing out that it will save the Customer a lot of money over the life of the project.

    D. Discuss the preferred schedule of status meetings with the Customer and include that data in your schedule and budget estimates for the project.

Chapter Notes:

_____

_____

_____

_____

_____

_____

_____

_____

_____

_____

_____

_____

The Final Exam

Chapter Fifteen

FINAL EXAM ANSWERS

Chapter Notes:

_____

_____

_____

_____

_____

_____

_____

_____

_____

_____

_____

_____

_____

1. A is the incorrect statement which makes Answer-A the best choice. Control Quality is generally performed prior to Validate Scope, not the other way around. The output of Control Quality - Verified Deliverables - serves as an input to Validate Scope, which then outputs Accepted Deliverables. Answer-B is true - they may be carried out in parallel. Answers-C and -D are true - both have inputs of deliverables and use inspection as a tool.

2. D. All four answers are good advice for Lupita; however, the best answer is Answer-D - to confirm that all project work has been completed and objectives met. That captures the goal of this process. Other items on her to-do list may include the final capture of lessons learned (note that lessons learned are collected throughout the project life), updating records, completing appraisals, and the like. All are important. But, Answer-D is the best choice.

3. D is the correct choice for this question. These answers are long and require a careful reading for accuracy. The problem with Answer-D is that a false conclusion is reached based on a correct phrase. The beginning phrase is accurate; however, the communications plan should be monitored, reviewed, and revised as needed throughout the life of the project. For example, the team may build a set of reports for key stakeholders weekly. After some time, key stakeholders may relax that requirement and back it off to monthly reporting. So, change the plan to reflect this revision.

4. A. The question fakes in the direction of Maslow's Hierarchy of Needs or Herzberg's Hygiene Factors. However, the statement in the question that Alex firmly believes he must be a hands-on, micromanager of his team carries the most weight. That clue should lead you to choose McGregor's Theory X and Y. Clearly, Alex represents Theory X. Answer-A is the best choice.

5. D. As part of Perform Integrated Change Control, the project manager will need to know when change has occurred, manage the changes, and influence the factors that cause change, but the project manager should not take on the attitude of denying change whenever possible. Some change is inevitable, and all change requests should be evaluated and not automatically rejected.

6. B is the correct answer. The obvious decoy in this set of answers is the process of Manage Stakeholder Engagement. As a project document, the Issue Log is an input to Manage Project Team, and that process belongs to the Executing Process Group.

7. C. Risk Categorization is a tool used during the process of Perform Qualitative Risk Analysis. The team may make use of a Risk Breakdown Structure (RBS) to look for potential sources of risk or the WBS to look for other areas of the project that may be affected by a risk. The purpose of the Risk Categorization tool is to help the team categorize each risk - to deepen the understanding of the risk, its impact, and its likelihood.

8. B is the best choice - these Resource Calendars indicate those resources and their availability that will be considered when developing the project schedule. Resource Calendars represents both internal and external (subcontractor) resources. These Resource Calendars are an output of the Conduct Procurements process as project documents updates.

9. A. The activity list is a decomposition of the WBS. It takes the work packages and breaks them down into activities that can be sequenced, estimated, and assigned.

10. D is the best choice - the stakeholder register is the output of Identify Stakeholders. Hopefully, the team included analysis on Kelly when this initiating process took place. If so, the team will be able to read the notes and recall the strategies suggested for managing this stakeholder.

Chapter Notes:

The Final Exam

Chapter Fifteen

Chapter Notes:

_____

_____

_____

_____

_____

_____

_____

_____

_____

_____

_____

_____

_____

_____

11. A - negotiation - is the best choice. Sandy is proactively negotiating with the program manager to get those resources that she has worked with in the past and now wants on her project team. Answer-B is not a bad choice either - this sounds like pre-assignment given the timing. But, Answer-B is not the correct choice: The question asks which tool most closely fits the description of the ACTIONS that Sandy took. Sandy's action in the scenario was Negotiation - based on her presenting a strong case. The Pre-assignment action of the program manager remains to be decided upon as a result of Sandy's negotiated position.

12. B is the best choice - Plan Procurement Management. This question has a lot of distracting information, but the key phrase or piece of information has to do with timing. The group is determining when to conduct a bidder conference. Plan Procurement Management is the process that involves determining an approach to procurements, selecting tools to use, and scheduling when to carry out these activities.

13. A. This is a straightforward question that requires you to know the definition of corrective action. Answer -B is more descriptive of rework. Answer -D is incorrect since corrective actions generally come in the form of change requests from monitoring and controlling processes.

14. C is the best choice, but let's take each answer into consideration. Answer A is not the best choice because it steps too far. There is nothing to suggest that attendance at the conference was mandatory. Answer B is not a terrible choice, but it is not reasonable to essentially hold another bidder conference after the first one. That is a waste! Answer D is a reasonable response, but this approach prevents Ben or the other firms from benefiting from Ben's questions. Ben's firm may ask a question and receive a response that helps all vendors understand the scope of work better. Go with Answer C - that is the most reasonable answer given.

15. Answer-B is the best choice. The Develop Project Charter process is used to validate or refine decisions made during the prior phase or iteration of this process. So, even the process that produces the Charter may be revisited, especially if the project has more than 1 phase. Answer-D comes in second place, but Answer-B is the best choice.

16. A. We are looking for the statement that is not true. Answer-A is a false statement about this topic of conflict resolution in teams. It should focus on the present and not the past. Answers-B, -C, and -D are true.

17. C. This is a nasty question that forces you to compare 4 answers and look for subtle differences. Answer-C is the best description or explanation of the Create WBS process. Answer-A is too vague and makes reference to requirements - not accurate. Answer-B mentions activities - those come after this process, so that is incorrect. Answer-D is not accurate - it mentions subdividing work packages further. In this process, the team decomposes larger deliverables progressively until work packages (the lowest level of decomposition) are achieved. Then, the team moves on to another process. Therefore, Answer-D is not accurate. Answer-C is the best choice.

18. B. The standards, policies, and procedures of the company are considered an organizational process asset. That makes Answer-B the correct choice. Answers-A, -C, and -D are all factors that may influence how she goes about acquiring staff - the cost of resources, the competency of resources, and the location of the project and the resources.

19. A. Read the end of the question carefully, and you will note that you are asked for a Process Group. That limits your choices to 5 valid responses. Now, consider the actions of the new team - they are carrying out Stakeholder Analysis, specifically to reach consensus on Bob and his level of influence. Stakeholder Analysis is a tool of the Identify Stakeholders process. That process is 1 of 2 in the Initiating Process Group. Answer-A is the best choice.

20. B is not a technique of this process (You may have selected it if you are familiar with some Agile methods). Answer-A is a technique of this process. Answer-C is a JAD session which is a type of facilitated workshop - listed as a technique. Answer-D is referring to modeling or prototyping - a very effective technique used in this process.

21. D. Tia and Anton are working in the process of Monitor Risks, and they are using the tool called Reserve Analysis (one of the techniques under Data Analysis). Answer D is correct.

Chapter Notes:

_____

_____

_____

_____

_____

_____

_____

_____

_____

_____

_____

_____

_____

_____

_____

_____

The Final Exam

Chapter Notes:

_____

_____

_____

_____

_____

_____

_____

_____

_____

_____

_____

_____

22. C is the correct answer. This question on ADR is obscure, but we want you to be exposed to it now - before the actual exam! ADR stands for Alternative Dispute Resolution - how the Buyer and Seller will manage any contract disputes or disagreements that may arise. Many contracts include ADR mechanisms or steps for clarity and planning. Conduct Procurements is the process that would use ADR as part of claims administration.

23. B. The procurement management plan, which is created in the Plan Procurement Management process, includes performance reporting specifications.

24. C is the best choice. Direct and Manage Project Work is the only process in this list where changes are implemented, corrective actions are carried out, and defects are repaired. Change requests are detected in other processes, documented, vetted, approved or rejected in other processes - but only implemented in this executing process.

25. B. In a functional organization, most of the power rests with the functional manager. Answer-B is the best answer because in this setting, it is likely the PM will run into more issues trying to obtain sufficient resources. Answer-A is not correct - the functional manager holds the most power. Answer-C is not correct - the PM wishes that the functional manager would share power! Answer-D is not correct - again, it describes more of a utopia than reality for the PM.

26. C. All 4 choices are extremely close here, but it is the approved project charter that formally initiates the project. The bottom line is that document must be signed by someone with proper authority to make the project official.

27. D. This long-winded question describes the process of Identify Stakeholders and the tools of expert judgment and stakeholder analysis that pertain. That process is one of two Initiating processes. Therefore, Answer-D is the best answer. Again, the question does not ask for the name of the process; it asks for the process group.

28. A is the best answer. The ultimate goal of this Define Scope process is to describe in detail the project AND the product this project will produce. You may think of it as describing the WHAT and HOW - what the project will produce, and how it will produce it. Answers-B and -C are not as complete as Answer-A. Answer-D starts out promising but gets out of whack when it skips ahead to the schedule baseline - not an accurate analogy.

29. D. This question draws on your knowledge of the quality management processes and your understanding of the tools. First, scan the answers for bogus terms and eliminate those. In this case, none of the answers involve made-up terms. Next, read the answers carefully. The sponsor is not concerned with theoretical conversations. Answers-A and -B fall into that category - whitepapers and categories of costs are not relevant to Samantha's specific project. That leaves Answers-C and -D. Answer-C compares a control chart from the current project with a prior project. Nothing in the question indicates that comparison would be meaningful to the sponsor of the current project. That leaves us with Answer-D - an updated checklist indicating when steps were carried out. Simple but effective. Answer-D is the best choice.

30. C. The key to this question is to recognize the process being described and to identify the related outputs. First, the question describes the process of Conduct Procurements. Answer C is the only correct combination of outputs - the Agreement (Contract) and a Selected Seller. All other choices include an output from the Plan Procurement Management or Control Procurements process.

31. D. Project Resource Management has 6 processes, and 3 of them are executing. The first of the executing processes is Acquire Resources followed by Develop Team and then Manage Team.

32. A. With an SPI this far below 1, you have a significant schedule delay, and you should report this to management. Answer-B is incorrect because you are doing quite well on cost, and there is no overrun. Answer-C is incorrect since it is your job to deal with scope change – not management's. Answer-D is incorrect because you cannot simply reject changes on the project. They must be evaluated thoroughly and fairly and sent through the change control system.

Chapter Notes:

_____

_____

_____

_____

_____

_____

_____

_____

_____

_____

_____

_____

_____

The Final Exam

Chapter Fifteen

Chapter Notes:

_____

_____

_____

_____

_____

_____

_____

_____

_____

_____

_____

_____

33. A. This one was extremely straightforward. The quality management plan is used to guide the Manage Quality process

34. C is the best choice. Answer-C actually defines the conflict resolution technique of smoothing or accommodating.

35. B. Prioritizing requests for change is one of many jobs of the project manager. Answer-A is not a good answer because of the wording that says turn the requests over to the board. That passive implication is not what you are looking for in the role of the PM. Answer-C is not a good choice. The requested changes may cause rework or a change to how plans are being executed now. Best to evaluate the changes now, so Answer-C is not a good move to make. Likewise, Answer-D is not a good choice. Your manager has placed you in the role to make decisions and set priorities like this one. Answer-D may sound reasonable, but assessing and prioritizing the 3 requests is the responsibility of the PM, not the manager of the PM. Answer-B is the best choice of these 4.

36. B. The correct sequence of processes would be: Identify Stakeholders, Create WBS, Monitor Risks, Close Project or Phase. All other choices misplace at least one component.

37. A is the best choice. Cost Aggregation is the tool. (Not Cost Aggravation!) The tool sums up costs starting at the activity level, up to work package, up to control account, up to total project. Each other answer has a problem in the sequence or the name of the tool.

38. C. The format of this question is unsettling. Two questions are asked. If you encounter a question like this on the actual exam, look for the second question to further clarify the first. In our example, the first instruction is more general; the second question asks specifically for the worst method. Now, you have an answer to seek from the choices. Answer-A is incorrect because punishment is not a conflict resolution method, but rather a form or power - though undesirable! Answers-B and -D are desirable methods, with Answer-D being a better option for conflict resolution. Answer-C is not a favored method and therefore the best answer to this question.

39. B. Tough question - answer B is the best choice. Trish has described the purpose of the monitoring and controlling process of the Communications knowledge area called Monitor Communications. Answer C is very tempting, but it does not list the name of a process; it lists an output.

40. B is the best choice. This question is very difficult. You must decide between CPI and SPI first. Then, you must select the best answer of the two that align with your choice! The CPI is considered the most critical EVM metric. That makes Answer-B the best choice.

41. A. The question is asking for the best definition out of 4 possible choices for critical chain. Ignore the drama with Fran and Mark and look for the best definition. The critical chain is a resource-constrained critical path. Answer-A is the best choice. Answer-B is wrong - critical chain starts with critical path and then introduces the factor of limited resources. That analysis often leads to a new critical path. They are not the same. Answers-C & -D include elements of truth mixed with false terms or ideas. Critical chain does include 2 types of buffers - the project buffer is placed at the end of the critical chain to protect delivery date; and, the feeding buffers mitigate the risk of feeding paths that may burn through their float and could cause a delay to the critical chain. So, feeding buffers are introduced at those points along the critical chain where feeding paths that are not critical intersect with the critical chain.

42. B is the best answer. The key word in the question is transfer. Hirdesh and Anton are discussing the transition steps - how Hirdesh's group will transfer the work product or deliverable to Anton's group for completion. This question describes a multi-phase project. The two are discussing how to Close the Phase from Hirdesh's group to Anton's. If Develop Project Management Plan had been a choice, it would have been a better answer since the PM Plan is an input to the process Close Project or Phase.

43. D is the best choice. Be prepared for lengthy answers that may require some time to read and review.

Chapter Notes:

The Final Exam

Chapter Notes:

_____

_____

_____

_____

_____

_____

_____

_____

_____

_____

_____

_____

_____

44. D. Work performance data (WPD) is a very common input to monitoring and controlling processes, often compared to the project plan to determine variances. (The result of such variance analysis is Work performance information or reports.) WPD is an output of Direct and Manage Project Work. "Lessons learned" are also collected during the life of the project to provide data/information for continuous improvement in the current project. Change requests approved as a result of lessons learned would also be implemented in an Executing process.

45. B. The term "baseline" causes grief for many test-takers. Memorize that the baseline (whether it is the scope baseline, schedule baseline, cost baseline, or performance measurement baseline) includes the original plan plus all approved changes. Once the budget change was approved, it should be added to the cost baseline.

46. D. At first glance, many people think that the wording of answer 'D' is impossible, but it is the correct choice. This problem should be solved in the usual 3 steps with one additional step at the end. First, draw out the network diagram based on the table. Your representation should resemble the one below:

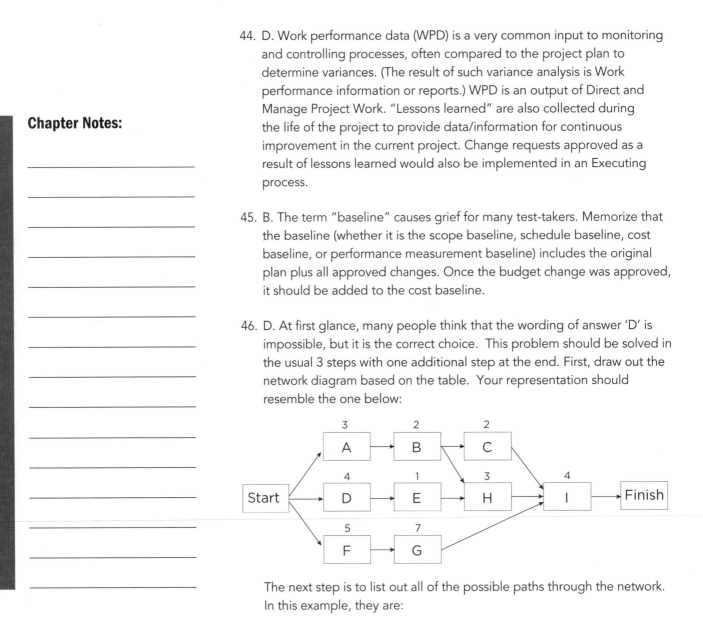

The next step is to list out all of the possible paths through the network. In this example, they are:

Start-A-B-C-I-Finish

Start-A-B-H-I-Finish

Start-D-E-H-I-Finish

Start-F-G-I-Finish

The third step is to add up the values associated with each path. Using the paths above, they are:

Start-A-B-C-I-Finish = 11

Start-A-B-H-I-Finish = 12

Start-D-E-H-I-Finish = 12

Start-F-G-I-Finish = 16

The final additional step is to increase the value of H from 3 to 7 and evaluate the impact. That would change the list to:

Start-A-B-C-I-Finish = 11

Start-A-B-H-I-Finish = 16

Start-D-E-H-I-Finish = 16

Start-F-G-I-Finish = 16

The answer, therefore, is that the critical path would change (there are now 3 critical paths), but the end date remains the same.

Moving from 1 critical path to 3 increases the schedule risk considerably, invalidating choice 'C'.

47. B is correct - $3,125,000. Planned value is the value of the work you planned to do at a given point in time. The first step is always to calculate the budgeted at completion. BAC is 50 stores X $250,000 per store = $12,500,000. Now calculate the planned value for 2 months of the 8-month project. Simply multiple the Budgeted At Completion by 2 and divide by 8. This yields $3,125,000. The interpretation of this is that you planned to earn $3,125,000 worth of value back into your project after 2 months of work.

Chapter Notes:

_____

_____

_____

_____

_____

_____

_____

_____

_____

_____

_____

_____

_____

48. D. Tough choices here, as all 4 represent valid outputs of this process. And, each argument is valid. However, if pressed to choose the one best answer, Answer-D is the choice. Resource calendars are vital to building a reliable schedule, as you need to know when resources are available, when they are on vacation or in training or working with another project team, and the like. Yes, all 4 answers are valid. However, the best choice is Answer-D - because of the importance to the project schedule - a key component of project success.

49. D. At least the PM is consistent - all six times, he has invited everyone to the change control party! Too many people, and not enough control. The actions of this project manager demonstrate a lack of understanding for performing integrated change control. It is a bad idea to invite the entire team (even when small) to a meeting to vet a change request. Perhaps a subset of the team is needed to weigh in or help evaluate impacts, but not everyone. And, certainly not the Customer along with mentors, friends, and family! Bad ideas - maybe Answer-A IS an appropriate course of action!

50. D. In the projectized environment, the role of project manager will most likely be a full-time position. As the power of the project manager goes up, so does the likelihood that the PM role will be full-time.

51. D. The key to answering this question correctly is understanding the project charter. It contains a summary milestone schedule and the assignment of the project manager. The stakeholder engagement plan will be developed in planning and not as part of initiating activities.

52. B. The fundamental question here is about inputs. You are asked to review the list and pick the one that doesn't fit. Answer-B is the best choice because the list of activities does not precede Define Scope - it FOLLOWS this process. Actually, it comes after Create WBS, too. Define Activities follows Define Scope; therefore, Answer-B is the best choice here. Answer-A refers to Requirements Documentation; Answer-C refers to the Risk Register; Answer-D is a real example of an Organizational Process Asset.

53. B. An important input to developing the schedule is the output of the Sequence Activities process. Project network diagrams convey task-to-task flow based on dependencies and logical relationships of tasks. Answer-A is incorrect because the schedule is used as an input to the Determine Budget process. Answer-C is incorrect because, even though reserve analysis is a tool used in estimating activity durations, the output of contingency plans is a result of active risk acceptance which does not impact schedule development. Answer-D is not the best answer in that quality planning is not as directly associated with schedule development as is sequencing the project activities.

54. A is the correct answer for this question. In the Plan Quality Management process, the team identifies quality standards and requirements for the product or project and documents how the project will demonstrate compliance. All 4 answers are valid Process names; however, only Plan Quality Management is correct.

55. D is correct. The similarities of these 2 tools can be striking which presents a challenge in keeping the purpose and uniqueness of the tools clear in your mind. Go into the exam with a visual of the tool and knowing how one differs from another. Some of these answers can be distracting - they sound good. However, Answer-D is the best choice. A Pareto Chart or diagram is a histogram that has been ordered or prioritized by frequency of occurrence.

56. A. The question asks what the first action should be. When an anticipated risk event occurs, follow the plan to address the risk. That should be the first action. However, some risks cannot be anticipated. If this risk of contractor bankruptcy was not identified, analyze the risk and put the best actions in place as soon as possible.

57. D is correct and the best choice. The Stakeholder Engagement Plan is created by Plan Stakeholder Engagement which is so straight-forward that you may shy away from the obvious choice! However, the fact remains that the Stakeholder Engagement Plan is the vital component here and best answer. Another important part of the overall plan is the communications management plan. However, that component of the plan is the second-best choice for this question about the process of Manage Stakeholder Engagement.

Chapter Notes:

_____
_____
_____
_____
_____
_____
_____
_____
_____
_____
_____
_____
_____
_____
_____

The Final Exam

Chapter Notes:

_____

_____

_____

_____

_____

_____

_____

_____

_____

_____

_____

_____

_____

58. C is the correct answer. Granted, several of these start to sound similar to each other; however, Answer-C is technically correct.

59. D is correct. First, consider that the question is describing actions taken in the Collect Requirements process. Two of the inputs to the Collect Requirements process are the project charter and the stakeholder register. Therefore, the two processes that create these must have taken place. They are outputs of Define Project Charter and Identify Stakeholders, so the correct answer is Answer-D. This would be considered an easy question on the exam; it is based on knowing the ITTOs in the process framework.

60. C is best. First of all, the scenario describes an opportunity or positive risk, not a threat. So, disregard Transfer and Mitigate because those are strategies for negative risks. That leaves Exploit or Share. Share is the strategy that involves teaming agreements, partnerships, and joint ventures to pursue opportunities or positive risks that may otherwise be out of reach.

61. B. Flowcharting is the best tool here - choose Answer-B. Barbara needs to uncover the bottlenecks - find the snags in the processes that are causing quality issues with the output. Flowcharting is a great tool for that purpose - it helps uncover failing processes. Barbara may find that one department is at fault, or the problems may be in the transition or handoff from one department to another. Or, quality issues may be due to something as simple as communication. Flowcharting the processes will help determine next steps. It is a technique of the Data Representation tool.

62. D. The project charter is developed very early in the life of the project - during project initiation (often with the aid of the PM). Timewise the charter precedes the in-depth analysis of stakeholders that would result in the stakeholder engagement strategy. Such a strategy might even be kept private by the PM - certainly not documented in the charter. The first 3 answers could be contained in the project charter - describing the business need - naming the sponsor (signature page) - and providing high-level schedules and budgets. Therefore Answer-D is the best choice.

63. C. Given the information presented in the question, the best advice to Vijay is to charge the training back to the project budget for GlobalCorp. GlobalCorp should pay for the development of a team member. Answer-C is the best choice. The question indicates that Vijay authorized the training and mentions no approval or communication with the client on this point. Answer-A is not a good choice, because Vijay did not ask the client before authorizing the training. Answer-B is not good advice - Vijay could get into trouble if he assumes his own PMO will pay for the training without asking first. Answer-D is not a good choice.

64. C. Brenda is in a tough spot - we can all sympathize. However, Answer-C is the best choice. When a project ends or is cancelled for some reason, the project manager should perform the Close Project or Phase process. Difficult to carry out with all the distractions, but that is the best choice for the exam! Answer-A is not a good idea - the decision has been made; Brenda should not fight the decision; don't waste company resources; shut down the project. Answer-B is a very natural and reasonable response; again, the first course of action needs to be to execute the close project process. Answer-D is no good - again, the decision has been made; follow the orders and shut it down.

65. B. One of the main reasons conflict arises on a project is due to communication, and one of the results of a project's communication lines being broken is that conflict increases.

66. D. First know that BCR stands for Benefit Cost Ratio. Project Solo has a BCR of 2.3 meaning that for every dollar of cost invested in the project, $2.30 of benefit or revenue will be realized. Answer-A is not good because we don't know what the other project choices are. One may have a BCR that is greater than 2.3. Answer-B is not a correct choice - that term is made up but sounds fancy. Answer-C is incorrect for the same reason as Answer-A - we don't know how this project stacks up against others. Note that the PM role includes helping with measuring the project's benefit in anticipation of the charter - and then helping to realize that benefit via the project execution.

Chapter Notes:

The Final Exam

Chapter Notes:

_____

_____

_____

_____

_____

_____

_____

_____

_____

_____

_____

_____

_____

67. A. Valid means of push communications include email, letters, press releases, voice messages, and faxes, to name a few. Answer-A - the knowledge repository - is an example of a pull communication method. Stakeholders would have to take action to go pull data from that source. Others are pushed out to them. Therefore, Answer-A is the best answer.

68. A. This is a difficult question because it presents 3 reasonable answers. Dismiss Answer C because risks are not the same as change requests. Answer A is the best answer because this is where you should start - add the risks to the register and document them. Answer B is a reasonable answer, but not the best choice as the PM should know how to proceed regarding risks on the project. Answer D is a very tempting choice as it plays off the favored tool of expert judgment. However, Answer D should be preceded by Answer A - document the risks first. An output of Monitor Risks is called Project Documents Updates and these Risk Register updates are the key component.

69. A is correct. If you got this one correct, give yourself a high-five. Changes and issues flow into and out of the process of Manage Stakeholder Engagement through the project documents and the project documents updates.

70. D. One of the challenges is to determine what the question is asking. In this case, the question describes activities carried out by George on behalf of his company in the Conduct Procurements process. The question is asking you to identify the outputs of this process. Find the one that is not an output. Answers A, B, and C are all valid outputs of Conduct Procurements. Resource Calendars may have tripped you up. Even those resources from contractors or Sellers should be included in your plans, so this is a valid output. Answer D is the best choice - Independent Estimates is a Tool, not an Output of this process.

71. A. Cutting the scope is a strategy for avoiding risk. Avoid or Answer-A is the correct choice. The definition given for the strategy of Avoid includes changing the project management plan in order to eliminate a threat entirely. This change of scope (impacting the scope baseline) qualifies.

72. A is correct. David McClelland proposed this motivational theory describing people's varying degrees of need for Affiliation, Achievement, and Power.

73. A is the correct answer - that's the right Process Group. The project manager is officially named and assigned in the project charter - which is one of the outputs of Develop Project Charter - an initiating process.

74. C. Assumption and Constraint Analysis - is the correct answer. As a part of the Identify Risks process, members of the team must check assumptions made during planning to validate them and, possibly, uncover more risks.

75. D is the best choice and offers the most logical explanation tied to the accompanying stage. Because of the potentially destructive nature of this stage, the PM would like for the team to move through the Storming stage with positive momentum. The PM will be more engaged and directive during this stage to help team members understand roles and boundaries and to preserve relationships and build trust. This can be a destructive stage and not very productive, from a PM's standpoint. Naturally, the desire is to move on.

76. A. First course of action is Answer A - review and amend the plan for the new risks this situation presents. Remember that you should look for a proactive approach to almost everything. Answer B is not advisable because you cannot simply decide to withhold payment if you are in a contractual relationship. Answer C may be something you would do; however, it is not the first thing you should do. Same is true for Answer D. That may be a next step, but first step is to plan for the risk.

77. D. Schedule constraints would not contain leads and lags for activities. 'A', 'B', and 'C' would all make sense to include as schedule constraints.

78. A. The key to answering this question correctly is to have a good understanding of what the Delphi technique is. Delphi is a means of soliciting the opinions of experts while hiding the identities of group members from each other. This prevents the group from forming a single opinion, being influenced by others, or from letting one person dominate the group. Therefore, Answer-A is the best choice here. The question is tricky because the other 3 answers are plausible and reasonable. They just don't relate back to the Delphi Technique.

79. D. Close Project or Phase from Integration was the process. The output of Final Product, Service, or Result Transition is the one you should have selected.

The Final Exam

Chapter Fifteen

Chapter Notes:

_____

_____

_____

_____

_____

_____

_____

_____

_____

_____

_____

_____

_____

_____

80. B is the correct answer. You may have chosen Answer-D - the issue list. The question and answer are vague here, and no information is given to distinguish the issue list as a private or public list… for all stakeholders or just for the team. Do not make an assumption. Look for a better answer. In this case, we have a better answer in Answer-B. Portions of the stakeholder register contain sensitive information, such as the assessment and categorization of stakeholders. Do you think one of your stakeholders will be happy to read that you have categorized him as having low influence? Also, the strategy for managing these stakeholders is included in the register, so those elements preclude you from posting that full document in a public place. Portions can be shared, but other portions of the stakeholder register should not be shared with all parties!

81. B is the bad description; therefore, Answer-B is the correct answer. The problem with Answer-B is the use of task-oriented (incorrect) instead of deliverable-oriented (correct). Answers-A, -C, and -D are all correct statements regarding the WBS.

82. C is correct. The common thread is continuous process improvement in the area of quality management.

83. D. In this case, the conflict is of a technical nature, so the best way the project manager could solve the problem is by using his or her technical expertise. 'A' is incorrect because legitimate power might stop the fight, but it wouldn't solve the problem. 'B' is incorrect because it also might stop the fight, but would not solve the problem. 'C' would probably be the least effective approach to solving this particular problem, since referent power is relying on personality or someone else's authority.

84. D. On the actual exam, you will encounter questions that have more than 1 correct answer. You have to pick the best from those correct choices. In this case, the definition of stakeholder is broad. Technically, Brandon may have many, diverse stakeholders to manage. Given these choices, the longer and more complete the list, the better the choice. Answer-C is a long list, but it includes the local PMI chapter president; we have no reason to believe he or she is involved in this project. Go with Answer-D.

85. A. The second of the three processes in Procurement Management is called Conduct Procurements. That process belongs to the Process Group of Executing. Answer A is correct.

86. D. One of the inputs to Control Scope is the Project Management Plan. 6 components of the plan are referenced here. They are as follows: the scope baseline, scope management plan, change management plan, configuration management plan, the requirements management plan, and the performance measurement baseline. Answer-D contains the most complete list and is the best answer. 2 of these components - the scope management plan and the requirements management plan - are created by the Plan Scope Management process.

87. B is the best selection of these 4. ROM stands for Rough Order of Magnitude estimate and is generally in the range of plus or minus 50%. That level of fluctuation is not acceptable for executing or controlling phases. That leaves us with planning or initiating as choices. Initiating is the more appropriate choice for a ROM estimate. Answer-B is the best choice. Caution: Even though these phases were named like the process groups - they are not the same thing!

88. B is correct. Members of the team are focusing on assigning estimates of duration to activities - how long tasks will take. That describes the process called Estimate Activity Durations. Ron has polled subject matter experts to determine their best estimate. He is reporting M = 12 days. It is reasonable to assume Ron is referring to M as the most-likely estimate as a part of a three-point or Triangular Distribution estimate. Answer-B is the best choice.

89. D. A Pareto chart or diagram is a form of histogram. A histogram is a bar chart. With a Pareto chart, that histogram is ordered or ranked from greatest to least. So, the data is the same - it is simply reordered to promote analysis. Histograms and Pareto diagrams are both examples of the Data Representation tool. Answer-D is the correct choice.

90. A is the best choice. A Pareto Diagram or chart is a histogram that shows ranked ordering of the causes of quality issues. This chart helps the team see where to focus attention - on those items that are contributing to the highest number of quality problems.

91. C. The term slack is synonymous with float.

Chapter Fifteen

92. C is correct. The tool of decomposition is described in the question, and that tool is used in 2 processes: Create WBS and Define Activities. Each answer has a slight inconsistency in it with Answer-C being the only exception. Answer-C does not spell out the name of the process, but the question does not ask for specific process names. The answer does describe what takes place in those processes that use the tool.

93. A. Regardless of the past, Daphne needs to be proactive and influence the root causes of change. Daphne should engage the Customer and discuss the reasons for the high number of change requests and the impact on the team and results. Answer -A is the best choice. Answers -B, -C, and -D take an incorrect approach to change requests. Future change requests should be allowed, naturally, and evaluated for merit. But, the bigger issue is reaching a common understanding with the Customer as to the approach to defining scope and managing changes to it.

94. C is the best answer of the four. The project charter is a formal document that authorizes the project. Jake is the sponsor. Jake has the authority to approve and fund the project. Answer-C is best here. Answer-A sounds nice but has no signature. Answers-B and -D skirt around the issue. Jake is the point of focus. He is the sponsor. When he signs the charter, Davicel has an official project.

95. A. TCPI is below 1 - that is good news, indicating that the team is performing better than expected when it comes to costs or spending efficiency. A TCPI below 1 indicates a CPI above 1 - all good. That eliminates Answers-B and -D. With remaining Answers-A and -C, we have to pick the preferred timing of the communication. The question indicates the level of uncertainty and risk during this phase and further indicates the active participation of the sponsor in initial planning. Therefore, Bob should communicate the latest news now - as soon as possible - to the sponsor. We have every reason to believe that she or he would be interested in this good development. Answer-A is the best choice.

96. B. The work authorization system (WAS) is a subset of the PMIS and is used during project integration management to ensure that work gets done at the right time and in the right sequence by the right people or resources. Answer-B is the best choice. This question is an example of how close these answers can be to each other. All 4 choices sound good, but Answer-B is the most accurate. This type of question is best prepared for by studying the Glossary of Terms in the back of this book. That will help you cement your understanding of key terms.

97. D. Plan Risk Responses would be the point at which you determine an appropriate response to the risks that have been identified, qualified, and quantified. Only after the risks are fully understood and analyzed would you make a change to the scope.

98. C is the correct choice and the statement that is true. A CPI of 1 means right on plan. Below 1 is underperforming, and greater than 1 is ahead of plan. TCPI is closely linked to the CPI. Mathematically, if the CPI exceeds 1, TCPI will be less than 1. If CPI is less than 1, TCPI will be greater than 1. Therefore, Answer-C is the best choice.

99. C is the correct answer. This tool does not belong in the process described. Risk probability and impact assessment is carried out in the prior process of qualitative analysis - not here in quantitative analysis. So, the team would respond to this member that this tool has already been used. The other 3 choices are valid data analysis tools of this process of quantitative analysis.

100. A. Assigning a team member to integration responsibilities sounds good; however, this description in Answer-A may imply a hands-off approach taken by the project manager that is very dangerous. Integration management is a vital discipline that should be performed by the project manager or at the direction of the PM, at the least. The PM needs to be aware of the information, work performance information, change requests, and project status that naturally flow into integration. Therefore, Answer-A is the best choice here. Answers-B, -C, and -D all describe true statements regarding integration.

Chapter Notes:

The Final Exam

Chapter Notes:

The Final Exam

_____

_____

_____

_____

_____

_____

_____

_____

_____

_____

_____

_____

_____

_____

101. D. This type of question makes the head throb. All 4 answers sound good and make a rational argument. However, we have to choose the best answer of the 4. That choice is Answer-D. Estimate Activity Resources is closely coordinated with Estimate Costs. Both processes focus on the quantity and type of labor, materials, and equipment to be used on the project activities. Therefore, Answer-D is the best choice.

102. B is the best choice of these 4. Answer-A is too limited - inspection is only 1 tool; many may have been used. Answer-C is broader but not on the point. Answer-C does not state that the quality process has been completed, just that some testing and analysis have taken place. If Answer-D used the word Accepted instead of Verified, then it would be accurate. Verified Deliverables are an input to Validate Scope. Accepted Deliverables are an output or result. Answer-B indicates that the Control Quality process has been completed generating Verified Deliverables that are now an input to this Validate Scope process. True statement

103. A is the most accurate statement and the best answer. This question is very difficult, as it requires an understanding of the differences in these two outputs of Determine Budget. When graphed, the project funding requirements will likely appear more as incremental steps up as opposed to a smooth S-curve. These steps represent the funding that typically takes place in a given month, quarter, or other period. Regarding Answer-D, note the use of the word Program instead of Project - that was tricky.

104. C is the best answer here. Answer-A is not as valid because the project managers make decisions on schedule change requests, not Sr. Mgmt. Answer-B is not best because the PM does not sign or authorize the project charter, though the PM may assist in the creation of the charter. Answer-D is not best because the Program Mgr does not make project task assignments - that is the role of the Project Manager. For the PMP Exam, be clear on the various roles and responsibilities.

105. D. When the project manager gets involved in monitoring and controlling project work, sometimes these types of issues will arise. The best course of action to deal with this conflict is to confront it head on, as soon as possible. The PM does not need to run to the functional manager - talk to Francis directly first! The PM does not need to involve the Sponsor - this is a job for the PM to handle. Don't attack Francis or deal with this issue in a crowd, like in a team meeting. This conversation should take place in a private setting so that the PM and Francis can have open, clear communication. Then, the PM can discuss the impacts of Francis's behavior on the team and the project.

106. A. You need to update the communications management plan. That item is not listed as a choice, so the best choice is the overall project management plan which contains this communications management plan as a component. Answer-A is the best choice.

107. C is the correct answer. Triangular Distribution is another name for the three-point estimate. Now, to decode the letters: P stands for Pessimistic, O for Optimistic, and M for Most-Likely in this formula. Therefore, it is accurate to say that M should be greater than O but less than P. Pessimistic will be the highest estimate; Optimistic will be the lowest estimate; Most-Likely will be somewhere between the other two.

108. D is the correct answer. Answer-D contains 1 item that does not belong - Delphi charts. Here is the important lesson to take from this question: look at the wide range of information stored in the WBS dictionary. And, notice that the WBS dictionary is obviously being updated after the Create WBS process has been performed once. Create WBS is iterative - an important point. Future planning efforts may lead to updates to the WBS dictionary.

109. B is the best answer here. Answers A, C, and D are all true, but answer B is too broad. Every element does not have to be unique (only the product, service, or result).

Chapter Fifteen

Chapter Notes:

_____

_____

_____

_____

_____

_____

_____

_____

_____

_____

_____

_____

_____

_____

110. C. This question is made difficult due to the similarity of answer choices. Answer C is the only answer that contains an invalid component - Make-or-buy decisions. Make-or-buy decisions are not relevant to contract language, though make-or-buy decisions is an output of Plan Procurement Management. This question scenario describes activities in the process of Conduct Procurements. Of these 4 choices, choose Answer C.

111. A. You may be advising Isabel to go meet with the sponsor and ask! That is great advice, but it is not a proposed answer. Given our choices, Answer-A is the best answer. Isabel wants to understand sponsor expectations. Those should be documented in both the stakeholder register and the communications management plan. Other answers are close, but Answer-A is the best choice given.

112. B. The 4 examples listed align with Voting, a tool of decision making, which makes B the correct choice. Unanimity - everyone agrees (unanimous decision). Majority - more than 50% support decision. Plurality - decision supported the most, even if it does not reach majority. Dictatorship - one person makes the decision for the group.

113. A. The process of Direct and Manage Project Work is where defects are repaired, documents are rewritten, reports are reproduced, corrective and preventive actions are carried out. Therefore, Answer-A is the best answer here. Yes, these problems are detected in other processes. Once flagged, the team determines the severity of the error or defect and those that can be salvaged are reworked in this execution process.

114. D. You cannot calculate the three-point estimate without knowing values for optimistic, pessimistic, and realistic. In this case, you are only provided with 2 of the 3 numbers, therefore the answer is unknown.

115. C is the best choice as it represents a valid combination of the correct process name and an appropriate tool or technique. EMV analysis (expected monetary value analysis) is often used along with decision tree analysis to apply probabilities of events to the cost or reward associated to that event. If you missed this question, it is likely that Answer-B tripped you up. The tool sounds correct, but the process is not correct.

116. A is the best choice of the four. The detailed analysis from a tornado diagram is not appropriate for this stage in risk management. The question describes the steps taken indicating that the current process is Perform Qualitative Risk Analysis. This process should not result in a tornado diagram. That is not appropriate until after further analysis has been performed in quantitative risk analysis using the tool of sensitivity analysis.

117. C. This question is a challenge because it tests both your knowledge of Inputs - Tools - Outputs and your practical application of project management. Answer-C is the best choice of the 4. First let us address the basic level of qualification. Answers-A, -B, and -C are valid tools to the Define Scope process. Answer-D (decomposition) is not; discard Answer-D as a choice. Answer-A lists expert judgment. It MAY be difficult to find the right expert, but that is not the best choice for this scenario. Answer-B lists the valid technique of facilitated workshops as part of the tool of interpersonal and team skills. It is true that the PM may struggle to get the right people in the sessions. Answer-C lists product analysis - that is a valid tool, but it will not align well with this project of gap analysis with reports as a deliverable. Therefore, Answer-C is the best choice as the least effective technique to use.

118. C is the best choice of the 4 answers. The question presents a scenario that sounds as if Ralph is in the process of Control Scope. The 4 answers describe items or inputs that may prove helpful to Ralph. Answer-C correctly identifies the requirements traceability matrix as an input and gives it the proper context. Answer-A is describing WPI but uses KPI - that's a common reference, but KPI is not mentioned in the PMBOK Guide. Answer-B incorrectly references the configuration management plan, a component of the overall project plan. Answer-D goes into the staffing required by the change request - making assumptions that we cannot validate given this question.

Chapter Notes:

The Final Exam

Chapter Fifteen

119. A. PMI has a strong opinion on this point. Success is delivering the defined, agreed-to scope. Nothing more; nothing less. Go with Answer-A - that's your best choice. Answer-B seems reasonable, but it goes back to the official scope. If it's not in scope, don't do it regardless of your schedule or budget. Answer-C wisely points to the need to assess risks that this new feature may present; however, that's a decoy. Don't gold-plate. Answer-D is not a good choice either. Stick to the scope.

120. C is the correct answer. Ignore any conflict or tension for resources and look at Camille's request. Show me the list of activities. Camille does not stipulate only those tasks on the critical path, or only those that have resource issues. Charles and Jose should provide the full list. That meets her request. Answer-C describes the complete list - all steps required to create work packages.

121. B. The work results (output) of the project may be products, services, or results. Answer-A is incomplete because work results could be a product, a service, or a result. Answer-C is incorrect because the work results don't have to meet quality specifications or pass acceptance criteria. Answer-D is bogus - the change control board reference is nice - but Answer-B is the best answer here.

122. C. This is sticky. Answer-C is the best choice - for the exam. Let's consider each alternative. Answer-A is a smokescreen - the PM should lead - there is no need to escalate to a manager. Answer-B is not a bad choice, but we don't have enough information to lead us there. Compressing the schedule by crashing adds expense and may not be effective, so this is not the first choice. Answer-D is a weak response - the head of a company does not wish to be troubled with this. Step up and lead. Go with Answer-C - treat Elisha like any other - look for an alternative - if none is found or reasonable, act in the best interest of the project's success.

123. B. Inspection is correct - Answer-B. The question describes the Validate Scope process. Inspection is 1 of only 2 tools of that process.

124. A is the false statement. Answers-B, -C, and -D are accurate. The first half of Answer-A is correct; however, the statement about the next process determining the quantities of resources is not true. That takes place in Estimate Activity Resources - both types and quantities are determined.

125. A is the correct answer. The communication styles assessment would take place in the prior process of Plan Communications Management. Now we are executing that plan, using the results of that assessment and other analysis.

126. B. The charter is developed after the business case and before the project plan. The business case is actually an input into the Develop Project Charter process as a Business Document. The project charter is an input into the Develop Project Management Plan process. Answers C and D are incorrect because the contract (or agreement) for performing the project is an input to the Develop Project Charter process and therefore precedes the charter.

127. C. This question describes the goal or purpose of the process named Manage Stakeholder Engagement. Answer-C is correct. Answer-A is made up. Answers-B and -D are not accurate answers.

128. B is correct - good interpretation of data for Chafik to pass along to key stakeholders. SPI below 1 indicates less than expected progress per the schedule. CPI greater than 1 indicates better than expected spending efficiency.

129. B. This question has tricky wording. Some of the questions on the exam may not ask directly for an input, tool, or output. They may ask indirectly, as this question does - what is the result of a process? An important output for Manage Communications is Project Communications.

130. D. The work performance information is all about how the work is being performed. Work in progress refers to the schedule, typically, and comes up in the topic of earned value. Answer-D is the best answer.

Chapter Notes:

_____

_____

_____

_____

_____

_____

_____

_____

_____

_____

_____

_____

_____

The Final Exam

Chapter Notes:

_____

_____

_____

_____

_____

_____

_____

_____

_____

_____

_____

_____

131. B. The first step with this question is to identify the process and focus on what the question that is being asked. The question describes the Manage Stakeholder Engagement process and asks for two inputs. The only accurate combination is in Answer-B - Issue log and Stakeholder Engagement Plan.

132. A. Accommodating or Smoothing is a technique of conflict resolution that looks to emphasize areas of agreement rather than areas of difference. In this example, the PM is essentially using the technique to keep the sponsor from focusing on the quality problem. That's bad leadership! Answer-A is correct. Accommodating or Smoothing is what is described here.

133. B. This question asks you to place the inputs, tools, and outputs in reverse order for a given process. Answer B does that correctly. Answer A is incorrect because it lists work performance measurements as an output of this process - it is not. Answer C's list does not match the question. Answer D lists 2 tools and no outputs.

134. A. Answers-B, -C, and -D are tools or techniques listed for the process of Determine Budget. Answer-A is the correct answer because earned value management is NOT a tool to develop the budget; EVM would come into play when you are controlling costs.

135. C is the correct answer. This question is a bit misleading by referencing Validate Scope and comparing it with a process in the Quality Management area. The tendency is to compare Validate Scope with Control Quality… not Manage Quality.

136. A. This problem should be solved in the usual 3 steps with one small bit of reasoning applied at the end. First, draw out the network diagram based on the table. Your representation should resemble the one below:

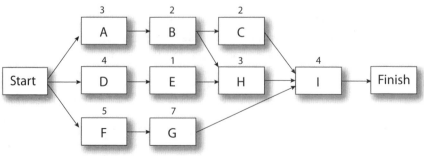

The next step is to list out all of the possible paths through the network. In this example, they are:

Start-A-B-C-I-Finish

Start-A-B-H-I-Finish

Start-D-E-H-I-Finish

Start-F-G-I-Finish

The last step is to add up the values associated with each path. Using the paths above, they are:

Start-A-B-C-I-Finish = 11 units

Start-A-B-H-I-Finish = 12 units

Start-D-E-H-I-Finish = 12 units

Start-F-G-I-Finish = 16 units

The question has asked for the path with the LEAST schedule risk, and that is represented by the shortest path (the one with the highest amount of float). The reason this path has the least risk is that tasks could slip the most here without affecting the critical path. In this case, it is Start-A-B-C-I-Finish, which corresponds to choice 'A'.

137. D is a false statement about the WBS. It implies that each work package will have 1 and only 1 associated schedule activity. That is not accurate. Answer-A is a true statement about the WBS. Answer-B is true - the number of levels will vary in a WBS depending on many factors, such as the industry and complexity of the project. Answer-C is an awkward, long statement but it is true. When the team is creating the WBS, the team keeps breaking down the project deliverables until they reach work packages or don't have enough information to continue at the present time.

Chapter Fifteen

Chapter Notes:

_____

_____

_____

_____

_____

_____

_____

_____

_____

_____

_____

_____

_____

_____

138. C is the correct choice because this is a false statement. Answers-A, -B, and -D are true about the stakeholder register. It is not a tool; it is created by Identify Stakeholders. Answer-C is close but not accurate. There are numerous Planning processes that have this input as a project document.

139. C. If you got this one correct, clap your hands. Answer-C is the correct answer to this tricky question. Answers-A and -D are very appealing answers, as both name a legitimate Process , and both are closely associated with deliverables. However, both Answers-A and -D refer to change requests and do not include Accepted Deliverables as an output. Answer-B is a made up name. Answer-C is correct - Validate Scope produces Accepted Deliverables which feed into the Close Project or Phase process.

140. D. The work authorization system is a formal, documented set of procedures designed to make sure work gets performed in the right sequence and at the right time. So, Answers-A and -C are true. The WAS is considered a component or subset of the overall project management system; therefore, Answer-B is true. Answer-D is false and therefore the correct answer. The WAS includes a tracking system and defines the levels of approval necessary to authorize work - by the PM, the Sponsor, or some other manager.

141. C. The wording of this question is a distraction. The first sentence adds very little helpful information. The question, in a round about way, is asking for the originator of the Theory X and Theory Y motivational theory. That is Douglas McGregor and dates back to the 1960s. Answer-C is correct. Answers-B and -D are decoys - correct names of the originators of other motivational theories, but not applicable to Theory X and Y.

142. A is the correct choice - not a desirable mindset or strategy for the leader of a team. Team members should compete as a team - not against each other as individuals. A zero-sum game (win-lose) is never as motivating as a win-win scenario. Answer-A is the best choice of the four given. The other three choices align with the process of Develop Team.

143. D. By the description given, Jonas appears to be in the Control Procurements process. But, the question asks you to place the processes in order. The correct order is in Answer-D - create the WBS, build the schedule, validate the work performed, close the contract, and close the project. Answer-D lists the correct order and the correct Process names.

144. D. Some of these questions are tricky, as they require a comprehensive understanding of the Processes. Not one of these answers is false. However, you are asked to pick the best answer. Answer-D is your best choice - it is the most complete and correctly addresses the interests of both Buyer and Seller.

145. B is the best choice as it is the most complete and accurate description of the process of Manage Stakeholder Engagement of those given. Answer-A is accurate; however, Answer-B provides a description that is richer - more complete. Answers-C and -D are inaccurate or incomplete statements as it relates to this process.

146. C. The purpose of Plan Quality Management is twofold: to identify the quality standards or requirements that must be met, and to document how the project will demonstrate compliance to these standards. Answer-C is the best description.

147. D. The first 3 answers are true statements. Answer-D is the correct answer to the question - it is very close but becomes a false statement with the inclusion of close out in the phrase. Identify Stakeholders is a continuous process - it takes place early and should be revisited throughout the project. Answer-D is the best choice.

Chapter Notes:

The Final Exam

Chapter Fifteen

Chapter Notes:

_____

_____

_____

_____

_____

_____

_____

_____

_____

_____

_____

_____

_____

_____

148. D. Did you take the time to calculate SPI? To calculate the schedule performance index, divide earned value by planned value (EV / PV). To determine EV, we need to know how much we have completed to date. The budgeted at complete is $1,800,000, and we are 25% complete. Therefore, EV = $1,800,000 x 25% = $450,000. Planned value is what we had planned to complete at this point. We are 5 months into a 20 month project, or 1/4 of the way through. 5/20 = 1/4 = .25 (25%), and our budgeted at completion of $1,800,000 x 25% = $450,000. Now, we can calculate the schedule performance index. It is EV divided by PV, or $450,000 / $450,000 = 1.00. Hey - we are right on schedule! IF you noticed that the 25% complete (actual) matched the 25% plan, THEN you knew the answer was 1. And, you saved time for other questions.

149. B. The resource management plan contains a recognition plan for team members.

150. D is correct. He would be wise to reference the process of Develop Team and the key tools of team-building activities, training, and recognition and rewards. Answer-C is nearly correct but attributes or associates McGregor instead of Tuckman to the 5 stages of a team. (Forming-Storming-Norming-Performing-Adjourning)

151. C. Identify Stakeholders and Develop Project Charter are the only two Initiating processes.

152. B is correct. Schedule Variance is calculated as EV-PV. In this example, we are given the PV and the SV, so we must solve for EV. SV=EV-PV; $15,000=EV-$105,000. So, EV=$120,000. Now, CV=EV-AC. So, CV=$120,000-$114,000. Therefore, CV=$6,000. Do not be surprised if you have to perform this type of calculation on the actual exam, using 2 formulas in order to reach the answer.

153. B is the best choice. Answer-B starts out well - reading through the contract looking for areas of weakness is not bad advice. However, the last half of the answer goes too far. Alysse should not waste her time or that of the procurement or legal department by attempting to create amendments to a contract. Writing contracts or amendments to the contract are activities best left to those who have formal training in that area. Answers-A, -C, and -D describe activities from the Control Procurements process.

154. B. Plan Communications Management uses a number of tools or techniques, and as the question states, one of those tools describes a formula for computing the number of communication channels. That tool is Communication Requirements Analysis. Answer-B is the correct answer.

155. A. The opportunity cost is not the difference in the two; it is what you missed by not choosing the other project. Because you invested in Project Green - you missed out on the present value (benefit) of Project Orange - $7.5 Million. The project manager's role provides assistance with this type of benefit measurement for project selection prior to chartering.

156. B is the best choice of the four. Remember that the focus on Manage Quality is carrying out the quality plans that have been made. So, quality control measurements are the proof or evidence that quality activities are occurring. The team can see the results of inspections, sampling, control charts, and the like and have confidence that quality plans are being carried out. The other answers lean to the understanding of the next process - that of Control Quality, where we focus on the product, not the process.

157. B is the false statement here. It is very close to true - it has 1 false element in it that invalidates the statement. The scope statement is not used to Collect Requirements because it will be developed later. Define Scope uses Requirements Documentation as an input; therefore, Answer-B is false and the best choice. Answer-A is a true statement - the Requirements Documentation and the Requirements Traceability Matrix are vital inputs to other processes. Answers-C and -D are both true statements.

158. B. Jamal has good reason to be disappointed, upset, and stressed. As a project manager, his first course of action is to begin the closure steps of the Close Project or Phase process. Answer-B is the best choice. The other answers may be logical steps - Jamal and his team may very well take these actions as a part of the close project process. Administrative closure includes a lot of documentation, so these steps may soon follow for requesting a formal notice and working with procurement to close out any related contracts. However, the first action needs to be administrative closure - carrying out Close Project or Phase.

Chapter Notes:

_____

_____

_____

_____

_____

_____

_____

_____

_____

_____

_____

_____

_____

_____

Chapter Notes:

_____

_____

_____

_____

_____

_____

_____

_____

_____

_____

_____

_____

_____

_____

_____

159. C. The project management information system (PMIS) is the one described in the question. 'A' is not a good choice because you don't have to have information technology from beginning to end in order to successfully deliver many projects. 'B' is a made up term. 'D' is not a good choice because the work authorization system (WAS) is used to make sure that the work is performed at the right time and in the right sequence.

160. A is the best choice. This description in Answer-A is more appropriate for a planning process, such as performing quantitative risk analysis. Answers-B, -C, and -D are all valid purposes for this process.

161. D. Communication is important at all points in the project, but it is critical during integration. When performing integration management, the project manager's job is primarily to communicate.

162. C. The key words in this question are "process group" - the question asks for a process group rather than the name of a process. This type of question can be tricky on the exam - it goes back to the basic PMI process framework. The work packages are completed and results are created during the executing process group. Other choices may have looked appealing - but the key words of process group make only Answer-C the correct answer. Watch carefully for these easy-to-make mistakes on the exam.

163. B. In a matrix organization, power is shared between the project managers and functional managers. In a strong matrix, the project manager is more powerful, while in a weak matrix, the functional manager has more power. In no circumstances would 'D' be correct, as the project coordinator is, by definition, weaker than a project manager.

164. C. The project organizational chart, showing positions and reporting relationships, is a part of the resource management plan

165. C is correct. In this situation, your preference would be to provide as broad a range as possible in the estimate. That would give your team the most room on either side of the estimate - high or low. Looking at the 4 choices, 3 are valid choices; Answer-D is a made-up term. From Answers-A, -B, and -C, Answer-C represents the broadest range. ROM stands for rough order of magnitude; some refer to it simply as Order of Magnitude. That preliminary estimate provides the least risk - broadest range - lowest stress to you, the project manager.

166. A. This question requires a deep and precise understanding of the processes and connections across knowledge areas. The Resource Management knowledge area has an Executing process named Acquire Resources that produces the Resource Calendars. That output becomes an input to the Develop Schedule process in the Schedule Management knowledge area. Answer-A is the correct answer.

167. B is correct - colocation is the tool described when team members come to the same location for a period of time. Colocation can be very effective when the team needs to focus to solve problems, complete phases, or reach milestones. Face-to-face communications are always the most effective.

168. D is the best choice. Francine is controlling the schedule by moving resources to those tasks that require more resources. Resource Optimization is the technique being described by this scenario. Note that resource optimization moves or reassigns resources to relieve pressure both from those resources and the tasks they are working. This scenario is a better description of resource optimization than the schedule compression technique of crashing. Crashing usually involves adding new resources (staff or contractors) to tasks. In this case, Francine is moving team members from one set of tasks to another. And, Rick is grateful!

169. D. The responsibility assignment matrix (RAM) does not include reporting relationships. Those are included in the project's organizational chart. 'A' is incorrect because the RAM does show who is responsible for what on the project. 'B' is incorrect because it shows roles on the project for the various team members. 'C' is incorrect because the RAM can be for either individuals or for groups (e.g., engineering or information technology).

Chapter Notes:

The Final Exam

Chapter Fifteen

_____

_____

_____

_____

_____

_____

_____

_____

_____

_____

_____

_____

_____

_____

170. A. Granted, this is a tough question. All answers contain some true elements, but there are decoys or extras in 3 of the answers. Answer-A is the best choice. The project plan is a formal document. It is created during planning, and is used to guide the execution processes, monitoring and control, and closure. It is a consolidation of the subsidiary planning processes. Answer-B is incorrect because it refers to a bogus term - the project measurement baseline. Answer-C is nearly correct, but it is an incomplete list and has contracts in it. Contracts are not a part of the project plan. Answer-D is incorrect because it is more like a hybrid of the definition of the work breakdown structure and change control than it is to the project plan.

171. A. The deliverables are the primary output of Direct and Manage Project Work - that's why we do projects. Answer-B is not a good choice here. Answer-C is appealing, but it says approved change requests - these change requests pop up during the process, but they are not approved or rejected until vetted in Perform Integrated Change Control. Answer-D sounds like Work Performance Information - but key performance information is not a term used as part of the processes of project management.

172. A. David is scratching his chin. The two data points don't reconcile. SPI is a measure of work efficiency. The increase in SPI indicates that the team was more efficient in the last period in spite of the extreme working conditions. Hard to reconcile! Answer-A is the correct interpretation.

173. B is the best choice. The question leaves 2 clues - that we are concerned with the Scope Management topic and specific monitoring and controlling processes. There are 2 M & C processes in this knowledge area: Validate Scope and Control Scope. Therefore, we can eliminate Answers-A and -D. Answer-B is the correct, short summary of this process of Validate Scope. Answer-D is not accurate for Control Scope.

174. C is the best of the choices. It correctly states that quality audits (a tool of Manage Quality) help to reduce the cost of quality and increase the likelihood that the Customer or Sponsor will accept the output of the project - the quality will meet the specifications. Answer-C is the only correct or true statement given.

175. D. All of the choices are valid in some cases about stakeholders, but Answer-D is more defining of the total concept of a stakeholder.

176. B is the correct answer. The Delphi Technique combines Expert Judgment with Data Gathering in order to identify risks without introducing bias. The word anonymous should tip off the reader - the Delphi Technique treats responses from experts anonymously and does not share a list of participants with the group. That practice encourages the experts to give a true opinion, one that is not influenced or biased by other participants.

177. C is correct - the project manager is ultimately responsible for the accuracy of the information that is being gathered and reported. The PM is responsible for the timeliness of the reports, as well. Other team members may be assigned tasks to help carry out the reporting of vital data; however, it is ultimately the responsibility of the leader of the team - the project manager.

178. C. Although several of these choices sound desirable, Answer-C is the best. The project manager is ultimately responsible for the work being performed by the team. That work should be approved and authorized and become a part of the baselines. If the team is working a change request that is not reflected in the baselines, that is bad! Bad for the team and the PM! Answer-A is not a good answer; the implication is that every project needs a change control board and the PM should establish it. Wrong - not every project requires a change control board. Answer-B is not a good choice because it is inappropriate and bad practice for all stakeholders to be updated on the status of change requests. Use a rifle (focused), not a shotgun (scattered) with that communication. Answer-D has a good sound to it, but the use of the words "quickly and decisively" should sound alarms in your head. First order of business is to evaluate, assess, or research the impacts of a change request. Not to snap off a decision. Given these choices, Answer-C is best.

Chapter Notes:

The Final Exam

Chapter Fifteen

Chapter Notes:

_____

_____

_____

_____

_____

_____

_____

_____

_____

_____

_____

_____

_____

_____

_____

179. D. This question is sticky - you read it and hope for an answer E that says ALL OF THESE. However, you won't find that option on the actual PMP exam. So, you must evaluate each answer and look for the "best" choice. Answer-D is the best choice. During Integration, the project manager's job involves solving problems and making decisions to keep the team focused on the work to be performed. It is not the team's job to do this - they look to the PM for leadership! The project manager should be resolving the issues and problems that come up and keeping the team focused on the work. Yes, team unity, communication, and resource allocation are all important. But, during integration, the PM needs to evaluate reports and inputs from all areas of the project, make decisions, solve problems, and provide clear leadership. Answer-D is the best choice.

180. D represents the correct combination - the first process of procurement is simply Plan Procurement Management. And, the input being described is called Requirements Documentation. Those specifications or descriptions of the product or feature desired may touch on several areas, such as the ones listed in the question, that may have an impact on the procurement selection and award process.

181. B. Based on the information given, Answer-B is the best. The tool of Resource Optimization includes Resource Leveling, which smooths out the distribution of work to resources. It optimizes the work and can be used to make sure that certain resources are not over-utilized. Yes, some of these other tools could be argued as a valid choice. But none is better than Resource Leveling in this scenario.

182. A. The Close Project or Phase process should be performed at the end of each phase or at the end of the project. Since that was not a choice, however, 'A' is closest to that. Remember that if the choice you want is not present, you should choose the best one from the list.

183. A is the best choice given. Clearly, this project is important to your organization. You cannot afford to leave Ted in this role. Move someone else into the role, and this time, make sure you assign the right person with the right skillset. Answer-A is the best choice because it focuses on your project. That sounds cold and ruthless, but for the exam your goal is project success first - do not sacrifice the project in order to train or develop staff. Answer-B may or may not be the best action. Ted may be very valuable in other areas of the project - the question does not provide that information. Answer-C does not solve the issue. Answer-D sounds nice, but you need to make a move with this key role.

184. B. Gather information before jumping to conclusions. Answer-B is the most prudent course of action. After that meeting, other actions described in other answers may be appropriate. But first evaluate your manager's thoughts and plans to see what project adjustments may or may not be required.

185. C. Do not be fooled by the use or non-use of capital letters. Know the process names and what they represent. Answer-C is the correct answer - the only process that is not a planning process is Identify Stakeholders, an Initiating process. A key role of the PM is maintain 2-way communications with the stakeholders—Identify Stakeholders is an important Initiating process for the success of the project as well as that of the PM.

186. A. This is a challenging question. Of these 4 statements, only Answer-A is true. Create WBS has 2 tools - decomposition and expert judgment; Validate Scope has 2 - inspection and decision-making; Control Scope has 1 - Data Analysis. Answer-B is incorrect - All 3 have the PM plan as a specific input. Answer-C is incorrect - Create WBS needs to occur before you can control the scope. Answer-D is incorrect - the Create WBS process is a planning process, not executing.

Chapter Notes:

Chapter Fifteen

Chapter Notes:

_____

_____

_____

_____

_____

_____

_____

_____

_____

_____

_____

_____

_____

187. D. The key factors of project success come back to the big 3 of scope, schedule, and cost. Work packages are the lowest element (most detailed) of the official scope of the project represented in the WBS; therefore, completing the work packages within the schedule and budget constraints of the project environment is the ultimate measure of success. Clearly, these other choices are desirable, as well. It's great to hit quality metrics, have customer acceptance, close contracts, and avoid lawsuits. Those are all positive things. Answer-D is the best answer of the 4 choices.

188. B. Monte Carlo Analysis is the common form of What-If Analysis. This technique makes use of a large number of variables that may impact activity durations. If a scenario plays out, then you can observe the schedule impact. Another scenario, a different result. And on and on the analysis goes. Answer-B is the best choice. Answer-A has that word weighted in it which is troublesome. Bad answer. Answers-C and -D involve risk concepts and other terms not appropriate to this discussion of a scheduling tool.

189. D. The project manager's job during integration is to solve problems and make decisions. It is not the team's job to do this! Their job should be to execute the work packages. The project manager should be fixing the problems that come up and keeping the team focused on the work.

190. B is correct. Tuckman's model describes 5 stages and indicates that how long each team remains in a stage fluctuates from team to team and project to project. Factors include leadership, team size, and team dynamics.

191. D is the best of these choices. Answer-A is too broad in the reference to the organization instead of a project. Risk management may certainly vary from project to project within an organization. Answer-B is too restrictive in that it lists threats explicitly. Answer-C is inaccurate - the risk register is not an output of this process.

192. D. Be prepared for long answers on the actual exam. In this case, the length of the answers may be greater than the length of the question. Read carefully. With this question, some of the answers actually list more than 1 justification. Read the full answer and make sure all of it is correct. Here, Answer-D is the false statement - the best choice for the question. Answer-D tosses in osmotic communications, a term from Agile practices, that refers to the benefits of communication that take place with teams working in the same workspace. That is just the opposite of the remote or virtual team. Don't be thrown off by the term. Answer-D is the correct answer.

193. D. The project charter is developed very early in the life of the project, often with the assistance of a PM. It's much too early to be specifying approaches for managing risk. Answer-D is the best choice - a "false" statement. Answer-A is true - it is appropriate that the project charter specify why the project is being undertaken and often even includes a business case. Answer-B is true - the project charter is the document in which the project manager is named. Answer-C is also a true statement. The project charter may specify known schedule milestones and a summary level budget.

194. B is correct. The term "generalizing specialist" is a term that comes from adaptive, or agile methodologies. It means that the team is cross trained and can do each other's work. Answer-C is not a good choice, since using generalizing specialists works best during integration activities.

195. D is correct. The meeting is best described as an audit, and audits are a tool of Manage Quality.

196. C. At the heart of the question, you are asked to tell what the arrows represent on an AON or Activity on Node diagram. Answer-A is incorrect - that statement describes an AOA - Activity on Arrow diagram. Answer-B is false - the arrow points to the subsequent activity. Answer-D is false - it has flipped the words predecessor and successor. Answer-C is true.

Chapter Notes:

The Final Exam

Chapter Fifteen

Chapter Notes:

_____

_____

_____

_____

_____

_____

_____

_____

_____

_____

_____

_____

_____

_____

_____

197. D is the best answer here. Remember the concept of progressive elaboration - this applies here. The processes are not set in stone; if you have a project plan, you can update it. Answers-A and -C are unnecessary. Answer-B throws in some Agile or Scrum concepts which do not apply in this context! Answer-D is the best choice.

198. A. You may get this type of ugly, vague question on the actual exam. Out of 4 messy choices, Answer-A is the best choice. It is a true statement - approved changed requests should be added to the appropriate baselines for scope or schedule or cost. Recall that a baseline is defined as the original plan plus all approved changes. Answer-B is not correct because the approved change should be added to the baseline. For analysis purposes, the baseline is most useful when compared against actual results - not against changes. Answer-C is an interesting choice - stating that approved change requests should be added to the project plan. You could argue that updates to the baseline would include these approved changes; therefore, they would be reflected in the project plan - it includes 3 baselines. That is true; however, Answer-A is still a better choice - more direct and a true statement. Answer-D is not correct for the same reasons that Answers-B and -C are not correct. Given this background, Answer-A is the best choice.

199. D is a partial truth, which makes it the best choice. In a quality audit, you should identify ALL gaps and shortcomings. Other statements in Answers-A, -B, and -C are accurate.

200. D. The Customer does not like email and has a preference for face-to-face meetings. Very well, plan accordingly. Answer-D is the best choice for this question about how to Manage Communications. ZXY Consulting should tailor the reports, frequency, and format to the needs of the Customer, their key stakeholder. One key role of the PM is to proactively promote 2-way communications with the stakeholders. Face-to-face is the most effective method.

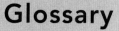

_____ **A** _____

Acceptance: The act of approving the deliverables. Acceptance is usually performed by the project manager and the customer or sponsor at the end of the project, project phases, or at predefined milestones. Acceptance of the product, service, or result is formal.

Accepted Deliverable: Deliverables that the customer has accepted as correct and complete. Accepted deliverables are the key output of the Validate Scope process.

Acquire Resources: An executing process focused on getting the right materials and the right people to work on the project at the right time.

Activity: Also called schedule activity. An activity is a task that must be performed in order to complete work on the project. Activities are created by further decomposing work packages. Under current guidelines, the primary difference between a work package and an activity is that a work package is a component of the scope and describes some aspect of the deliverable, while an activity describes the work that must be done in order to complete the work package. Schedule activities are first defined, then sequenced and estimated for duration.

Activity Attributes: The informational components that accompany each schedule activity. These may include information on dependencies, leads and lags, assignments, accountability, requirements, constraints and assumptions.

Activity Duration Estimates: The length of time an activity is expected to take to complete. Duration estimates are often expressed as a probability range.

Activity List: The list of all schedule activities to be performed, derived by decomposing the work packages into their schedule components. The activity list is a primary output of the Define Activities process.

Activity on Arrow (AOA): A type of graphical project network diagram where schedule activities are represented by lines with arrows. The lines are connected by nodes, usually represented by circles. AOA diagrams are seldom used in practice today and have been replaced by AON (see next entry).

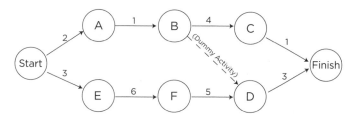

Glossary

Activity on Node (AON): A type of graphical project network diagram where schedule activities are represented by nodes (usually rectangles), and their interdependencies are represented by lines with arrows.

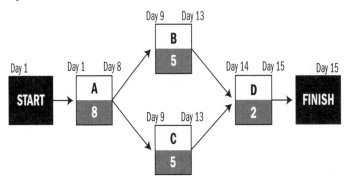

Activity Resource Estimates: The material and human resources that are expected to be required to complete an activity. Resource estimates are often expressed as a probability range.

Activity Resource Requirements: The resources required to complete the activities in the activity list. Typically these are physical, human, and organizational resources but do not include financial resources.

Actual Cost (AC): Also know as Actual Cost of Work Performed (ACWP). A term used in earned value management. Actual cost represents the amount that has been spent by the project up to a point in time. It is often contrasted with earned value to show the difference between the amount of value earned on the project (represented by earned value) and what was spent to earn that value (represented by the actual cost).

Actual Cost of Work Performed (ACWP): See Actual Cost

Adaptive: The agile approach that values responding to change over following a plan. Adaptive methodologies constantly seek solutions that deliver maximum value to the customer, and they recognize that the customer and the team's understand is likely to evolve and change with each deliverable.

Affinity Diagram: A visual tool that groups individual items into categories.

Agile: A way of managing projects that embraces uncertainty and breaks the project into very short phases, referred to as iterations. Agile methodologies empower the team and keep plans fluid and adaptable.

Agile Epic Story: A large user story that may span multiple iterations, multiple projects, and even multiple products.

Agreements: A document, defining intentions around the project or some component of the project, that has been accepted by both parties. It is helpful to think of agreements as contracts for purposes of the exam.

Allowable Costs: Costs that are allowed under the terms of the contract. Typically, allowable costs become relevant under certain types of cost-reimbursable contracts where the buyer reimburses the seller's allowable costs. If there are non-allowable costs in a contract, the buyer is not obligated to reimburse the seller for these.

Alternatives Analysis: A data analysis technique used in several processes to identify multiple possible approaches to solving a problem.

Analogous Estimating: Also known as "Top-Down Estimating." An estimating technique that uses the historical information from previously performed activities that are similar in nature, to estimate the effort, duration, or cost needed to complete an activity.

Analytical Techniques: A logical approach that looks at the relationship between outcomes and the factors that can influence them.

Application (exam): The application for the PMP or CAPM exam which requires the applicant to document an adequate combination of education and experience in project management. The application must be received and processed by the Project Management Institute before the applicant is eligible to schedule his or her certification exam.

Arrow Diagramming Method: The method that produces activity on arrow (AOA) diagrams. See Activity On Arrow for more information.

Assumption: Anything that is considered to be true while planning. Assumptions should always be documented and validated, and they are often closely linked to constraints.

Assumption Log: A list of all uncertainties that are treated as true for the purposes of planning.

Assumptions Analysis: A review of the risks and an analysis of the factors that were treated as true for planning purposes to see if those are still valid.

Attribute Sampling: A way of measuring quality where the results for each item or attribute are evaluated to either true or false to represent whether or not the item met quality standards. Contrast with Variable Sampling.

Audit: A structured review of the process and activities to evaluate which ones should be improved. The goal of the audits is to improve both the acceptance of the product and the overall cost of quality.

Autocratic: A decision making technique where one person has authority and takes responsibility for making a decision for the project or team. Autocratic decision making can be an efficient way of reaching a decision; however, it commonly increases risk related to the quality and the adoption of the decision.

B

Backlog: The list of user stories that are used in agile projects. Backlogs should be kept well-groomed, which means that they are ordered by priority, with the highest priority items kept at the top of the list.

Backward Pass: A technique used to calculate slack, or float, that begins with the last node of a project network diagram and logically works backward to the start. Using the backward pass technique, each schedule activity's late start and late finish dates are determined.

Bar Chart: A term in project management that equates to a Gantt chart. In a bar chart, horizontal bars represent lengths of time for schedule activities. A calendar of dates represents the horizontal (X) axis.

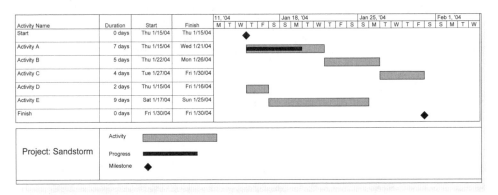

A bar (Gantt) chart

Baseline: The original approved scope, cost, or schedule, plus all approved changes. Baselines represent the approved plan, and they are especially useful for measuring how actual results deviate from the plan. It is important to remember that baselines can, and typically do, change throughout the life of the project as changes are approved. Baselines occasionally apply to other measured areas such as performance and quality.

Basis of Estimates: The backup detail showing how cost or schedule estimates were derived, where they came from, who was involved, what information was used, and what estimating technique was used.

Benchmarking: Using data from other projects, departments, or organizations to measure performance of the project or product.

Benefit Cost Ratio: The ratio of the expected benefits and the anticipated costs. A higher BCR is more desirable.

Benefits Management Plan: The plan that communicates the expected size of benefits to be realized by the project and when and how those benefits will be delivered.

Bottom-up Estimating: A technique for estimating overall project duration, effort, or costs by estimating the lowest levels of the schedule or work breakdown structure (WBS) and aggregating those numbers up to the summary nodes on the WBS. Bottom-up estimating is widely considered to be a relatively accurate, but often tedious, technique for estimating. This technique is the opposite of top-down or analogous estimating.

Bidder Conference: A meeting for potential sellers to come and understand the work they are considering bidding on. In a bidder conference, all bidders are given the same information and are kept on a level playing field.

Brainstorming: A technique to gather ideas that involves getting ideas from many participants in a rapid-fire and non-judgmental environment. Ideas are not evaluated until after they have all been gathered.

Budget: See Cost Baseline

Budgeted at Completion (BAC): The planned (budgeted) amount for the total project. The BAC represents what the project should cost at the point it is completed if everything proceeds according to plan.

Budgeted Cost of Work Performed (BCWP): See Earned Value

Budgeted Cost of Work Scheduled (BCWS): See Planned Value

Buffer: Extra time or money added to the schedule or budget to allow for unanticipated overruns. Buffers are useful since they allow for some slippage without affecting the overall schedule or budget.

Burn Rate: The rate at which the project consumes financial resources. The burn rate factors in any income the project generates. It represents negative cash flow. Burn rates are often used by agile projects as a way to budget costs for planned iterations.

Business Case: The social, economic, or business outcomes that justify undertaking this project or part of the project.

Business Documents: An input that includes the business case for the project and the benefits management plan.

C

Cause-and-Effect Diagrams: Also known as an Ishikawa diagram, or a fishbone diagram. Cause and effect diagrams graphically show the relationships between causes and effects. They are primarily used in risk and quality to help uncover the causes of risks, problems, or issues.

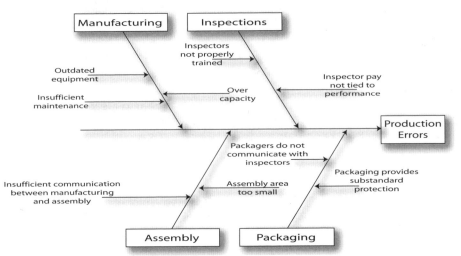

An example of a cause and effect diagram

Certified Associate in Project Management (CAPM): A project management credential created and managed by the Project Management Institute. The CAPM is for anyone who works on a project, can demonstrate the required education, and can demonstrate an adequate understanding of the *PMBOK® Guide*.

Change Control: Deliberately managing change to a project, whether that change is to the scope, cost, schedule, or quality baseline. In change control, change requests go through a formal process before they are approved or rejected. See Perform Integrated Change Control in chapter 4 for more information on the specific process associated with change control.

Change Control Board: A group with formal responsibility for evaluating project change requests. The change control board makes up a part of the overall change control system.

Change Control System: The procedures for evaluating and managing requested changes to the project. This system varies from project to project and from organization to organization.

Change Log: The list of all changes, whether or not they were requested, made to the project. The change log is used as an input to various processes to ensure that the impacts of changes are properly reviewed and evaluated.

Change Request: Any requested change to a documented baseline. Change requests are typically only implemented once the scope, cost, schedule, or quality is "baselined." Since change requests are formal, before project baselines exist a less formal method is generally used. Change requests are processed according to the change control system.

Charter: The document that formally starts the project. The charter typically is issued by the sponsor and names the project manager. Additionally, it may list the high-level project requirements, the high-level milestones, and a summary-level preliminary budget. The charter is a formal document created in the Develop Project Charter process. It authorizes the project manager to expend organizational resources in order to accomplish the project objective.

Checklist: Any set of procedural instructions used to ensure that product or component quality is achieved. Checklists are used in the Manage Quality and Control Quality process.

Claim: An issue with performance against the contract brought by one party against another. Claims could be made by the buyer against the seller for non-performance, or by the seller against the buyer for untimely payment. Claims must be resolved before the contract can be properly closed out.

Close Project or Phase: The closing process that administratively closes a phase or the overall project. In Close Project or Phase, all final project documentation and project files are completed, and lessons learned are documented.

Closing Processes: The process group, containing only one process, that focuses on closing out the project or an individual phase. This process group focuses on releasing resources, delivering the product, and gaining formal stakeholder approval.

Coach: An agile servant-leader role that exists to help the team follow the process and who works to help identify and remove any obstacles.

Collaboration: Working together and sharing tools and information to create a work product or result.

Collect Requirements: A planning process in scope management that documents the stakeholders' needs for the project. The resulting requirements documentation focuses on how the requirement, once it is built, will satisfy the underlying need or meet the opportunity that drove it.

Collocation: The act of physically locating everyone on a project team in the same space or general area. Collocation is used to break down distance barriers and facilitate team-building. A war room where all project team members work together is an example of collocation.

Common Cause: A reason contributing to a quality problem that is usually considered acceptable. Common causes are looked at as unpreventable, or if they are preventable, the cost of prevention would not justify the benefit. Contrast with Special Cause.

Communication: The act of accurately encoding, sending, receiving, accurately decoding, and verifying a message. Communication between a sender and a receiver may be formal, informal, oral, or written.

Communication Channels: The number of possible formal or informal paths of communication on a project. The concept of communication channels is particularly helpful in understanding how the addition of a small number of people to a project team can complicate the project manager's job of controlling communications. The formula for calculating communication channels is: [n (n-1)] ÷ 2 ,where n = the number of people in the communication model.

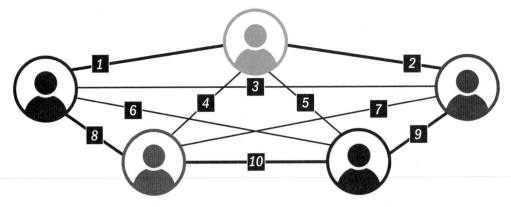

Communication Model: The formal paths of communication that will be used on the project. The traditional communication model involves a sender, a receiver, and a message, and both sender and receiver have responsibilities as to how they act upon the message.

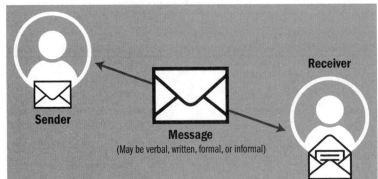

Communications Management Plan: The component of the project plan that specifies communications requirements and how those requirements will be addressed by the project. The communications management plan describes what communications will be provided, to whom, in what format, and how often.

Compromise: A method of negotiating where both parties give up something in order to reach an agreement. Compromise is considered to be lose-lose.

Conduct Procurements: The executing process in procurement management, where the seller responses are gathered, a seller is selected, and the contract is awarded. Conduct Procurements will only be performed on projects that procure goods or services from outside the organization, but on those projects it may be performed multiple times as needed.

Conflict: Difference of opinion or agenda on a project among team members or stakeholders. While not all conflict can be resolved to everyone's satisfaction, it is primarily the project manager's job to drive conflict resolution so that the project is not jeopardized.

Consensus: A group decision technique where the group agrees to support an outcome, even if the individuals do not all agree with the decision.

Constraint: Any external factor that limits the ability to plan. The most common constraints are scope, schedule, and cost, but they could be any factor, such as the law, quality, weather, or resource availability. Constraints and assumptions are often closely linked.

Context Diagram: The generic term for a use case diagram that shows systems and the "actors" that interact with each system. Each actor may be a user or another system.

Contingency: Also known as reserve, contingency is padding time and/or money to the project's schedule or budget to help manage overruns. Contingency may or may not be communicated to project stakeholders, and it may be added at an activity level, at any node on the WBS, or even at an overall project level.

Contingency Theory: A theory by Fred Fielder that states that the set of skills and attributes that helped a manager in one environment may actually work against them in another environment.

Contingent Response Strategies: A way of making a plan related to risk that only activates if certain conditions occur.

Contract: A legal document that specifies the relationship between two parties. In project management, these two parties are most often referred to as buyer and seller.

Glossary

Contract Change Control System: The formal system for managing changes to the contract so that all changes are tracked and processed, and all relevant parties are notified of the changes.

Control: See Monitoring and Controlling

Control Account: Also known as a "cost account," a control account is a node on the WBS where the scope, schedule, and cost are measured. Control accounts contain one or more work packages and are used to measure earned value. A project may have numerous control accounts placed on the WBS at nodes where it would be particularly meaningful to measure the earned value of those parts of the project.

Control Account Manager: The individual accountable for the delivery of the work contained in the Control Account to the scope, budget, and schedule.

Control Account Plan (CAP): The plan for how a given control account will be performed and measured. Since each control account is a division of the overall project, each CAP functions essentially like a mini-project plan for that division of work.

Control Chart: A specialized chart used in statistical process control to help determine whether or not a process is in control. Control charts are often associated with control limits, specification limits, means, standard deviations, and the rule of seven.

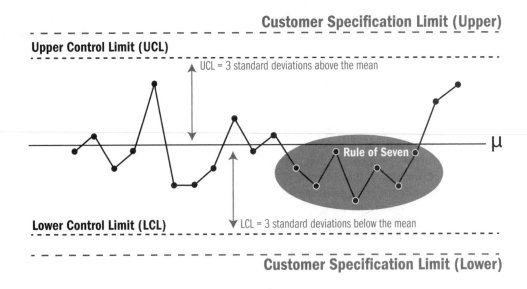

Control Costs: The process to monitor and control project costs to ensure they align with the plan. Control Costs is proactive to anticipate change and risk factors, as well as reactive to actual factors that affect project costs.

Control Limits: The upper and lower limits, used in statistical process control, that determine whether or not a process is in control. Upper and lower control limits are set at prescribed intervals and measured in standard deviations, above and below the mean. As long as the data points fall between the control limits, the process is in control.

Control Procurements: The monitoring and controlling process performed by the buyer to ensure compliance by the seller or other party. Control Procurements compares performance against terms and conditions specified in the contract to make certain that the seller meets his or her contractual obligations. The seller's performance is typically rated or evaluated by the buyer and is communicated back to the seller.

Control Quality: The monitoring and controlling process that focuses on work product quality. Control Quality is different from Manage Quality in that Control Quality inspects actual work products and tests them against requirements, while Manage Quality looks at the overall quality process to ensure that it is being followed and that it is working effectively.

Control Resources: The monitoring and controlling process within resource management that makes sure the flow and usage of physical resources lines up with the resource management plan.

Control Schedule: A monitoring and controlling process where the planned schedule is compared with the work performance information. If the project is ahead of schedule or behind schedule, corrective action in the form of change requests or updates to the plan may be necessary.

Control Scope: A monitoring and controlling process that ensures that changes to the scope baseline are properly controlled.

Corrective Action: Any action taken to bring future results in line with the plan. Corrective action may change the plan, or the way the plan is executed.

Cost: Any project expenditure. Costs are tracked on numerous levels, but usually tie back to a chart of accounts and nodes on the work breakdown structure.

Cost Account: See Control Account

Cost Aggregation: The practice of rolling activity cost estimates up to the work package level and the control account level.

Cost-Benefit Analysis: An analysis of potential scope changes and the forecasted benefits of making these changes and the costs involved. Quality is the section on the exam where this is most relevant, and in quality management, benefits should always outweigh costs.

Cost Forecasts: Cost estimates adjusted for performance. There are several ways to do this, including using the Estimate At Complete, the Estimate To Complete, the Budgeted at Completion, the Cost Performance Index, and others.

Cost Baseline: Also known as the budget. The cost baseline is a time-phased plan for when funds will be disbursed on a project. It helps the performing organization anticipate cash flow needs for the project life-cycle. Accuracy is dependent upon a well-defined project scope and schedule, although a summary-level cost baseline is typically supplied with the project charter before the scope and schedule are fully defined.

Cost Management Plan: The plan for how project costs will be measured, monitored, and controlled. The cost management plan is created in the Plan Cost Management process.

Cost of Quality (COQ): The sum of all project costs expended associated with achieving quality. Cost of Quality includes a complete analysis that includes planning, execution, control, the costs of potential alternatives, and the costs of quality failure.

Cost Performance Index (CPI): Expressed as CPI = EV÷AC, the CPI is an earned value calculation borrowed from the discipline of cost accounting. The CPI can be useful for predicting future performance based on previous history, as well as for plotting trends over time. Conventional wisdom dictates that a CPI >= 1 is preferable since that indicates that the project is earning value at a cost that is better than planned, while a CPI < 1 is undesirable since it indicates that performance lags the plan.

Cost-Plus-Fee (CPF): Also known as Cost-Plus-Percentage-Of-Cost (CPPC), it is a type of contract where the buyer pays the seller's costs for performing contractual duties plus a fee that is tied to the costs. Typically this fee is calculated as a percentage of costs. This contract type places a large portion of the risk on the buyer, as the seller stands to be financially rewarded when costs run high.

Cost-Plus-Fixed-Fee (CPFF): A type of contract where the buyer pays the seller's allowable costs for performing contractual duties plus a fixed sum for performing the work. The buyer bears much of the risk by paying the seller's allowable costs; however, this contract type places some of the burden on the seller, since the seller's profit is fixed regardless of how long or expensive the contract work is.

Cost-Plus-Incentive-Fee Contract (CPIF): A type of contract where the buyer pays the seller's allowable costs for performing contractual duties plus an incentive fee tied to the seller's performance. The incentive is often calculated by the seller's performance at keeping costs down. This contract type distributes the risk between the buyer and the seller.

Cost-Reimbursable Contract (CRC): A type of contract where project costs incurred by the seller are reimbursed by the buyer. In addition, the buyer typically pays the seller an additional fee for the seller's profit. Cost-reimbursable contracts often include incentives to the seller to keep costs down, where the seller would share a percentage of the cost savings with the buyer. The share of risk distributed to the buyer and seller depends upon the specifics of the contract.

Cost Variance: Commonly abbreviated as CV, cost variance is the earned value minus the actual costs, expressed as CV = EV-AC. Cost variance is useful to represent how project spending is tracking against the plan. A positive cost variance is generally considered to be a good thing, and a negative cost variance indicates overspending and is considered to be undesirable.

Crashing: Applying additional resources to one or more activities in order to complete the work more quickly. Crashing usually increases cost more than risk and can lead to the law of diminishing returns as resource allocation passes optimal levels. Compare with Fast Tracking.

Create WBS: The planning process for creating the work breakdown structure. This process decomposes all of the work necessary to perform the project and organizes it into the work breakdown structure (WBS). The WBS dictionary, which provides expanded information on the WBS, is also an output of this process.

Criteria: Objective measures for acceptance or judging quality.

Critical Activity: Any schedule activity that appears on the project's critical path. An activity is designated as critical if its delay would delay the overall project assuming all other activities finished as planned.

Critical Chain Method: A technique for managing a project's schedule that focuses on managing the constraints caused by limited human and material resource availability. Based on the Theory of Constraints, the critical chain method manages schedule buffers and emphasizes flexibility and keeping all resources fully working.

Critical Path: One or more combinations of activities from start to finish in a project network diagram, any one of which delayed would delay the completion of the entire project.

Critical Path Method: A technique of schedule analysis, where the schedule activities are evaluated to determine the float (or slack) for each activity and the overall schedule. The critical path method uses forward pass, backward pass, and float analysis to identify all network paths, including the critical path. The reason this technique is known as the critical path method is that the path of least flexibility and highest risk (i.e., the critical path) is identified so that it may be managed appropriately.

Customer: The individual or organization who will accept the project's deliverable. The role of customer should not be confused with the sponsor even if the same person fills both roles.

D

Data: The term generally referring to raw data. Data, when processed, becomes information, and that is eventually transformed into reports.

Data Analysis: Any technique used to analyze raw data, including alternatives analysis and reserve analysis.

Data Gathering: Any technique used to solicit and document ideas such as brainstorming, expert interviews, focus groups, questionnaires and surveys, and benchmarking. Data gathering techniques may be oriented toward a high quantity of ideas or higher quality ideas.

Data Representation: Any means of depicting data visually in order to aid in its comprehension by team members, customers, the performing organization, or other stakeholders.

Decision Making: Any one of numerous tools such as voting or multicriteria decision analysis, used to drive to a decision.

Decision Tree: A tool used in risk management to analyze risk and the expected monetary value of a decision or event to evaluate the outcome of certain scenarios. Decision trees are used to evaluate uncertainty.

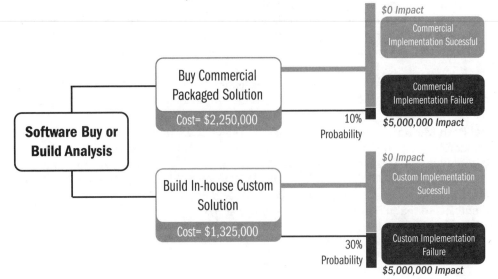

Decomposition: A technique for progressively breaking down the scope into smaller and smaller components. Decomposition is performed on nodes of the work breakdown structure and typically stops when the decomposed pieces are small enough to be assigned and estimated for time and cost. These smaller nodes (work packages) are later decomposed further into schedule activities.

Defect: An issue when the project's product, service, or result does not match the documented scope. Defects are often costly and require rework.

Define Activities: The planning process that takes work packages from the work breakdown structure (WBS) and further decomposes them into schedule activities.

Define Scope: The planning process that results in the project scope statement. The goal of this process is to develop a detailed understanding of the scope and to document that understanding.

Deliverable: A part of the product, or the product itself, that is presented to the customer or stakeholders for acceptance.

Delphi Technique: A form of expert judgment where a group of stakeholders is asked a question or opinion in a way that prevents the people being polled from knowing who the others are. Named after the blind oracle at Delphi in ancient Greece, the Delphi Technique is often used to prevent highly-opinionated stakeholders from influencing the rest of the group.

Dependency: A relationship between two or more activities where one activity must be started or completed before another related activity may be started or completed. Considering two activities of "Purchase Laptops" and "Configure Laptops," the start of activity "Configure Laptops" might be said to be dependent upon the finish of activity "Purchase Laptops." A Dependency may be mandatory, discretionary, or external to the organization. It is also known as a logical relationship between nodes. See entries on Start-Finish, Start-Start, Finish-Finish, and Finish-Start.

Design for X (DfX): A methodology where design is applied to the top priorities, including Design for Cost (DfC), Design for Assembly (DfA), Design for Manufacturing (DfM), Design for Logistics (DfL), Design for Serviceability (DfS). Design for X is a tool of Manage Quality.

Design Of Experiments (DOE): A technique using data analysis to determine optimal condition. It is most often used when there are multiple variables to be considered, and this technique analyzes how factors influence and change these variables. An engineer might use DOE to evaluate and determine the right combination of transmission gearing, wheel size, and tires for a new automobile within the cost constraints he or she has been given.

Determine Budget: The planning process where the individual cost estimates are compiled into the cost baseline. The cost baseline is a time-phased representation of costs so that stakeholders can see what funds will be needed and when they will be needed.

Develop Project Charter: An initiating process where the project charter is produced. This process typically occurs very early in the project, but also may take place at the beginning of each project phase. The output of this process formally authorizes the project to begin, names the project manager, and provides resources for the project.

Develop Project Management Plan: The planning process in which all subsidiary components of the project plan are integrated into a single plan that will drive the rest of the project. The subsidiary components include: the Requirements Management Plan, the Scope Management Plan, the Schedule Management Plan, the Cost Management Plan, the Quality Management Plan, the Resource Management Plan, the Communications Management Plan, the Risk Management Plan, the Procurement Management Plan, the Stakeholder Engagement Plan, the Schedule Baseline, the Cost Baseline, the Scope Baseline, the Change Management Plan, the Performance Measurement Baseline, the Project Life Cycle Description, Development Approach, and the Configuration Management Plan.

Develop Schedule: The planning process where the activities are arranged on a calendar to create a schedule. The project schedule may take several forms and have varying degrees of detail.

Develop Team: The executing process of enhancing the project team. Develop Team focuses on improving the overall sense of teamwork and the individual skills and abilities of the project team members.

Diagramming Techniques: Various means of depicting a system or a virtual concept such as a business or system process flow using drawings to show entities, relationships, and interactions.

Dictatorship: A group decision technique where one person makes the decisions for the entire group. This technique is generally not viewed favorably when it comes to the exam.

Direct and Manage Project Work: A high-level executing process as part of integration management that focuses on carrying out the project plan. Direct and Manage Project Work is closely tied to the process Monitor and Control Project Work, where the performance and quality of the execution is measured against the plan.

Direct Cost: A cost, usually measured and reported in Control Procurements, that is a direct project expense. Direct costs may include salaries of project workers, materials, and other expenses that are solely for the project. They do not include overhead or shared expenses. Generally, direct cost data is collected and reported as part of the Direct and Manage Project Execution process and becomes part of the Work Performance Information.

Document Analysis: A technique used in five processes. For example, document analysis is used in the Collect Requirements process to review existing documentation in order to gather requirements for a new product. An organization's marketing literature developed for a product that does not yet exist would be an example of a document that would be used for analysis.

Dummy Activity: A part of Activity On Arrow (AOA) project network diagrams where a "false" schedule activity is assigned a duration of 0. A dummy activity, represented as a dashed line between two circular nodes, is used to create logical relationships.

Duration: The amount of time needed to complete a schedule activity or work package. Duration is different from effort, since duration is concerned with calendar time, while effort is concerned with work hours. For example, a schedule activity that takes 8 workers 5 days, would require 40 days of effort, but may be possible to complete in the duration of only one workweek. Durations are estimated during the Estimate Activity Durations process.

E

Early Finish Date (EF): Used for schedule activities on project network diagrams, the early finish date is the earliest date possible that an activity could be completed given all of the constraints, durations, and logical relationships that exist within the schedule.

Early Start Date (ES): Used for schedule activities on project network diagrams, the early start is the earliest date possible that an activity could start given all of the constraints, durations, and logical relationships that exist within the schedule.

Earned Value (EV): Also known as Budgeted Cost of Work Performed (BCWP), Earned Value is a cost accounting term representing the value of the work that has actually been completed up to a point in time. Earned Value (EV) is different from Actual Cost (AC) because EV measures what was actually done and how much that is worth, which is different from what has been spent. For instance, if the project spent $100,000 but got $200,000 of value out of that, the EV would be $200,000, while the AC would only be $100,000.

Earned Value Management (EVM): The cost accounting technique of measuring work completed (earned value) against the plan (planned value). There are various calculations to show past performance and to predict future performance.

Economic Value Add: The total value a project creates for shareholders.
EVA = After tax profits – (capital invested X costs of capital)

Effort: The amount of work needed to complete an activity. Effort is different from duration, as duration measures how long something will take on a calendar. For example, 240 man hours of effort might only take one calendar week of duration to complete if enough resources. Effort is estimated during the Estimate Activity Durations process.

Enterprise Environmental Factors: Any factor outside of the project's control that influences the project. This could include organizational attitudes, culture, reporting relationships, government, the economy, laws, etc.

Estimate: A numerical representation of cost or time. Estimates should always specify the confidence and expected margin of error. For example, an early estimate for the design of a software database might be represented as follows: Database Design, Preliminary Estimate = 92 hours +/- 50%.

Estimate Activity Durations: The planning process that estimates how long a schedule activity should take. These estimates may be expressed as a specific number (e.g., 2 weeks) or as a range (e.g., 1 to 3 weeks). Activity durations are derived through a variety of methods, but are generally a function of the amount of work to be done, the resources applied to the task, expert judgment, and historical information.

Estimate Activity Resources: The planning process that estimates the material and human resources needed to perform a schedule activity to completion. This process may be performed before, after, or in parallel with the process of Sequence Activities.

Estimate At Complete (EAC): The forecasted amount a project should cost at its end, factoring in all of the performance metrics that have occurred at this point in the project. At a project's beginning, the Estimate at Complete (EAC) should be equal to Budgeted at Complete (BAC); however, if the project performs better than expected, or if risk occurrence is lower than expected, EAC could be lower than BAC. Conversely, if there are performance or risk problems with the project, the EAC may well trend higher than the BAC. There are numerous methods for calculating EAC and the closely related ETC. For the purposes of exam preparation, use the formula of EAC = BAC ÷ CPI.

Estimate Costs: The planning process of estimating the costs of activities which have not been performed. Estimate Costs is performed after the scope has been defined, the activities have been decomposed, and the duration and resources for each activity have been estimated. The cost estimates are later mapped back to the work breakdown structure and are used to create the budget.

Estimate To Complete (ETC): The forecasted amount it will take to finish a project from a point in time going forward. The Estimate To Complete (ETC) factors in known performance metrics. The ETC answers the question "how much more will it cost us to complete the project at this point?" There are numerous methods for calculating the ETC and the closely related EAC. For the purposes of exam preparation, use the formula ETC = EAC - AC.

Executing Process Group: One of the five process groups. All of the 49 project processes and activities are organized into one of five process groups, Initiating, Planning, Executing, Monitoring and Controlling, or Closing. 10 of the 49 processes are executing. All executing processes and activities focus on carrying out some aspect of the project plan, and on most projects, the majority of project costs are expended during executing processes.

Exit Gate: A logical point at the end of a project phase, where an independent party reviews that phase's deliverables to determine whether or not they were completed successfully and the subsequent project phase should be initiated. Exit gates are also commonly referred to as stage gates, phase gates, or kill points.

Expectancy Theory: A motivation theory that states that team members make choices based on their expected outcomes.

Expected Monetary Value (EMV): A method to calculate the value of potential future outcomes, factoring in the possible costs and probability of events. Decision tree analysis is one method that uses expected monetary value.

Expert Judgment: Using knowledgeable groups or individuals to assist in project decisions. Expert judgment is a highly favored technique within project management.

Expert Power: The power that comes through possessing a level of expertise.

F

Facilitated Workshops: A meeting or series of meetings where a facilitator works with project stakeholders from various disciplines to determine requirements. Joint Application Design (JAD) and Quality Function Deployment (QFD) are examples of specific types of facilitated workshops.

Facilitation Techniques: A technique used in integration management to move early stakeholders toward consensus on the broad goals of the project.

Fast Tracking: Performing project activities in parallel that would have been performed in sequence. It is most often the discretionary dependencies that are discarded in order to fast track activities. Fast tracking usually results in the project schedule being completed in a shorter time frame, but it typically increases risk.

Feedback: Verbal and nonverbal communication cues that a speaker must monitor to determine whether the listener is receiving and comprehending the message.

Final Report: The summary of the project including information on performance, scope, cost, schedule, quality, and risks. The final report may be written at the end of the project or after each phase.

Finish Date: The date that an activity is predicted (or permitted) to finish, based on the analysis of the schedule. The early finish date of a schedule activity is calculated by performing a forward pass on the project network diagram, and the late finish date is calculated by performing a backward pass.

Finish-to-Finish (FF): The logical relationship between nodes in a project network diagram. A finish-to-finish relationship between two schedule activities (e.g., activities T and W) indicates that regardless of when activity W starts, it cannot finish before activity T does.

Finish-to-Start (FS): The most common logical relationship between nodes in a project network diagram. A finish-to-start relationship between two schedule activities (e.g., activities D and E) indicates that the successor activity (activity E) cannot be started until the preceding activity (activity D) has finished.

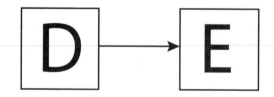

Firm-Fixed-Price Contract: See Fixed-Price Contract

Fishbone diagram: See Cause-and-Effect diagram

Fixed-Price-Incentive-Fee Contract: A type of contract where the seller is paid a fixed price for the contract but can also earn an incentive fee, paid by the buyer, for achieving predefined targets related to the seller's contract performance.

Fixed-Price Contract (AKA Lump Sum): A contract that specifies a fixed price for the deliverable paid by the buyer to the seller. Firm-fixed-price contracts transfer primary risk to the seller, since the seller is paid one price regardless of costs, efforts, or any other potential uncertainty. Firm-fixed-price contracts are also referred to simply as fixed price contracts. A purchase order is one example of a fixed-price contract.

Float (slack): The amount of time a schedule activity could be delayed without impacting the finish date of the project.

Flowcharting: A graphical, logical representation of a sequence. In project management, flowcharts are most often used in the area of quality to determine how one set of inputs may lead to one or more outcomes.

Forcing: Exerting power to gain compliance. Forcing is not a favored method of problem solving since it does not deal with the underlying problem(s) that led to conflict.

Forward Pass: A technique for calculating the early start and early finish dates of schedule activities. The forward pass is part of the critical path method and is paired with a backward pass to determine activity and schedule float and the critical path.

Free Float: The amount of time a schedule activity may slip without impacting the start of any other activities. Free float is often confused with float, but it is different in that float is concerned with disrupting the finish date of the project and the critical path, while free float is concerned with disrupting the planned start or finish date of any successor schedule activity.

Functional Manager: A manager of a department or functional group within an organization. Functional managers are vital to most companies since they have deep expertise within a given area and perform the human resource management duties for the employees of their departments. Project managers experience most of their conflict with functional managers.

Functional Organization: A very common type of organization that has strong (vertical) departments, organized around function or expertise. In a functional organization, the functional manager generally has more organizational power than the project manager, and the project manager may struggle to receive significant support, recognition, or authority.

G

Gantt Chart: See Bar Chart

Gatekeeper: The person responsible for evaluating the project deliverables between phases at the phase exit gates. The gatekeeper is preferably an impartial person from senior management who does not work directly on the project.

The term "gatekeeper" also has a usage in resource management to describe a constructive team role where a person works to ensure that others are involved in a discussion or a process.

Generalizing Specialist: A type of team member favored on agile projects. Generalizing specialists are highly interchangeable, which favors the agile practice of committing to a package of scope. If one generalizing specialist falls behind, another can usually step in to help. Generalizing specialists are usually seasoned professionals.

Gold Plating: The practice of adding more scope than the customer requested and more than the team has planned for. Gold plating increases risk and is not a favored practice.

Grade: A way of evaluating the product's suitability for use. In project management low grade may be acceptable, depending on the application; however, low quality is never acceptable. For example, a project may call for producing a consumer-grade refrigerator. Producing a higher grade refrigerator would not only be uncalled for but would likely incur unjustified higher expense. While grade traditionally applies to physical items (e.g., steel, foodstuffs, video monitors), it may also apply to non-physical items (e.g., software encryption or communication signals).

Ground Rules: Rules of conduct that apply to the entire project team. Ground rules are adopted by the team to establish behavioral norms among the members.

Group Creativity Techniques: Techniques used in meetings and workshops such as brainstorming, mind mapping, and the nominal group technique to generate creative thinking and potential solutions.

Group Decision-Making Techniques: Techniques used by the project manager to move the group toward consensus or decision. The four popular group decision-making techniques for the exam are Unanimity, Majority, Plurality, and Dictatorship.

H

Hammock Activity: An activity that summarizes other schedule activities. While the project execution occurs at the lower (sub) activity level, hammock activities are used for tracking and reporting purposes. Most times, a hammock activity groups activities that would not be related through the work breakdown structure.

Herzberg's Motivation-Hygiene Theory: A theory of motivation that divides factors into either hygiene factors or motivational factors. Hygiene factors, such as a paycheck, do not provide motivation; however, motivation factors, such as achievement or responsibility, do motivate but will not work without the presence of hygiene factors.

Histogram: A statistical tool that uses a column chart to show frequency of occurrence of a particular item. For instance, a histogram showing the ages of a group of people might show the number of people from 0 up to 10 years of age as the first bar, the number of people 10 up to 20 as the second bar, and so on. Histograms are widely used in quality management to determine statistical trends and identify issues or problems. See Resource Histogram.

Historical Information: Any information from previous projects that has been archived by the performing organization. Historical information can be used to help evaluate future project decisions.

Historical Information Review: A tool used in the Determine Budget process. When using historical information, past data or project results are considered to estimate or forecast budgets for the current project. For example, a project to build a road might be estimated at a certain amount of money per kilometer based on similar projects.

Glossary of Terms

I

Identify Risks: The planning process of anticipating all of the risks that could happen on the project. Common tools used to facilitate risk identification include checklists, brainstorming ,SWOT analysis, and expert judgment.

Identify Stakeholders: The initiating process where all of the groups or people who will be considered on this project are identified. The resulting stakeholder register documents their names, their interests, and their involvement on the project.

Implement Risk Responses: An executing process that carries out the risk management plan to respond to the identified project risks.

Imposed Date: A date that is provided to the project and may not be moved. An imposed date may come from internal sources, such as senior management, or external sources, such as a government entity. Imposed dates are treated as constraints during Estimate Activity Durations and Develop Schedule.

Independent Estimates: Estimates generated by experts outside of the project for the purposes of comparing with those from the team. When used as part of procurement, independent estimates involve parties that do not intend to bid on the project, therefore presumably making them less likely to be biased.

Indirect Cost: A cost, usually tracked as part of a contract, that is not expended directly for the project's benefit. Indirect costs include such things as overhead and management expense that may be shared by things other than a single project. How indirect costs are tracked and accounted for varies depending on the organization or the contract.

Influence Diagram: A chart showing how a set of influences may affect outcomes. The diagrams depict the components that go into the decision-making process. Influence diagrams are used as a tool in the Perform Qualitative Risk Analysis process, along with simulation and decision tree analysis.

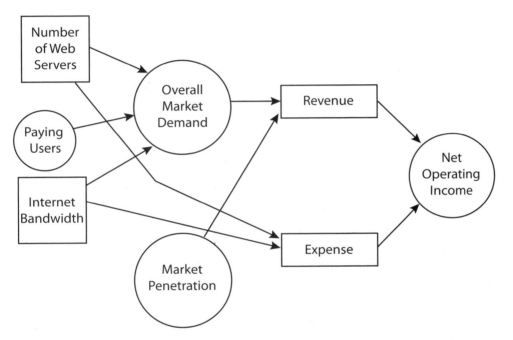

Influencer: Stakeholders who can positively or negatively affect the project due to their ability to influence the customer, the performing organization, or the project team.

Information: Data that has been organized and processed to make it more meaningful. Data eventually becomes information and information is finally processed into reports.

Information Management: Using a system to allow the team to capture and share tools, documents, templates, etc.

Information Management Systems: A way to collect, manage, and distribute project information. A project portal or collaboration site could be examples of information management systems.

Interpersonal and Team Skills: The ability to lead people and develop a team without resorting to formal authority.

Glossary

Initiating Process Group: The processes that take place early in a project or project phase. Initiating processes are involved with starting (chartering) the project or phase and the identification of stakeholders. Only two of the 49 processes are initiating processes.

Input: Something needed or used by a process to create the outputs for that process.

Inspection: Reviewing the functionality or suitability of a product, service, or result against the requirements. The desired result of inspection is acceptance.

Internal Rate of Return: A way to look at the project's anticipated returns as an interest rate.

Interviews: A meeting between a business analyst and a user, key stakeholder, or expert to gather and document requirements.

Invitation for Bid (IFB): See Request for Proposal

Ishikawa Diagram: See Cause-and-Effect Diagram

Issue: An unresolved threat or problem on the project, or a point of disagreement.

Issue Log: A document where all stakeholder issues can be recorded. The issue log is an important artifact for tracking, communicating, and managing issues.

Iterative: An approach to planning, execution, and control that breaks execution into relatively short cycles and reassesses the plan after each cycle.

Iteration Burndown Chart: A chart used on agile projects to show progress during each iteration. Burndown charts communicate how many user stories have been completed during an iteration and how many remain.

K

Kanban Board: Literally "signboard". A Kanban board is a task board that originated with Lean Manufacturing, used to provide information on where user stories are in the workflow. As user stories are completed, more work is "pulled" from the backlog onto the Kanban board.

Kill Point: See Exit Gate

Knowledge Area: One of the competency domains within project management. The 49 processes of project management are grouped into ten knowledge areas.

Knowledge Management: Increasing knowledge within the organization by encouraging the team to interact and share.

L

Lag: Changing the finish-to-start relationship between two schedule activities so that the dependent activity cannot start until a given amount of time after its preceding activity finishes. Given that activity B (erecting a building frame) cannot start until Activity A (pouring concrete) has finished, if 3 days of lag time were applied to activity A (e.g., to allow the concrete to cure), then activity B could not start until 3 days after activity A finishes. Lags are used to represent calendar time that must elapse when no actual work is taking place by project resources. (Contrast with "lead" below.)

Late Finish Date (LF): The latest possible date a schedule activity can finish without impacting the critical path, assuming all estimated durations are accurate. The late finish (LF) is calculated as follows: LF = EF + Float, or by performing a backward pass on the project network diagram.

Late Start Date (LS): The latest possible date a schedule activity can start without impacting the critical path, assuming all estimated durations are accurate. The late start is calculated as follows: LS = LF − DURATION + 1, or LS = ES + Float, or by performing a backward pass on the project network diagram.

Life-Cycle Costing: A method of looking at the total cost of ownership of an item rather than only looking at the cost to the project.

Lead: Changing the finish-to-start relationship between two schedule activities so that the dependent activity can start before the preceding activity finishes. Given that activity B cannot start until Activity A has finished, if 2 days of lead time were applied to activity B, then activity B could start 2 days before activity A finishes. Leads are used to efficiently manage the schedule and get a head start on certain activities where possible.

Lean: An agile methodology that focuses on eliminating all waste and any activities that do not add value. One goal of Lean is to have every activity performed by the team deliver value to the customer.

Leading: The act of establishing a direction, aligning the team to that vision, and motivating and inspiring them.

Legitimate Power: Also known as formal power, legitimate power is positional power where the project manager has authority and the backing of the organization.

Lessons Learned: The formally documented information the team has acquired during execution of the project. Lessons learned specifically focus on variances in the project and document how the team would plan or execute differently if they had a specific component of the project to perform again. The lessons learned register documents the current project, while the lessons learned repository stores information for all projects in the organization

Level of Effort (LOE): Supporting work that does not produce an actual deliverable such as support or follow-up activities. Level of effort is often difficult to measure effectively and to relate back to a product or service. It is tracked and reported at a high level.

Logical Relationship: See Dependency

M

Majority: A group decision-making technique where a simple majority of votes is enough to make a decision. Many political elections are examples of the majority technique, where anything over 50% is sufficient to decide the outcome.

Make-or-Buy Analysis: A technique used in Plan Procurement Management. Make-or-buy analysis looks at the component of the project to determine whether it is rational to make it internally or to buy it from an outside vendor. Several factors go into this decision; however, all other things being equal, buying is favored over making.

Manage Communications: The executing process where information is distributed to the stakeholders according to the communications management plan.

Managing: The act of assembling and working with teams and organizing and executing tasks to deliver key results.

Manage Project Knowledge: An executing process that leverages lessons learned on previous projects and captures lessons learned on the current project.

Manage Stakeholder Engagement: The executing process where the project team communicates and works with stakeholders to ensure their needs are addressed and their issues are resolved.

Manage Quality: The executing process that focuses on the overall quality activities to ensure that all of the plans are being followed and that the project meets the quality requirements. Contrast with Control Quality.

Manage Team: The executing process of directing the project team to complete the work of the project plan, monitoring their performance, and working to improve performance and resolve issues where necessary.

Market Research: Looking outside of the performing organization to gather information about current trends and capabilities in the industry. Market research is a data gathering technique used in the Plan Procurement Management process.

Maslow's Hierarchy of Needs: A theory of human motivation by Abraham Maslow that states that lower needs such as food and clothing must be satisfied before higher needs such as esteem and self-actualization may be achieved.

Matrix Organization: An increasingly popular organization that is a hybrid between a functional and a projectized organization. A matrix organization provides a project manager with control over the projects, while preserving the functional manager's control over departments. The project manager "borrows" resources from one or more departments for a temporary project, while the functional manager performs administrative and human resource duties for the resources.

McClelland's Three Needs Theory: Also called Achievement Theory, this theory states that in order to be motivated, people have needs for Achievement (nAch), Power (nPow), and Affiliation (nAff) that must be satisfied.

Meetings: Live or online sessions where the participants exchange information, collaborate in real time, and drive to decisions. A meeting is a common tool used frequently in processes. Each stakeholder who attends should have a clearly defined role pertaining to the meeting and expectations of the meeting.

Methodology: A set of steps to manage a project. Methodologies are an organization's specific implementation of the processes of project management. They typically include checklists, procedures, and document templates.

Milestone: A notable event in the project. A milestone may be a date, a project deliverable, or any significant point of interest.

Milestone Schedule: A high-level schedule that shows only significant schedule points. A milestone schedule is often supplied along with the project charter, where the milestones become schedule constraints.

Activity Name	Duration	11, '04	Jan 18, '04	Jan 25, '04	Feb 1, '04	Feb 8, '04	Feb 15, '04
Marketing Studies Complete	0 days	◆ 1/15					
Requirements Gathered	0 days		◆ 1/23				
High level design	0 days			◆ 1/30			
Prototype ready	0 days					◆ 2/9	
Detailed design	0 days						◆ 2/16

Project: Firestorm	Milestone ◆

A Milestone Schedule, With Four Milestones Represented

Mind Mapping: A means of visually depicting relationships between items to help understand relationships.

Modeling: An approach used in schedule management and risk management. Modeling and simulation can help identify problems or areas of risk with the project before they actually occur. What-if scenario analysis and Monte Carlo analysis are examples of modeling techniques.

Monitor and Control Project Work: A high-level integration process used to ensure that the project work being performed matches the plan. If the results do not line up with the plan, either the way the work is being performed is altered, or the plan is changed to reflect a more realistic scenario.

Monitor Communications: A monitoring and controlling process, performed throughout the project, that compares the project communications with the communications management plan and makes any needed adjustments.

Monitor Risks: The process that reviews the risks that have and have not occurred on the project and evaluates how the execution of the risk management plan lines up to the plan itself.

Monitor Stakeholder Engagement: A monitor and controlling process that ensures that the right stakeholders are involved on the project at the right level and in the right way.

Monitoring and Controlling Processes: One of the five process groups. Monitoring and controlling processes constitute 12 of the overall 49 processes which generally measure the work results against the plan and make adjustments or take corrective action where variances exist.

Monte Carlo Analysis: The risk management technique used to compute large numbers of possible scenarios and identify areas of high risk. Monte Carlo analysis is almost always performed by computer due to the high numbers of scenarios considered. The output is a range of possible schedule due dates and costs.

Multicriteria Decision Analysis: A way of rating or assigning values to different dimensions of the project.

N

Negative Float: A situation that occurs when an activity's start date occurs before a preceding activity's finish date. Negative float is an indication of a scheduling issue.

Net Present Value: The same as present value but NPV also subtracts out the costs.

Networking: The tool used to build or leverage existing relationships to help complete the project work.

Node: A point on a project network diagram. In activity on node diagrams, a node represents a schedule activity, while in activity on arrow diagrams, a node is simply a connecting point.

Nonverbal Communication: Ways of communication that do not involve words or vocalizations such as body language, expressions, hand motions, or posture.

O

Observation and Conversation: A preferred way of getting in touch with the team and staying attuned to the progress and morale of the team.

Observations (Job Shadowing): Watching product users or subject matter experts work as a way to gather scope and requirements.

On-Demand Scheduling: An agile approach where teams use a Kanban board showing work in progress. Technically work is not scheduled in advance. Instead, work is "pulled" from the board when resources become available or when work is completed.

Operations: Ongoing activities needed to continue business. Operations are not considered part of a project, but they often are considered part of a program.

Opportunity: Anything that could have a positive impact on the project's scope, schedule, or cost. Opportunities are also considered as risks to the project, as they represent uncertainty.

Opportunity Cost: The value of a project that was not performed so that another one could be. Opportunity cost is typically calculated by taking the value of the best alternative that was passed up.

Organization Chart: A chart that shows the reporting relationships among a group of people working for an organization or for a project.

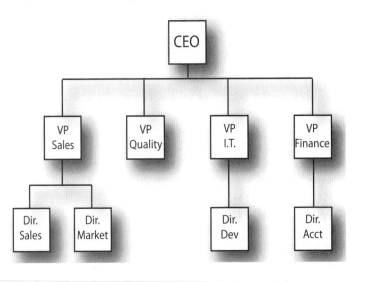

Organizational Breakdown Structure (OBS): A chart that relates work packages to the parties in the organization responsible for their completion.

Organizational Process Assets: All historical information or knowledge that an organization has at its disposal, which may be used to help future projects. Examples of organizational process assets would include templates, forms, research results, work breakdown structures, quality standards, benchmarks, previous plans, contracts, etc.

Output: Something coming out of a process. For example, in the process Create WBS, the work breakdown structure is part of the scope baseline, which is the output.

P

Paralingual Communication: Communication that is vocal but not verbal such as the tone of voice, volume, or pitch.

Parametric Estimating: Using organizational process assets such as historical data to formulate estimates based on past performance or results. Parametric estimating is considered to work best on highly linear and scalable components with adequate historical information. The better the parametric model and the information coming in, the more reliable the parametric estimate will be.

Pareto Chart: A column chart, or histogram, used in quality management to show problems and help the team to know where to focus their efforts based on frequency of the problem.

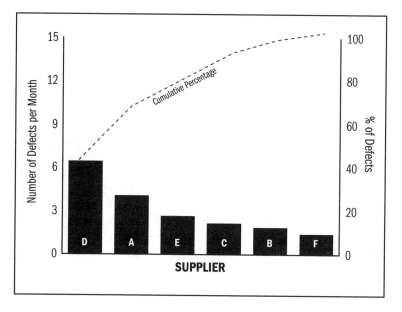

Path: A series of schedule activities that have a relationship that carries through from the project's start to the finish.

Path Convergence: A point at which two or more network paths converge.

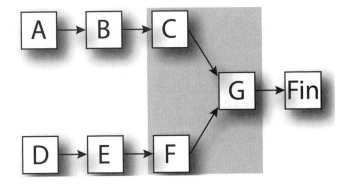

Payback Period: The amount of time it will take for an organization to recover its financial investment in a project based on the value the project is expected to provide.

Percent Complete: An estimated or actual value showing how much of the activity's work has been completed. Percent complete is sometimes used to report on various levels of the work breakdown structure as well.

Perform Integrated Change Control: The monitoring and controlling process where requested and unrequested changes are reviewed according to the change control system. Perform Integrated Change Control focuses on changes to the product, service, or result as well as the organizational process assets that endure past the project.

Perform Qualitative Risk Analysis: A planning process to look at non-quantifiable aspects of each risk. Perform Qualitative Risk Analysis prioritizes the risks using the probability impact matrix, according to which risks have the highest factors of likelihood and potential impact.

Perform Quantitative Risk Analysis: The planning process where all risks are analyzed and assigned a value as it relates to the risk's impact on the project. Risks are typically quantified in terms of potential impact on budget or schedule so they may be weighed against the risk tolerance of the key stakeholders.

Performing Organization: The organization responsible for executing the project. A project manager typically works for the performing organization to manage planning, execution, monitoring and controlling, and closing activities. While the project sponsor typically works for the performing organization, the customer may or may not.

Personnel Assessment Tools: Surveys and assessments to give the project manager and the team greater insight into team member working styles and preferences. A personality assessment would be one example of a personnel assessment tool.

Phase: A grouping of project activities. Many projects are divided into two or more phases in order to provide a point where the deliverables can be evaluated. Phases are separated by exit gates or kill points where someone who does not directly work with the project (the gatekeeper) evaluates the deliverables to determine whether or not the next phase is initiated. Phases should not be confused with process groups.

Plan Communications Management: The planning process that analyzes the project, the stakeholders, and the communications needs of the project and creates the communications management plan.

Plan Cost Management: The planning process that creates the cost management plan, which is the plan that guides the activities in the other three cost management processes.

Plan Procurement Management: The planning process where the project team performs make-or-buy analysis and decides what goods and services will be created or performed internally and what will be procured from external sources. Additionally, the procurement documents are created, and potential sellers are identified.

Plan Quality Management: The planning process where quality targets are identified. Plan Quality Management also determines how these targets will be met and spells out how the other two quality processes (Manage Quality and Control Quality) will be carried out.

Plan Resource Management: The planning process that determines how the project will be organized and staffed in terms of the personnel and how the physical resources will be acquired. The resource management plan is the primary output of this process.

Plan Risk Management: The process that creates the risk management plan. Plan Risk Management focuses on planning for the six subsequent risk processes.

Plan Risk Responses: The planning process that determines how each identified risk will be mitigated, avoided, transferred, shared, exploited, enhanced, or accepted.

Plan Schedule Management: The process that creates the schedule management plan, which shows how the remaining schedule management processes will be carried out.

Plan Scope Management: The process in the scope knowledge area that plans how the other five scope management processes will be carried out. The two major outputs of this process are the scope management plan and the requirements management plan.

Plan Stakeholder Engagement: The process that plans how the team will relate to stakeholders and the involvement stakeholders will have on the project.

Planned Finish Date: The date a schedule activity should be finished if that activity's work begins on time and is completed according to plan.

Planned Start Date: The date work on a schedule activity should begin according to the plan.

Planned Value (PV): Also known as the Budgeted Cost of Work Scheduled (BCWS). An earned value management term representing the value that should have been realized on the project at a given point in the schedule. Planned Value (PV) is contrasted with Earned Value (EV). See Earned Value for more information.

Planning Package: A node on the WBS where the scope is understood but there are no detailed schedule or cost estimates. Planning packages are often given to outside groups to perform the work.

Planning Processes: The process group containing all of the processes associated with planning or creating a plan. 24 of the 49 processes of project management are planning processes, which accounts for more than any other process group.

Plurality: A group decision-making technique where the largest block of individuals decides the outcome. Plurality differs from Majority in that plurality does not require more than 50% to be in agreement. For example, if 30% vote in favor of outcome A, and 30% in favor of outcome B, and 40% in favor of outcome C, outcome C would carry the group because it represents the largest block. It is not uncommon for the plurality technique to employ a run-off between the two options that received the highest votes until one option receives a true majority.

PMBOK: Different from the *PMBOK® Guide* , the PMBOK is an acronym for the project management body of knowledge, which includes the sum of all knowledge in the profession of project management.

PMBOK® Guide: The ANSI Standard for project management. *PMBOK® Guide* is an abbreviation for the full title of the standard, which is "A Guide to the Project Management Body of Knowledge." The standard is defined as being applicable to most projects, most of the time.

Portfolio: A group of projects and programs intended to achieve a business result. A portfolio usually refers to all of the projects and programs in an organization.

Position Description: A document describing the responsibilities of a specific project team role. For most positions, the position description should be created in advance of filling the position. This document can be a useful tool for recruiting.

Precedence Diagramming Method (PDM): The technique that uses the analysis of logical relationships to create Activity on Node diagrams. See entry for Activity on Node for more information.

Present Value: An economic calculation that calculates how much future payments are worth in today's currency. Present value is always smaller than the sum of future payments due to the time value of money.

Prevention: The concept, in quality management, that states that quality cannot be inspected into a product but should be planned in from the start in order to avoid problems.

Preventive Action: Action taken proactively in order to prevent or avoid anticipated future problems. Preventive action is tied to risk management.

Probability and Impact Matrix: A graphical risk analysis tool that plots the likelihood (probability) of each risk event on the Y (vertical) axis, and the risk event's potential impact on the X (horizontal) axis. The X and Y values are multiplied together to give a risk score. Risks with the highest scores are prioritized higher for analysis and response.

Procedure: A set of rules to be followed in order to achieve a desired result.

Process: A set of inputs, tools, and techniques, used together to produce one or more specific outputs for the project. There are 49 processes of project management which make up the core of the *PMBOK® Guide*. Each process is organized so that it belongs to one knowledge area and one process group.

Process Group: An organization of the 49 processes of project management by overall function. Every process is assigned to a single process group according to whether its purpose is initiating, planning, executing, monitoring and controlling, or closing the project.

Process Improvement Plan: The quality management plan for how activities will be reviewed and analyzed so that efficiency improves as the project progresses.

Procurement: Buying goods or services from outside of the organization. Procurement is generally treated as a formal activity.

Procurement Management Plan: The component of the project plan that is used to manage one or more contracts that exist on the project. The procurement management plan details the types of contracts to be used and governs how changes to the contract will be managed, how claims will be processed, and how contract-related communication will be handled. Any information known about the procurement process will be detailed in this plan, and it should specify the process by which any contract(s) may be updated.

Product: The primary deliverable of the project. Projects may produce products, services, or results, and these must be accepted by the customer or sponsor.

Product Life Cycle: The different market phases of a product. Not to be confused with project life cycle.

Product Scope: All of the requirements and functionality necessary to create an acceptable product, service, or result.

Product Scope Description: A document that describes the characteristic of the project's product. The product scope description is progressively elaborated. Its main purpose is to help create a common understanding of the product among stakeholders.

Program: A group of related projects, managed together, usually to realize some common efficiencies. Programs may also include ongoing operations, which individual projects do not have.

Program Management: Coordinated management of two or more projects in order to realize common efficiency.

Program Management Office: The group within the performing organization responsible for establishing program standards, supporting with expert knowledge, and providing templates and a repository for organizational process assets and other historical information. The actual authority of program management offices varies according to organization and industry.

Progressive Elaboration: An iterative approach where planning occurs in cycles rather than up front. Projects which use progressive elaboration typically do some planning, some execution, some monitoring and controlling, and then repeat that cycle.

Project: A time-limited undertaking to deliver a unique product, service, or outcome. In this definition, "unique" means that it has never been performed by this organization before. Projects do not include ongoing operations, although they do need to consider them up front.

Project Calendar: A calendar that is specific to this project, factoring in the constraints of all participating organizations and geographical and demographic regions. Project calendars show which days will be working days and which ones will be non-working.

Project Charter: The document that creates the project. Although it may be created by the project manager, it is signed by the sponsor, and it names the project manager and gives him or her the authority to manage the project.

Project Coordinator: The project role that is weaker than a project manager in terms of authority. A project coordinator can typically assign project resources but is not authorized to spend project funds. When the role of project coordinator exists on a project, it is in the place of a project manager. Project coordinators report to someone from senior management who has ultimate responsibility for the project.

Project Expeditor: The project role that has some project responsibility but little organizational authority. Project expeditors ensure that tasks are completed on time and that the project is progressing as planned; however, they cannot assign project resources or spend project funds. Project expeditors report to someone from senior management who has ultimate responsibility for the project.

Project Funding Requirements: The amounts of funds that will be required and the dates those funds will be required in order to perform the project. Project funding requirements are tied to the schedule and the cost baseline.

Project Life Cycle: A group of project phases specified by an organization's project management methodology. The project life cycle is made up of all of the project phases, viewed as a whole. Projects are divided into phases in order to create logical management and decision points. See Phase for more information.

Project Management Information System (PMIS): The system used to support management of the project. It serves as a repository for information and a tool to help with communication and tracking. The PMIS supports the project from beginning to end.

Project Management Office (PMO): A group within the performing organization responsible for providing standards and guidance to projects and project managers. The role and responsibility of the PMO varies from organization to organization, with some PMOs directly accountable for project success.

Project Management Plan: The plan for how the project will be managed. The project management plan is a formal, approved document composed of the other planning documents. Once approved, the project management plan is placed under control. The project management plan is also known, more succinctly, as the project plan.

Glossary

Project Management Professional (PMP): A project management certification managed by the Project Management Institute.

Project Management Software: Software to automate and assist the processes of project management, including the gathering, storing, updating, and reporting of information and the calculating of schedules and budgets.

Project Management System: All of the processes, people, tools and techniques, and methodologies used to manage the project. The project management system should be described in the project plan.

Project Manager: The role of the person ultimately responsible for the project. The project manager has the authority to spend project budget and to assign project resources in order to realize the project's goals.

Project Network Diagram: a graphical way of depicting schedule activities, their dependencies, and sequence. The most common form of project network diagram is an Activity on Node diagram where the nodes are represented by rectangles and the dependencies are represented by arrows that connect the nodes.

Project Network Node: a rectangle within an *activity on node* project network diagram that represents an individual schedule activity.

Project Organization Chart: A graphical chart depicting reporting relationships of all team members, specifically for this project. A project organization chart may differ from the standard organization chart in that it is not unusual for a project manager to have someone who ranks higher than him in the organization reporting to him on the project.

Project Plan: See Project Management Plan

Project Schedule: A central component of the project management plan that prescribes when activities should take place and in what order - also known as the schedule baseline.

Project Scope: All of the work to be performed on the project. The project scope is documented in the project scope statement and the work breakdown structure.

Project Scope Statement: The document that states the project requirements by describing objectives, deliverables, boundaries, and acceptance criteria.

Project Selection Methods: Any of the calculations that organizations use to choose to initiate a project. Most of these are financial calculations to help determine priority.

Projectized Organization: An organizational structure that is arranged around projects. In a projectized organization, the project manager also fills the role of functional manager for the project team, meaning that the human resources report directly to the project manager. Projectized organizations give the project manager a great degree of control and authority; however, that control comes with more administrative responsibility that can reduce the project manager's ability to focus on the actual project.

Prompt List: A list used by teams to facilitate a risk review. A prompt list helps identify new risks that might have occurred by giving a list of categories for the team to review.

Prototypes: Functional or non-functional incomplete models of a product to allow stakeholders to interact with it and refine design before it is constructed.

Pull Communication: Forms of communication where the sender might post information that must be pulled down by the receiver. A blog post could be one example of pull communication. Contrast with Push Communication.

Punishment Power: Also known as coercive power, it is the ability to punish a team member if a goal is not met. Punishment power is not viewed favorably in the field of project management.

Push Communication: Forms of communication where the sender actively delivers the information to the receiver. A sent email would be one form of push communication. Contrast with Pull Communication.

Q

Quality: Conformance to specifications.

Quality Control Measurements: The results after the tools and techniques of Control Quality have been applied.

Quality Management Plan: The plan which specifies how the quality policy will be implemented on a project. The quality management plan is a component of the project plan.

Questionnaires and Surveys: A technique used in Collect Requirements to gather scope from a large group of stakeholders. This data gathering technique is also used in Control Quality and Identify Stakeholders.

R

Referent Power: Power based on charisma or persuasive ability or based on an alliance with a more powerful person in the organization.

Regulation: A requirement that must be followed, issued by an authority.

Reports: The final form in the transformation from data to information to reports. Reports should always be actionable.

Request for Information (RFI): Also known as a RFI, a request for information is issued by a buyer to potential sellers to supply information relevant to the procurement process.

Request for Proposal (RFP): A formal document, issued by the buyer to potential sellers. Potential sellers respond to the request for proposal with a proposal for how they would satisfy the buyer's request. The response should answer all of the questions asked by the buyer in the RFP.

Request for Quotation (RFQ): A formal document, issued by the buyer to potential sellers. An RFQ typically requests pricing on pre-existing products or offerings. Potential sellers respond to the request for quotation with pricing.

Requirement: Something that the product needs to do or an attribute it needs to have. Requirements should be documented in advance.

Requirements Documentation: A document that ties each deliverable back to the underlying need it will address.

Requirements Management Plan: The plan that tells how the requirements will be gathered, prioritized, documented, measured, and traced. The requirements management plan becomes part of the project management plan.

Requirements Traceability Matrix: A table showing the stakeholder or origin that produced each requirement and the functionality that will address that requirement. This is a useful document since projects may have difficulty remembering how and why a particular requirement came to be.

Reserve: Time or funding that is added to the schedule or budget to protect against overrun. Reserve is used so that the project manager can deal with routine overruns without having to reformulate the cost or schedule baselines after each individual slippage.

Reserve Analysis: A technique used to determine how much cost or schedule reserve is appropriate for a given activity, work breakdown structure node, or time or funding category.

Residual Risk: Risks that remain after planning has been completed. All projects carry some residual risks.

Resources: People, organizations, or materials that can be used on a project.

Resource Breakdown Structure (RBS): A graphical organizational chart that groups resources together by their function. For example, an RBS might show all of the database designers grouped together, and all of the programmers. Within the programmers node, they may be further subdivided by the software language in which they program. This is useful for resource leveling. The RBS is most often used for human resources but may also include material resources. See Resource Leveling for more information.

Resource Calendar: A calendar that shows the dates project resources will be in use on the project and days when they will not be used. This facilitates making these resources available to other projects or needs within the organization.

Resource Histogram: A column chart that graphically represents when a resource will be in use on the project. Resource histograms provide a good visual representation of how project resources will be used over time.

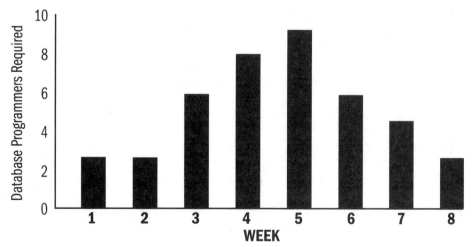

Glossary

Resource Leveling: The technique of making the resource requirements match up with the organizational realities. Resource leveling effectively means adjusting the requirements to meet what the organization can supply, and negotiating with the organization to make sure it can supply the project's resource needs. All of this takes place within the cost and time constraints imposed upon the project. One application of resource leveling would be to try to ensure that all resources work a 40 hour week and that no overtime is incurred.

Resource Optimization Techniques: Using optimization techniques such as resource leveling and resource smoothing to match the schedule for when a task needs to be completed to a resource's availability.

Resource Smoothing: Adjusting the number of resources to help keep resource usage relatively level. When resource smoothing is used, the critical path and the completion date do not change even though individual activity durations likely will move.

Responsibility Assignment Matrix: A grid where the work packages are represented in the rows, and the resources are represented in the columns. Each cell shows what responsibility (if any) a particular group of resources will have in relation to a work package. A R.A.C.I chart is a specific type of R.A.M..

Retrospective: An agile meeting held after the development in an iteration is complete. The point of a retrospective is for the team to review the process and the results and to identify opportunities to improve them for the next iterations.

Return on Investment: The percentage that shows what return an organization earns by investing in a project.

Return on Investment Capital: A calculation that answers the question "for every dollar of capital the organization invests, how much should we earn in return?"

ROIC = Net Income (after tax) from Project ÷ Total Capital Invested in the project

Reward Power: The power to offer a reward, recognition, or incentive to team members.

Rework: Anything done to make a product or service conform to specifications.

Risk: Any unknown on the project. Risks may be positive or negative.

Risk Acceptance: The decision to deal with the risk if and when it occurs. When risk acceptance is employed, no additional planning or steps will be taken before the risk event occurs.

Risk Audits: Periodic reviews of risk events to see if the events that were anticipated are the ones that are occurring and if new risks have become apparent. Risk audits are concerned with how effective the overall risk process is.

Risk Avoidance: Taking steps to eliminate the project risk. Moving a project site from a potentially hazardous location would be an example of risk avoidance.

Risk Breakdown Structure: A graphical chart showing risks organized into categories. The organization of a risk breakdown structure will vary from project to project.

Risk Database: The risk database contains all information on identified risks throughout the life of the project. The risk database will be used by future projects to assist in risk analysis.

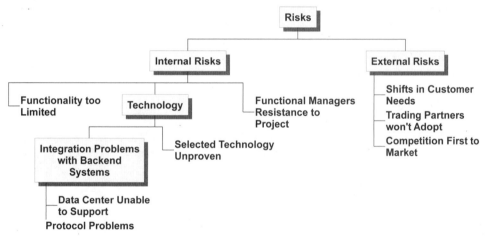

Risk Enhancement: A risk management strategy for making a positive uncertainty even better for the project. For example, if labor rates for work in another country came in at 75% of what was expected, a risk enhancement strategy might be to move even more work to that location to capitalize on the resource.

Risk Exploitation: A risk management strategy for making a positive uncertainty more likely to occur.

Risk Management Plan: The component of the project plan that shows how subsequent risk processes and activities will be performed.

Risk Mitigation: Looking to decrease either the likelihood of an identified risk's occurrence, or its impact on the project if it does occur.

Risk Parameters: The measures of a risk's urgency, proximity, dormancy, manageability, controllability, detectability, connectivity, strategic impact, and propinquity.

Risk Reassessment: Cleaning up the risk register by removing risks that are no longer relevant and adding any new risks that have been identified.

Risk Register: The document containing all identified risks relevant to the project. The risk register, which is a component of the project plan, contains information about each risk and is updated throughout the project.

Risk Report: A summary document that examines the factors that are contributing to risk and the high-level information on identified risks.

Risk Transference: The risk response technique of shifting the risk to another entity, usually a subcontractor or a vendor specializing in that type of risk. Firm fixed-price contracts would be one type of risk transference, as would be purchasing an insurance policy that protected the project.

Role: The part a person will play on the project. For example, a senior person in the organization may play a junior role on a given project.

Rolling Wave Planning: A planning technique that does not seek to answer all questions or plan all project activities at the beginning. Instead, only imminent project activities are planned in detail, while activities further in the future are planned at a higher level.

Root Cause Analysis: A technique that places a premium on understanding the underlying reasons behind a problem rather than focusing on the problem or symptom. Root cause analysis is used in quality management as a tool to prevent future defects.

Scatter Diagram: A chart that plots events against a dependent and an independent variable to identify correlation and spot trends. Scatter diagrams are most often used in quality management, specifically in the Manage Quality and Control Quality Processes.

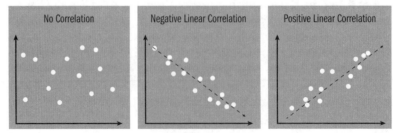

Three different scatter diagrams

Schedule Activity: See Activity

Schedule Baseline: The original schedule plus all approved changes to it.

Schedule Data: Supporting information related to the schedule that would not appear on the schedule network diagram.

Schedule Network Analysis: The techniques of performing a forward pass or a backward pass through the schedule to determine early start, early finish, late start, and late finish dates along with float and free float.

Schedule Compression: Work to reduce the overall calendar time for a project. Crashing and fast-tracking are examples of schedule compression techniques.

Schedule Forecasts: Updated projections for the activities and overall schedule based on performance and actual data.

Schedule Management Plan: The plan for how the project schedule will be measured, monitored, and controlled. The schedule management plan is created in the Plan Schedule process.

Schedule Tool: A software tool that uses schedule data and manual adjustments to automatically calculate and update the schedule.

Scope (product or project): May refer to product scope or project scope. The product scope contains all of the requirements, features, and attributes the product, service or result needs for successful acceptance. The project scope contains all of the product scope plus any other items needed to successfully perform the project.

Scope Baseline: The combination of the scope statement, the WBS and the WBS dictionary. When these documents are put under control they become the scope baseline.

Scope Management Plan: The plan, created in Plan Scope Management, that describes how the other five scope management processes will be carried out.

Scope Statement: A narrative description of the scope. The scope statement contains the goals of the project, the product description, the requirements for the project, the constraints and assumptions, and the identified risks related to the scope. It should also include the acceptance criteria and any items that are out of scope that would be helpful to document.

Scrum: A type of agile framework that breaks the project into 21 day cycles called sprints. The team pulls work from a prioritized backlog and a retrospective is held at the end of each sprint.

Self-organizing Teams: The agile practice of assembling a team, usually made of generalizing specialists, and allowing the members to determine how their efforts would be best put to use. Self-organizing teams are highly autonomous and often do not have anyone with the role of project manager on them.

Seller Proposal: A potential seller's response to a buyer's request for proposal. These are used as an input into the Conduct Procurements process.

Sequence Activities: The planning process of Sequence Activities takes the schedule activities from the activity list and sequences them according to the order in which they must be performed. This is accomplished by determining which activities are dependent upon other activities. This process produces project network diagrams as its primary output, and these are used later to create the schedule.

Seven Basic Quality Tools: Seven tools used frequently in quality management. They are: cause-and-effect diagrams, flowcharts, check sheets, Pareto diagrams, histograms, control charts, and scatter diagrams.

Sigma: The Greek symbol σ that represents one standard deviation from the mean. In quality management, a higher number of sigmas (e.g. Six Sigma) represents very high quality, since, at that level, everything within six standard deviations of the mean would be of acceptable quality.

Sponsor: The person responsible for funding the project. The sponsor is typically someone from senior management and may or may not be the same person as the customer.

Smoothing: Also called Accommodating, smoothing plays down the problem and diverts attention to things that are going well. Smoothing is not a favored means of problem solving since it does not deal with the underlying problem(s) that led to conflict.

Special Cause: The reason contributing to a quality problem that is considered to be generally preventable. Contrast with Common Cause.

Stage Gate: See Exit Gate

Stakeholder: Anyone who may influence the project or who has an interest in the project, whether that interest is positive or negative.

Stakeholder Engagement Plan: The component of the project management plan that specifies the requirements and expectations for stakeholder communications and their desired participation on the project.

Stakeholder Register: A table that documents all of the project stakeholders, their interest on the project, and often their importance on this project.

Standard Deviation: A representation of how diverse or scattered a data set is. In quality management, a low standard deviation is generally preferred, since it shows that results are predictable and the process is delivering products that are consistent.

Start-to-Finish: A logical relationship between nodes in a project network diagram. A start-to-finish relationship between two scheduled activities (e.g., activities A and B) indicates that regardless of when activity B starts, it cannot finish until Activity A begins.

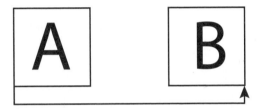

Start-to-Start: A logical relationship between nodes in a project network diagram. A start-to-start relationship between two scheduled activities (e.g., activities Q and R) indicates that activity R cannot start until activity Q starts.

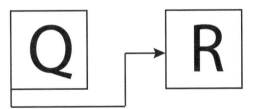

Statement of Work (SOW): The narrative description of the project's product, service, or result. The statement of work is intended to foster a common understanding among stakeholders.

Statistical Sampling: Using a representative sample to draw statistical inferences about a larger population.

Strategies for Opportunities: Ways to deal with potential positive occurrences on the project, including escalation, exploitation, sharing, enhancing, and acceptance.

Strategies for Threats: Ways to deal with potential problems on the project including escalation, avoidance, transference, mitigation, and acceptance.

SWOT Analysis: An technique used to gather and categorize strengths, weaknesses, opportunities, and threats about a population. Strengths and weaknesses are internal, while opportunities and threats are external to the organization.

System: The rules, processes, procedures, people, and other elements that support an outcome or process. Several systems are defined in project management, including the project management information system, the change control system, and the work authorization system.

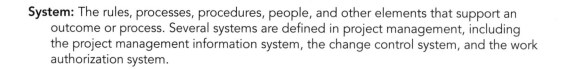

Task: A schedule activity. Some project management resources treat a task as a sub-activity, or a further decomposition of a schedule activity; however, for the purposes of the exam, you should think of the two terms as being equivalent.

To-Complete Performance Index (TCPI$_c$): The performance the project would need to achieve to end on target. In this case, a lower index is good, since it means that you could underperform and still meet your target, while an index of greater than one is bad since you are essentially saying that you would need to overperform against the plan in order to meet your goals or targets.

Team: The entire group responsible for planning, executing, and monitoring and controlling the project. The project team typically involves the sponsor as well. Agile teams are empowered to make decisions for the project and often include the customer as a part of the team.

Team-Building Activities: Exercises designed to strengthen the sense of team. Team building works best when the activities are begun early, and the focus should last throughout the project.

Team Performance Assessments: Evaluations conducted to gauge a team's effectiveness.

Template: A document that serves as a starting point for a particular output. Examples of templates include documents with mandatory headers and placeholders, complete examples from previous projects, or commercially available documents. Templates are often provided by the project management office, and they may be generic or specific.

Theory X: A management theory that presumes that workers must be closely and constantly supervised in order to get maximum results.

Theory Y: A management theory that assumes people are naturally motivated and may be trusted to do good work.

Threat: Anything that potentially jeopardizes the project's planned scope, time, or cost. Due to their uncertainty, threats are considered to be risks. Also see Opportunity.

Three-Point Estimate: A technique for estimating duration or cost. The three-point estimate uses a pessimistic, optimistic, and realistic estimate to calculate. The formula most often associated with the three-point estimate is a simple average, expressed as follows: Estimate = (Pessimistic + Realistic + Optimistic) ÷ 3.

Time and Materials Contract (T&M): A type of contract where the buyer reimburses the seller for the seller's time at a predefined rate, and for material expenses the seller incurs on the project. A pure time and materials contract shifts the primary risk to the buyer, as there are no direct financial incentives for the seller to control labor or material costs.

Tolerance: The limits a project sets for quality acceptance.

Top-Down Estimate: See Analogous Estimate

Tornado Diagram: A graphical chart used in Perform Quantitative Risk Analysis. Tornado diagrams show how sensitive the project is to risk by depicting the effect of a single variable change, while holding all other variables steady.

Change in project cost due to a 10% change in labor costs with all other project costs held constant.

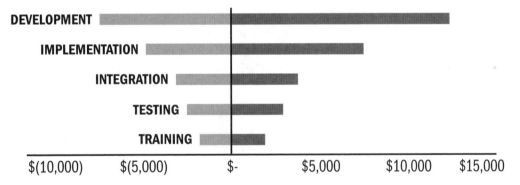

Total Float: The sum of all time that an individual activity can slip from its early start date without affecting the finish date of the project.

Total Quality Management (TQM): A philosophy of quality management that focuses on bringing quality into the entire organization. TQM became popular in the second half of the twentieth century by expanding the view of quality beyond the product to include all people and processes within an organization. Feigenbaum, Deming, Juran, Crosby, and Ishikawa are considered to be the primary architects of TQM.

Training: Efforts to build the capabilities of the individuals and the team. Non-project-specific training should generally be paid for by the functional manager or the department.

Trend Analysis: A statistical forecasting technique to predict results related to scope, time, or cost by plotting a trend line based on previous performance. Run charts are often used in trend analysis to create trend lines.

Trigger: A warning sign that a risk has occurred, is occurring, or is about to occur.

Triple Constraint: The intersection of scope, time, and cost on a project. The triple constraint emphasizes that one of these cannot change without affecting at least one of the other two.

U

Unanimity: A group decision technique where everyone on the team must agree with the decision before a decision is made. A jury is a common example where unanimity is used.

V

Validate Scope: The monitoring and controlling process of inspecting project deliverables and gaining their formal acceptance from the appropriate stakeholders.

Value Engineering: Trying to decrease costs, increase profitability, improve quality, shorten the schedule without changing the scope of an item.

Variable Sampling: A method of quality management where the results for each item or attribute are ranked on a scale to show the degree to which they meet quality. Contrast with Attribute Sampling.

Variance: A difference between the plan and the executed results.

Variance Analysis: A tool used frequently in controlling processes to look at the difference between the plan and the results and to understand the contributing factors.

Variance at Complete (VAC): The difference between what was budgeted and what is forecasted to have been spent. The VAC is calculated by subtracting the estimate at complete from the budgeted at completion, or VAC = BAC - EAC.

Vendor Bid Analysis: An analysis of what the project should cost performed by aggregating individual vendor bids.

Verification: Inspecting the product, service, or result to ensure that the processes and deliverables meet quality requirements.

Verified Deliverable: Deliverables that have been compared with the documented scope to ensure that all of the work was completed. Verified deliverables flow out of the Control Quality process.

Virtual Team: A team that is geographically distributed. Virtual team members may never actually meet in person and will use collaboration tools to share information and do their work.

War Room: A centralized room for project planning that may also be used for execution and other project activities. A common use of the war room is to co-locate the team for a period of time.

Withdrawal: A means of conflict avoidance which practices avoidance in the hopes that the problem will resolve on its own. Withdrawal is not a favored means of problem solving since it does not deal with the underlying problem(s) that led to conflict.

Work Authorization System: Part of the overall project management information system (PMIS), the work authorization system is used to ensure that work gets performed at the right time and in the right sequence. It may be an informal e-mail sent by the project manager to a functional manager, or a formal system to get an assigned resource released to complete scheduled work.

Work Breakdown Structure (WBS): A graphical, hierarchical chart composed of nodes that are logically organized from top to bottom. The WBS represents all of the work and only the work to be performed on the project. Each node on the WBS has a unique number used to locate and identify it.

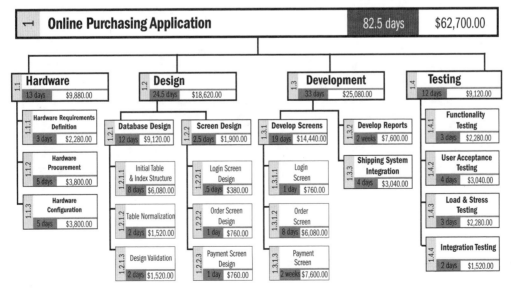

Example WBS

Glossary of Terms

Work Breakdown Structure (WBS) Dictionary: The WBS dictionary is a companion document to the work breakdown structure (WBS). Since the WBS is a graphical chart, there is not room for all of the supporting information and attribute information that accompanies each node. Therefore, the WBS dictionary provides a place for this information and is organized so that it corresponds back to each node on the WBS. Supporting information found in the WBS dictionary may include the following: time and cost estimates, the person or group responsible for the deliverable, due dates, further descriptions, etc.

Work Package: The lowest hierarchical level of the work breakdown structure. Work packages represent deliverables on the project and should be small enough to estimate for cost and duration. Work packages are further decomposed into activities for further estimating and scheduling purposes.

Work Performance Data: Raw, unprocessed data about how the team has executed the work. Compare with work performance information.

Work Performance Information: Processed information on how the work is being performed, gathered during the executing processes. Work performance information begins to flow as soon as the work is executed. Among other things, it includes the status of deliverables, how things are performing against cost and schedule goals, and how the product measures up against quality standards.

Work Performance Reports: Useful and often actionable formats of work performance information.

Workaround: A response to an unplanned risk event.

Index

Symbols

A

Index

B

C

Index

Index

Index

Index

E

F

Index

J

K

Index

N

O

Index

P

Q

R

Index

Use the key inside the back cover flap to access:

https://insite.velociteach.com/book_key/keynote.htm

PMP Exam content, additional questions, and study aids

If your book did not come with a Key to InSite on the inside back cover, it may not be authentic. If you do not have a Key to InSite, you may purchase one at http://insite.velociteach.com